THE CROSLAND LEGACY

"A most timely and topical study of a politician who was also one of Labour's outstanding theoreticians… vital reading for all interested in Labour's future."
Eric Shaw, University of Stirling

"Crosland's revisionist credo continues to be a lodestar for Labour Party 'modernisers'. In this pithy and insightful work Patrick Diamond critically explores the reasons for its enduring legacy."
Hugh Pemberton, University of Bristol

"Tony Crosland continues to fascinate nearly forty years after his untimely death. This new study is authoritatively written by someone who was a senior party advisor turned academic and deserves to be read seriously by scholars and activists alike."
Kevin Hickson, University of Liverpool

THE CROSLAND LEGACY

The future of British social democracy

Patrick Diamond

First published in Great Britain in 2016 by

Policy Press
University of Bristol
1-9 Old Park Hill
Bristol
BS2 8BB
UK
t: +44 (0)117 954 5940
pp-info@bristol.ac.uk
www.policypress.co.uk

North America office:
Policy Press
c/o The University of Chicago Press
1427 East 60th Street
Chicago, IL 60637, USA
t: +1 773 702 7700
f: +1 773 702 9756
sales@press.uchicago.edu
www.press.uchicago.edu

British Library Cataloguing in Publication Data
A catalogue record for this book is available from the British Library.

Library of Congress Cataloging-in-Publication Data
A catalog record for this book has been requested.

ISBN 978-1-4473-2473-7 paperback
ISBN 978-1-4473-2475-1 ePub
ISBN 978-1-4473-2476-8 Mobi

Cover design by Soapbox design
Front cover: image kindly supplied by Getty
Printed and bound in Great Britain by Clays Ltd, St Ives plc
Policy Press uses environmentally responsible print partners

Contents

About the author

Patrick Diamond spent ten years in various roles at the heart of British government, including Head of Policy Planning and Senior Policy Adviser to the Prime Minister, Group Director of Strategy, Equality and Human Rights Commission, and Special Adviser to the Cabinet Office. He is now Lecturer in Public Policy at Queen Mary, University of London, Executive Chair of Policy Network and was Gwilym Gibbon Fellow at Nuffield College, Oxford. He writes extensively for numerous UK and European newspapers, publications and other media outlets.

Preface

At key junctures in British political history, the most gifted politicians have exerted a decisive influence on the future direction of their parties. This book examines the impact of one political figure and socialist theoretician, the former Cabinet Minister, Anthony Crosland, now best remembered as the author of *The Future of Socialism*. Crosland played a pivotal role in recasting the Labour party's identity and doctrine in the decades following the Second World War. Sixty years on, the re-examination of Crosland's ideas is particularly apposite as the current Labour party undergoes a dramatic change in its philosophy and political trajectory from New Labour under Tony Blair and Gordon Brown in the 1990s to fresh leadership in the 2010s and beyond. The scale of Labour's 2015 poll disaster plunged the party into despair, but the crisis in Labour's fortunes was evident as the financial crash in 2008 and subsequent electoral defeats underlined the party's abject failure to revitalise the social democratic project.

Against that backdrop, this book addresses Crosland's influence on ideological change in the Labour party over the last 60 years. His effort to remake the party was inevitably a contentious and fraught process while the impact of revisionism was uneven and provisional. At crucial turning-points in the 1970s and 1980s, the party chose to ignore Crosland's most resounding message: Labour must retain an original 'cast of mind' distinguishing between 'means' and 'ends', facing up to the consequences of a changing economy and society. At times, the fault lay squarely with Crosland's generation who were unwilling to confront the 'forces of conservatism' within the British labour movement. Their deferential attitude towards the organised working class encapsulated in the symbols and myths of Labour's 'proletarian sectionalism' hindered the full development of the revisionist project. The willingness to speak truth to power with unflinching honesty captured in Crosland's confrontation with the Fabian legacy of Sidney and Beatrice Webb was qualified by abiding affection for, and loyalty towards, the ascendant institutions and prevailing cultures of the labour movement. This contradiction inhibited ongoing revision of the party's doctrine and policies, preventing Labour from evolving into a social democratic party at the cutting edge of the new society. Any historian of the labour movement must be alive to subtleties and contradictions. The tension between the urge to reject outdated shibboleths on the one hand, and devotion to the movement on the other, is the central paradox of the revisionist tradition, a thread running throughout the previous 60 years of Labour's politics: the book will examine how it is imprinted on Crosland's life and political career.[1]

The present context is a poignant moment to reassess Crosland's legacy. There are some in the party who fear that Jeremy Corbyn's victory in 2015 heralds a regression away from social democracy, a rejection not only of New Labour but the parliamentary strategy advocated by revisionists since the early twentieth century. The Corbyn ascendancy repudiates Crosland's influence, much as Ralph Miliband sought to achieve in the early 1960s with the publication of *Parliamentary Socialism*. Corbyn's aim is to demonstrate to the Left that the Labour party is not an inherently flawed political movement, a moderate and pragmatic electoral device destined always to compromise its beliefs to accommodate itself to capitalism.[2] Corbyn wishes to transform Labour 'into a socialist party free from the constrictions hitherto imposed by its leaders', notoriously prone to 'conspiratorial socialisation' and seduced by the trappings of high office.[3] At the same time, the political momentum propelling Corbynism is borne of growing antagonism towards financial capitalism and profound dissatisfaction with contemporary representative democracy: 'a pervasive sense that old models both of economics and politics have broken down'. Fiscal retrenchment since 2010 that combines cuts in the fabric of the state with greater economic inequality has fuelled demands for a radical political alternative rather than an 'austerity-lite' agenda.[4] The Corbyn project galvanised the party's core supporters, leading to a sharp rise in membership during an era in which social democratic parties across Europe are being hollowed out. As Andrew Gamble has noted, Corbyn's victory draws a line under the New Labour years, obliging moderate forces to rethink centre-left politics for the 'new hard times'. This effort will entail restating the case for Labour as a governing party pursuing social reforms that are capable of making a practical difference to the lives of working people, rather than Labour as a party of protest whose marginalisation from power surrenders control of the British state to the Conservatives.

For that reason, Crosland's appeal is likely to remain even though *The Future of Socialism* was published in 1956, and he died almost 40 years ago. This volume argues his legacy deserves to be thoroughly re-examined. More than a decade since Labour last won an outright parliamentary majority and nearly ten years after the most disruptive financial crisis since the 1930s, 'the world is changing around us. If there was ever a time for reappraisal, it must surely be now.'[5] Crosland understood that the party needed an explicit strategic purpose: a guiding mission of what it was for enabling Labour to acquire power through the democratic electoral process governing effectively in a world of rapid change.

All that said, historians and commentators might ask why yet another book is needed to address the life and career of a 'second-rank' post-war politician who never became party leader, Prime Minister or even Chancellor of the Exchequer. Crosland has attracted attention as an unconventional politician who enjoyed a colourful and enigmatic personal life. Much, inevitably, has been written about a figure who stood out in the post-war Labour party for his political courage, his willingness to confront unpalatable truths, and his insouciance. In their perceptive personal histories, Crosland's biographers, his wife Susan, and the historian, Kevin Jeffreys, examine the paradox of a man fiercely private and diffident behind the scenes, but also a charismatic, even magnetic public personality.[6] Understandably, neither addresses the relationship between the development of ideas in the Labour party and Crosland's legacy. That is the principal concern of this volume.

Numerous books were produced about Crosland's influence as a socialist intellectual who inspired generations of Labour politicians. These include a collection of essays published shortly after the Conservative party's victory in 1979.[7] A similar volume was made available after Blair's 1997 triumph, addressing the contention that New Labour was a definitive break with the social democratic tradition.[8] The academic literature has revisited Crosland's impact on the modernisation process in the 1980s and 1990s, notably through articles by Martin Francis and Mark Wickham-Jones.[9] Additional work by Raymond Plant, Matthew Beech and Kevin Hickson assesses Labour's political thought while analysing the elaboration of revisionist ideas.[10] Similarly, David Riesman offers an exhaustive overview of Crosland's legacy as an economist and political theorist.[11] Finally, the former Cabinet Minister, Peter Hain, has turned to *The Future of Socialism*, mapping out a future direction for the Labour party in the wake of the financial crisis and great recession.[12] There is an extensive literature in place: so is there a compelling case for a further volume on Crosland's legacy? This monograph's aim is to address his ongoing relevance and impact on the Labour party. Despite the voluminous literature, Crosland's thought has seldom been related to the contemporary debate about political strategy and ideology on the centre-left of British politics. Moreover, there is surprisingly little work that probes and interrogates Crosland's inheritance. The relationship between political parties and ideas in post-war Britain alongside the decisive role of intellectuals is similarly underexplored.[13] An assessment of Crosland's influence obliges us to consider the political environment he inhabited, both within post-war society and the institutional structures of the Labour party. The volume makes use of a variety of sources including interviews with leading contemporaries of Crosland. Historical archives are drawn upon that shed light on his ideas and relationship with his party, alongside the extensive use of primary and secondary documentation.

My interest in Crosland's legacy, nonetheless, goes beyond scholarly inquiry. Steven Fielding has written that 'the sound of grinding axes is almost deafening when reading most studies of the [Labour] Party...objectivity is something to which even the most apparently disinterested academic can merely aspire to'.[14] As Callaghan, Fielding and Ludlum note: 'The study of the Labour party is especially prone to interpretive dispute because it is inherently politicised.'[15] If I have any political affiliation within the Labour tradition, I consider myself to be a Croslandite revisionist. Why? First and foremost, Crosland believed that Labour should be a party of government capable of exercising political power. Accompanying his analysis were credible and achievable policy reforms rather than Utopian schemes that stood little chance of being implemented. Secondly, Crosland acknowledged that for all Labour's pride in the 1945 Government, the party had failed to realise its potential in British politics: this meant addressing the underlying causes of Labour's anaemic electoral performance. The party had to make a broad-based, radical appeal to the whole nation, north and south, working-class and middle-class, forging a new progressive alliance in British politics. Thirdly, Crosland not only produced a rigorous analysis of structural change; he was motivated by a moral commitment, namely his desire for a fairer, more equal society. In recent decades, that passion to right what is wrong in Britain has palpably been lost. Finally, Crosland recognised that the Labour party had to learn from the world beyond Britain's shores. He remains an alluring politician since he had a logical and reasoned view of what Labour should stand for, examining how the party should adapt to new realities if it was to put its principles into effect.

I would like to thank the many people who have helped in the preparation of this book, especially those who were kind enough to grant me interviews including Lord Andrew Adonis, Mr David Coats, Lord Bernard Donoughue, Lord Bruce Grocott, Lord Roy Hattersley, Mr Dick Leonard, Lord David Lipsey, Professor David Marquand, Lord Raymond Plant, Lord Giles Radice, Lord Bill Rodgers and Professor Tony Wright. I have benefited greatly from conversations with Professor Andrew Gamble, Dr Helen Thompson and Dr James Ellison. Professor Tim Bale and Professor Michael Kenny at Queen Mary University of London, along with three anonymous referees, provided extensive and insightful comments on the draft. The librarians in the Crosland archive at the London School of Economics (LSE) were assiduous in making various documents available; I am grateful for permission to quote from Crosland's papers, and to David Higham Associates for using extensive extracts from *The Future of Socialism*. The staff team at Policy Press, notably Alison Shaw, Emily Watt and Laura Vickers, were helpful and efficient throughout.

Patrick Diamond
December 2015

ONE

Introduction: Crosland's Legacy

Tempora mutantur, et nos mutamur in illis ('Times change and we will change with them'). (Revisionist credo)

Socialism, as I see it, is a society where everyone starts equal with an equal chance and there are no upper and lower classes...it should mean a state of affairs in which every single citizen has the chance to live the same sort of graceful, cultured and comfortable life that only the lucky few can live today: a life with beauty in it, with leisure in it, with art in it, the sort of life that William Morris wrote about and longed for: in which people can forget about all these miserable economic problems and concentrate on the things that really matter. (Anthony Crosland, 1950[1])

The most fundamental ideal of those who shared his outlook was social justice – but it was an ideal in no way inspired by class hatred. They were equally devoted to democracy and personal freedom. They were for the rational and practical, and suspicious of large general ideas which on examination turned out to have no precise content...They wanted to get results.

They were realistic in politics and critical of armchair politicians who, not understanding what the British electorate was really like, were forever making bad judgements. Above all, while accepting the ultimate emotional basis of moral valuation, they had great faith in the power of reason both to find the answers to social problems and to persuade men to see the light. They were for the pursuit of truth to the bitter end, through the patient and unswerving application of logical thought. They wanted no barriers of prejudice to obstruct the free working of the mind or blunt the sharp edge of intellectual integrity. (Hugh Gaitskell, 1955[2])

Introduction

Anthony Crosland was the British Labour party's revisionist *par excellence*. His most influential work, *The Future of Socialism*, has been described as the bible of Labour revisionism.[3] This book examines Crosland's legacy: the impact of his incisive and penetrating writings on the Labour party's doctrine and strategy in post-war Britain. The party absorbed Crosland's ideas into its political identity in the 1950s and 1960s, searching for a revitalised purpose having accomplished the immediate tasks of post-war reconstruction and social reform. By the time of Harold Wilson's victory in 1964, Labour was ostensibly a moderate and forward-looking party of government. This study addresses the nature of the political influence that Crosland exerted almost 40 years since his death; it asks what more he has to impart to social democratic parties as the certainties of the post-war age have passed into abeyance. The Cabinet Minister, Richard Crossman, observed that Labour in the years after 1945, 'lost its way not only because it lacked maps of the country it was crossing, but because it thought maps unnecessary for experienced travellers'.[4] Others have been more forgiving: the leading Fabian intellectual, G.D.H. Cole, welcomed the fact that the party was, 'so undefined in

2

its doctrinal basis as to make recruits readily among people of quite different types'.[5] Labour emerged in the early twentieth century as an idealistic but pragmatic movement putting its faith in gradualist reform; it eschewed abstract theories of society and state: only a minority owed even marginal allegiance to Marxism. Crossman's view in 1956 was that expediency had become debilitating: 'If challenged to say in a single sentence what is wrong with British socialism, I should reply that it is bookless.'[6] Friedrich Engels remarked that 'indifference to theory is one of the chief reasons of the slow progress of the English working-class movement'.[7] In essence, Crosland agreed; he objected to Labour's 'anti-doctrinal and anti-theoretical bias': a coherent identity and governing programme were essential if Labour was to emerge as a viable contender for power, rather than remaining a party of protest.[8] Only by developing this prospectus could Labour seize the title deeds to the future, claiming its rightful place as the natural party of government.

Given that he was a practising Labour politician as well as an eminent socialist theoretician, Crosland's impact on the British Left has been considerable. As Maurice Kogan writes:

> Although other leading members of the Labour Party have attempted to contribute to the Party's stock of ideas – R.H. Tawney, John Strachey, as well as Roy Jenkins come to mind – Crosland stands out as one who operated as an intellectual of the highest calibre whilst playing a full part in the politics of the party and of the polity at large... Crosland was a supreme one-off – in the quality of his intellect, in his determination to put it to direct policy uses, in his ability to sustain an argument in long-haul works of distinction and analysis, in avowal of social and personal values that still present a challenge to our existing political leaders.[9]

According to his former political adviser, David Lipsey: 'Crosland still had a vision of what Labour should be doing to make society better...that is one reason why his influence persists despite the fact the world he inhabits has changed.'[10] Few writers since Tawney have had such a mesmerising effect on subsequent generations of practising Labour politicians and theorists. More surprisingly, his influence has not been confined to the 'usual suspects', an assortment of Gaitskellites, modernisers and reformers who have sought to update the party's appeal after electoral defeat. Leading figures across the party from Roy Hattersley to Gordon Brown tried to lay claim to Crosland's inheritance, acquiring political credibility by emphasising their affinity to Croslandism.[11] In a foreword to the fiftieth anniversary edition of *The Future of Socialism*, Brown positioned himself as Labour's leading contemporary revisionist, emphasising how Crosland's work inspired him: 'When I first read Crosland's book, it was this passion against injustice and the anger about the unfairness of low levels of mobility allied to gaps in economic opportunity that made the greatest impression on me.'[12] Crosland conferred the imprimatur of social democratic authenticity, and an affinity with the moderate socialist tradition that made identifying with him a political asset, particularly after Neil Kinnock had begun the tentative process of party modernisation in the 1980s.

What is more surprising is that Crosland's impact persisted despite the fact that the social democratic prospectus he championed had been discredited during the crisis years of the 1960s and 1970s. Post-war confidence in 'quasi-Keynesian' fine-tuning, macro-economic management and rising public expenditure vanished by the late 1970s. Doubt gripped the British policy-making establishment: Keynesianism had been dismissed as 'the revolution that never was'; a return to the laissez-faire strategy of the inter-war years appeared inevitable. As a consequence, Crosland's 'post-capitalist' analysis was strongly criticised in a climate inhospitable to social democracy. There had been substantial changes in British society and the economy after the Second World War, indeed, since *The Future of Socialism* was published. By the time of Crosland's passing, the post-war age promising an optimistic and propitious future of rising economic growth and personal prosperity was drifting towards industrial crisis, sharpening ideological polarisation and growing political instability. The eruption of Celtic nationalism had the potential to undermine the legitimacy of the British state while shattering traditional political allegiances, none of which were scenarios considered by Crosland. Since that time, structural change in the economy has advanced apace: Thatcherism and New Labour have further reconstructed the British political landscape.

Labour's fascination with Crosland might be considered an expression of weakness rather than strength. According to Mark Wickham-Jones, 'such attempts by both critics and advocates of New Labour to capture Crosland's mantle reveal a shared insecurity about the party's intellectual identity'.[13] New Labour figures were circumspect about their party's roots. The politicians, notably Blair, were determined to deny past associations with so-called Old Labour, which they blamed for the party's disastrous performance in the 1980s and early 1990s. New Labour defined 'Old' Labour as encompassing the trade unions, left-wing activists, unpopular Labour councils, the Wilson and Callaghan governments, the party's 'cloth cap' image, even the egalitarian philosophy of Gaitskell and Crosland.[14] Whereas New Labour stood for dynamism and growth, 'Old' Labour promulgated the traditional politics of the welfare state and redistribution.[15]

Despite this historical amnesia, Crosland's continuing status as an intellectual reference point has been remarkable. In the wake of the party's 2015 defeat, *The Financial Times* insisted Labour needed to, 'reawaken the modernising impulse in the party's past, championed by figures such as Tony Crosland', if the party was to re-emerge as a plausible contender for power in British politics.[16] Labour in the post-war years failed to provide an answer to the question Crosland posed in the mid-1950s: how should the party adapt its approach in a society characterised by material affluence, the rise of consumerism, declining deference, and a craving for personal freedom?[17] Crosland's response was that Labour would never succeed as a conservative party; British social democracy had to be a force for radical social reform rather than conspiring in the traditionalism and inertia that enveloped British national life after 1945. In the 1940s and 1950s, Crosland occupied the position of an intellectual 'enfant terrible' defiantly questioning Labour's most sacred myths and cherished shibboleths. Like his revisionist hero, the German social democrat Eduard Bernstein, Crosland was fearless in confronting Labour's dangerous drift towards doctrinal sterility. In subsequent decades, however, Crosland was eager to position himself as a 'party man'. Affection for, and loyalty towards, the structures and rituals of the labour movement increasingly qualified his willingness to speak truth to power, accompanied by growing acknowledgement of his political ambition. This paradox limited the scope for a heretical critique of the party's programme, particularly after Labour's demoralising defeat in 1970. That inherent conflict between the pull of loyalty to traditional institutions and a radical 'cast of mind' is the central contradiction of the party's revisionist tradition embodied in Crosland's life and political career; it weaves a delicate thread through 60 years of Labour history.

Why exactly does Crosland still matter in Labour's politics? Crosland was one of few figures in the post-war era who conveyed a confident sense of the party's purpose. He remains, for all the criticisms of his theories and policies, a crucial influence by which the quality of Labour's ideas and leadership ought to be judged. First, he articulated more persuasively than any other post-war theorist why equality should be the centrepiece of Labour's ideology rather than state ownership. Nationalisation was no longer the most effective instrument for advancing social justice and the public interest. He argued equal opportunity was 'not enough'; it was only through pursuing equality 'on many fronts' that individuals would be free and society more just. Since Crosland's death, inequality has risen to the top of the political agenda in the rich market democracies.

The second factor in Crosland's relevance is his advocacy of a revisionist strategy prepared to face up to the world as it was, not as post-war socialists wished it to be. This realism meant coming to terms with sociological change and affluence:

it involved adapting the Labour party to society, rather than struggling to adapt society to the Labour party. Since its inception, Labour struggled to establish itself as a credible governing party having endured a succession of electoral defeats in a predominantly 'conservative century'. The party's support has been regionally concentrated in 'heartland' seats; the state socialist policies of the 1930s and 1970s never secured the allegiance of a majority of voters, and the continuing presence of the Liberal party divided the 'progressive vote'.[18] Only where Labour has built support outside its 'core' constituencies, restrained its inclination towards state socialism, and matched the appeal of its 'progressive rival' has the party proved itself capable of securing a parliamentary majority.[19] Labour has, at crucial junctures, turned to revisionism in offering a way out of the electoral and political abyss. The party after the 2010 and 2015 defeats confronts a crisis of electability, as well as purpose.

The third point is Crosland foresaw that developments in European social democracy, as well as the liberal progressivism of the United States following the presidency of Franklin Delano Roosevelt (FDR), could constructively influence the British Left. Throughout Europe, social democratic parties had discarded the obsolete commitment to state ownership of the means of production. American liberalism provided an alternative route to a decent society centred on equal citizenship and social rights, overseen by an activist government that maintained full employment while tackling the unjustified concentration of economic and financial power. For Crosland, this was a signpost to the future.

The final and most compelling reason for Crosland's ongoing significance is that he gave the Labour party a persuasive, electorally appealing character, acknowledging that ethical socialism was at its core a marriage of individual freedom and social justice. This identity owed an obvious debt to the New Liberalism of T.H. Green and Leonard Hobhouse. The connection with liberalism was essential given that the British political tradition had its roots in the philosophy of Hobbes and Locke, the imperative of local self-government, and, above all, the commitment to liberty free from arbitrary interference by the state. In Crosland's view, the Labour party had to accept the prevailing currents of that political tradition. He utilised the New Liberalism which was increasingly amenable to social democratic doctrine, emphasising the potential of an interventionist government to enhance personal freedom. The development of the collectivist state could advance the cause of radical progressive and libertarian reform. Labour's relationship with social liberalism remains vital today.

In pursuing ideological revitalisation, Crosland turned to the rich heritage of ideas and traditions centred on liberal socialism and radical social liberalism. He adopted a constructive, forward-looking approach to the development of Labour's programme rather than promising, like so many of his opponents, merely to defend the gains of the past. At critical turning points in post-war history, Labour has been willing to draw from Crosland's inheritance of theories, concepts and rhetorical motifs. The book considers the continuing relevance of the political and theoretical legacies he bequeathed to the Labour party and British social democracy.

Croslandite social democracy and the role of ideas

John Maynard Keynes noted that ideas were so important 'the world is ruled by little else'. Ideas are 'the set of key organising principles and axiomatic propositions that drive the programmatic vision of socialist parties. [They are] invoked by socialist politicians to propose solutions for concrete policy problems in the economic, social or cultural realm'.[20] Samuel Beer defines ideas as 'orientations or premises of action'.[21] Ideas are a precursor to political mobilisation: the role of ideas in political parties has to be taken seriously.[22] The contribution of parties and politicians to the development of ideas is central to our understanding of the Labour party. The book examines the influence of Crosland's ideas on Labour since the Second World War.

In particular, this book focuses on how ideas permeate political parties and infuse the agenda of governments. Ideas are not merely about the process of governing: they are 'weapons in the struggle for power'. Politicians use ideas to undermine prevailing economic and political orthodoxies, a necessary starting-point for sustained electoral success. Gramsci observed that intellectual leadership was needed to achieve 'domination' in political life.[23] As such, 'ideas shape the way we understand interests, are the inspiration for the construction of political and social institutions, and are the currency of our discourse about politics'.[24]

The study of ideas alludes to the interaction between agency and structure in British politics: intellectual historians examine the pre-eminent role of individual actors, tracing ideologies that emerge from a particular canon and tradition of thought.[25] The structural context in which ideas are developed has generally been prioritised by political scientists. There are, nonetheless, approaches that examine how structure and agency are interwoven: for instance, the origins of social democracy in Western Europe are found in the changing structure of late nineteenth century capitalism. The market economy evolved in each society according to a unique legacy of institutions and cultures: national political movements developed their interpretations, forging a distinctive political language framing the arguments made by social democratic parties.[26] In *The Future of Socialism*, Crosland sought to shift Labour's appeal onto more propitious territory in the light of the transformation of capitalism and the emergence of a materially affluent society. There is merit in understanding the post-war Labour party by addressing political thinkers, their interpretations of structural change in the social and economic landscape, and the ideas they elaborated. This is consistent with Leonard Hobhouse's view that:

> The onward course of a movement is more clearly understood by appreciating the successive points of view which its thinkers and statesman have occupied than by following the devious turnings of political events and the tangle of party controversy.[27]

This analytical viewpoint emphasises that spatial 'Left/Right' models of party ideology are often inadequate: rather than straining to locate political movements on a static Left/Right spectrum, ideologies have to be disaggregated into their component ideas. Parties are not just electoral machines garnering votes among a fluid and volatile electorate that has cast aside the old tribal loyalties. Ideas matter in politics: they help politicians to define strategic priorities focusing their efforts; ideas convey clarity of purpose; they build coalitions for change undermining vested interests; and ideas enable political parties to grasp the impact of economic and social change.[28] Moreover, ideas are crucial to achieving, then exercising, political power. Politics is the struggle to make a framework of ideas the accepted 'common-sense' or dominant consensus, as the revisionists sought to achieve during the 1950s and 1960s. The former Chancellor of the Exchequer, Nigel Lawson, wrote in his memoirs: 'Never, never underestimate the importance or the power of the tide of ideas. No British government has ever been defeated unless and until the tide of ideas has turned against it.'[29] The role that ideas play in political parties remains of vital importance. Crosland's legacy illuminates a more general theme: the relationship between politicians, ideas and intellectuals in British politics.

As a prominent politician and intellectual, Crosland articulated the revisionist case with audacity and eloquence, justifying his pre-eminent status in shaping ideas in post-war Labour politics. *The Future of Socialism* was a transformative contribution to social democratic thought given the anti-theoretical bias and pragmatic gradualism that prevailed throughout Labour's political development. During the first half of the twentieth century, writing on the British Left with the exception of Tawney and Durbin has been dismissed as 'textbooks of social democratic economics...as dull as ditch water with no broader vision or picture':

> There was no great rival to Crosland in the breadth of what he had to say. The attraction of [*The Future of Socialism*] was that it talked about a great deal more –

education, the liberalisation of morality, as well as the claim that there was socialism that didn't have to be rooted in Marxism.[30]

Labour has relied heavily on Crosland as a source of inspiration since the 1950s; we might share his former Parliamentary Private Secretary, Dick Leonard's view that:

> To a shaming extent, the Labour party (or at least its moderate wing) have been living off the intellectual capital (of *The Future of Socialism*) ever since. Many of its concepts have become such common coinage that few of those who trade in them are aware of their origin.[31]

According to Leonard, the continuing interest in Crosland's ideas has been a blessing and a curse. The clarity and rigour of his thought made him stand out as one of the great socialist theoreticians as subsequent generations admired and celebrated his work. The Labour peer David Sainsbury remarked: 'The recent Labour government suffered from not having a credible, alternative political economy to neo-liberalism...no one had produced a new progressive political economy since Tony Crosland wrote *The Future of Socialism* in 1956.'[32] Richard Reeves argued in 2009: 'Labour is in urgent need of intellectual renewal. The last significant piece of sustained thinking by a Labour politician on what it means to be on the Left was *The Future of Socialism*, published by Crosland over half a century ago.'[33] Crosland's ongoing presence in the Labour party since the 1950s has been noteworthy while underlining the paucity of contributions from elsewhere in the social democratic tradition.[34]

Labour in the post-war years

Understanding Crosland's ideas means considering his distinctive purpose given the situation the party confronted after 1945. *The Future of Socialism* was concerned with advancing a rationale for Hugh Gaitskell's leadership while affirming Labour's commitment to central tenets of the post-war settlement.[35] *The Future of Socialism* was 'the central text of the Gaitskellite revisionism of the 1950s'.[36] Gaitskell defeated Herbert Morrison and Aneurin Bevan in the 1955 leadership contest following Attlee's retirement; Gaitskell believed the central lesson of the 1931 crisis was that Labour must behave as a responsible party of government, justifying his decision to introduce NHS charges on 'teeth and specs' in the 1951 budget. Following the 1955 and 1959 defeats, the leader rejected the pre-eminence accorded to nationalisation. But despite embracing the revisionist outlook, Gaitskell lacked a coherent programme of reform or policy direction of his own, relying on Crosland to forge a new strategy as Labour visibly floundered after successive election disasters.

Crosland was a passionate believer in Gaitskell's ability, convinced that Labour's intellectually formidable and principled leader had the potential to be a great Prime Minister. He was anxious to play the central role in Gaitskell's 'kitchen cabinet' of advisers. Crosland still grew doubtful about Gaitskell's judgement: he was a polarising figure; the leader's ability was sorely tested by his fractious and volatile party. In the meantime, Gaitskell's leadership came under attack from the Left, never reconciled to Bevan's defeat in 1955 and provoked by the suspicion that Gaitskell was prepared to ditch the sacred principles of socialism: to the Bevanites, Clause 4 was a commitment to fight for the underdog against the barbarities of the capitalist system. The leadership was wilfully neglecting the achievements of the Attlee Government. The Bevanites viewed 1945–51 as the epitome of socialist progress following the Government's comprehensive programme of nationalisation, a tenacious commitment to improving the material circumstances of working people.

The Future of Socialism has to be read not only for its intellectual virtuosity but as motivated by a political aim: winning the battle for the party's soul on behalf of Labour's revisionist tradition while giving the party a fresh rationale in an age where capitalism was being restructured; working-class living standards had risen after years of rationing and austerity. Establishing Labour as a credible governing party was Crosland's core mission, enacting reforms that would attract the majority of voters. As the 1950s progressed, he sensed Labour was out of touch with an affluent Britain moving on from the ravages of war; the party had lost its way. In this context, *The Future of Socialism* was greeted by a tide of praise and adulation. Crosland's work stood out: no figure on the British Left had produced a prospectus that compared in its polemical style, analytical power and programmatic sophistication. According to the former Head of the Number Ten Policy Unit in the 1970s, Bernard Donoughue, *The Future of Socialism*:

> [W]as wonderfully inspiring because I had lived through the great days of the Labour Attlee government and had been aware of how it died of exhaustion. By the mid-1950s, Attlee was just going as leader; Bevin was dead; Morrison, who was a wonderfully creative figure in Labour history, was finished. For a while it seemed the only vital force was on the Left with the Bevanites...When Crosland's book came out it gave us huge hope that the future would be with democratic socialism. It was intellectually thorough, politically relevant, and inspiring.[37]

The insight that socialism was about equality rather than nationalisation and a planned economy left an indelible mark; it had far-reaching implications for the party's ideology and strategy. Labour's debate in the 1940s and 1950s had been about how much nationalisation was desirable and whether voters would support it; British socialism's belief in planning to promote industrial efficiency made it distinctive. But public ownership was becoming increasingly unpopular while the legacy of ration books and wartime austerity meant that planning was tainted. If equality was now the goal of democratic socialism, Labour was able to accept a greater role for the market: social democracy and the price mechanism need not be in conflict.

The proposition that socialism was about equality affirmed the close relationship between two distinctive traditions in British politics: radical liberalism and social democracy. Crosland's doctrine was a marriage of individual freedom and social justice with its roots in liberal socialism spanning Green, Hobhouse, Keir Hardie and Ramsay MacDonald. Crosland's ideas reacquainted the Labour party with that diverse liberal tradition. Political liberalism in Britain draws together numerous thinkers, political movements and ideological traditions from J.S. Mill to Hobbes, from the radical Liberal Prime Minister, Lloyd George, to the Liberal leader, Jo Grimond.[38] Within that liberal tradition is British social liberalism, a vital and distinct creed. Edwardian social liberalism drew on the writings of Green, Hobhouse and J.A. Hobson to emphasise the pursuit of positive liberty alongside the essential role of an enabling state in liberating the poor and dispossessed. Roy Hattersley portrays Green as 'the first philosopher of social justice'; although the link is never explicitly made, there is an apparent affinity between Green and the vision of post-war socialism adumbrated by Crosland.[39] Crosland drew on Hobhouse's ethic of liberal socialism, emphasising the state as the critical instrument promoting the liberty and freedoms of the individual against the constraints imposed by unfettered market capitalism. Similarly, Hobson insisted that the aim of the New Liberalism was: 'The realisation of individual liberty contained in the provision of equal opportunities for self-development. But to this individual standpoint must be joined a just apprehension of the social...the insistence that these claims or rights of self-development be adjusted to the sovereignty of social welfare.'[40]

Liberal social democracy gains control of democratically accountable institutions to counter injustice, promoting equality throughout society in the name of national citizenship, mobilising the power and resources of the state.[41] There is a thread running through Green and Hobhouse to William Beveridge, Keynes, T.H. Marshall and Crosland, emphasising the inclusive nature of citizenship where each of us can exercise inalienable civic, political and social rights.[42] This vision of social welfare and equality ran counter to the goal of a state-controlled economy. The commitment to wholesale nationalisation inspired numerous socialist traditions in Britain, particularly the Labour party of the inter-war years which acquired a sense of ideological direction from Clause 4; by the 1950s, however, state ownership was being surpassed by the revisionist emphasis on equal citizenship.

The revisionist challenge to the traditional wing of the party was stark, repudiating an emphasis on the conflict between capital and labour in the ownership of productive assets, motivating currents of socialist thought from syndicalism to Marxism.[43] Like Bernstein, Crosland insisted liberal social democracy was not a 'half-way house' between Marxism and classical liberalism; it was a distinctive ideology in which the state reformed markets in the public interest reconciling social justice with economic efficiency, viewing human welfare as being as important as wealth creation and the pursuit of profit.[44] As Sheri Berman has written, the foundations of gradualism are to be found in Bernstein's democratic revisionism emphasising the imperative of class cooperation, alongside the central role of parliamentary politics. Crosland drew upon this heritage having proclaimed himself in a letter to his Oxford friend, Philip Williams, to be the modern Bernstein.[45]

Crosland and where Labour goes next

The year 2016 marked the sixtieth anniversary of Crosland's seminal work, *The Future of Socialism*. This volume revisits Crosland's legacy in the wake of one of Labour's worst defeats since 1918. A process of fundamental questioning is underway about the future of British social democracy. Since the publication of David Marquand's book, *The Progressive Dilemma*, in the early 1990s, there has been a lively debate about constructing a credible alternative to Conservatism in British politics which, after all, dominated the twentieth century.[46] In the last hundred years, Labour governed for only 33 years; out of 25 general elections, the party won just five with convincing majorities. But the battle is not just to win future elections: Crosland's point was that Labour must have a coherent idea of what it was for, a vision of the change it sought to bring about in British society. Rather than harking back to the past, either the 'golden age' of the post-1945 settlement or the era of governance inaugurated by Labour's 1997 landslide victory, Labour has to be a forward-looking party addressing new economic and political realities. The issue of how to re-discover the party's original appeal preoccupied Crosland and the Labour revisionists throughout the 1950s and early 1960s and is relevant today.

Crosland grew frustrated by his party's strategic ineptitude but refused to be pessimistic about the centre-left's prospects. There were always obstacles and adversities in an age of fiscal constraint, growing taxpayer resistance, rising material affluence, increasing scepticism about the state and declining faith in established democracy. He recognised that social and economic change, nonetheless, creates renewed possibilities for social democratic politics: ultimately a new economic and political landscape enables the Labour party to forge different coalitions of support, establishing a revitalised centre-left consensus in British politics. The question that bedevils the party today as it did in Crosland's era is whether it can step outside the confines of its prevailing doctrine and institutions, making the broad appeal that the revisionist analysis entails. Can loyalty and fidelity to the labour movement be sacrificed to enable the party to move beyond the constraints imposed by traditional class structures and political cultures without undermining the rationale for the party's existence? The revisionists provided an answer to the conundrum of how Labour should appeal to the mass electorate on which it depended for victory. However, they were more often reluctant to follow through their analysis: the revisionists feared they would tear the movement apart, as was evident in the turbulent period after Labour's 1959 defeat. This paradox of intellectual honesty set against enduring party loyalty was present throughout Crosland's career.

Crosland's relevance to the current debate about ideas on the British Left scarcely needs to be restated. His revisionist analysis remains pertinent to the pre-eminent questions confronting the party, particularly after the shattering defeats of 2010 and 2015. Labour's crisis is one of underlying purpose. It has no widely shared understanding of what the party is for or merely what Labour exists to achieve in British society bringing to mind Morrison's aphorism that socialism is merely what a Labour government does; Crosland desperately sought to convey direction to his party in the dying days of Attlee's Administration. The predicament gripping Labour is an overwhelming confusion about its political objectives. This problem afflicts social democratic parties across Europe who are torn between remaining 'communitarian' movements with a special relationship to the working class, and accepting their position as 'cosmopolitan' liberal parties embracing the diversity of modern society but no longer providing a traditional bulwark against the dehumanising capitalist system. It is far from unmanageable for a political party to retain its liberal and communitarian instincts as Labour did with some difficulty under Attlee, Wilson and Blair. But Labour will continue to flounder until the existential question of the party's rationale and identity is resolved. There is no tactical shortcut back to power; the party's electoral and political recovery depends on addressing fundamental questions in a changing economy and society:

- What should Labour's primary aims be: the optimisation of economic growth with the greatest achievable measure of social justice; the extension of personal freedom, classlessness, and opportunity for all; maximising the sum of human happiness irrespective of the rate of growth?
- Which inequalities should most concern the British Left? How important is equality of outcome in an affluent society; what should equality practically entail today?
- What can the modern state plausibly achieve and what are the limits of central government's power; how far should political power be decentralised to localities and citizens?

- Where should the balance be struck between personal liberty and mutual obligation relating to civic institutions such as the welfare state?
- How should individualism and diversity be reconciled with a commitment to social cohesion and civic responsibility? What, if any, notion of British identity can be reconstructed to give space to burgeoning national, regional and local identities?
- How far should culture be at the forefront of politics?
- What is the most effective international response to globalisation; what role should the European Union (EU) play in the development of social democracy?
- Finally, how far can British social democracy draw strength from the liberal tradition emphasising individual freedom, alongside the ethical socialist tradition centred on solidarity and the common good?

The political context in which Crosland authored *The Future of Socialism* is reminiscent of Labour's current predicament. The party in opposition in the 1950s had little idea of where to go next, befuddled by the emergence of post-war affluence and the electoral success of One Nation Conservatism. Attlee's ministers had tremendous achievements to their credit: the post-war administration virtually abolished mass unemployment creating a universal welfare state and National Health Service (NHS) free at the point of need. Crosland wrote that it was, 'a record of reform and advance and improvement such as no government of this country has ever equalled before'.[47] The Blair and Brown governments secured full employment and improved Britain's public services following decades of under-investment. The NHS, on the brink of a major crisis in the early 1990s, was revived as a national institution. Crosland acknowledged that Attlee's New Jerusalem paradoxically forced Labour to look backwards rather than towards the future. As Crosland feared, 'political parties often pay a harsh penalty for their own successes'.[48]

New Labour's modernisation discarded time-honoured shibboleths, fulfilling Gaitskell's mission to remove the formal commitment to nationalisation from the party constitution.[49] The leadership was determined to pitch its tent on the so-called centre-ground of British politics to marginalise the Conservative party, in so doing abandoning doctrine altogether; as a consequence, Labour's underlying purpose and identity was obscured. By rewriting Clause 4, New Labour sought to remove the ambiguity about the market economy that dogged the party throughout the twentieth century; however, it struggled to formulate an alternative identity.[50] Blair initially sought to locate his party within the communitarian tradition, drawing on the ethical socialism of Hardie, Tawney and John McMurray, alongside the social liberalism of Green, Hobhouse and Charles Masterman. But New Labour struggled to reconcile the rediscovery of community with its embrace of the global market which undermined national identities and communal solidarities, weakening the political legitimacy of the social democratic state.

Post-war revisionists including Gaitskell and Crosland accepted the market economy but were suspicious of capitalism's insatiable appetite for wealth creation and creative destruction. The market generated revenues for state spending through economic growth; the revisionists acknowledged that private ownership and competition were preferable to state control. But they did not embrace capitalism without qualification, in stark contrast to Peter Mandelson's infamous remark that Labour was 'intensely relaxed' about people becoming 'filthy rich...as long as they pay their taxes'. The financial crash erupted in 2007–08, but Labour discarded its ethical critique of markets and capitalism in the 1990s, a critical pillar of European social democracy throughout the twentieth century. As the crisis struck, Labour's self-confidence was shattered and its economic credibility severely depleted. The Conservatives reconstructed the politics of the crisis, defining the central issue as excessive public debt flowing from a bureaucratic and 'overloaded' state rather than ineptly regulated markets and financial institutions.[51]

Labour struggled in vain to come to terms with the crash and the electoral bloodbath that followed. Now the party is perplexed and disorientated. Political support for the two established parties of Left and Right across the United Kingdom is probably lower than at any point since 1918. This electoral fragmentation might indicate a critical juncture similar to Dangerfield's *Strange Death of Liberal England* following the First World War. One hundred years later, British politics is witnessing the decline of the two-party system after a general election in which a different political party won in each of the four constituent nations of the United Kingdom.[52] If Labour is to develop a revisionist project in a cold climate for social democracy and the Left, it will have to confront the forces insidiously undermining the British state and threatening to pull UK politics apart.

The structure of this book

The structure of *Crosland's Legacy* is as follows. The introductory chapter has presented an outline of Crosland's work, examining the context facing the post-war revisionists in reinvigorating the Labour party as the aims of the Attlee Government were realised. Chapter Two turns to the question of Crosland's legacy as a socialist minister and theoretician, providing an overview of his career. It reflects on the ups and downs of Crosland's time in politics, and what made him stand out as a Labour politician and socialist intellectual. This perspective is necessary to consider the extraordinary nature of Crosland's appeal. At times, he conveyed the impression of being a wayward character lacking the discipline required to advance his career; in 1951, his brother-in-law, the historian A.J.P. Taylor wrote a concerned letter:

> You're extremely able; have a high reputation as an economist; and speak exceedingly well. You ought to be a junior minister by now; & would have been if it wasn't for drinking too much. I know on the very best authority that Attlee has said as much. He won't give you an appointment, because he has seen you drunk too often in the smoking room.[53]

As a consequence, Crosland's career 'had a promise that was never quite fulfilled'.[54] Crosland's aversion to the House of Commons was legendary: 'He disliked the low level of argument, the exchange of party platitudes. Nor did he care for the bickering and back-stabbing that then – even more than usual – characterised the Parliamentary Labour Party'.[55] Susan Crosland attests that her husband remained ambivalent about a political career; he gained intellectual fulfilment from writing. Crosland never rose to the top of the greasy pole of British politics, thwarted in his efforts to seize the prized post of Chancellor of the Exchequer. At crucial moments such as 1974 and 1983, Croslandite social democracy appeared doomed, symbolised by Crosland's disastrous 1976 leadership bid in which he polled just 17 votes in the parliamentary party.

Astonishingly, Crosland's influence endured, nevertheless; as an obituary in *The Times* noted, his impact was, 'greater than the offices he held'.[56] This is because his writings combined analysis with iconoclasm, his ideas were a cut above the rest, and he articulated them with style and verve; Crosland's legacy is the focus of the four chapters that follow: Chapter Three examines Crosland's role in forging a social democratic philosophy given the primacy he accorded to equality; Chapter Four explores his position as a liberal progressive in a traditionalist party wedded to the vague doctrine of British socialism; Chapter Five turns to the influence of Western European socialism and American liberalism in shaping revisionist ideas, alongside Labour's view of Britain's role in the world; Chapter Six considers Crosland's status as a revisionist and policy strategist in the post-war Labour party.

Chapter Seven then reflects on the debate about ideas that has shaped the Labour party since the 1980s and 1990s. Retrospective commentaries have oversimplified Crosland's arguments, as *The Future of Socialism* attained a mythical status in Labour's doctrinal debates; like Keynes, views are attributed to Crosland that he never held. Finally, Chapter Eight addresses the future of the Labour party and British social democracy. The British Left has struggled to come to terms with the post-2008 crisis and great recession; the politics of the 'new hard times' are especially harsh because of receding faith in the political system and antipathy towards representative democracy. National identity and the constitutional status of the United Kingdom rose up the political agenda following the 2014 Scottish independence referendum. Since 2010, Labour sought to frame a new political agenda in the aftermath of an unprecedented 13 years in government. In the 2015 election, the party suffered a shattering defeat, among the worst in its history. If there was ever a time for sustained rethinking employing an original 'cast of mind', it is surely now. The concluding chapter draws the threads together, considers major criticisms of Crosland's analysis, and highlights his ongoing influence and relevance to social democracy.

Conclusion

For 60 years, Croslandite arguments and analysis have been circulating throughout the Labour party's discourse about social democratic strategy. In arguing that socialism was about equality and freedom rather than nationalisation of the commanding heights of industry, Crosland established an ethical belief system ostensibly bridging Gaitskell's Labour party in the 1950s with the party of Blair, Brown and Miliband in the 2010s. Since *The Future of Socialism*, Labour has drawn extensively from Crosland's rhetoric and narrative; as the result of social and political change, however, a multitude of issues facing the party now were barely considered in the 1960s and 1970s. The aphorism of revisionists that the original ideas and insights of one generation are the stultifying orthodoxy of the next still holds true.[57] The task is to draw on Crosland's insurgent 'cast of mind', developing the party's strategy and political identity for the 'new hard times'.

Henry Drucker contended the Labour party evolved by developing a 'doctrine' and an 'ethos'; the doctrine concerned ideas and how they might adapt to changing social and economic circumstances; this was the exclusive preserve of the revisionists. The party's ethos, on the other hand, related to shared beliefs and collective interests, Labour's 'common culture' and group loyalty focused on exploitation and the suffering inflicted on the industrial working class.[58] Crosland was infamously a 'stereotypical middle-class revisionist', who acquired an awareness of the party's ethos through his relationship with the South Gloucestershire and Grimsby Labour parties: 'he was a genuine egalitarian who preferred his Grimsby workers to fellow intellectuals'.[59] Nevertheless, Crosland discovered that reconciling ethos and doctrine in a left-wing movement is a precarious undertaking. The revisionists absorbed a romantic image of the organised working class and the prevailing culture of British labourism: this steadily undermined their effort to remake the Labour party. Revisionism produced bursts of intellectual creativity positively affecting Labour's electoral fortunes and governing credibility, but the revisionists were visibly in retreat by the 1970s. The paradox of the revisionist tradition was the relentless search for political reason and truth on the one hand, set against enduring loyalty to the movement on the other. Crosland's experience as a Labour minister and socialist theoretician encapsulated this quandary. The chapters that follow examine the contradictions and schisms it provoked.

TWO

Crosland: the socialist theoretician as hero

The difficulty lies, not in the new ideas, but in escaping from the old ones. (J.M. Keynes, 1936[1])

The party appears to the outside observer to be less prepared in spirit for the many awkward problems which it will have to face as soon as it reaches office than it was even in 1945, when its whole task was enormously simplified by the existence of a comprehensive set of wartime controls and a lot of civil servants sitting ready in their offices with long experience of working them. (Andrew Shonfield, 1960[2])

The revisionist case against more statist versions of socialism was not new: its combination of reason, passion, and parliamentary gradualism had been present within the British Labour Party from the start, for passion could as well inspire parliamentary gradualism as anti-parliamentarianism. (Brian Harrison, 2009[3])

Introduction

Anthony Crosland has been an iconic figure for generations of British social democrats; next to Aneurin Bevan he was 'the most exciting Labour politician of the twentieth century'.[4] His writings conveyed the qualities of political relevance and intellectual élan that were in short supply in the British Labour party. Crosland had exceptional abilities ensuring that he stood out as Labour's pre-eminent 'scholar-politician'. This chapter charts the highs and lows of his career against the rise and fall of British social democracy. There were prolonged periods in which Crosland's career stagnated, particularly following Wilson's ascent to the leadership in 1963. During the 1970s, Croslandite social democracy was imperilled: its political economy was disintegrating in the face of global financial pressures; revisionism had little to say about the surge of Celtic nationalism and the incipient crisis of the British state. After defeat in 1979, the party moved sharply to the Left; in its 'wilderness years', Labour regressed by attempting to revive an outdated state socialism centred on nationalisation and the siege economy. Nonetheless, Crosland ensured later generations understood the necessity of updating the party's identity following profound changes in the social structure of Britain.

This chapter assesses his legacy as a socialist politician and intellectual: there are two essential themes. The first is Crosland's life and career, providing a biographical overview of how his ideological beliefs emerged, the wavering fortunes of his experience as a minister, and his relationship with significant political developments after the war. The second theme examines what made Crosland stand out on the post-war Left: his influence continued because he was an admirable political figure and prized Labour theoretician. What made Crosland of such appeal to successive generations; why has he sustained an extraordinary hold over sections of the Labour party; why do rival factions still fight over his memory? The chapter traces the source of Crosland's enduring fascination and charisma. His writings conveyed the depth of his personality, central to his political ideas; Crosland lived his life by values, his enjoyment of pleasure and his abiding hatred of class inequalities. As an intellectual, he set out to influence and affect the real world; as a politician, he sought to do what was right in principle rather than most expedient. Crosland had authenticity, a depth of character and vision that captivated many in the Labour party and beyond.

Crosland: his life and career

Anthony Crosland was born on 29 August 1918 in St Leonards-on-Sea into an upper middle-class English family; his father, Joseph Beardsell Crosland was a senior civil servant; his mother, Jessie Raven, lectured in Medieval Languages at Westfield College in the University of London.[5] Crosland was educated at Highgate School followed by Trinity College, Oxford where he read Greats.[6] Trinity College was, 'a typical incubator of the English ruling classes before the war'; the majority of undergraduates attended public schools notably Winchester and Eton; Crosland mixed with students educated in state grammar schools who worked conscientiously and had little money for high living.[7] He saw active military service in the Second World War as a member of the Royal Welsh Fusiliers and the Parachute Regiment in Italy, France and North Africa; he then returned to Oxford and secured a First-class degree in Politics, Philosophy and Economics (PPE). He became a Fellow of Trinity College from 1947 to 1950 where he taught economics to future stars including Anthony Wedgwood Benn and sought to convert 'Tory Old Etonians' to Keynesianism: 'Students remember Crosland's style fondly and particularly appreciated his ability to explain potentially abstract theoretical economics with frequent reference to their real life applications.'[8] He made an impact as President of the Oxford Union and as a leading figure on the Left. According to the former Cabinet Minister, Bill Rodgers, 'He had a style which young people very much appreciated... he was glamorous and very clever. [Crosland] talked highly intelligently and was very provocative in his style' as a regular speaker at Fabian Society summer schools.[9]

Despite the promise of a prestigious academic career, Crosland's focus had already shifted to Labour politics in Whitehall and Westminster where his rise owed much to being one of the former Labour Chancellor, Hugh Dalton's, favoured protégés. The Labour-supporting City financier, Nicholas Davenport, has memorably described Crosland's relationship with Dalton; Davenport regularly welcomed both of them to his stately home in Oxfordshire:

> Hugh [Dalton] had asked me specially to invite his young friend who was the economics fellow of Trinity College. 'I want to see how he behaves when he is drunk', he said. Tony came in his bright red sports car, wearing the red beret of the Parachute Regiment. We had an entertaining evening of drink and talk and Tony drove back to Oxford as steadily as he had come. He could obviously hold his drink. As he drove away I could see in Hugh's eyes the rekindling of his romantic love for gallant and handsome young men. After another weekend occasion, when Tony had left abruptly to catch a train with a girl to London, leaving Hugh and me alone to dine, Hugh actually refused to eat or speak. He paced about the room as if he had been jilted as a lover.[10]

The former Labour Prime Minister, James Callaghan, recalled meeting Crosland in the late 1940s:

> I wondered how he would go down in politics, and I asked him tactfully whether he was sure that he would feel at home away from the Oxford atmosphere. I then had the first taste of what we all got to know very quickly afterwards: he brushed me swiftly aside and left me in no doubt about what he intended to do. Fortunately, he attracted the attention immediately

of people much more important and with better judgement than myself, especially Hugh Dalton.[11]

According to his former Parliamentary Private Secretary, Dick Leonard, Crosland was in many ways, 'An Olympian figure. Blessed with an intelligence which was several notches higher than any other politician, with film star good looks, an incisive writing and speaking style and apparently brimming with self-confidence, it was almost written in the stars that he would rise to great heights.'[12] The Labour parliamentarian, Giles Radice, recalls:

> When I was young, Tony Crosland was one of my political heroes. I was attracted i) by his intellectual glamour; ii) by his insouciance and devil-may-care attitude symbolised for me by his collection of brightly coloured braces and iii) by his romantic attachment to his Grimsby constituents, of whom he was immensely proud.[13]

He was aggressively promoted for parliamentary selection by Dalton and elected Member of Parliament for South Gloucestershire in 1950. At his adoption meeting, Crosland memorably told local party members that the Attlee Government disproved the Tory charge that Labour was unfit to govern; the Conservatives were no longer the natural ruling party in British politics.[14] Following an unfavourable boundary review ahead of the 1955 election, he hastily moved constituencies to Southampton Test. Crosland believed he would be offered the winnable seat of Itchen, but was forced to contest the other Southampton constituency; despite a glowing reference from Dalton in his election literature, Crosland was defeated in a dismal result for Labour nationally:

> No young man on either side of the House has been more understanding, or more quickly made his mark in the last two parliaments. A gallant paratrooper in the war, an inspiring teacher at Oxford University and in

Adult Education, a man of deep convictions and wide
social sympathies, he would be an ideal representative
of the great town and port of Southampton.[15]

Absent from the House of Commons during the 1955–59
Parliament, Crosland was secretary to the Commission
examining the future of the Co-operative Society. The
1958 Co-operative Society conference defeated most of
the recommendations.[16] Symbolising the mood of stubborn
resistance to change on the Left, Crosland concluded that
the Commission had been 'a bitterly disappointing failure'.[17]
All that said, he found the Co-operative connection useful
in advancing his political career, counteracting his 'louche,
revisionist, Oxford-educated reputation'.[18] Without the
distraction of parliamentary business and constituency
responsibilities, Crosland completed his ground-breaking
treatise on *The Future of Socialism*.

During the 1950s, there were fears among his political
allies that Crosland might squander his talents; one friend
remarked: '[Tony] is so reckless, so uncalculating, he'll never
get anywhere'.[19] Crosland disliked the House of Commons and
found the lifestyle of parliamentarians unappealing. He was
thought to be 'ambivalent' about whether to stand again in
1959.[20] Crosland admitted: 'There was a time when I probably
did waver about a political career. I wasn't absolutely certain
that I wanted to come back in 1959.'[21] Tony Benn, a close
friend and pupil from Oxford, remarked:

The main trouble is his strict non-conformist
background. His parents were Plymouth Brethren and
against them he has been in constant revolt. His years
in the war gave him the excuse for thinking that his
youth had gone and he has been trying to catch up
since 1945. At thirty-nine it is rather silly. But he is fact
a rather kind man. He taught me economics as a favour
in the evenings and we went to the cinema together.
Without his recommendation I would never have got
Bristol South-East and without the redistribution in my

favour he would never have lost South Gloucestershire. He is unusually gifted as an economist and has a very clear mind with a very great faith in the power of reason. But the proof of his unhappiness is his curious death wish, which he showed when in the Commons, and which now takes the form of affecting to be bored with current politics. If he gets back into Parliament he will get high office. If he does not, then his life could be a very tragic one.[22]

One of Crosland's protégés, Roy Hattersley, accepts that his colleagues viewed Crosland as patronising and aloof, influenced by a 'romantic view of the Labour party and the working classes. Rather like Tony Benn his view of the working classes was shaped by the fact he hadn't met any until the war.'[23] He drank a great deal, acquiring the reputation of being a dilettante; Brian Harrison commented: 'It would have been surprising if these leading revisionists had not carried at least some liberal ideas on personal conduct from their private into their public lives.'[24] Nonetheless, Crosland continued to work long hours: 'fun' was only permitted after completing a long day's work.[25] Susan Crosland noted that when *The Future of Socialism* was being written, 'the puritan's self-discipline predominated in his life: he preferred to work at home and until he finished the task he had set himself, playtime could not begin'.[26] Crosland was a remarkable combination of the Fabian rationalist and the hedonist libertarian: this was the paradox of his complex personality. He developed a reputation as an unpredictable dinner guest: Roy and Jennifer Jenkins stopped inviting him to their parties because he was so rude to their friends; they continued to see a lot of him, but always on his own.[27] Rather than wearing suits to dinners as was the convention in the 1960s and 1970s, Crosland would arrive sporting a red paratrooper's sweater and red slippers.[28] As Noel Annan remarked: 'No politician among us ever said more forcibly to the world *je m'en fous*.'[29]

For all its frustrations, a political career had temptations: 'I wanted to be involved in the actual process of taking decisions and making policies. This seemed to me, and still seems to me, more satisfactory than writing books about them from an Oxford chair.'[30] Crosland's prominence in the party owed much to his friendship with Gaitskell, who Crosland allowed to use his Kensington flat in pursuing an affair with the society hostess, Ann Fleming.[31] Susan Crosland (a former journalist on the *Manchester Guardian*), his second wife after a brief marriage to the heiress Hilary Sarson, wrote that '[Gaitskell] was deeply attracted to Tony Crosland's combination of intellectual astringency and unabashed insistence on the right to private enjoyment.'[32] The *New Statesman* pilloried Crosland as 'Mr Gaitskell's Ganymede', an accusation with distinctly homoerotic overtones.[33] In the wake of his defeat at Southampton Test, Gaitskell was 'absolutely desperate' to get Crosland back into the House of Commons. After the 1955 election, Kenneth Younger, then MP for Grimsby and Shadow Foreign Secretary, announced he was leaving to be appointed Director of Chatham House. Given his experience, Younger expected Gaitskell to make every effort to dissuade him from departing the frontbench; he was taken aback when the leader's first words were: 'You'll be leaving Grimsby then: will they take Tony?'[34] Gaitskell found Crosland's personality 'immensely attractive'; he remained enormously impressed by his judgement on economic policy; the Labour leader was 'highly dependent' on his protégé during the arduous internal struggles of the late 1950s and early 1960s.[35] In the meantime, Crosland was buoyed by his marriage to Susan, a close personal and political relationship described as 'a great meeting of minds'.[36]

In 1959, Crosland was returned as MP for Great Grimsby by 101 votes, holding the seat in five successive general elections. His selection owed much to his effervescent and flamboyant personality, impressing party members and constituents with his willingness to address the most pressing issues facing a port on the East Coast of England. Crosland even agreed to spend five days and nights on a North Sea fishing trawler.[37] According to James Callaghan:

Although he always carried the aura of the university don even into his local Labour Club, it was never resented. On the contrary, this characteristic was greeted with rather affectionate amusement, because in Grimsby they knew him for what he was. They knew that he was not a humbug and that when he insisted on watching *Match of the Day* every Saturday, no matter how busy he was, it was not a pose; he genuinely enjoyed it. His charm and his bump of irreverence were as much a part of his private life as they were part of his public personality.[38]

Crosland conveyed genuineness of character, accompanied by real understanding of the problems afflicting working-class communities; he never pretended he was anything other than an upper middle-class Oxford educated economist:

When he first came to Grimsby some of the railwaymen imagined he was another public school academic come to teach the lads socialism. Then they met him and discovered he knew the problems sometimes better than they did, even though they were the ones that lived with them. His personality struck them more than the Oxford accent. They knew he didn't jump on bandwagons: he had joined the Labour party when he was sixteen. He'd been in the army, knew how to get on with people. He was a bloody big man. He liked a pint. He could sling stuff back at them. The differences in accents were then forgotten: they didn't hold his academic advantages against him.[39]

Bryan Magee writes that Crosland was 'a stimulating gossip, full of warm yet waspish humour…When we drank in the evenings we tended to get solidly drunk, yet our conversations retained a worthwhile level of content up to a surprisingly advanced stage.'[40] Magee found Crosland an 'acutely vulnerable' man, but also 'startlingly open about his feelings'. Roy Hattersley recalls that: 'Crosland had more élan than any other politician

I have ever known…life was a great charge for Tony. That was one of things that made him very attractive.'[41]

Crosland's ministerial experience

Crosland's mentor, Hugh Gaitskell, tragically died in January 1963 at the age of 56 having contracted the rare autoimmune disease, lupus erythematosus.[42] Without patronage at the top of the party, the revisionists were bereft. Crosland's relations with Wilson were dismal; he supported Callaghan and then George Brown in the second ballot for the leadership. Bill Rodgers recalls Gaitskell's death 'left Tony in danger of drifting'. Wilson came from Labour's Left having resigned from the Attlee Government with Bevan and John Freeman in 1951 following the imposition of NHS prescription charges; he was hostile to revisionism and critical of Gaitskell's efforts to rewrite Clause 4 which he equated to removing 'genesis from the Bible'. Having become leader, Wilson espoused an ambiguous commitment to industrial modernisation aligning science with socialism, appealing to the new class of professional and technical workers. Wilson acquired the reputation of being a 'skilled conciliator' of Left and Right, who avoided confronting cherished shibboleths. The leader intended that his party should postpone indefinitely, 'any consideration of the need for an intellectually articulated and justified strategy' while acknowledging that in 1964 Labour had to offer a programme of national renewal and modernisation rather than an 'old-fashioned' socialist programme.[43]

Although Wilson acknowledged the importance of accommodating the Labour Right, he preferred to promote other modernisers; Crosland was disparaged as an ardent Gaitskellite, ensuring Roy Jenkins gained preferment from Wilson throughout his career. Giles Radice believes that Jenkins, who had been subordinate to Crosland, subsequently gained the edge in the race to succeed Wilson.[44] Crosland's ambition to become Chancellor of the Exchequer was thwarted on three occasions: in 1967 as he was passed over in favour of Jenkins; in 1974 when Denis Healey was preferred; and again in 1976 when Callaghan with whom Crosland enjoyed a political friendship decided to stick with Healey who had survived the International Monetary Fund (IMF) crisis. Wilson and Crosland disagreed over economic policy, particularly Crosland's view in 1964 that devaluation was inevitable. He irritated the Prime Minister with 'his intellectual squeamishness and inverted snobbishness'.[45] Wilson had a coterie of allies on the Bevanite Left, notably Richard Crossman and John Freeman; he had little need for Crosland's brain. He turned to Keynesian economists such as Nicholas Kaldor and Thomas Balogh as an alternative to the distrusted civil service machine.[46]

Following Labour's victory in the 1964 election, Crosland was appointed Minister of State at the Department of Economic Affairs (DEA) under George Brown. He became Secretary of State for the Department of Education in 1965, where he fought to abolish the 'iniquitous' 11-plus favouring comprehensive education. Crosland moved to the Board of Trade in 1967, and the Department of Local Government and Regional Planning in 1969. Following Labour's defeat in 1970 and narrow victories in February and October 1974, Crosland returned to the Cabinet as Secretary of State for the Environment (1974–76), and then Foreign Secretary (1976–77), a post in which he served with distinction. A senior Foreign Office official, Sir Michael Butler, wrote that had he lived, 'Crosland would have been one of Britain's great foreign secretaries'.[47]

According to Dick Leonard, 'Wilson's long tenure of the leadership substantially blighted Crosland's prospects.'[48] It was not just a matter of personal animosity. Crosland's performance as a minister raised doubts among Wilson's circle: he was rarely accused of incompetence but was said to be reluctant to take difficult decisions, commissioning research and advice rather than acting decisively.[49] In reforming housing policy in the 1970s, there was speculation that 'the Secretary of State himself was not giving a strong enough lead. Originally promised for the autumn of 1975, a year later the Review had run into the sand and ended as a feeble package.'[50] David Lipsey accepts that

Crosland had two major faults: 'he wanted to think everything through whereas [Roy] Jenkins would go with his prejudice'. Furthermore, Crosland separated himself psychologically from Jenkins; as a result, 'he paid far too much attention to party policy' particularly on housing and local government.[51] Crosland would have brought the rigour of a trained economist to the Treasury, but Wilson was convinced he lacked the acumen, decisiveness and common touch necessary to enhance Labour's reputation for economic competence.

Wilson still grew to admire Crosland according to the former Head of the Downing Street Policy Unit, Bernard Donoughue. By the mid-1970s, some considered Crosland to be Wilson's favoured 'heir'; after all, Jenkins had defied a three-line whip over Europe.[52] Crossman believed Crosland was effective in Cabinet: 'what matters in cabinet government is personality'.[53] With his economic expertise, Crosland brought a strategic perspective to the entire government acting as 'a real, active Cabinet Minister'.[54] He remained close to Callaghan, who made him Foreign Secretary having secured the leadership in 1976. Callaghan intended to swap Healey for Crosland as Chancellor, a decision never implemented because of Crosland's untimely death in 1977.

It is difficult to avoid the conclusion that by the early 1970s, Crosland's career was stalling. He had always had a mixed reception within the Parliamentary Labour Party (PLP); Crossman wrote: 'I don't suppose there's any man who is more disliked and out of touch with the parliamentary party than Denis Healey, unless it's Tony Crosland. Both of them are arrogant and despise their colleagues.'[55] In the 1972 deputy leadership contest, Crosland received 65 votes. He topped the Shadow Cabinet elections in 1970, but did progressively worse over the next four years, punished by acolytes of Jenkins for his decision to abstain on Britain's entry into the European Community.[56] Bill Rodgers, one of the leading Jenkinsites in the 1970s, argues that Crosland paid the price for being 'extremely self-centred': 'Tony was our hero, but stage by stage we transferred our loyalty, support and affections [to Roy Jenkins], because Tony had no loyalty to his own friends.'[57]

In the 1976 leadership contest, Crosland finished at the bottom of the ballot having attracted the support of 'a motley collection of screwballs and crackpots'.[58] His reputation in the parliamentary party declined after 1971 reflecting the shift to the Left in the PLP and trade unions, alongside his breach with the Jenkinsites. Crosland even failed in his 'modest aspiration' of being elected to the constituency section of the National Executive.[59] Bernard Donoughue observed: 'There is always something of the detached, amused Oxford Don about him'.[60] Crosland had no hope of securing the leadership as 'he has too little committed support'.[61] According to his allies: 'The real problem in crude political terms was that he was in the middle – so he was the least disliked of all the candidates but had little chance of getting through the first ballot.'[62] Crosland had no discernable political base whereas Jenkins had the pro-European faction; Callaghan had the trade unions; and Michael Foot had the organised Left.[63] Crosland's advance within the Labour party had been halted by the time of his death.[64] With the support of his wife, Susan, Crosland attempted to carve out a role as a mainstream Labour politician more instinctively in touch with the grassroots than Jenkins; but he scarcely succeeded in redefining his image as a 'party man'.

Crosland as socialist theoretician

Giles Radice recalls that although he greatly admired Crosland as a minister, 'It was his role as a socialist writer and theoretician which had the most impact on me. Indeed his great book *The Future of Socialism* shifted my whole approach to politics. Even now, fifty years later, the brilliance and sharpness of Crosland's mind stands out from its pages.'[65]

The Future of Socialism gave the Labour party a new perspective and vision, escaping from the cul-de-sac of Clause 4 and the Attlee era.[66] Crosland's other major writings included *Britain's Economic Problem* (1953), *The Conservative Enemy* (1962), and *Socialism Now* (1974) accompanied by an impressive array of Fabian pamphlets, academic papers and newspaper articles.[67] However, *The Future of Socialism* was

Crosland's most celebrated and renowned work, offering a persuasive and incisive presentation of social democratic ideas. The disappointment of defeat in 1955 had enabled him to focus on producing this great work of socialist theory: 'When he was writing, it was almost impossible to lure him into social company of any kind. He would concentrate intellectually for fourteen, fifteen hours a day.'[68] Intense intellectual energy drove Crosland's life in this period:

> On entering the flat at 19 The Boltons one felt that the atmosphere was charged. The furnishings themselves were donnish. Books lined a long wall, and manuscripts were systematically organised in piles on the seat of the sofa, on its arms, along the floor directly in front of it. Depending on the stage of writing he'd reached, further piles might be carefully set along the back of the sofa.[69]

The political analysis and strategy that Crosland developed inspired later generations of Labour politicians and intellectuals.[70] John Stratchey commended *The Future of Socialism* as, 'the product of a cultivated and humane intelligence...no-one must in future take part in the controversy on socialism without having read it'.[71] Ralph Miliband, a prominent Marxist critic of Crosland, still described *The Future of Socialism* as 'the bible of Labour revisionism'.[72] Henry Drucker writes that Crosland's book was 'the sole British socialist tract since the Second World War to achieve an international audience'.[73] According to Roy Hattersley:

> *The Future of Socialism* was right for the time. There was a lot of people, me included, who wanted the Labour party to have a body of belief on which it based its policies, what Tony [Crosland] called an ethical framework. There was a great shortage of that. The only theory around was Marxism which we rejected without knowing what to put in its place... *The Future of Socialism* produced a theory that was immensely

suitable for what we were looking for. We all believed
the Labour party was about equality.[74]

More recently, *The Future of Socialism* was hailed as 'the book
that influenced the British Left more than any other in the
last century'.[75] It was a 'focused and intellectually innovative'
piece of writing, as well as 'formidably well informed'; the
book was deliberately 'oriented towards the practical'.[76] The
Future of Socialism was a revisionist tract intended to offer a
revitalised concept of British socialism for the post-Attlee
era.[77] The Left could not be satisfied if Labour was merely 'the
party for defending 1945–51 and a little more'.[78] Crosland's
generation was more iconoclastic in assessing the record of the
post-war governments. In the *New Fabian Essays*, Roy Jenkins
and Crosland insisted Attlee's ministers had been insufficiently
radical in tackling the inequalities that bedevilled Britain in
the inter-war years. The aim of 1945 was 'a fairer deal for
the working man' rather than a social revolution leading to
a fundamental redistribution of wealth and power. Labour's
programme in the 1945 manifesto, *Let Us Face the Future* was all
but complete by 1950: the party's ageing, exhausted leadership
had little new to offer the country beyond the 'consolidation'
of public ownership.[79] Facing up to such a predicament, '*The
Future of Socialism* was a radical tract which gave the Labour
party new perspective and vision allowing it to escape from
the orthodoxies of Clause 4 and the Attlee Government.'[80] The
Bevanite Left was content merely to entrench the domestic
achievements of the 1945 administration.

Crosland's mark on the Labour party and the intellectual
life of the British Left is unusual. The extent of his impact
remains surprising; it was not clear in the 1950s that Crosland
was set to exert such influence. The British labour movement
was notoriously circumspect about intellectuals. Crossman
noted that around the Labour party there was a 'fear and
suspicion of ideas and the intellectuals who produce them.
Just as intellectuals are potential traitors, so the new ideas
they put forward are always by nature assumed to be anti-
socialist, until you can show that they are not.'[81] In the 1930s,

mavericks like Stafford Cripps fuelled mistrust of intellectuals by promulgating apparently eccentric ideas. Dalton, Hilary Marquand, Evan Durbin and Gaitskell were viewed more positively, deploying their scholarship in diligently serving the party and the trade unions. But suspicion towards socialist intellectuals continued; for that reason alone, it is important not to overemphasise Crosland's immediate impact in the 1950s.

When his treatise was published, it was greeted by a chorus of acclaim, but the impact of the book was initially hard to discern. According to the historian Martin Pugh although it was read widely and revered in academic circles, '*The Future of Socialism* was one of those influential books that never quite enjoyed the influence it deserved.'[82] Sales of the book were high but far from spectacular.[83] *The Future of Socialism's* impact came belatedly as its publication coincided with the Suez crisis and the Soviet invasion of Hungary; it took a decade for Crosland's work to get the attention it deserved.[84] As a middle-class intellectual and leading architect of the permissive society, Crosland never built a substantial following in a predominantly working-class party; his reputation as a Gaitskellite and revisionist limited his impact, particularly under Wilson.[85] That Crosland was out of step with the party's prevailing working-class culture is overstated as an argument; he was assiduous in accommodating himself to the party's 'proletarian sectionalism'; nonetheless, his books were addressed to a party contemptuous of theoretical debate. Inevitably, the process of hammering out ideas to develop an alternative programme for the affluent society was undertaken by a narrow circle of Labour intellectuals and politicians.

Rather than imposing a rigid doctrine, the purpose of Crosland's revisionism was to understand how the world was changing and how Labour's politics must adapt. In post-war Britain, living standards were rising and material poverty was declining after a long period of rationing and austerity. The era of affluence contrasted markedly with the mass unemployment and social deprivation of 'the hungry thirties'. The revisionist challenge was to develop strategies for a more prosperous society.[86] The mass industrial working class of factories and coal mines inhabiting close-knit communities was disappearing, with it the solidarities that socialism took for granted: relative industrial decline, the rise of new service industries, the clearance of slums and the construction of suburban estates and new towns meant that traditional political allegiances fragmented. In this heady atmosphere of structural change in British society, Crosland drew on Bernstein's revisionism, separating the 'ends' and 'means' of socialist doctrine; means were institutional reforms required to bring about ends, the fundamental aspirations of democratic socialism: 'timeless values which functioned as moral imperatives'.[87] Of course, social change is never objective and in Crosland's revisionism it is interpreted through an ideological lens; the social and economic landscape was always politically constructed. Like R.H. Tawney, Crosland believed:

> A political creed…is neither a system of transcendental doctrine nor a code of rigid formulae. It is a common conception of the ends of political action, and of the means of achieving them, based on a common view of the life proper to human beings, and of the steps required at any moment more nearly to attain it.[88]

Instead of viewing nationalisation and public ownership as the only plausible agents of British socialism, they were redefined as flexible policy instruments; Crosland depicted socialism as timeless, 'spiritual' egalitarian beliefs fulfilled by the goal of 'democratic equality' requiring intervention by the state to equalise the distribution of opportunities cultivating a classless society:

> The socialist seeks a distribution of rewards, status and privileges egalitarian enough to minimise social resentment, to secure justice between individuals, and to equalise opportunities. And he seeks to weaken the existing deep-seated class stratification, with its concomitant feelings of envy and inferiority, and its barriers to uninhibited mingling between classes.[89]

The breadth and quality of scholarship means *The Future of Socialism* is justifiably seen as a landmark book in the development of post-war social democracy.[90] It was not astonishingly original: *The Future of Socialism* still articulated a comprehensive agenda of social reform going beyond conventional economic and industrial questions, an impressive breadth of vision for its age.[91] Crosland's revisionist tract provoked and unnerved the Labour Left, prompting inevitable accusations of heresy and betrayal; *Tribune's* headline was 'Socialism? How Dare He Use the Word!': if Labour listened earnestly to Crosland, *Tribune's* reviewer insisted, the party would be 'set firmly and inexorably on the road to decline'.[92]

The suspicion and paranoia stirred by Crosland's treatise were not in the least surprising: *The Future of Socialism* departed radically from Labour orthodoxy. Crosland offered an uncompromising critique of the traditional arguments for nationalisation; he restated the aims of democratic socialism as ethical values rather than the commitment to class struggle, which had animated Labour's fight on behalf of the underdog since the early twentieth century; socialism as a battle of 'them against us', a perpetual class war, was consigned to the 'dustbin of history'.[93] Crosland insisted that socialism had no 'precise, descriptive meaning' equated with state ownership. Socialism was about enduring ethical ideals: a belief in equality, a classless society, the commitment to fellowship and cooperation. He highlighted pre-eminent objectives, notably a guarantee of universal social welfare: 'a socialist is identified as one who wishes to give this an exceptional priority over other claims on resources'; and the goal of equality: 'the most characteristic feature of socialist thought'.[94] Crosland defined an egalitarian philosophy for the centre-left in terms of opportunity and outcome: public services and private enterprise should work together to achieve social equality.[95] The strategy for post-war social democracy was to distribute the proceeds of growth between personal consumption and living standards on the one hand, and investment in state services and the public sector on the other.[96]

Reviewing Crosland's later work, *The Conservative Enemy*, Barbara Castle attacked his conviction that 'we can get rid of the evils of society without changing what Socialists have always believed to be the source of those evils: the private ownership of the means of production and their deployment in obedience to the profit motive'.[97] Despite vehement criticisms, Crosland was established as the leading revisionist theoretician. In reacting so divisively to his heresies, the Left underlined Crosland's radicalism, strengthening the book's currency. Richard Crossman bemoaned his 'diabolically left-wing' programme which outmanoeuvred the Bevanites. More than just the leading revisionist, Crosland emerged as a top Labour politician.[98] His biographer, Kevin Jeffreys, wrote that *The Future of Socialism* was 'a slow-burner, its influence growing steadily over the course of the next decade'.[99] Stuart Hall, the New Left's leading light, remarked that 'few of us imagined, when Mr Crosland began to construct his house of theory in *The Future of Socialism*, that he would become the architect of the party in the sixties'.[100] It is noteworthy that 60 years after *The Future of Socialism's* publication, Crosland's book remains the yardstick against which contributions to British social democratic thought are assessed.[101]

Crosland's reformulation of socialism influenced the 1964–70 and 1974–79 Wilson–Callaghan governments, laying the foundations for subsequent revisionism: the emergence of New Labour in the late 1980s and early 1990s owes an unacknowledged debt to *The Future of Socialism*. The revisionist attitude to the public–private sector relationship was pragmatic and instrumental: state intervention should take place within a dynamic market economy upholding the legitimate role of private enterprise.[102] Economic growth was essential to reduce economic inequalities and improve social welfare. The increment from growth would fund an expansion of state services, making progress towards equality without disillusioning those on high incomes: post-war social democracy depended on sustaining economic growth, a new alignment between production and distribution.[103] Crosland admitted that redistribution was 'easier and less painful with a large and growing national cake than with a small one'.[104] The revisionist prospectus was, nonetheless, subsequently undermined by the absence of a credible strategy for rebuilding the productive base of British capitalism, a weakness underlined by the collapse of the Wilson Government's National Plan and the 1966–67 devaluation crisis. Crosland was less inspirational and audacious during the 1964–70 and 1974–79 Labour governments than in the 1950s; there was little prospect of producing a revisionist treatise to rival *The Future of Socialism*.[105] This retreat led some to question why Labour should look back to Crosland for inspiration: to a politician of mixed achievement and questionable political judgement who died in the 1970s, and whose ideas were thoroughly discredited by the time of Margaret Thatcher's victory.

Crosland: his influence and appeal

On the contrary, Crosland's unique combination of personal qualities and intellectual credentials expose a vacuum contemporary politicians have struggled to fill. These attributes have even greater currency in an age when political figures are regarded as professional careerists and technocrats with little interest in weighty and thoughtful debate about ideas. It has been said of Crosland that 'the manner in which he conducted himself in politics are deemed to have been as important as his specific ideas': this included a constructive approach to political debate, minimising partisan conflict.[106] Crosland was without the hatred and malice that infected other front-rank parliamentarians during the battles of the 1950s and 1960s.[107] Gaitskell's conduct was said to have been 'in standing contradiction to those who wish to believe that only men with cold hearts and twisted tongues can succeed...He took the cynicism out of politics.'[108] Exactly the same epithet could be applied to Crosland.

There have been numerous front-rank Labour politicians and many British socialist theoreticians; Crosland achieved the rare distinction of being both. He was 'the scholar-politician of the movement'[109] possessing a 'remarkable and enduring appeal' with his 'curious, swashbuckling quality...combining intellect, glamour and arrogance in roughly equal proportions'.[110] Crosland was a unique combination of an inspiring thinker as well as a practising politician, respected academic writer as well as a committed man of action rallying Labour's moderate wing in defence of Gaitskell's leadership. As Secretary of State for Education, Crosland was unusual in his capacity 'to turn ideas into action'.[111] Despite being preoccupied at the highest levels of government (in an age when the demands on members of parliament were, it must be said, less onerous than today) he continued to publish and write extensively. This was an unusual combination of talents, emulated rarely before or since. Wilson was a gifted statistician who worked with Beveridge on his plans for social insurance; but his intellectual outlook was technocratic and administrative, conveying little interest in political ideas. Other revisionists of Crosland's generation such as Jenkins and Healey were scarcely political theorists, despite their literary and cultural hinterland. Healey positively eschewed what he called 'intellectualism', while Jenkins abandoned labourism for the language of 'the new centre' during the 1970s.

Much has been written about the experience of intellectuals in political life: Max Weber concluded that academics were too thin-skinned to pursue political careers.[112] Crosland never suffered unduly from a lack of confidence. He was dismissive of the mass media, 'extremely loath to accept that television had become an expected link between politicians and public'; his former PPS, Christopher Price, once remarked 'The trouble with you on television, Tony, is that you look so bored.'[113] Nevertheless, he had an unrivalled capacity to promote new thinking with his formidable reputation that combined 'authoritative egalitarian anger with no-nonsense realism'; he quickly attracted a following of admiring supporters in public life.[114] Reisman's verdict that Crosland would have 'made a greater contribution to the future of socialism if he had remained with his books and not opted for the rainbow of action' neglects his qualities of charisma and audacity, his impeachable honesty and rigorous approach to the conduct of politics.[115] To his supporters, Crosland had an intellectual spirit; a certainty of moral purpose; a fearlessness in taking on received wisdom while addressing new social problems; as well as an audacity in forcing Labour to rethink its mission in an acquisitive age.

He had virtues that appear ever more necessary 40 years since his death. For good or ill, these have vanished from modern politics shaped by the global '24/7' news media cycle, the imperatives of technocratic management, and a policy process characterised by the 'end of ideology'. The perception of politicians is as venal, unprincipled, immoral, and even corrupt. According to David Runciman, there is a perception that 'compared to previous generations, we live in an age of political pygmies', reinforcing the suspicion that current politicians lack genuine ballast and stature.[116] Crosland, on the other hand, was a figure 'of genuine substance and experience' with remarkable qualities, accompanied by a vast cultural and artistic hinterland.

There is an ongoing debate about the quality of statecraft in British politics. Peter Clarke categorised the skills of leadership from William Gladstone to Margaret Thatcher as rational persuasion, executive efficiency, charismatic oratory, party organisation, institutional power-broking and 'high political scheming'.[117] Crosland did not possess all of these attributes and was disinterested in political manoeuvring. But he left a significant mark because his 'outlook and gifts chimed in with the contemporary mood, anticipating rather than simply echoing it'.[118] Clarke reminds us that success in politics is a combination of structure and agency: individual flair and aptitude are decisive, but the structural conditions must exist for political talent to catch the tide. It was Labour's paralysis after 1951 that afforded Crosland the opportunity to exert intellectual leadership in the party; nonetheless, he stood out for several reasons:

The politics of principle and the politics of power

Crosland bridged the politics of principle with the politics of power. His approach drew on Bernstein and Tawney, attesting that there was no trade-off between political ethics and competing for office through the democratic electoral process. Crosland insisted the Labour party was electable without abandoning its core beliefs. The revisionist strategy drew a distinction between policy 'means' that were for a particular historical era and 'ends', socialist values providing a signpost to the future. Crosland's vision of the interlinked nature of liberty and equality bestowed Labour with a strong social democratic identity. Crosland argued that the party must be alive to social change, but there was no inherent conflict between principles and power.

He was willing to challenge conventional wisdom to create a more equal and just society, making the case for social reforms such as a 'property-owning democracy' and home ownership dismissed previously as Conservative party ideas. He advocated an extension of personal freedom and the easing of moral regulation through legislative reform. Nevertheless, according to David Lipsey, he was scathing of the proposition that Labour should embrace superficially popular policies such as reducing income tax merely to court favour with the electorate. Measures were judged by whether they advanced social democratic values, eschewing the 'opinion-survey driven socialism' which characterised New Labour's modernisation in the 1990s. Crosland's outlook has appeal in an age when politicians are perceived as devoid of belief, concerned only with winning the support of the non-aligned median voter in a predominantly middle-class society.

A distinctive vision of the just society

Crosland provided a unique vision of social justice and the good society. He left a significant mark because Crosland wanted Labour not only to be a responsible governing party but to offer a compelling and uplifting vision of a just society:

Labour had to develop a majoritarian national project with a natural appeal wide enough to attract a solid base of electoral support. Traditional Fabianism focused on means such as central planning and state ownership which became obsolete in the decades following the Second World War. The peroration in the final chapter of *The Future of Socialism* is one of the finest in any twentieth century political tract. It defined socialism not merely as a transformation in the economic system, but as enhancing quality of life and widening the capacity for human fulfilment; Labour's purpose should be to enrich 'personal freedom, happiness and cultural endeavour; the cultivation of leisure, beauty, grace, gaiety, excitement, and all of the proper pursuits, whether elevated, vulgar or eccentric, which contribute to the varied fabric of a full private and family life'.[119] The breadth of Crosland's ambition has appeal in an age when politicians are perceived as focused on short-term politics and policy, disinterested in an ambitious view of the good society and economy.

The potential of democratic politics

Crosland was strongly committed to parliamentary politics and representative democracy. Drawing on Bernstein's revisionism, he believed in the capacity of parliamentary democracy to transform British society through gradualist social reform. Nonetheless, he became more and more attached to the traditional structures, rituals and institutions of the Labour party. Marquand has written that the party was for Crosland:

> The unquestioned structure that gave meaning to his life; the embodiment of a commitment that was now beyond argument. His loyalty to it was not, as party loyalty so often is, a superficial matter of convenience, or habit, or personal ties. It sprang from the deepest recesses of his complex and elusive character.[120]

Crosland was repeatedly criticised for being sentimental about British working-class life, especially the labour movement.

One of his parliamentary allies, Donald Dewar, complained about the attention he devoted to 'second-rate' trade union regional secretaries.[121] He admired the labour movement's maturity in embracing the parliamentary road to socialism. It was the party's steadfast commitment to parliamentary democracy in the early twentieth century that gave Labour the opportunity to transform British society. The revisionists believed that parliamentary sovereignty was the vehicle for achieving socialism: by winning power at Westminster, the measures necessary to build a fairer, more equal society could be enacted. A later generation of parliamentarians including John Mackintosh and Marquand attacked Crosland for being too conservative in his attitude to the Westminster model. But Crosland's optimism about the potential of political leadership and parliamentary democracy has appeal in an era when faith in representative democratic institutions is deteriorating, when electoral turnout is declining, and the level of participation in formal democratic politics, such as party membership, is waning.

Crosland as enlightenment rationalist

Finally, Crosland's legacy stands out in the contemporary Labour party and among the liberal intelligentsia since he was a rational empiricist, committed to values of tolerance upholding the legitimacy of dissent. Having been taught at Oxford by A.J. Ayer, Crosland was influenced by logical positivism. He came to believe that 'moral values, though they could be reasoned about, were decided independently of any theory about society'.[122] The Oxford school of analytical philosophy's approach was *de rigueur* among twentieth-century revisionists, particularly Gaitskell and Jay. Logical positivism separated empirical facts based on objective evidence from value judgements, the product of human values and emotion. As such, Crosland: 'Adopted the orthodox logical positivism of the immediate post-war world. Morality is a matter of individual choice, moral propositions are merely the evincing of a positive emotional reaction towards something...it is all a matter of emotion and opinion and choice.'[123]

Crosland insisted that 'every opinion needed to be based on evidence (and therefore on knowledge rather than emotion) from which any inference needed to be logically justified. For him, everything was also, or he thought it ought to be, a matter for rational demonstration.'[124] As Crosland's mentor, Gaitskell believed in the pursuit of truth 'to the bitter end'.[125] This created an intriguing blend of political traits: Gaitskell and Crosland were both private men who had a reputation for being cold and unemotional; but Crosland particularly was also warm, witty and charismatic; in spell-binding and passionate speeches to the Labour conference, Gaitskell pledged to 'fight, and fight, and fight again, to save the party we love'. Crosland had an ethical view of the good society but was reluctant to impose his moral philosophical outlook. Gaitskell and Crosland were not opposed to religious faith in politics, but insisted that public institutions should be governed by liberal principles of tolerance and equality. Logical positivism has lost authority in the academy since the 1960s; nonetheless this philosophical outlook has attractions in an age when secular rationalism is under attack, amid growing concern about the role of religious belief in modern civic life.

Conclusion

The historian Ben Pimlott presciently remarked that Crosland was one of few figures from the post-war era with whom Labour politicians were not embarrassed to be associated.[126] During the 2010 leadership election, one of the contenders, David Miliband, announced that Crosland was the politician who inspired him most. The victor, Ed Miliband, referred to Crosland's ideas in his speeches having addressed the 2006 Memorial Conference celebrating the fiftieth anniversary of *The Future of Socialism*. Leo Panitch, a close friend of Ralph Miliband's, noted with irony that, 'people are saying of David and Ed that they are the inheritors of Croslandism in the Labour party'; Ed went so far as to say that 'in the household in which [we were] brought up, Crosland and his ideas were not popular – his critique of Marxism, his views on public ownership'.[127] Crosland's impact on both Miliband brothers underlines how far his influence permeated throughout the party.

This chapter has considered Crosland's role as a moderate socialist politician and Left theoretician tracing his influence on the Labour party since the Second World War. Having never acquired the great offices of state as Prime Minister or Chancellor of the Exchequer, Crosland's ministerial career is seldom judged an unequivocal success. He experienced undoubted highs and triumphs as well as innumerable setbacks and disappointments. Nonetheless, this book will examine how Crosland's ideas acquired a life of their own which has had an impact on subsequent generations. Before he died, his thinking had purchase since Crosland was close to the leadership, particularly Gaitskell, although he also left an imprint on Wilson's modernisation strategy; his political thought was presented in a form that could be readily digested by party audiences: *The Future of Socialism* is strikingly well written and his books had political relevance as well as intellectual vivacity. The influence of protégés such as Giles Radice and Roy Hattersley who then disseminated Croslandite thought in a cold climate for social democracy explains Crosland's impact after his death; other factors were the manner in which Crosland's ideas were debated in party institutions such as the Fabian Society; the 'timeless' quality of Crosland's analysis marrying economic theory with social justice; as well as the paucity of the next generation of theoreticians, particularly after the SDP's 'breakaway' in 1981.

The next chapter will begin the task of examining Crosland's legacy in the post-war Labour party by analysing his contribution to Labour's strategy and programme as an egalitarian social democrat. It was in establishing equality as the centrepiece of democratic socialism that Crosland's influence has been greatest. The chapters that follow address Crosland's commitment to radical liberalism in a devoutly socialist party; the influence of Europe and America on the development of British socialism after the Second World War; and Crosland's status as a political strategist: in Labour's politics, the revisionist *par excellence*.

THREE

Egalitarian social democracy: 'Is equality of opportunity enough?'

In Britain, equality of opportunity and social mobility, though they lead to the most admirable distribution of intelligence, are not enough. They need, not to be played down, as some sociologists would have us do, but to be combined with measures, above all in the educational field, to equalise the distribution of rewards and privileges so as to diminish the degree of class stratification, the injustice of large inequalities, and the collective discontents which come from too great a dispersion of rewards. (Anthony Crosland, 1956[1])

I came to hate and loathe social injustice, because I disliked the class structure of our society, because I could not tolerate the indefensible differences of status and income that disfigure our society. (Anthony Crosland, 1956[2])

Introduction: Crosland's legacy and egalitarian social democracy

Crosland's *Future of Socialism* inspired the debate in the post-war Labour party about the nature of equality. His revisionism involved a vigorous commitment to egalitarian social democracy: equality was at the front and centre of Crosland's analysis. His work offered a reference point for what kind of equality mattered in Britain: equality of opportunity where all citizens could rise through the class and occupational structure as far as their talents would take them; and equality of outcome ensuring the distribution of disposable income and resources accords with fundamental principles of social justice. Since Crosland understood equality as the pre-eminent value, his views on egalitarianism are discussed extensively in *The Future of Socialism*. According to Dick Leonard, Crosland offered: 'The most persuasive, eloquent and comprehensive presentation of the values of democratic socialism so far attempted'.[3] Roy Hattersley insists that Crosland crystallised what equality ought to mean to the party: 'We all believed the Labour party was about equality. Crosland gave substance to that by defining equality in an acceptable way. Tawney had talked about equality not being uniformity and encouraging diversity, but only Tony up to that point had given thought to the different forms of equality.'[4] His views have acquired additional significance since *The Future of Socialism*'s was published as more recent generations of Labour politicians have fought to acquire the Croslandite mantle. The chapter will address Crosland's ongoing influence on British social democracy, and what equality ought to mean in today's society. Despite arguments surrounding Crosland's definition of equality, his influence on the party's concept of egalitarianism has been profound.

While Crosland articulated his conviction that 'equality of opportunity is not enough', he struggled to resolve the question of what the Left ought to mean by equality and social justice. As a result, confusion about the relationship between equality and the ends of social democracy in Labour's thinking persists. This chapter examines the debate about what kind of equality social democrats should pursue. It opens by reflecting on the Attlee Government's legacy, considering the position adopted by Crosland on the question of how the Left should define equality. Providing a robust definition mattered as equality would supersede nationalisation as the primary goal of socialism in the post-war years. Lurking beneath the dispute is a debate about equality of opportunity and the emphasis on social mobility, which Crosland considered necessary but not sufficient to construct a truly classless society. His concept of 'democratic equality' was intended to marry together outcome with opportunity. Labour modernisers were later accused of emphasising equality of opportunity at the expense of outcomes: redistributing opportunities is less contentious than the redistribution of resources which explicity penalises the better-off. Crosland believed that the ideal of equality was compatible with a winning electoral strategy in an affluent society; redistribution would occur through rising living standards and sustained growth minimising resentment among the middle class. After 1997, Blair insisted his Government's success ought to be judged by whether Labour created a 'genuine meritocracy'. However, the danger is that radical equality of opportunity merely 'legitimises inequality'.[5] Meritocracy leads to a 'winner takes all' culture: a distribution of income which undermines equal opportunities, focused on a narrow measure of equal worth.[6]

It is necessary to address significant criticisms of Crosland's vision: some political theorists insist that he had little original to say about equality. The Fabian Society averred in the late 1940s that 'socialism is about equality. A passion for equality is the one thing that links all socialists; on all others they are divided.'[7] *The Future of Socialism* did not advance the debate significantly beyond the position developed by Tawney and the post-war Fabians. Crosland's perspective rested on 'value or ethical judgements of a non-economic character' contrasting with the economic and welfare arguments adumbrated in the inter-war years by Keynes and Durbin. Keynesianism 'legitimised the doctrine of equality' demonstrating that 'economic expansion depended on broadening the base of consumption through a diffuse distribution of income and wealth'.[8] Keynesian theories constituted a powerful attack 'on the free market doctrines of the day'.[9] In conrast, Crosland's analysis contained a series of omissions and inconsistencies: the question of whether equality was the ultimate purpose of socialism or just the means to the end of enlarging human freedom in a capitalist society was never clarified. Tawney relied on Christian doctrine to give his views moral legitimacy, but Crosland's secularism meant that this option was scarcely available. He struggled to articulate the ethical basis of his position: what made equality vital in human societies? Crosland turned to John Rawls' *Theory of Justice*[10] with its argument that inequalities were justified only where they benefited the least advantaged; but this was undertaken after Crosland's major works had been published: in any case, there were fundamental discrepancies in Rawls' justice theory.

In attaching importance to the 'ends' of social democracy, namely equality and social justice, Crosland rejected the views of conservative philosophers, notably Michael Oakeshott, who insisted that the pursuit of abstract ideals should be abandoned in favour of the 'common-sense intimations' of everyday life.[11] Oakeshott emphasised the importance of upholding tradition and moral order; resolving abstract claims to a just income distribution would merely intensify social conflict. In *The Future of Socialism*, Crosland remarked that the Labour party preferred the communitarianism of Keir Hardie which offered 'a more reliable foundation than the theories of Lassalle and Kautsky'; ethical socialism put less emphasis than he was to do on theoretical principles of justice and equality.[12] In contrast to the communitarian tradition which emphasised 'the brotherhood of man', Crosland put equality at the forefront of socialism. As he soon discovered, however, equality was 'a highly complex and contested social ideal' in the economic climate of post-war Britain, where disputes erupted over the distribution of the fiscal dividend from growth.[13] Then, after Crosland's death, under Conservative governments in the 1980s and 1990s inequality rocketed to levels he never anticipated in the relatively propitious circumstances of the early post-war decades.

Equality and the Attlee governments

In making the case for a more equal society, Crosland assumed that the traditional arguments for redistribution were losing their relevance: fiscal measures introduced by the Attlee governments after the Second World War meant income differences were narrowing.[14] More redistribution would scarcely improve human welfare: taxing the income of the very wealthy (then a relatively small section of society) would produce marginal gains for the working class. Crosland's ambition to revive contemporary socialism meant overcoming the sense of exhaustion enveloping Attlee's Administration, developing a new approach to the pursuit of equality through fiscal mechanisms combined with state intervention.

The inter-war generation of Tawney, Cole, Durbin and Dalton formulated a socialist prospectus for the 1945 Government which the historian Kenneth O. Morgan hailed as 'without doubt the most effective of all Labour governments, perhaps the most effective of any British government since the passage of the 1832 Great Reform Act'.[15] In striving for equality, Attlee's ministers had adopted a blend of resource use planning and Keynesian demand management: sustaining an adequate level of purchasing power to maintain full employment, while emphasising planning 'from the ground up – giving an appropriate place to constructive enterprise and private endeavour in the national plan'.[16] According to Adam Przeworski this 'held out the prospect that the state could reconcile the private ownership of the means of production with democratic management of the economy'.[17] During Cripps' tenure as Chancellor after 1947 and Gaitskell in 1950–51, Labour downgraded the importance of central planning to focus on a coherent financial strategy.[18] Ministers were determined to re-establish Labour's reputation for economic competence after the financial crisis of 1931.

As Alan Warde has noted, subsequent interpretations of the Attlee governments' performance on equality were polarised: those who adopt a fundamentally optimistic view of the 1945 governments insist that Labour created the foundations of a new social order; full employment and the welfare state radically modified the capitalist system. The Labour Administration altered the terms of social relations strengthening the bargaining-power of workers in relation to capital while augmenting social security.[19] The party's 1918 programme was broadly implemented realising the inter-war demands of the labour movement for government intervention, full employment, social security and a wide-ranging public sector. As Crossman wrote:

> The Government has fulfilled its historic mission. The nationalisation of half a dozen major industries, the construction of an all-in system of social security and a free health service, and the tentative application of planning to the national economy – the achievement of these reforms seemed to have exhausted the content of British socialism.[20]

The Left newspaper, *Tribune*, concurred: 'Few would have thought that so much could have been done so soon.'[21] The 1945 victory created a heroic myth about socialist planning which held Labour in thrall ever since. Even the Thatcher governments' disposal of nationalised assets, the most conspicuous symbols of the post-war settlement, left intact pre-eminent Attlee-era institutions, notably the National Health Service, as well as public bodies including the Arts Council, the new towns, and the National Parks, all of which left a lasting imprint on national life. According to Paul Addison, the post-war social settlement hastened the erosion of traditional class divisions: differences in dress, housing, consumption patterns and social habits between manual and non-manual workers noticeably blurred, although new patterns of class stratification were to emerge over the course of the late twentieth century. Crosland wrote that although the Attlee

Government ostensibly achieved its mission 'people perhaps scarcely realise today. Memories are feeble; the changes are quickly taken for granted and accepted as part of the status quo.'[22] The electorate was not inclined to reward Labour for past achievements: in 1950–51, they wanted to know where the party intended to lead Britain in the future.

The Attlee governments confronted major obstacles in pursuing their egalitarian aspirations. Ministers had few precedents from which to draw: the only Labour governments had been the minority administration of 1924 and the 1929 MacDonald government, culminating in the disastrous split of 1931; the programme developed in the 1930s contained radical proposals but was bedevilled by ambiguities, notably the inability to develop a viable model of nationalisation; the period in which Attlee's ministers had served in the wartime coalition reinforced their cautious instincts; yet the scale of post-war reconstruction and unmet need was unprecedented in British history, requiring transformational reforms.[23]

The Attlee governments had critics too, notably voices on the British Left. Labour after 1945 had enabled a revived private sector, particularly the City of London, to resume its dominant position from the inter-war years; the social reforms Attlee's ministers enacted were only modestly ameliorative (Warde, 1982). Property rights were left undisturbed while Labour's nationalisation programme was limited. Attlee's preferred model of state ownership, the 'public corporation', transferred power to the managerial class rather than workers. The Foreign Secretary, Ernest Bevin, was criticised for pursuing a pro-Atlanticist strategy abandoning all pretence of a socialist foreign policy. Like the 1931 administration, the Attlee Government confronted significant opposition from 'the bureaucracy, the Bank of England, the banks, the great financial institutions, most of industry...and the dead weight of conventional wisdom'.[24] According to Crossman, Britain was scarcely a more equal or a more classless society by the end of the 1940s; writing in the *New Statesman* he declared:

> In the history of the British Left there can seldom have been an administration so conservative in its solicitude for the stuffier constitutional conventions, so instinctively suspicious of all suggestions for popular participation in decision-taking and workers' control, and so determined to damp down the fiery demands for a new social order that had won them the election…If in 1931 the MacDonald government was killed by the aristocratic embrace, in 1951 the Attlee government quietly expired in the arms of the Whitehall establishment.[25]

Even more perturbing, the Government ran out of steam with little momentum for radical socialist reforms to advance equality.[26] Following its 1951 defeat, which the Labour leadership assumed would be a temporary loss of office, the party collapsed into a state of nervous exhaustion, paralysed by indecision: Labour was unable to develop as the natural governing party emulating the political dominance achieved by social democrats in countries such as Sweden.[27] By the early 1950s the Conservative party, comprehensively defeated in 1945, was on the road to recovery. Labour lost the 1951 and 1955 elections not only because it mislaid middle-class votes; working-class support for the Tories was decisive as it had been in the inter-war period.[28] Beveridge's biographer Jose Harris has written:

> Labour ultimately lost its post-war hegemony, not to rival pragmatists but to a party that, temporarily at least, took seriously the analytical and polemical weapons offered by political theory. It seems plausible to infer that negligence and sentimentalism in these areas were of some contributory significance in old Labour's long-term demise.[29]

By linking socialism rigidly to state planning and nationalisation, Labour lost its way by the early 1950s. In advancing the cause of a more equal society, too little progress was made.

Crosland's argument that socialism was about equality rather than central planning was a blinding flash of truth in 1956; it had far-reaching implications for Labour's doctrinal purpose.

Crosland's view of equality

Crosland's ambition was to formulate 'an egalitarian principle of distributive justice' constructing an unambiguous divide between Left and Right in British politics despite previous ideological convergence. The Conservatives' acceptance of the post-war settlement was a fundamental pillar of their electoral strategy in the 1950s and 1960s: Labour's commitment to equality enabled it to make a distinctive and radical appeal as a 'broadly-based, national, people's party'.[30] *The Future of Socialism* rejected any straightforward commitment to equality of outcome. The aim was to combine equality of opportunity with more equal outcomes: a concept of 'democratic equality'.[31] This meant that inequalities were justified 'if, and only if, differential rewards work to the benefit of the community as a whole and we can assume that access to jobs which command differential rewards would be on the basis of genuine equality of opportunity'.[32] The commitment to equality is about more than an equal opportunity society or a 'pure meritocracy': socialists are concerned not merely with giving everyone an equal chance, but narrowing material differences in disposable income and life-chances between 'the privileged and the rest'.[33] This claim relates to a further theme in Crosland's work: the relationship between equality and liberty. The socialist's principle ideal is equality, but equality is the means of guaranteeing 'positive' freedom for all. He acknowledged that without greater equality in the distribution of material resources, many citizens would be unable to lead fulfilling lives, a position that Tawney elucidated in the early twentieth century drawing on T.H. Green's notion of positive freedom:[34]

> The doctrine which throws all its emphasis on the importance of opening avenues to individual

advancement is partial and one-sided. It is right in insisting on the necessity of opening a free career to aspiring talent; it is wrong in suggesting that opportunities to rise, which can, of their nature, be seized only by the few, are a substitute for a general diffusion of the means of civilisation, which are needed by all men, whether they rise or not.[35]

As Kevin Hickson has indicated, Crosland elaborates three essential arguments to justify the pursuit of equality in modern society through parliamentary politics and social reform.[36] Firstly, too much inequality will constrain the development of skills and talents that are vital to the success of the whole nation, creating 'social waste' and unfulfilled potential:

The British class system involves a definite social waste, since it selects its leaders badly. If social mobility is low, as it must be in a stratified society, and people cannot easily move up from the lower or the middle reaches to the top, then the ruling elite becomes hereditary and self-perpetuating; and whatever one may concede to inherited or family advantages, this must involve a waste of talent.[37]

This position attacks the market liberalism of Hayek and the claim that inequality is necessary to encourage risk-taking and entrepreneurship, the engine of a productive capitalist economy. Inequalities by the 1950s were less extreme than is the case today: the Thatcher experiment made British society markedly more unequal than in the post-war years. That was the result not only of discretionary changes by governments including cuts in the top rate of income tax and reductions in social security benefits for poorer households, but underlying structural changes which made market economies more unequal: the weakening of labour's bargaining power; an increase in rewards at the top of a global market for the highly educated; the impact of globalisation and trade liberalisation; even the increasing likelihood that individuals with university degrees will enter into relationships and marry one another. These factors all contributed towards the growth of inequality after 1979. In the late 1970s, the richest 1 per cent earned 6 per cent of all marketable incomes in the UK; by 2010, the figure had reached nearly 15 per cent.[38]

The next argument that Crosland advanced was that rewards earned by the wealthy have to be justified by what Rawls termed 'the difference principle': inequalities are legitimate only where they benefit the least advantaged. This reasoning is referred to by Crosland as 'a just distribution of privileges and rewards' under which a particular element of inequality is justified:[39]

> No socialist has disputed the need for a degree of inequality here, both because superior talent deserves some rent of ability, and because otherwise certain kinds of work, or risk, or burdensome responsibility will not be shouldered. Thus one should pay differentially high rewards to the artist, the coal miner, the innovating entrepreneur, and the top executive.[40]

A transparent system was required to justify the distribution of rewards. Grossly unequal remuneration polarised the income distribution, increasing the 'social distance' between the rich and the rest of society. Research demonstrates the price of inequality is borne by the entire national community through externalities from rising crime and social disorder, to climate change and increased ill-health: the best predictor of how countries perform 'is not the differences in wealth between them, but the differences in wealth within them... the evidence shows that even small decreases in inequality, already a reality in some rich market democracies, makes a very important difference to the quality of life'.[41] Crosland was concerned about a society in which individuals from diverse social backgrounds no longer mixed because the distance factors created by income and wealth inequality were too high. The principal justification for the post-war welfare state was to weaken social stratification, encouraging the intermingling of the classes.

Crosland's final argument for equality is that too much inequality undermines society's ability to achieve social justice alongside an equal distribution of opportunity. This contention prefigured subsequent research which demonstrated that social mobility is lower in countries that have higher levels of income inequality.[42] Crosland argued that: 'every child has a right, as citizen, not merely to "life, liberty and the pursuit of happiness", but to that position in the social scale to which his native talents entitle him: [every child] should have, in other words, an equal opportunity for wealth, advancement and renown.'[43] For this reason 'existing inequalities offend against social justice'.[44] Redistribution increases the 'sum-total' of freedom and personal fulfilment since the poorest benefit most from increasing purchasing power, alongside enhanced opportunities such as decent education and well-funded health provision.[45] Crosland advances a utilitarian case for moderate redistribution by fiscal means.

Crosland's revisionism was intolerant of grotesque and obscene levels of inequality, but he was reluctant to prioritise equality of outcome through the redistribution of income alone. Crosland accepted that redistribution had limits as an egalitarian strategy, particularly if high and continuous levels of economic growth were no longer sustainable. Despite his reputation for advocating 'tax and spend' policies, Crosland was wary of pursuing 'pure' equality of outcome: he understood that equality would undermine economic efficiency and productivity if the confiscation of income and wealth were pushed too far. He acknowledged that inequalities might be necessary to mobilise the talents and skills of those with ostensibly more to contribute. Even in the context of Britain in the 1950s, taxation had limits: 'The most adventurous entrepreneur will become apathetic if he finds that all the rewards of his endeavours are taken in taxation by the state.'[46] Nevertheless, he warned of the dangers where 'the ruling elite becomes hereditary and self-perpetuating'.[47] Despite the emergence of a 'post-capitalist' society, Britain was still a class-ridden country which bred antagonism and resentment, weakened social solidarity, reinforced stratified class divisions, and acted as a barrier to fluidity and social mobility.[48]

The desire to tackle the injustices of class inequality underlines the emphasis given by Crosland to educational reform: democratising access to the public schools and entrenching the comprehensive principle in state education was 'the main engine in the creation of a more just society'.[49] According to Crosland 'the school system in Britain remains the most divisive, unjust and wasteful of all the social aspects of inequality'.[50] Grammar schools had been designed to educate middle-class pupils to a high standard, while secondary modern and technical schools were starved of resources, reinforcing entrenched social and class divisions.[51] The purpose of comprehensivisation was not to eliminate competition from the system 'but to avoid the extreme social division caused by physical segregation into schools of widely divergent status'.[52] On public schools, Crosland's initial aim was to make 75 per cent of all places open to non-fee payers:[53] '[t]o eliminate their divisive influence on society, the schools must accept a socially mixed entry.'[54] More radical proposals were muted, such as requiring that Oxford and Cambridge colleges give fewer places to pupils from public schools, as well as the elimination of tax privileges.[55]

Crosland was determined to proceed consensually over grammar schools, building on the successful reform of the Swedish system: 'It was fundamental to his view of democracy that reform would be more lasting if it could be achieved voluntarily.'[56] A Labour government should restate its 'preference' for comprehensives 'actively encouraging local authorities' to reorganise provision; where the tripartite system continued, public spending would narrow the gap between the grammar schools and secondary moderns; enabling more late transfer to grammar schools would weaken the 'last chance' nature of the 11-plus examination. If the school leaving age were raised to 16, resources could be focused on 'education priority areas', schools in deprived communities with a disproportionate concentration of pupils from poorer families.[57] Crosland opened up educational opportunity further by enshrining the binary principle in higher education, launching a new generation of polytechnics to enhance the quality of technical and vocational training.

Crosland, equality of opportunity and social mobility

Even if the philosophical and theoretical insights were less than innovative, Crosland bequeathed to the British Left a path-breaking account of the political strategy of equality. He justified initiatives to reduce inequality in the income distribution and opportunity structure of society. Crosland emphasised the importance of educational opportunities that would erode class differences and liberate the innate talents of all citizens. As such, he laid the foundations for a majoritarian social democratic project, adopting an inclusive framing of the case for a just society, centred on mobilising the abilities and contribution of everyone. Nonetheless, the British centre-left has remained confused and befuddled by the pursuit of egalitarian ideals: the bewilderment can be traced back to Crosland who never satisfactorily answered the questions: equality of what?[58] And equality: how?

New Labour emphasised the goal of equality of opportunity. This approach was electorally expedient: it avoided apparently unpopular measures such as redistribution and higher taxes. Crosland believed that social mobility and equal opportunity were insufficient. In *The Future of Socialism*, Crosland writes: 'Equality of opportunity and social mobility, though they lead to the most admirable distribution of intelligence, are not enough.'[59] He advanced a 'strong' account of equal opportunities drawing on Tawney, which did not merely enable the most talented and able to escape the confines of their social class, but secured better provision for every citizen 'by virtue of being human'. This equality of regard was enshrined in the principle of comprehensive education and a universal welfare state. Crosland understood social mobility as necessary but not sufficient to achieve a more equal and just society.[60] He wrote in *Socialism Now*:

> By equality we mean more than a meritocratic society of equal opportunities, in which the greatest rewards would go to those with the most fortunate genetic endowment and family background – what Rawls has subsequently called the 'democratic' as opposed to the 'liberal' conception.[61]

The evidence from recent developments in post-war Britain is that Crosland was right to be cautious about social mobility as the primary egalitarian objective of the Labour party. Social mobility has proved notoriously hard to measure; it has not been easy to improve the overall level of social mobility in Britain despite decades of educational reform; and since Michael Young's seminal work on *The Rise of the Meritocracy* (1958), commentators have questioned whether social mobility is a desirable goal for the Left.[62]

Social scientists disagree about whether social mobility has risen or fallen in Britain since 1945. Some economists argue earnings mobility has declined since the 1970s and 1980s, implying that children are more likely to receive salaries similar to their parents: according to LSE research, 'there has actually been a fall in the degree of social mobility over recent decades. Children born to poor families are now less likely to break free of their background and fulfil their potential than they were in the past.'[63] Men and women in the 1970 birth cohort earned incomes closer to their parents than the 1958 generation. The expansion of higher education disproportionately benefited those from middle-class backgrounds; more pupils from low income households stayed on at school, but university graduation rates rose only marginally among working-class students. Between 1986 and 2000, there was a 26 per cent increase in university degrees among the richest fifth of households compared to 3 per cent in the bottom fifth; this implies that increasing the supply of university places has not yet equalised access to higher education.[64] Improving access to educational provision does not necessarily strengthen earnings mobility, advancing equality of opportunity. The claim that more education necessarily produces a society centred on upward mobility is increasingly threadbare.

Sociologists, notably John Goldthorpe, insist that there is little evidence that social mobility declined after the Second World War. Mobility might have improved since the 1950s due to the increasing supply of middle-class jobs and the growth of the salariat rather than society becoming more fluid and democratic.[65] Goldthorpe distinguishes between absolute and relative social mobility: since 1945, total mobility has risen as more professional and white collar jobs have been created. Over the last 60 years, the proportion of the workforce employed in skilled, professional and technical occupations rose from 25 per cent to 44 per cent.[66] Electorally, this was counterintuitively to Labour's advantage, creating a new cadre of altruistic public service professionals and middle-class managers committed to public duty, replacing the declining industrial proletariat.[67] Crosland foresaw 'a new labour aristocracy of salaried, white collar, technical and similar workers', the basis of Wilson's winning electoral coalition in 1964 and 1966.[68] These groups created the conditions for the rise in absolute mobility. In contrast, relative social mobility in Britain 'remains essentially unchanged'.[69] According to Goldthorpe, there is no evidence that grammar schools were effective in boosting mobility: changes in the economic and occupational structure determine levels of mobility, rather than policies designed to alter the take up of post-16 education.[70] Social mobility began to slow down in the 1980s and 1990s as the rate of growth in professional employment and occupational upgrading similarly declined.

Since Crosland's time, social mobility has been predominantly shaped by the structure of the economy and labour market. New Labour believed that increasing the supply of skills and human capital in the global economy would attract more high-wage, high productivity jobs. Pervasive structural forces undermined this strategy: firstly, emerging market countries are producing more skilled graduates, highly trained but also cost efficient to employ; secondly, digital technologies and automation are reducing the demand for qualified workers in professions such as accountancy, law, medicine and the social services. Goldthorpe highlights the capacity of middle-class families to ensure that their children can access professional employment, even where they are less skilled and have fewer qualifications. Since education in the jobs market is a 'positional good', high income parents use additional resources as a form of 'defensive expenditure' (for example, spending on extra tuition, music lessons and sport), exploiting social networks to preserve their children's advantageous position in gaining middle-class jobs.

Even where these children do not succeed at school, they acquire essential 'soft skills' and cultural capital which enable them to compete for managerial positions in the service industries.[71] The rise of inequality and the reproduction of social and political elites is further encouraged by an increase in 'assortative mating' where individuals from similar educational backgrounds are more likely to marry one another: in the United States, for example, the proportion of men with university degrees who marry women graduates has risen from 25 to 48 per cent since the 1970s.[72] As the authors of a recent US study conclude: 'The implications of assortative mating for income inequality are greater now than they were in 1960.'[73] In so far as governments have increased mobility, they struggle to reduce inequalities in life-chances using conventional instruments of state intervention. The Labour governments after 1997 introduced a range of measures including a dramatic expansion of early years' education; income subsidies for the poorest households with children through tax credits; Education Maintenance Allowances (EMAs) to improve school staying-on rates; and expanding the availability of higher education and apprenticeships. Nonetheless, the evidence indicates that mobility is lower in societies such as the United States and Britain with greater levels of income inequality.

Finally, there is an ethical debate about whether it is worth living in a truly meritocratic, socially mobile society.[74] If the rich alongside those at the top of the occupational ladder believe that they earned their rewards on merit and effort alone, they are less willing to support arrangements that help the least fortunate.[75] Crosland's exchange of views with Michael Young, a close friend and leading sociologist, illuminated this problem. As Young remarked: 'If meritocrats believe, as more and more of them are encouraged to, that their advancement comes from their own merits, they can feel they deserve whatever they get...So assured have the elite become that there is almost no block on the awards they aggrogate to themselves.'[76]

In a competitive and acquisitive society, attributes beyond the calculus of the market are essential for social cohesion and stability: caring for family members while actively contributing to community life are always in danger of being undervalued. Crosland wrote in the 1950s that 'competitive social relations' were at risk of undermining 'fellowship and social solidarity': socialists should retain the ethical aspiration of a more fraternal, cooperative society.[77] Crosland acknowledged that while the Left might succeed in equalising opportunities 'all pervasive competition' undermined the common good.[78] The mainstream parties in Britain have increasingly favoured social mobility. New Labour sought to appeal to 'aspirational' median voters, emphasising its commitment to equal opportunity. For Crosland, equality of opportunity meant raising everyone up, improving circumstances throughout society; a society with less material inequality was necessary to ensure genuinely equal opportunity, the platform for greater fluidity in the class structure. John Goldthorpe avers that the Scandinavian countries are more likely to succeed in improving social mobility, focusing on job security for wage-earners, prioritising full employment, and reducing income differentials through redistributive fiscal policies. Economic growth centred on promoting advanced technologies, sectoral innovation and infrastructure investment is more likely to improve occupational upgrading.[79]

The critique of Croslandite egalitarianism

Crosland's posthumous reputation as one of the most influential thinkers on the post-war British Left stood the test of time.

His credibility as an egalitarian theorist may well have been overstated, however, reflecting the paucity of political thought within British social democracy. The synthesis adumbrated in *The Future of Socialism* between equality of outcome and opportunity offers a useful starting-point, but is never developed while there are some conceptual ambiguities and misunderstandings. The Gaitskellite revisionists failed to clarify what they meant by equality, advancing the concept little beyond Tawney's interpretation in *The Acquisitive Society* (1921) and *Equality* (1928).[80] There was ambiguity in *The Future of Socialism* about whether equality was a means to the end of personal freedom and fulfilment, or whether equality was the overriding objective. Crosland's aim was to maximise the productive potential of capitalism while at the same time reducing inequalities to the 'lowest practicable level'; however, the revisionists had a tendency to confuse 'meritocratic' and 'incentive-based' arguments in their justification for inequalities of reward.[81] By the time *Socialism Now* was published, Crosland drew on Rawls' 'difference principle' to bolster his position. According to Plant, 'When Crosland saw that Rawls was quite close to what he was arguing he just rested the intellectual case for equality on a Rawlsian view.'[82] Plant goes on: 'There were various elements of that: the difference principle; the idea of desert – you can only take credit for what you can take responsibility for; and the idea that in a highly meritocratic society, he is indebted here to Michael Young, all sorts of human values would be lost.'

Nonetheless, there are evident limitations to Rawlsian theory. Michael Sandel noted that the 'difference principle' and 'veil of ignorance' were defensible only by accepting the premise that an individual can exist outside their social and historical context.[83] This position involves a form of 'extreme individualism' which pays too little attention to how an individual's views are shaped and constituted by the community of which they are a part. The critique of Rawls has grown in resonance, particularly if we consider what has taken place in the industralised economies since the 1970s and 1980s: the rise of a particular view of individualism has made a range of inequalities legitimate that are manifestly not in the interests of the least advantaged. The ideal of 'pure' meritocracy has proved an influential ideology in rich market democracies centred on the claim that talent and scarce attributes of high intelligence and ingenuity should be infinitely rewarded.

The weaknesses of Rawls' position are replicated in Crosland's analysis taking insufficient account of the relationship between the individual and society, as the New Liberals had sought to do at the turn of the twentieth century. This debate alludes to the relationship between equality and solidarity in post-war Britain. The corporatist model which emerged in the aftermath of the Second World War followed by Thatcherite individualism in the 1980s demonstrated that the cause of equality could be undermined by the dwindling of solidarity: too little belief in the public interest and the denigration of social obligation. Labour revisionists failed to confront the structural problem afflicting the twentieth century party: the industrial wing of Labour, a movement ostensibly committed to assisting the underdog, was comprised of trade unionists who sought to defend the sectional claims of their members. These relatively well protected working people (usually men) were labour market 'insiders' with privileges and economic status. The poorest were usually labour market 'outsiders' who lacked formal political and workplace representation, particularly efficient trade unions. The Attlee Government improved the absolute position of the worst-off immediately after the Second World War, but mounting economic pressures in the 1950s and 1960s encouraged the unions to defend sectional interests and wage differentials, undermining the achievement of social justice.[84]

Crossman noted how the trade unions pressurised the 1964–70 Wilson governments into focussing on increasing real wages rather than spending on public services.[85] Revisionists, too, exhibited trenchant loyalty towards the labour movement by the late 1960s; they were reluctant to question the growing strength of trade unionism illustrated by Crosland and Jenkins' withdrawal of support for Barbara Castle's 'In Place of Strife' White Paper in 1969. These sordid compromises meant that Labour governed in the post-war decades drawing on a 'threadbare series of doctrines'.[86] The party sought to create a fairer, more equal society using the traditional fiscal levers of high politics, ignoring the capacity of powerful producer interest groups to override the claims of the vulnerable. The ethic of solidarity and the common good was not sufficient to moderate the competing claims of group interests embodied in the trade unions, alluding to the inherent tension between personal freedom and equality. As Plant reminds us, 'Whereas Rawls' book is about the potential conflict between equality and personal liberty, Crosland doesn't recognise that as an issue'.[87]

Of course, the revisionists were attempting to win an existential battle within their party: they regarded equality as the pre-eminent socialist value undermining the primacy accorded to nationalisation and state ownership. Crosland objected to 'the defeatist left-wing belief' that society would only become more equal if the state controlled the means of production and distribution: too much emphasis was given to seizing 'the commanding heights' of industry overstating the importance of ownership for egalitarian outcomes.[88] In *The Conservative Enemy*, Crosland wrote: 'The commanding heights of private privilege and social separatism', played a greater role in generating social inequalities than ownership of 'the steel or chemical industry'.[89] Socialists ought to focus on reforming the public schools: 'This privileged stratum of education, the exclusive preserve of the wealthier classes, socially and physically segregated from the state educational system, is the greatest single cause of stratification and class-consciousness in Britain.'[90] Crosland's ambition was 'to secure a more equitable distribution of educational resources between different classes of the nation' fuelling his ambition to develop the comprehensive school system.[91]

What mattered to Crosland were the 'distance factors' attenuated by inequality: status, deference and class demarcations that reinforced barriers making society less economically efficient and socially just. However, it is difficult to deny that 60 years since *The Future of Socialism*, Crosland underestimated the ability of market liberalism to undermine the pursuit of equality, rolling back the gains of the post-war settlement. Plant believes that Crosland was too dismissive of his intellectual adversaries; for instance, he refused to take New Right figures such as Hayek seriously. Crosland wrote: 'No one of any standing now believes the once popular Hayek thesis that any interference with the market mechanism must start us down the slippery slope to totalitarianism.'[92] In an interview with Samuel Brittan in the 1970s, he dismissed the views of New Right theorists as 'froth'; their growing prominence 'didn't presage some fundamental shift in how British intellectuals thought about economic policy and the role of the state'.[93] On that, Crosland was proved profoundly wrong.

As the 'rhetoric of reaction' and counter-revolution against collectivism gained momentum, Croslandite revisionism provided a weak defence since the case for equality had little coherent philosophical or moral underpinning.[94] Crosland believed that for all its limitations, the Attlee Government advanced British society irreversibly towards equality. Socialism would be brought about by abolishing class-based inequalities, but in any case a new system of 'progressive capitalism' was emerging.[95] This shift was not merely a consequence of social reform; structural change and the development of a 'post-capitalist' society were redefining the ideological consensus in British politics. In the post-1945 era, Crosland wrote, 'ostentation is becoming vulgar; rich men tend to disclaim their wealth; and a general modesty in consumption becomes the fashion. This naturally reinforces the trend towards equality in outward style of life.'[96] The scale of income inequality in the rich market democracies since the 1970s and 1980s indicates that Crosland was, to say the least, unduly optimistic about social change.

Crosland, equality and New Labour

Despite these limitations, Crosland's influence has endured in the dispute about what form of equality Labour should pursue, a debate that has generated controversy and disagreement on the British Left since the Second World War. This argument about why equality matters arose again in the 1990s and counterposed the then Chancellor of the Exchequer, Gordon Brown, with Labour's former Deputy Leader (now Lord) Hattersley. In Hattersley's view, Crosland adopted an ideological position on equality which held true regardless of social change and the need to come to terms with Thatcherism. In Crosland's writing, 'there were always absolutes – that public expenditure had virtue in its own right, that equality was what socialism was about, that redistribution of wealth mattered even in a modern society.'[97] New Labour's refusal to raise state benefits while ensuring a fairer distribution of rewards through increasing the top rate of tax contradicted Crosland's egalitarianism. Hattersley concluded in 2001: 'At this moment Labour stands for very little that can be identified with social democracy'; New Labour no longer believed that 'higher public spending is best paid for by a redistributive and progressive form of taxation…the commodification of public space has become an aggressive Blairite objective'.[98] Hattersley was a tireless opponent of another New Labour obsession: choice in public services. He wrote: 'The articulate and self-confident middle classes will insist on receipt of superior services. The further down the scale a family comes, the less likely it is to receive anything other than the residue which is left after others have made a choice.'[99]

As Chancellor, Brown did not rely exclusively on traditional redistribution but pursued 'dynamic' equality of opportunity through policies such as tax credits for the working poor, welfare-to-work and public–private partnerships. The platform of modest increases in National Insurance and income tax to fund a rise in the state pension and child benefit was perceived to be culpable for Labour's 1992 defeat. In revisiting the debate about 'tax and spend', Brown invested in tax credits designed to improve the relative position of low income families, borrowing from the Clinton Administration's Earned Income Tax Credit (EITC). He introduced new programmes to guarantee a minimum income for poorer pensioners, significantly reducing the prevalence of poverty. Brown did not reject equality of outcome; according to Plant:

> Having become Chancellor, Gordon Brown rather liked the idea that he was Crosland Mark II. He gave the impression that the Blairites were emphasising equality of opportunity without remembering the Crosland argument that [equality of opportunity] was not enough. It was politically useful for Brown because it gave the impression he was more radical and more to the Left than Blair.[100]

The Secretary of State for Education and Employment between 1997 and 2001, David Blunkett, similarly insisted his reforms of secondary education 'modernising the comprehensive principle' were consistent with Crosland's belief in equality of opportunity. In 2001, Crosland's widow, Susan, attended the launch of Blunkett's White Paper in the House of Commons emphasising his proposals were at one with Crosland's vision in the 1960s: an end to narrow academic selection in schools. Mrs Crosland told a BBC news programme that in her view 'change was a good thing': her husband was the leading architect of the comprehensive revolution but also a pragmatist who believed that 'if it's not working for some reason, then change it'.[101] Blunkett's proposals led to a further confrontation with Hattersley, who insisted that Labour's reforms were undermining Crosland's legacy, encouraging diversity of provision while giving a new role to private providers.[102] The Prime Minister's spokesman, Alistair Campbell, inflamed the row by referring to New Labour's mission to abolish 'bog-standard' comprehensives creating a new cadre of academy schools, faith schools and specialist schools independent of Local Education Authority (LEA) control. For Hattersley, this was an absolute betrayal of Crosland's egalitarian legacy in post-war education.

By the early 1970s, Crosland had begun to have reservations about traditional egalitarianism; in *Socialism Now*, he identified the electoral dilemma faced by the 1964–70 governments: how to share the proceeds of growth between public expenditure and personal consumption among wage-earners.[103] Labour's dilemma was acute: since the 1950s, British voters under successive Conservative governments became used to rapid improvements in the standard of living after years of wartime rationing and austerity. As Crosland's disciple, Hattersley insisted that 'Socialism is about equality and we cannot have greater equality if we cut public spending.'[104] In examining the record of the Wilson governments, however, Crosland regretted that higher public expenditure had not achieved equality given the tendency of the 'sharp-elbowed' middle class to benefit disproportionately from the expansion of public services. In 1976, Crosland observed: 'a shift from private spending to public spending does not necessarily increase equality'.[105] It should not be assumed that public expenditure would lead automatically to greater equality: for instance, because richer people often died later they were disproportionate beneficiaries of state pensions and welfare services.[106] Research demonstrated that the middle class gained more from the post-1945 welfare state than the less privileged in society:[107]

> They demand more resources for the schools in their areas; they complain vociferously if they have to wait for their operations; they demand that the state intervenes to subsidise the price of rail tickets from their commuter homes to their work. Too often these pressures have been successful; and in consequence the distribution of public spending has been tilted away from the areas of the greatest need towards those which generate the loudest demands.[108]

The positive impact of egalitarian policies such as comprehensive schooling and the expansion of social housing were less evident by the late 1970s.[109] This scepticism highlights the fact that Crosland was prepared to re-think traditional egalitarian claims in the light of changing circumstances. Lipsey and Leonard point to Crosland's obsession with the need to adapt to a changing economic and social landscape: no particular instrument such as progressive taxation was sacrosanct in fulfilling democratic socialist objectives.[110] Crosland's egalitarian strategy has been interpreted too narrowly: it offered a general reference point rather than a fixed programme which must be rigidly adhered to. He noted in the 1950s that significant inequalities in Britain resulted from 'the ownership of inherited capital' rather than 'earned incomes'.[111] Inherited wealth made society less efficient, in danger of being dominated by private privilege.[112] Crosland advocated reform of inheritance tax focusing not only on the size of the estate but the taxation of each bequest to an individual, augmented by capital gains tax and a wealth tax.[113] Moreover, *The Future of Socialism* challenged the traditional obsession of the Left with economic and distributional concerns. In the inter-war years, revisionists had confronted the MacDonald Government's failure to respond adequately to the 1931 financial crisis by developing a comprehensive programme of economic reforms; but questions of culture, the shared environment, and quality of life were rarely considered. In contrast, Crosland adopted a pluralistic understanding of equality which went beyond the realm of economics and income.

Crosland saw himself in the 1950s as a strident opponent of the Webbs' mechanistic vision of socialism wedded to anachronistic state control. Nonetheless, he still believed that enlightened intervention by the state would fashion the just society.[114] By the late 1990s, politicians including Brown and Blunkett were confronting the need radically to 'modernise' and update the social democratic agenda in the light of new developments. The post-war state of Attlee and Beveridge would not be resurrected in late twentieth-century Britain. It was this legacy of post-war social democracy that New Labour ruthlessly abandoned. Crosland was writing against the backdrop of Britain in the 1950s building on the gains of the Attlee era. By the 1990s, Britain had experienced two decades of Thatcherism: an age of collectivism had morphed into an age of individualism. New Labour became aware of the political constraints on egalitarianism, abandoning the language of equality; Blair insisted in the mid-1990s: 'I think one of the tragedies of the Left was that it allowed the term 'equality' to really become a term of abuse about levelling down.'[115] Crosland's concept of equality and a genuinely classless society were ambitious, contrasting with New Labour's defensive and cautious strategy. Blair's party chose to emphasise using the resources of the state to give everyone an equal chance, eschewing the Thatcherite view that society ought to be ruled by market forces. New Labour was, nonetheless, reluctant to countenance the wide-ranging redistribution of income and wealth. Electoral expediency was partly the motivation, but also Britain was not as class-bound as it had been in the mid-twentieth century: there is no longer a rigid demarcation between manual and mental labour; the disappearance of traditional class identities undermined the traditional arguments for redistribution.[116]

The dispute between Hattersley and the modernisers continues in the form of contemporary discussion of inequality, the role of progressive taxation, and the political sustainability of the post-war welfare state. Labour's record on inequality since 1997 has been criticised because too little progress was made in narrowing the gap between rich and poor. New Labour's modest and piecemeal reforms failed to overturn profoundly polarising forces arising from the changing nature of global capitalism. While equality was relegated as a major preoccupation of the Left, the UK was becoming increasingly unequal. Since the 1970s, the top 1 per cent had seen their share of gross disposable income more than double, returning the income distribution to pre-war levels accompanied by greater transmission of social advantage between the generations.[117] Atkinson noted that unequal outcomes in the parent's generation were creating more unequal opportunities for their children.[118] Crosland's perspective in the 1950s was that managerialism and new methods of production were taming capitalism: the market economy was no longer as rapacious or 'red in tooth and claw'. Today, the 'great moderation' has been superseded by the resurgence of shareholder capitalism; the globalisation of capital, labour and product markets; a culture of runaway rewards disproportionately benefiting the winners of globalisation; and a powerful financial sector able to exercise influence over democratic decision-making in areas such as taxation policy. At the same time, Crosland's optimistic assessment in the context of post-war affluence that British capitalism would generate sustained growth and rising living standards across the income distribution did not prove well-founded.

In government, Labour not only refused to introduce more radical measures; according to critics, it failed to make the moral case for a more equal society. There is a renewed emphasis on addressing inequalities of wealth and income highlighted in the work of Richard Wilkinson and Kate Pickett in *The Spirit Level*.[119] Thomas Piketty's influential volume on *Capital* has examined long-term changes in which western societies have become increasingly unequal in the distribution of income, property and wealth.[120] According to Piketty's data, wealth inequality has increased in capitalist economies as the rate of return on capital exceeds the annual rate of growth.[121] Market capitalism rewards the owners of property and assets rather than those earning wages. Much of the rise in inequality over the last 30 years is attributed to rising property values and land prices. The ownership of land and property, still taxed at a lower rate than income, is beneficial; this results in reduced labour productivity, capital investment and living standards.[122] Against the backdrop of inequality, there are renewed concerns about the sustainability of the welfare state in the light of demographic pressures; the rise of tax resistance alongside antipathy to 'free-riding' among the tax-paying majority; and the demise of the contributory National Insurance principle devised by Beveridge in the early 1940s for a world of full employment and male breadwinners (Atkinson, 2015).

Social democrats, notably Hattersley, have accused Blair's party of replacing the commitment to equality with 'communitarian liberalism'. In Hattersley's view, the willingness of the modernisers to travel lightly unencumbered by ideological baggage suited Blair's expedient motives, appealing to the median voter in Middle England but sacrificing the party's core beliefs. It was politically convenient not to take equality seriously, as New Labour lacked the political will to confront the wealthy. The claim that New Labour's strategy was diametrically at odds with the post-war governments is hard to sustain, however. While New Labour might have acted cautiously on equality, this encourages a 'golden age' view of past governments.[123] In the *New Fabian Essays*, Crosland chastised Attlee's ministers for doing too little to advance equality; in *Socialism Now*, he despaired at Wilson's failure to translate growing public expenditure into a more egalitarian society. While Crosland was 'fundamentally committed to economic expansion and against conventional Treasury 'stop–go' policies',[124] he failed to acknowledge that international economic circumstances constrained previous Labour administrations.[125] The 'stop–go' cycle of fiscal expansion and deflation following balance of payment crises eroded Labour's reputation for economic competence alongside its fiscal room for manoeuvre, undermining the party's ability to pursue egalitarian strategies. In an essay published shortly before his death, Crosland speculated that Labour would have to adopt a more pluralistic definition of social equality: there were limits to what formal action by the state could achieve by altering the distribution of income and wealth. It was not enough to rely on higher taxes and public spending in an age of heightened fiscal constraint where, as Crosland infamously reminded a conference of local government leaders, the 'party' of rising government spending was over.[126] New Labour has been accused of abandoning traditional beliefs for electoral calculation: the revisionist's view of equality exhibited serious weaknesses well before 1997, however, failing to enunciate an adequate moral basis for equality that would have countered the pressures to constrain public spending.

As we have seen, Crosland was reluctant to spell out the moral underpinnings of his view of equality, writing in *The Future of Socialism* that whether equality was accepted would depend on 'the moral predilections of the reader'.[127] His argument for egalitarian measures rested on the claim of 'mutual dependency': the success of the privileged few depends on the contribution of the majority who deserve a fair share of society's rewards.[128] This position is consistent with the practical case for equality as 'self-interest': individuals pay into collectivist institutions to insure themselves against catastrophic risks of illness, unemployment, old age, and unexpected loss of income. They want to live in a society no longer scarred by excessive inequality leading to social disorder, high crime rates, the growth of social resentment and entrenched class divisions, alongside the breakdown of inter-generational mobility.[129]

The limitation of Crosland's position was his reluctance to make the case for equality, redefining the dominant political discourse. This weakness came to matter more as the inhospitable climate for egalitarianism grew in the 1980s. Marquand goes further, indicating that Crosland was incapable of defining the moral basis on which equality could be said to matter:

> Are you deriving it from Christianity as Tawney does? Tawney says the important thing about human beings is their similarity by incarnation to God; a very powerfully-held position, but the Crosland generation had been brought up only on PPE [Politics, Philosophy and Economics] at Oxford University. So where does that leave you?[130]

British social democracy is comprised of two fluid and loosely configured traditions: statism and ethical socialism; the emphasis in ethical socialism on fraternity and fellowship was marginalised by the mechanistic redistribution that dominated Labour's post-1945 programme.[131] Crosland favoured 'mechanical' rather 'than' moral reform,[132] believing that social change would be brought about through a democratic and interventionist state; for him transforming the consciousness and moral values of citizens was implausible. As a consequence, post-war social democracy put too much faith in statist mechanical change: the gradual redistribution of resources was insufficient to transform society.[133] Today, government's capacity to engineer social change is questioned: the advocates of communitarianism urge a return to the ethical socialist tradition of mutualism and the common good, rejecting any attempt to create egalitarianism through the levers of the central state imposing change from the top down.

Crosland's egalitarian legacy

The previous section briefly illustrated how Crosland's analysis resurfaced in the Labour party since the late 1970s: critics allege that the New Labour governments adopted a 'Croslandite' tax and spend strategy relying on redistribution by stealth through the fiscal increment from growth. Labour struggled to contain inequality where the rules of the game were skewed favouring financial markets and asset accumulation. New Labour's strategy was stretched to breaking point in the aftermath of the 2008 crisis as the consequence of higher borrowing and an unsustainable deficit: the liberal growth model driven by strong performance in the service industries, especially the financial sector, no longer appeared sustainable. Moreover, Labour inherited ideas about distributive fairness from Crosland's era which contradicted deeply held public sentiments about welfare and migration. The electorate's views had become harsher and more punitive since *The Future of Socialism*; there was little sympathy towards a 'something for nothing' welfare system.[134] Crosland did not foresee that a backlash against the social democratic state was a possibility, culminating in the Conservative party's 1979 victory and their political dominance throughout the 1980s and 1990s.

It remains the case that Crosland's critics have failed to acknowledge the sophistication and depth of his arguments. The Croslandite model was not wholly dependent on a benevolent social democratic state redistributing the fruits of growth. He presupposed a host of regulatory institutions, from collective wage bargaining to effective trade unions, which he saw no reason to justify in the 1950s.[135] They were treated as central planks of the post-war settlement. Crosland acknowledged that any viable strategy of redistribution required interventions to ensure greater equality in the primary distribution of income, rather than relying on taxes and benefits. To assert that he emphasised only redistributive taxation and public expenditure ignores the breadth of the arguments in *The Future of Socialism*, alongside its rationale for social democracy in an affluent society. Crosland was writing at a particular moment in post-war history. The policy-making establishment exhibited great confidence in Keynesian economic management. In contrast, many in the Labour party still believed the goal of socialism was the overthrow of capitalism; Crosland emphasised the permanence of the mixed economy with a significant private sector: social democracy should aim to reconcile capitalism with social justice. He sought to persuade the party not to treat the capitalist system as the enemy.

Crosland was sceptical about communitarianism, which attempted to challenge the dominant role of the state in Labour's doctrine and programme, while recapturing the ethical socialism of solidarity and mutual responsibility. Along with other leading revisionists such as Gaitskell and Jay, he expressed doubts about whether altruism, cooperation, and fraternity aided Labour's advance as a prospective governing party (Jones, 1996). From the 1930s, revisionists adopted increasingly utilitarian arguments for equality centred on Keynesianism, emphasising the compatibility of greater material equality with productive efficiency in a capitalist economy; they were never prepared to embrace a communitarian position since the repressive norms of traditional community life conflicted with their libertarian principles.[136] New Labour espoused a communitarian ethic in the new Clause 4, an alternative to both Attlee-era nationalisation and the egalitarian values of Crosland's revisionism. However, Labour struggled to translate communitarianism into a workable programme. New Labour sought to impose a new ethic of rights and responsibilities in the welfare state. Blair emphasised the importance of 'strong families'. But in government, efforts to define a coherent policy came to little. Labour was determined to avoid errors made by the Conservatives over 'back to basics' in the 1990s, eschewing moralising rhetoric then struggling to identify credible policies. Inequality was the major issue that returned with a vengeance in the aftermath of the financial crisis, giving credence to the view that the New Labour era in British politics was finally over.

Conclusion

Despite concerns about the growing gap between the wealthy and the poorest in society, there has rarely been an appetite for large-scale redistribution alongside radical progressive taxation in Britain: the UK lacks the egalitarian culture that prevails elsewhere in Northern Europe. As a consequence, even in 1945 Labour politicians felt constrained; the temptation was to pursue social democracy by stealth when the party was in power. Crosland's approach anticipated the dilemmas faced by New Labour in the 1990s:

> The social democrat is interested in the relative position of the worst-off. But you had to pay attention to the absolute position of the better-off otherwise they won't vote for you. What you can do is to have policies that reassure middle-class aspirations and gives them confidence their incomes will be maintained.[137]

That said, 'Crosland underestimated the capacity of market liberalism to unwind the gains of the post-war settlement'.[138] He was a utilitarian reluctant to spell out a moral argument underpinning his view of equality. In *The Future of Socialism*, Hayek's theories were dismissed as 'implausible...in a British context' and 'thoroughly discredited'.[139] Crosland had no intuitive sense that the theories of neo-classical economics might once again become influential in British politics.[140] Keynesianism had dominated the academic and political debate in Britain until the 1970s.

Meanwhile, the Labour governments after 1997 lacked any strategy to reshape attitudes in the aftermath of Thatcherism. When the economy was growing, it was possible to redistribute incomes without political cost. When adverse circumstances reappeared after the crash, support for redistributive measures crumbled. For many on the Left, this was surprising and perturbing. After all, the crisis was supposed to revive support for the state and with it, redistributive measures. That was not how things turned out: since the Second World War, voters' support for redistribution had been higher the further they were down the income scale; since 2008, however, those on low and high incomes have been converging in their hostility to redistribution.[141] Among UK citizens, 60 per cent believe 'ordinary people do not get their fair share of the nation's wealth', but only 39 per cent agree in principle that government should 'redistribute income from the better-off to those who are less well-off'.[142] It may be that those on low incomes fear that they will be caught by punitive taxes; the state is perceived as too incompetent to redistribute efficiently. Electorates are concerned, even incensed, by the growth in rewards enjoyed by the super-rich and the scale of inequality; but voters are invariably hostile to state intervention. Meanwhile, egalitarian measures are more vulnerable where the British Left is bereft of a moral case; the rationale for equality:

> [W]ould always unravel under the power of an alternative set of ideas...there was a strong need for a defence of egalitarian social democratic values. The whole project since 1956 had not been defended on intellectual grounds. It was just seen as what the Labour party historically had stood for without trying to rethink the case.[143]

Crosland does not formulate a rigid doctrine of equality: his analysis illuminates tensions and dilemmas that still bedevil social democratic parties. *The Future of Socialism* never offered a thoroughly worked out philosophical position: there is no explicit moral theory of why equality matters to the Left. This ambiguity has advantages, of course: others have had the opportunity to take on and develop Crosland's thinking.[144] Nonetheless, his attempt to define a powerful and economically coherent case for equality proved elusive. Equality was the centrepiece of Crosland's socialism yet in an aside he declared that he did not want to support an egalitarian position that made society 'dull', 'drab' or 'colourless'.[145]

Consequently, Labour should be cautious about an ideology of equal outcomes, even in the wake of the financial crisis and rising concern about inequality in Britain and the United States. Crosland's political insights are still worth heeding. He argued that governments have to tackle a range of inequalities, highlighting important questions about egalitarian strategy. In what circumstances should social democrats focus on equalising the distribution of disposable incomes and purchasing power (equality of outcome)? Should the Left ensure that citizens can ascend the class and occupational structure as far as their talents take them (equality of opportunity)? Should they concentrate on enlarging the public realm in which money matters less, where services are distributed according to need not ability to pay (equality of regard)? Crosland was a pragmatic thinker: Labour would have to combine judiciously equality of outcome, opportunity and regard.

In reconciling liberty and equality, Crosland believed equality mattered where it advanced the freedoms of the individual within an active and stable community, enabling people to lead lives they had reason to value. Whatever the limitations of Croslandite egalitarianism, like Tawney he defined an ethical framework in which people are 'equally enabled to make the best of such powers as they possess'.[146] Crosland was influenced by the New Liberalism of Green, Hobhouse and Hobson, alongside the socialism of Tawney and Durbin, who insisted that equality and liberty were indissolubly linked: 'The problem of a just society is not the single problem of economic equality, but the much more difficult problem of achieving simultaneously in one society both equality and liberty', Durbin wrote in the 1940s.[147] Durbin's book, *The Politics of Democratic Socialism*, prefigured Crosland's revisionism arguing it was 'radically false...to suppose that the dynamic element of social life is...that of class struggle and class warfare'.[148] The essence of the civilised and democratic society was cooperation between the classes: socialism meant nothing 'except within a framework of liberty for the individual and representative democracy'.[149]

In Durbin and Crosland's vision, social democracy would marry the emphasis on collective action, state intervention and the provision of public goods with the right to autonomy and liberty, upholding the individual's freedoms and citizenship rights within a diverse and open society. The emphasis on positive liberty remains a compelling rationale for the Left in British politics: equality is the means to the end of enlarging the individual's rights, choices and freedoms in the new society. It involves not only the redistribution of income but a fundamental redistribution of power where every citizen has access in Tawney's words 'to the means of civilisation'.[150] The dilemma for the centre-left since the Second World War has been that British society is barely comprised of 'egalitarian citizens'. Even in 1945, Labour's victory resulted from suspicion of the Conservatives, and did not represent the electorate's full-throated conversion to socialism.[151] The weak affiliation with egalitarian sentiments is confirmed by social attitudes surveys. Crosland acknowledged that the majority of the British working class were not socialists, and unlikely ever to become so.[152] He aimed to spell out a concept of equality that enabled the Labour party to win elections and govern authoritatively, forging a broad-based, radical appeal. Such a prospectus relied on reconciling equality with freedom and libertarianism on the British Left. Not surprisingly, the radical liberal tradition left an indelible mark on Crosland's revision of post-war social democracy; the influence of that tradition on the Labour party is the central theme of the chapter that follows.

FOUR

Crosland and liberal progressivism: the politics of 'conscience and reform'

I would like to see action taken both to widen opportunities for enjoyment and relaxation, and to diminish existing restrictions on personal freedom. (Anthony Crosland, 1956[1])

Growing prosperity and sophistication bring to the forefront other issues, tending to cut across class lines, such as the rate of growth, educational opportunity, urban and amenity planning, consumer protection, the role of the mass media, and libertarian reform. (Anthony Crosland, 1962[2])

Introduction: Crosland's legacy and progressive liberalism

Crosland's mission was to equip his party with a powerful social democratic identity drawing on the liberal as well as the socialist heritage within the British political tradition. Social democracy was at heart a marriage of individual freedom and social justice: socialism was the 'legitimate heir' of liberalism.[3] Despite the commitment to collective ownership of the means of production in Labour's constitution, socialism's 'threadbare doctrines' were inadequate in the wake of the 1951 defeat: for Crosland, liberalism was essential in reviving Labour as a credible party of government. The revisionists sought to rejuvenate British socialism assimilating prescient arguments from the New Liberalism, which tentatively permeated Labour's thought from the late nineteenth century. The relationship between Crosland's vision of socialism and the liberal tradition is the central focus of this chapter. Labour was a traditional party of the Left that in the past had given preference to state socialist policies. In contrast, the final peroration of *The Future of Socialism* captures the libertarian mood of post-war Britain, articulating the desire for fewer legislative controls, an easing of austerity, alongside support for individual freedom and tolerance of diversity in private life. Crosland was determined that the Conservative party should not be allowed to own the language of liberty and consumerism in the post-war world. That was, to say the least, a controversial aim for many in Crosland's party.

This chapter assesses the nature of Crosland's commitment to the radical liberal tradition, alongside his critique of Clause 4 socialism. The revisionists were convinced that the clause was detrimental to the party's electability after the Attlee Government's defeat: it defined Labour's purpose anachronistically as state ownership and nationalisation. This outdated position encouraged damaging uncertainty about Labour's objectives, making it a less pragmatic and effective party.[4] The state socialism embodied in Clause 4 encouraged Labour to break with the progressive liberal tradition, which until the 1920s had been a major influence on the party's development. By acknowledging the importance of liberty and the growth of individualism, Crosland confronted the legacy of Fabianism embodied in the writings of Beatrice and Sidney Webb who shaped the party's doctrine and identity in the late nineteenth and early twentieth century. His rejection of Fabian socialism with its emphasis on the state bureaucracy directing and overseeing capitalism was pivotal. The chapter dissects Crosland's legacy by exploring the nature of the New Liberalism and its ambiguous relationship with revisionism: the similarities between *The Future of Socialism* and the New Liberalism have rarely been acknowledged. This uncertainty is hardly surprising: the extent to which British socialism should draw from the liberal tradition is fiercely contested, particularly in the modern Labour party. In the light of this, the inadequacies of British liberalism are addressed. Commentators attest that cultural and economic liberalism has led to civic atrophy in western democracies: by reconnecting the party with the liberal tradition, Crosland allegedly distanced Labour from its ethical socialist roots in fellowship and the common good. Crosland's position, however, is subtle and nuanced; he conceived social democracy as an association of individual freedom and social justice. Strengthening the individual's ability to lead a life they had reason to value, enabling them to access 'the means of civilisation', should never be at the expense of collective obligations: a moral commitment to one's fellow citizens and the national political community.

Crosland's liberal progressivism

Crosland's reputation as the revisionist *par excellence* and his unyielding commitment to equality are among his most renowned beliefs. But as this chapter makes clear there is another dimension of his legacy: liberal progressivism. This concept of progressivism is drawn from Richard Hofstadter's work on *The American Political Tradition* referring to 'the popular humanistic language of the progressive tradition' that defined the presidency of Franklin Delano Roosevelt in the United States.[5] The term 'progressive' is dismissed as an anodyne, catch-all appeal to enlightenment values; in Crosland's revisionism, it inferred a belief in the liberal democratic state as the engine of social progress, advancing the public interest and liberating individuals from the restraints of unfettered market capitalism. The notion of progressivism has 'connotations of social justice, state intervention and [liberal] alliance with Labour'.[6]

In the early 1950s, Crosland rejected 'old-fashioned' methods of state control but believed in government's capacity to ameliorate a host of economic and social problems from unemployment to inadequate teaching in schools. This position contrasted with the market liberalism of Hayek and Niskanen that dominated the 1980s and early 1990s in the name of limited government. Crosland's revisionism was untroubled by the structure of the state; he was sceptical about constitutional reform insisting that Labour must accommodate itself to the existing political order. Whereas previous generations of radicals and socialists remained sceptical about the state, Crosland had little reason to question its neutrality and effectiveness.[7] This complacency was by no means exceptional: Attlee's ministers accepted the political establishment and its institutions almost without qualification, as did Wilson, Callaghan and Blair. Crosland's thought is associated with a truncated phase of post-war political history in which the state and collectivism enjoyed unprecedented prestige.[8] This approval of the state was encapsulated in Jay's work, *The Socialist Case* (1937), which urged the expansion of indicative planning. He insisted:

> Housewives as a whole cannot be trusted to buy all the right things, where nutrition and health are concerned. This is really no more than an extension of the principle according to which the housewife herself would not trust a child of four to select the week's provisions. For in the case of nutrition and health, just as in the case of education, the gentleman in Whitehall really does know better what is good for people than the people know themselves.[9]

Addison notes that by the mid-1950s, British society was characterised by a scale of state intervention markedly greater than in the inter-war years.[10] The growth of the state led to fears that liberties were being eroded by the leviathan of socialist bureaucracy. In Crosland's progressivism, social democracy was concerned with ethical and moral values. While orthodox Marxists and Fabians advocated state control of the economy inducing a transformation of capitalism, Crosland saw socialism as a humanitarian critique of an unequal, class stratified society.[11] Whereas Marx saw morality as a bourgeois delusion, Crosland understood moral values as the essence of socialism; politics was the art of persuading citizens to look beyond their self-interest to acknowledge the common good: Crosland's writings put democratic socialist ideals at the centre of Labour's identity.[12] In a society where traditional allegiances were dissipating, he recognised that for Labour to realise its electoral ambitions, it had to make a broad-based and radical appeal forging a new progressive alliance in British politics.

Crosland's assimilation of the New Liberalism was not only an attack on Marxism, but on the belief in pragmatism and 'muddling through' epitomised by the Labour Right and Morrison's commitment to 'consolidation'. This hard-headed world view accepted the party's threadbare ideology as a virtue, instead of carving out a distinctive ethical framework and body of belief providing guidance in changing times.[13] If Labour grasped the scale of social change in post-war Britain, it could forge a new progressive coalition. As with the generation of revisionists who preceded him, especially Tawney, Durbin and Dalton, Crosland acknowledged his party's ambiguity about the role of the market economy made it less likely that a coherent economic and political strategy could be forged. Having dreamed that capitalism might one day be supplanted, the apparent resilience of western capitalism in the post-war years demoralised the Left. At the end of the 1950s, Denis Brogan commented:

> Everywhere, 'capitalism' has shown astonishing powers of adaptation and recuperation, and in 1959 the prospects of what is now the traditional 'Left' look bleaker than they did in 1919 or 1945. All over Europe, democratic socialism is in retreat or is stagnant. And defeated three times in a row, the British Labour

party that cast itself in 1945 with such confidence
not only as the rightful heir of the radical tradition in
Britain, but the natural leader of the resurgent left in
liberated Europe, asks itself with distress...what has
gone wrong?[14]

By the mid-1950s, Crosland acknowledged ambitious social
reforms were only viable in Britain if the private sector was
sufficiently vigorous and dynamic to finance them. Labour's
attitude of suspicion, even contempt towards private wealth,
profit-making and competitive enterprise was unsustainable.
Crosland believed that capitalism would survive: post-war
reforms had transformed the system; equal citizenship and
the welfare state mitigated the indignities and instabilities of
markets. Even more to the point, Labour's prospects depended
on its ability to secure a reputation for economic competence
among a fluid electorate: the party had to demonstrate that it
could manage the market as efficiently as the Conservatives.
In this climate socialism had to be recalibrated, no longer
standing for the victory of one class or sectional interest over
another, but for a classless society in which citizens had duties
as well as rights, a conception of social democracy that stretched
back to Bernstein.[15]

Crosland was not conventionally viewed as a 'liberal';
indeed, liberalism was scarcely mentioned in his writings. *The
Future of Socialism* contains only glancing references to the work
of Keynes and Beveridge; Hobhouse and Green, meanwhile,
are never referred to. Hardly surprisingly, the liberal dimension
of Crosland's legacy has been underplayed. After all, Crosland
wore his liberal values lightly throughout his career, despite
his commitment to the permissive social reforms of the 1960s
and 1970s. In the heat of battle between the 'revisionists'
and 'fundamentalists', Crosland, Gaitskell and Jenkins faced
the accusation that they were 'rootless liberals' lacking any
commitment to the Labour party and British socialism.

Crosland's purpose was to re-think the strategy and doctrine
of the Labour party, an institution to which he demonstrated
tribal loyalty. The party's emergence as a serious contender

for power during the early twentieth century entailed a breach with liberalism, even if certain ideological influences remained. The creed that shaped Crosland's thought was not 'the mid-[nineteenth] century liberalism of the Utilitarians and Mill', but the tradition of liberal reform combining 'empirical science' with social 'ethics'.[16] As Alan Grimes has written: 'The doctrines of 'peace, retrenchment and reform, with freedom of trade and freedom of contract', died with Gladstone in 1898.'[17] In its place, the New Liberalism accorded a decisive role to the active state. Crosland focused on rigorous intervention to tackle social problems, where individual self-development was predicated on 'an ethical truth that man can only realise himself as part of a community'.[18] Crosland shared a belief in 'social action via the state – not as necessary evil, but as the just and right way of attaining human ends'.[19] Crosland's view of liberty and equality as indissolubly linked can be traced back to Green, Hobhouse, Hobson and Trevelyan.

The ethic of liberal progressivism centred on the politics of 'conscience and reform' constitutes Crosland's most significant contribution to the post-war British Left. His emphasis on 'a new, more humane practice of socialism...which did not rely on 'total abstinence and a good filing system'' was rooted in the commitment to positive freedom that has stimulated reformist social democracy in Britain for over half a century.[20] Leonard and Lipsey conclude that Croslandism displayed an unparalleled ability to withstand the 'quirks' of political fashion by virtue of its 'radical humanitarianism'; they are justified in arguing that Crosland's 'creed of equality and liberty still contain the seeds of a rich harvest'.[21] Before this ethic of liberal humanitarianism could flourish, however, the remaining residues of Clause 4 socialism had to be expunged from Labour's identity and doctrine.

Clause 4 socialism

The central point of attack in Crosland's revisionism was Clause 4 socialism. The intellectual genesis of the clause and its political implications are hard to pinpoint. Ralph

Miliband overemphasises the extent to which the Labour party unambiguously adopted a socialist ideology in 1918. The author of the statement of 'Party Objects', Sidney Webb, once described immodestly by his wife Beatrice as 'the intellectual leader of the Labour party',[22] initially sought a less confrontational formulation of socialism. The Webbs were influential in enabling the Labour party to develop its ethical instincts into a programme of political action:

> The Webbian influence was thus notable because, at the time when the Labour party was looking for an intellectual lead, there was ready to hand a complete and relevant body of ideas, well-founded in research, elaborately explored, and fully worked out in terms of the detailed institutional and policy aspects of the process of social change envisaged.[23]

The early Fabians had contempt for Marx and Marxism; it must be said the feeling was mutual: Lenin once described the Fabians as 'filthy froth on the surface of the world labour movement'.[24] Nonetheless, Sidney Webb alongside Arthur Henderson as the Labour leader in the aftermath of the First World War were compelled to accommodate syndicalist and Guild Socialist thought initially inspired by British Marxism into their formulation of party doctrine. Webb proposed the following statement as the basis of Clause 4: 'To secure for the producers by hand or by brain the full fruits of their industry by the Common Ownership of all Monopolies and essential Raw Materials'.[25] This formulation restricted the objective of state ownership to the utilities and basic industries. Under pressure from increasingly radical elements in the trade unions, a new formula drafted by Webb and Henderson was stipulated proclaiming Labour's strategic goal to be 'the common ownership of the means of production, distribution and exchange'. The meaning of 'common ownership' was deliberately obscure to elide differences between syndicalist advocates of workers' control, and the Fabian preference for state-run monopolies. This uncompromising and radical draft was directed at the entire productive economy. Pelling described it as 'a striking demonstration of the leftward trend in the unions', but Clause 4 did not end the uncertainty over Labour's doctrine.[26] The clause was regarded as vague and internally contradictory even in the 1920s; according to Tawney, Clause 4 was directly culpable for the ineptitude of the 1929 Labour government:

> The gravest weakness of British Labour is one which it shares with the greater part of the world, outside Russia...It lacks a creed...It does not achieve what it could, because it does not know what it wants...This weakness is fundamental. If it continues uncorrected, there neither is or ought to be, a future for the Labour Party.[27]

It has been said that the strength of Clause 4 was its ambiguity: the statement of party objects enabled Labour to break with its dependence on liberalism without imperilling the party's fragile doctrinal accord. Clause 4 allowed the fractious coalition of working-class sectional interests and middle-class intelligentsia to survive, imputing whatever meaning into the clause they wished. For pragmatic trade unionists such as J.H. Thomas, Clause 4 meant little; to politicians such as Bevan, the infamous passage was a signpost on the road to a socialised and planned economy.[28] Crosland captured this point himself:

> [T]he leadership, both Left and Right, tended to speak with two voices – one for the electors and another for the Party militants; it never, for example, sought to amend the Party constitution with its apparent commitment to 100 per cent public ownership. The Left-wing leaders, especially, were schizophrenic on the subject of nationalisation; intellectually they accepted a mixed economy, emotionally they still clung to the dogma of wholesale public ownership. The result was a series of very confused voices.[29]

The logic of the clause was replacing the 'anarchy' of laissez-faire capitalism with a rational economic order focused on collectivism and central planning articulated in the accompanying policy statement, *Labour and the New Social Order* (1918). This document 'was of great importance because it formed the basis of Labour Party policy for over thirty years – in fact, until the general election of 1950'.[30] Pelling contends that Clause 4 equipped Labour with a 'greatly improved constitution' enabling the party to make a national appeal: 'a practical programme which in domestic affairs was a compromise between Marxian Socialism on the one hand and the piecemeal social reform of the Chamberlain-Lloyd George type on the other'.[31] In the inter-war years, even non-socialist advocates of 'national efficiency' argued for 'case-by-case' nationalisation where private sector competition was no longer working in the public interest: electricity and gas; the coal mines; the railways; and London transport.

Labour's adoption of the clause in the aftermath of the First World War nonetheless reflected the transformation in socialist ideology which had taken place since the late nineteenth century: 'From liberal humanitarianism to aggressive exclusivism, from the emphasis on the dignity of the individual to that on the power of collectivities', socialism in Western Europe was becoming 'invested with combative emotionalism'.[32] Nowhere was this 'emotionalism' more apparent than in the Labour party where British labourism increasingly cultivated a sectarian outlook of righting wrongs against the ruling class. Labour was not alone in this: Lloyd George as Liberal Chancellor between 1909 and 1914 mounted a 'class war' against the landowning aristocracy and the 'idle rich'. After 1918, Labour's dogmatic attachment to Clause 4 reinforced its reputation as the 'anti-intellectual party'; Nairn observed that Labour had developed 'not...in response to any theory about what a socialist party should be; it arose empirically, in a quite piecemeal fashion, like so much in British society before it'.[33] In *The Future of Socialism*, Crosland referred to the party's 'marked anti-doctrinal and anti-theoretical bias'.[34] Even in 1945, the party's programme amounted to a series of piecemeal domestic reforms 'held together by a diffuse ethical yearning for socialist utopia'.[35]

As such, it was far from obvious that Clause 4 allowed the party to develop its credentials as a serious contender for power. The statement of aims asserted that the existence of profit denied workers access to what was rightfully theirs, underlining the eternal struggle between capital and labour while positioning the party in opposition to the essential principles of the market economy.[36] Profit was an 'evil' rather than necessary to produce long-term investment and growth; the clause reiterated that Labour existed to fight for class interests rather than the public interest.[37] The party's programme focused on public ownership and the nationalisation of productive assets. In the words of Tawney, Clause 4 ensured that the party, 'drugged itself with the illusion that, by adding one to one, it would achieve the millennium, without the painful necessity of clarifying its mind, disciplining its appetites, and training for a tough wrestle with established power and property'.[38] Writing in *The Conservative Enemy*, Crosland acknowledged that in the 1930s and 1940s there had been a legitimate case for nationalisation, promoting cooperative social relations, ensuring a fairer distribution of wealth, and advancing towards a more classless society; by the mid-1950s, however, the traditional rationale appeared questionable. Attlee's ministers had disagreed about the model of public ownership required to manage the assets and industries identified in Labour's 1945 programme. Inequality would be addressed through progressive taxation and social reform rather than by transforming the structures of ownership.[39] Crosland advanced these criticisms in the decades after the Second World War.

Despite the success of the 1945–51 governments, the revisionists believed fundamental weaknesses in the party's strategy remained, originating in Clause 4 socialism. In the first half of the twentieth century, Labour struggled to articulate the institutional machinery that was required to bring about its overarching aim of reforming capitalism. In the 1930s and 1940s, theoreticians notably Tawney, Cole, Dalton, Meade and Durbin developed new approaches to central planning inspired by the apparent success of the Soviet five year plans. Labour was continually exposed to conflict, however, since the leadership found it impossible to agree on a British model of nationalisation, public ownership and indicative planning.[40]

Until the end of the First World War Labour was a 'small parliamentary grouping' defending the sectional interests of workers and trade unions; the various socialist societies and unions comprising the party 'could agree on no positive programme'.[41] Above all, the socialist commonwealth they envisaged as an alternative model of society remained elusive and ambiguous. Clause 4 signalled Labour's objective of transformation towards a new social order, achieved through parliamentary democracy rather than violent revolution and political upheaval. The immediate result, however, was ideological obfuscation; the long-term consequence was the failure of Labour to articulate a credible governing strategy.[42] Barbara Wootton has elegantly summarised this deficiency in the doctrinal basis of the party:

> It has long been a joke against socialists that they answer every question and dispose of every criticism by a reference to 'the abolition of the capitalist system', but that if pressed, they would as often as not be quite unable to explain in precise terms what exactly was to be understood by that phrase: what were the features which made the capitalist system capitalist.[43]

The response of the revisionists by the late 1950s was to urge the explicit demotion of Clause 4: nationalisation was no longer necessary to ensure economic efficiency and social justice; it was increasingly unpopular with an electorate in thrall to post-war affluence and modernisation. Ruminating in his diaries, Patrick Gordon Walker concluded:

> I am sure that to win the next election we must drop nationalisation in the sense of a commitment or a threat. But it will be hard to do. Perhaps we must change the constitution first. This would also help

us to change the image of our association with the trade unions. They must appear in a new and more modern light – and less the masters of the party – if we are to win.[44]

As Lawrence Black noted: 'For Tony Crosland, affluence afforded a post-materialist focus in which the Webbs and Fabian emphasis on efficiency would yield to a more relaxed pluralism of full enjoyment besides employment and aestheticism, not asceticism.'[45] Gaitskell memorably told the 1959 party conference: 'Let us remember that we are a party of the future, not of the past; that we must appeal to the young as well as the old – young people who have very little reverence for the past. It is no use waving the banner of a bygone age.'[46] According to Mackintosh, British socialism was acquiring: 'A deeply conservative outlook based upon fear of change; it expects that the inevitable burden of adjusting to modern methods will fall predominantly on the workers so that the first priority is to defend the positions already won by the Labour Movement.'[47]

Leading revisionists including Gaitskell, Dalton, and Jay, as well as Crosland, agreed that nationalisation should be justified in industries and sectors 'case by case'. In a 1952 lecture, Jay argued for public ownership of chemicals and engineering alongside greater state investment in industry. [48] Nonetheless, Jay had already downgraded the importance of public ownership in his book, *The Socialist Case*, insisting the priority for future Labour governments was the redistribution of income and social security; this led Cole's review of the book to conclude: 'there is very little in it of what most people habitually think of as socialism'.[49] In his Fabian pamphlet on 'Socialism and Nationalisation', Gaitskell similarly urged a pragmatic and realistic approach to public ownership.[50] This was spelt out by Tawney in 1944 when he argued a transformation in the ownership structures of industry:

Does not necessarily mean indiscriminate nationalisation, which is merely one method, though an important method, of achieving that result...The truth is, of course, that the transference of property to public hands is a means not an end.[51]

Even Left-wing parliamentarians accepted that a transfer of ownership need not entail the imposition of state monopolies: 'Nationalisation should be used much more *flexibly* than in the past.'[52] The problem with defining public ownership as the party's principal objective was it created ambiguity about a Labour government's programme, limiting social democracy's appeal. By the end of the 1950s, Crosland was convinced the party had shown 'appalling uncertainty' about which industries it wanted to nationalise; it was seen as a threat to any sector in private hands.[53] The party changed its mind between 1951 and 1959 over whether the sugar, cement and chemical industries ought to be brought under state control. Other sectors notably machine tools, aircraft, electrical engineering and meat wholesaling made fleeting appearances in the party's nationalisation programme; Crosland singled out Labour's *Industry and Society* (1957) document as especially damaging with its 'vaguely threatening references' to nationalise the top 600 companies.[54] This uncertainty was exploited by the Conservatives who published a pamphlet in 1958 entitled 'They've got a little list' detailing the 500 British companies the party was threatening to bring under government control.[55]

The Future of Socialism sought to contest the assumption that Clause 4 provided Labour with an intellectually coherent strategy. Crosland insisted that the statement of party objects weakened Labour's appeal in the light of rising material affluence and consumerism in the Britain of the 1950s. As Addison recounts, the Attlee governments state planning and wartime controls led to a backlash among voters tired of regulation and bureaucracy, the emergence of 'a host of sweeping and arbitrary powers' enforced through the monolithic state.[56] Increasingly, 'there was a discernible Puritanism in Labour's preference for collective social provision over personal consumption, and an appeal to materialism in the Conservative rhetoric of tax-cutting and setting the people free'.[57] According to Magee, the

Labour party contained 'a disproportionately high number of people who equate the world and the flesh with the devil – sabbatarians, vegetarians, teetotallers – people who tint with grey everything they touch'.[58] Crosland condemned the Left's 'pharisaical attitude to the lives of others'.[59] He was determined to resist the retreat into tribalism and statism that reinforced Labour's political sterility.

Crosland and the Webbs' socialism

Although a believer in the active state, Crosland was concerned about its impact on individual freedom, just as unfettered market capitalism imperilled the liberties of citizens,[60] reminding fellow socialists: '[T]hey have anarchist blood in their veins, and that it is no part of their creed always to back the state against the individual'.[61] As the British socialist tradition evolved in the early twentieth century, it became increasingly anti-libertarian highlighted by the Webbs' fascination with Russia, alongside Wilson's claim that the party 'owed more to Methodism than to Marx'. As the pendulum swung from the individual to the collective, Crosland demanded:[62]

> A complete reversal of the Webb tradition. When socialists were all utopian anarchists, and liberals were all home rule dissenters, it was necessary to preach that a good filing system was more useful than an active conscience and to turn young socialists into good researchers and bureaucrats. But today, many of us are economists well-versed in fact-finding research, incipient bureaucrats and administrators. What we lack now is some of the fire and idealism, utopian though it often was, which the Webbs so much suspected. The morality of the Webbs...really would if universally influential make the socialist state into the dull functional nightmare which many fear.[63]

Crosland's antipathy to the Webbs' socialism was uncompromising. At a Fabian Summer School, he was rebuked by Margaret Cole (Beatrice Webb's biographer and the wife of G.D.H Cole) for criticising the Webbs' bureaucratic and elitist vision.[64] A programme of liberalisation was required affirming Crosland's view that liberty and 'freedom from controls' were as important as traditional concerns with solidarity, cooperation and fraternity.[65] Anthony Wright attests that Tawney's 'discussion of equality in terms of equal worth and social solidarity has different foundations from a liberal approach concerned with identifying the criteria of "fairness" and social justice';[66] Crosland was adamant that equality and individual freedom were interdependent. His estrangement from the Webbs reflected differences of personal temperament and character: 'The theoreticians in the Labour party were rather a grim lot', Roy Hattersley reminds us; 'The Webbs on honeymoon with their blue books. Tony wasn't about that. He was about having a drink, chasing women, having a good life. [*The Future of Socialism*] appealed to the middle class – all that stuff about opera, parks and flowers.'[6]

Jay, a committed Keynesian, took the view that public ownership should not be extended any further;[68] his conclusion was that Labour should concentrate on improving access to social security: 'This is a form of socialism which the public will both understand and desire, in the more affluent society into which we are now moving – a fairer sharing of the nation's wealth at home and abroad.'[69] Rita Hinden insisted that socialism must involve 'advance on many fronts': not just ownership and equality, but an extension of civil liberties, education reform and the expansion of the welfare state, alongside the goal of a property-owning democracy. Democratic socialism developed as an economic doctrine under the influence of Marxism; Crosland was critical of the narrowness of the British Left. In a speech in the late 1940s, he insisted:

> Economic redistribution will have gone as far as practicable, but distribution of opportunities for a cultured life will not. So the main emphasis will be on housing standards, town planning, new towns, the

clearance of old industrial areas, education. None of this will be accomplished until the background of comfort, beauty and culture in everybody's life is equal to what it is now for a person born of wealthy parents. This is the ultimate socialist ideal.[70]

Peter Jay observed that by the early 1970s: 'Fewer and fewer of the public problems about which we actually get excited – the Common market, urban motorways, incomes policy… the control of broadcasting, Concorde, conservation, and immigration can be satisfactorily solved by applying the socialist's catechism.'[71] *The Future of Socialism* elucidated an alternative libertarian position:

> The fight against uniformity and homogeneity in leisure life will then be the main battle – abolish Lord Chamberlain, abolish divorce laws, bring flagellation back into sex, have open air cafes open all night – lights, dancing, gaiety, culture and no talk of economics, politics or the need for a New Fabianism.[72]

Crosland made a plea for a more open, tolerant, and liberal society:

> We need not only higher exports and old-age pensions, but more open-air cafes, brighter and gayer streets at night, later closing hours for public houses, more local repertory theatres, better and more hospitable hoteliers and restaurateurs, brighter and clear eating houses, more riverside cafes, more pleasure gardens on the Battersea model, more murals and pictures in public places, better designs for furniture and pottery and women's clothes, statues in the centre of new housing estates, better-designed new street lamps and telephone kiosks and so on ad infinitum.[73]

Crosland articulated this liberal appeal in a remarkable speech to the South Gloucestershire Labour party on the eve of the 1950 general election:

> The ultimate ideal of socialism seems to me essentially a moral and not a material one. It is nothing to do with nationalisation of the means of production, nothing to do with any particular economic policy. It has something to do with a just and moral and equal society, in which it is no longer true that half the people live in cramped ugly houses and the other half in spacious and beautiful ones, in which half the people leave school at 15 to go into factories and the other half have all the advantages of Eton and Oxford.[74]

Towards the end of his career, Crosland adopted a broad-based conception of the social democratic ideal:

> I still believe the fundamental point very strongly that socialism is not simply a matter...of higher old age pensions and nationalising whatever it is. It must have some connection with our total way of life, and use of leisure and the rest of it.[75]

This is captured by Roy Jenkins' biographer, John Campbell, who claimed that:

> [*The Future of Socialism*] was less an economic blueprint than a manifesto for a new definition of socialism, based not on the old dogmas of public ownership and planning – now relegated to possible means rather than defining ends – but rather on increased equality, the breaking down of class barriers and wider opportunities for personal fulfilment.[76]

Crosland aimed to instil: 'the generous cultural vision of William Morris for the dour mechanistic socialism of the Webbs'.[77] An assortment of intellectuals influenced *The Future of Socialism*: Cole and Tawney from the socialist tradition alongside the liberal heritage of Keynes and Beveridge.[78] Crosland participated in a diverse intellectual community encompassing A.J.P. Taylor, A.J. Ayer, Michael Young and Daniel Bell. He had ties with scholars and academics from the United States and continental Europe. Crosland's liberal progressivism alongside his economic and political analysis drew on an eclectic variety of influences.

The emphasis on liberty was counter-balanced by the revisionist's uneasy relationship with fraternity and fellowship. Crosland made reference to community and the co-operative ideal throughout *The Future of Socialism*.[79] 'Few will quarrel with this ethical aspiration towards a more fraternal and co-operative society.'[80] Nonetheless, he was sceptical about imposing traditional solidarities on post-war Britain that restrained consumerism insisting 'there is nothing immoral about working-class materialism'.[81] Crosland's outlook was shaped by sociology and economics: it was in sociology rather than economic theory that 'the significant issues for socialism and welfare will be increasingly found to lie'.[82] Having been taught at Oxford by Ayer, the author of *Language, Truth and Logic*, his philosophical stance rested on logical positivism.[83] This rationalist outlook made Crosland wary of moralism. In *The Future of Socialism*, Crosland makes no reference to moral distinctions between the 'deserving' and 'undeserving' poor. He represented 'a strand of scientific rationalism in socialist thinking that threads back to Saint-Simon'.[84] The belief in the 'rational ordering of society' inspired Michael Young's 'nightmare vision' of a meritocracy driven not by unfettered market capitalism, but 'scientific positivism' and a 'hierarchy of intelligence'.[85] While Young emphasised the importance of family and community life, revisionists struggled to foresee what commitment might arise from an abstract and utopian communitarianism of the Left as we saw in Chapter Three. Crosland was scornful of middle-class intellectuals condemning the materialism and hedonism of working-class communities. The priority was 'a change in cultural attitudes', alongside 'government legislation', removing 'socially imposed restrictions on the individual's private life and liberty'. This legislation was 'intolerable, and should be highly offensive to socialists'.[86] By the early 1970s, Crosland was insisting on 'an everlasting need for vigilance in the defence of liberty'.[8]

This scepticism about central bureaucracy echoed past concerns among revisionists about the impact of central planning and state control on personal freedom. Additional measures were necessary to democratise the state, preventing dictatorship and oligarchy by strengthening parliamentary accountability.[88] In particular, Crosland was doubtful that nationalised industries could be supervised adequately by Parliament. Ministers had many duties and responsibilities: they were unable to run industries from Whitehall. To avoid excessive interference, managers ought to have autonomy to operate public enterprises at 'arm's-length' from the central bureaucracy.[89] Crosland insisted that during an era in which individualism was growing, Labour had to remove the residue of the Webbs' Fabianism from the party's identity. Labour must re-connect with the liberal tradition: liberty and equality would supplant the traditional socialist preoccupation with the planned economy.

Crosland and the New Liberalism

The British liberal tradition was inevitably a diverse and eclectic creed; its relationship with socialism and the Labour party has been heavily contested. Labour believed it was necessary to break with liberalism in the early twentieth century, securing independent working-class parliamentary representation while establishing its credentials as a majoritarian party.[90] Ralph Miliband concluded that Crosland's goal was to return Labour to its pre-1918 position: an ideology devoid of socialism that allowed the party to pursue power without concern for principle.[91] Historians have given Miliband's view credence: although the links between the Labour party and liberalism declined in the first half of the twentieth century, revisionism 'was more a development of radical liberalism than a revision of socialism'.[92] Theoreticians, notably Green and Hobhouse, had a 'remarkable influence' on British socialism's development; their ideas 'permeated social thought in England...they infiltrated the Fabian Society and came to exert some influence on the newly formed Labour party'.[93] By 1894, the Rainbow Circle was embracing 'progressives of all shades of opinion'; the aim was to develop 'a consistent body of political and economic doctrine which could be ultimately formulated in a programme of action'.[94] Key figures included William Clarke, Charles Trevelyan, John Hobson and Ramsay MacDonald. In 1896, the New Liberal *Progressive Review* was launched; the journal sought to articulate why economic and social inequality was economically inefficient as well as morally unjust.[95] The evidence of interchange between the Labour party and the Liberal party throughout the twentieth century is in fact considerable: for instance, Peter Sloman demonstrates figures on the Left of the Liberal party in the early 1950s sought to emphasise the vital role of the state. They were influenced by Crosland's book, *Britain's Economic Problem*, drawing on its 'more radical reading of Beveridge and Keynes'.[96] In turn, the impact of Keynes and Beveridge on the Attlee Government's post-war reforms was significant. This transmission of ideas brings to mind Campbell-Bannerman's declaration that the Labour party and the Liberals were 'both elements in the progressive forces of the country' who would achieve more together by working in partnership.[97]

Unlike other Gaitskell acolytes, Crosland was sceptical that the breach with 'old style socialism' should be achieved by publicly renouncing Clause 4. In battling to rewrite Clause 4 at Labour's 1960 conference, he conceded the revisionists 'made a frightful mistake' by antagonising the traditional wing of the party.[98] Crosland nonetheless agreed that the Webbs' formulation of party doctrine was ill-conceived and outdated; British socialism should draw on an array of traditions including radical liberalism. He sought an enlightened marriage between the concept of socialism which he was developing in the 1950s, and the New Liberalism defined by its 'generous benevolence toward everything human, with a desire for a universal embrace, for tearing down all walls of segregation, with a determination to lay the foundations for a truly open society'.[99]

Miliband's accusation that the revisionists were returning Labour to its pre-1918 situation devoid of an explicit commitment to socialism misunderstands the Attlee Government's significance. Whereas Gaitskell and Crosland's antecedents including Tawney, Dalton and Durbin believed in radical social transformation as a response to the mass unemployment experienced by the working class in the inter-war years, post-war revisionists insisted that the Attlee governments had forged a new age of full employment, social security and political stability; as a consequence, Labour should accept the existing class structure, but advance equal rights across British society.[100] The lodestar was ameliorative social reform rather than transformative social revolution. This commitment to evolutionary change was advanced in the *New Fabian Essays*, subsequently developed in *The Future of Socialism*. As Alan Warde has written, Crosland's revisionism meant a breach with orthodox socialism and sustained dialogue with radical liberalism:[101]

- Firstly, British socialism was reinterpreted by revisionists as an 'ethical ideal' centred on human relationships, rather than an alternative economic system. It was Labour's first leader, Keir Hardie, who insisted socialism was 'at bottom a question of ethics or morals. It has mainly to do with the relationships that should exist between a man and his fellows.'[102] The 1945 Government had addressed numerous problems that arose after 1918, creating public institutions to eradicate poverty promoting social security and welfare. Old class antagonisms were replaced by a spirit of consensus and cooperation.
- Secondly, the fundamental goal of nationalisation was relegated. Public ownership was no longer necessary to ensure full employment. The 'capitalist ruling class' were replaced by managers and bureaucrats rarely fixated on the profit motive. Within this climate of managerial capitalism, trade unions had the freedom to bargain with employers without fear of state interference or manipulation of wage-setting. As Warde puts

it: 'Social reformism condoned the sectional-corporatism of the trade unions', incorporating organised labour within the revisionist's strategy. This approach culminated in the unlikely trade union endorsement of Gaitskell over Bevan in the 1955 leadership election, a decision further motivated by the desire to defeat Communism within the labour movement.

- Thirdly, the revisionists were committed to equality as the ethical ideal of socialism; but inequality and class were not structural relationships borne of economic exploitation as Marxists had presumed. Class differences led to social stratification which encouraged resentment and inferiority: it was these attitudes that socialism had to modify. The revisionists like the New Liberals were committed to a more equal distribution of wealth, but concluded that unequal rewards were inevitable; the profit motive was necessary for freedom and prosperity. These diverse intellectual currents led to ambiguity about equality and meritocracy within revisionism: what kind of acquisitive society would emerge if equality of opportunity was pursued to its limits? If socialism was about human relationships, what was the long-term effect of consumerism and individualism on social solidarity?
- Fourthly, the revisionists countenanced interference with the market mechanism where it upheld the public interest, believing in the preservation of private property rights. Although government intervention was necessary, it should be restricted so as not to curtail human ingenuity, the engine of a dynamic capitalist economy. The revisionists did not oppose strategic planning by the state but remained suspicious of any departure from the precepts of modern liberal ideology: individuals should be free to shape their own opportunities and life-chances. In *The New Fabian Essays*, Crosland and Jenkins had underlined the importance of market competition.
- Fifthly, Crosland's generation were committed to parliamentary politics and responsible government. Social reform had to be achieved by a parliamentary strategy which upheld democratic norms and institutions. This approach understood politics in terms of 'ethics rather than power or interests';

revisionists were suspicious of the corporatism characterising the Wilson–Callaghan years. The revisionists emphasised class conciliation through ethical ideals; corporatists understood society as comprised of opposing sectional interests. Both Crosland and Jenkins reluctantly opposed Castle's *In Place of Strife* reforms in 1969, and were cautious about a statutory incomes policy. In 1956, Crosland insisted: 'A national, centralised wage policy is, in the first place, impractical and unwise. It goes against the British tradition of Trade Union autonomy and independence of government control.'[103]

- Finally, the revisionists adopted a 'realist' strategy in international diplomacy, questioning the concept of a socialist foreign policy, the notion of Britain as a 'third force' between Soviet Russia and the United States. Healey elaborated the realist position in his *New Fabian Essay* on 'Power Politics in the Labour Party'. It meant a steadfast commitment to membership of the North Atlantic Treaty Organisation (NATO) and the maintenance of the Atlantic alliance. America remained the best guarantor of political freedom and democracy.[104]

By drawing on the heritage of radical liberalism under the guise of revisionism, the Labour party was able to shape decisively the post-war settlement.[105] In the nineteenth century, British liberalism fractured as the doctrine of laissez-faire was questioned; the expansion of the urbanised working class led to vocal demands for public intervention in health, housing, education, and in alleviating material deprivation (Warde, 1982). The New Liberalism emphasised 'positive freedom', an ethic of equal citizenship to liberate the most disadvantaged, influencing generations of reformers and social democrats:

> From T.H. Green, through Hobhouse, Hobson and T.H. Marshall to Crosland, a basic conceptual structure survived. This structure comprised a language of social and civil rights, a conception of modern history as the development of citizenship and a common culture,

an individualist notion of liberty, and a central critical concept of equality.[106]

This notion of positive freedom was developed by Tawney in 'We Mean Freedom':

> There is no such thing as freedom in the abstract, divorced from the realities of time and place. Whatever else it may or may not imply, it involves a power of choice between alternatives – a choice which is real, not merely nominal...because a man is most a man when he thinks, wills and acts, freedom deserves the sublime things which poets have said about it; but, as part of the prose of everyday life, it is quite practical and realistic. Every individual possesses certain requirements – ranging from material necessities of existence to the need to express himself in speech and writing, to share in the conduct of affairs of common interest, and to worship God in his own way or refrain from worshipping Him.[107]

According to this ethic of positive freedom, the purpose of politics was to nurture and release human potential, guaranteeing equal rights for all citizens. There was still a determination to uphold the central axiom of liberalism: the starting-point for all forms of political action is the individual. Recognising the primacy of the individual was not antithetical to the public interest which defined Green's 'liberal-idealism'; the individual and the community existed in 'unstable equilibrium': individuals developed through their relationship with others, having an organic link to society.[108] This was elaborated by Crosland in emphasising the importance of public institutions, notably comprehensive schools and the welfare state, bringing citizens together across class lines to create spheres of provision where private interests did not predominate.

Stefan Collini has demonstrated how Green and Hobhouse undermined the classical liberal view that state expansion imperils freedom: Green developed the notion of positive liberty; Hobhouse focused on how inequalities unjustly constrained entire classes of individuals. According to Guido de Ruggiero, 'The best formulation of the new English liberalism of the twentieth century...is that of Hobhouse. Here we find the teachings of Mill and Green in a modernised form.'[109] The concept of political and economic rights wedded to national citizenship emerged out of the radical liberal tradition, justifying state intervention without curtailing liberty.[110] Hobhouse's mission was 'to turn nineteenth century liberalism in the direction of twentieth century social reform while still preserving the fundamental base of individual freedom'.[111] Hobhouse sought to justify reform not by advancing 'a collectivist theory of community' but instead by affirming 'traditional liberal principles'.[112] In this sense, it is important not to exaggerate the disjuncture between classical and social liberalism:[113] both affirmed individual rights were the focal-point of political action. So too did early socialists including Hardie and MacDonald, although there was ambiguity given the demands of socialism for cooperation and collectivism.[114]

The next generation of New Liberals, notably Beveridge and Keynes, influenced Labour's ideas about economic policy and the welfare state. Though Keynes and Beveridge were both liberals, there was still 'a major difference in their approach to the post-war world'; Keynes sought to revive market capitalism through social reform, whereas Beveridge was sympathetic to greater state intervention and collectivism.[115] However, both kept their distance from the Labour party; Keynes dismissed Labour's 'doctrinaire state socialism' concluding: 'The intellectual elements in the Labour party will never exercise adequate control.'[116] He stated:

> I do not believe that class war or nationalisation is attractive or stimulating to modern minds...the true socialism of the future will emerge from an endless variety of experiments directed towards discovering the respective appropriate sphere of the individual and

the social, and the terms of a fruitful alliance between these sister instincts.[117]

As the twentieth century progressed, the mood of intolerance on the British Left towards both the Liberal party and liberal ideology was considerable.[118] This hostility was the consequence of party competition between Labour and the Liberals, as well as a misinterpretation of liberal doctrine, conceived as a mid-nineteenth century free market philosophy based on utilitarianism and the early writings of John Stuart Mill. As Freeden has remarked, the New Liberalism was a distinctive creed inspiring Lloyd George's reforming administration of 1906–14. This position acknowledged the individual's role within the community, asserting the claims of 'the social' over narrowly individualistic concerns.[119] Hobhouse argued that human life was 'essentially relational in its fundamental features'.[120] In his polemic on *Liberalism*, Hobhouse invoked an 'organic view of society' inherited from Green arguing that 'such a fulfilment or full development of personality is practically possible not for one man only but for all members of a community.[121] There must be a line of development open along which each move in harmony with others.'[122] The essence of the New Liberalism was positive liberty:

> Liberty is an end – or the end – in politics…Liberty means the ability to do what one chooses; but also he holds that as a man cannot wholly escape the influence of other individuals, of groups and of society at large, there may be cases in which the state can intervene with coercive measures which, while reducing the freedom of the person coerced, increases the freedom of others who were perhaps in the power of the person legislated against.[123]

Hobhouse, in turn, rejected: 'Laissez-faire liberalism on the one hand, and doctrinaire, economically deterministic socialism on the other…he sought to justify in theory that which was largely achieved in substance in both England and the United States half a century later: the rudiments of the liberal welfare state.'[124]

This conception of freedom echoes Green's definition of liberty: 'the positive power or capacity of doing or enjoying something worth doing or enjoying'.[125] Society is comprised of 'a community of mutually interacting beings', in which 'there is always the possibility of the state intervening to prevent coercion and so increase liberty'.[126] The New Liberals were attracted by 'the moral appeal of socialism', particularly a guaranteed minimum income and a just distribution of wealth; it was necessary to constrain market forces through state intervention to permit the expansion of social provision. New Liberals were not 'non-socialist progressives': they drew upon socialist ideas about ownership and the organisation of industry.[127] Hobhouse lamented 'the traditions and class distinctions [that] kept many good liberals outside Labour'.[128] Like Crosland, the New Liberals were sceptical that collectivism and state ownership would on their own create a fairer society.[129] According to Hobhouse: 'If the change from individualism to socialism means nothing but an alteration in the methods of organising industry it would leave the nation no happier or better than before'. His colleague, John Hobson, agreed: 'A so-called socialism from above, embodying the patronage of an emperor or of a small enlightened bureaucracy, is not socialism in any moral sense at all.'[130] The divergence between socialism and liberalism during the twentieth century was not merely the consequence of the party system institutionally dividing Labour and the Liberals, but substantive differences of attitude towards economic management and the state bureaucracy. The New Liberals were especially doubtful about the Labour party's institutional relationship with the unions:

> There is possible a distinctive kind of socialism viz. one based not on the Trade Unions but on the community and social service. The constitution of the Labour party binds it tight to the Trade Unions and their sectional selfishness, a most serious defect.[131]

By the end of the First World War, the Edwardian progressive alliance had been shattered: Labour was becoming electorally ambitious and increasingly committed to socialism; the adoption of Clause 4 had imposed a 'clear dividing line' which 'liberals could not cross without becoming socialists, and renaming their liberalism'.[132] Leading members of the Liberal party responded differently: while some joined Labour many defected to Baldwin's Conservative party emphasising that socialists and liberals were by no means always natural bedfellows; after the 1920s, Liberal politicians frequently sided with the Conservatives against 'socialism'; others, including Keynes, wanted Labour to enter into progressive co-operation and drop the pretence of class struggle; to some extent 'the governing assumptions of Edwardian progressivism lived on in MacDonald's Labour party' although the 1931 crisis led to a further breach between socialism and liberalism; Labour opted for an uncompromising programme of state planning and nationalisation in response to the economic crisis.[133]

The New Liberalism and Fabianism criticised traditional Marxist prescriptions for economic organisation,[134] but Hobhouse, like Crosland, rejected the Webbs' emphasis on enlarging central bureaucracies, 'the temptation to hail any and every extension of state authority, whatever its principle or its object, as a triumph for socialism'.[135] The Fabians had too little respect for democracy, always tempted to force through change 'by packing and managing committees instead of winning the popular assent'; the triumph of Fabian expertise would ensure that 'all that was human in socialism vanishes out of it'.[136] The Fabians believed in socialism's inevitability, but Hobhouse asked himself: 'If Socialism is coming of itself, why should anyone incur the obloquy of calling himself a Socialist, or put himself to any trouble in securing the advent of the inevitable?'[137] Many Fabians had been sympathetic to imperial wars, but the New Liberals, notably Hobson, C.P. Scott, Clarke and Hobhouse, rejected the defence of Empire.[138] Hobson provided additional anti-Fabian ammunition, charging that Fabianism was dependent 'more and more upon the wire-pulling and intriguing capacity of the enlightened few'.[139] Hobhouse and Hobson had similarities to Crosland in their scepticism towards Fabian socialism.

In laying the foundations of revisionism, Hobhouse developed a 'socialistic' conception of the New Liberalism entailing a rigorous separation of ends and means. Tawney prefigured Crosland by defining socialism in terms of ethical values giving primacy to equality and social justice.[140] According to Peter Clarke: 'The New Liberalism professed to be a means of adjusting the apparently competing claims of collectivism and individualism, democracy and knowledge, social forces and rational progress. On this basis it saw room for wide and fruitful co-operation with Labour as part of a progressive movement.'[141]

This movement gave birth to liberal socialism with Tawney as the link between the New Liberalism of Green, Hobhouse, Hobson and Graham Wallas; the Labour revisionists of the inter-war period including Durbin and Dalton; and the post-war generation of Jay, Jenkins, Gaitskell and Crosland. Tawney resisted the conflation of socialism and state ownership, insisting 'like other summary designations of complex political forces, Socialism is a word the connotation of which varies, not only from generation to generation, but from decade to decade'.[142] Tawney's advice was 'to treat sanctified formula with judicious irreverence, and to start by deciding what precisely is the end in view'.[143] Crosland maintained the distinction between institutional means and principled ends; he was 'dogmatic on the fundamentals and flexible on details' focusing on a concept of liberty that was about removing 'bad' restrictions increasing the sum total of human freedom and happiness.[144] To quote the former Liberal Prime Minister, Herbert Henry Asquith, the aim of politics was 'to equalise opportunities no less than to curtail privileges; to make the freedom of the individual a reality and not a pretence'.[145]

The period between 1918 and the 1950s can be viewed as an aberration in Labour's history: the party sought to establish a doctrine and identity which constituted a decisive break with the radical liberal tradition. Edmund Dell portrays the decades between the end of the First World War and the emergence of post-war Britain as a period in which the party embraced an explicitly socialist ideology giving primacy to state ownership of productive assets and industries.[146] Similarly, Harrison observes that Labour experienced 'a statist and class-conscious diversion from the pragmatic, libertarian, and undoctrinaire Edwardian radical/Liberal reforming alliance whence it had come'.[147] In the late 1950s, as Labour endured three successive defeats in an age of affluence accompanied by an apparent yearning for personal freedom, the party reacquainted itself with core elements of the liberal tradition under the guise of revisionism. As Desai remarked:

> The relationship of the revisionist or social democratic intellectuals to the Labour party can be traced to the turn of the century when their intellectual forebears, the Fabians and Progressive Liberals, first began to move towards Labour.[148]

Crosland was a pivotal figure in recapturing the radical tradition. As an ambitious politician aspiring to the party leadership, he wore his liberal credentials lightly.[149] Nonetheless, he naturally identified with a liberal conception of socialism; his writings constitute a persuasive examination of the indissoluble nature of equality and liberty. In the late 1950s, he complained repeatedly to Gaitskell that Grimond's Liberal party was seizing the mantle of progressive reform, attacking the hereditary status of the House of Lords and the dominance of the public schools.[150] In *The Conservative Enemy*, Crosland praised progressive liberals outside his party acknowledging 'an idealistic or forward-looking minority of non-socialists has sympathised with, and even sought to further, some of the aims of the socialist or working-class movement'.[151] Figures such as Charles Dilke and Lloyd George alongside 'non-socialist intellectuals' from Hilaire Belloc to John Ruskin inspired social democratic institutions, notably the welfare state. They affirmed Britain's unique political structure 'based as it is on a long liberal tradition...exceptionally tolerant of dissent'.[152] This stance emphasised Crosland's admiration for the parliamentary system and Westminster model of democracy. Radical social reforms were compatible with 'our parliamentary institutions, our liberal tradition, and our national character strongly attached to personal freedom'.[153]

Crosland was a champion of liberal progressivism, promoting Labour as a libertarian party on the Left advancing the individual's rights and freedoms against legislative restraint. He established a careful balance between liberty and collectivism; liberal socialism was concerned with developing a model of the state to ensure greater equality while preserving the institutions and freedoms of democracy.[154] Crosland warned of 'the inevitable growth of a state bureaucracy impinging heavily on the lives of individual citizens',[155] drawing on the writings of Dalton and Durbin who cautioned of collectivism's excesses in the 1930s. He was lucid as well as insistent:

> The aim of socialism is to give greater freedom to the individual. British socialists have never made an idol of the state, demanding the individual should be sacrificed to it...State action is advocated by socialists not for its own sake, but because it is necessary to prevent the oppression of the individual by others.[156]

Crosland summarised his position in *The Future of Socialism*: 'My conclusion is that men and women will be more free, not less free, under socialism. Freedom will be more widely disseminated. There will be no attempt to impose rigid uniformity.'[157] This outlook indicates sympathy towards the primacy of the rational individual accompanied by scepticism towards an arbitrary growth in the size and scope of government.[158] Like Gaitskell and Jenkins, Crosland did not believe that state ownership of the means of production and a planned economy would produce an inherently more equal and just society. Like the New Liberals, Crosland also rejected the views of Herbert Spencer and Hayek that all forms of state intervention were detrimental to liberty. The state was necessary to encourage self-development and equal opportunities among the least advantaged, qualifying without imperilling property rights or the sovereignty of free markets.[159] Liberalism was given a fresh lease of life in the 1950s and 1960s not only by Grimond's party but through the aegis of Labour and the revisionist wing (Warde, 1982). Grimond sought a realignment of the Left acknowledging that Gaitskell and Crosland in their opposition to a centrally planned economy blurred the distinction between the Liberals and Labour.[160] In a lecture given in the mid-1970s, Crosland warned:

> We must take seriously the fears about the growth of state power, especially given the *penchant* of some socialists for the continual spawning of giant new institutions under centralised control. We should not forget that a change from private control to state control is socialist only if control is democratic; a transfer from a private bureaucracy to a public bureaucracy in no way furthers the aims of socialism. We should not be in the business of creating endless giant Leviathans managed by armies of bureaucrats; and we must therefore heed this warning...The fact is that we want democratic control over all concentrations of power; and here the socialist tradition is far more relevant than a Conservatism which is obsessed by state power alone.[161]

John Mackintosh and David Marquand criticised Crosland for his self-satisfaction about the British political system predicated on Lord Hailsham's concept of 'elective dictatorship'. Crosland scorned the cause of political reform and participatory democracy:

> [Crosland] does say in *Socialism Now* that he would be against constitutional and political reform that led to an artificially contrived idea of equality of participation because 'we don't want more and more people engaged and fussing about'. He had great scepticism

about big claims for increased participation that many constitutional reformers wanted to lay claim to.[162]

Crosland was doubtful that the majority of the population were interested in influencing the decision-making process since most voters:

> Prefer to lead a full family life and cultivate their gardens. And a good thing too. For if we believe in socialism as a means of increasing personal freedom and the range of choice, we do not necessarily want a busy bustling society in which everyone is politically active, and fussing around in an interfering and responsible manner, and herding us all into participating groups. The threat to privacy and freedom would be intolerable.[163]

Nonetheless as a practising politician, Crosland was conscious of the decline of faith in the British political and governing system. By the mid-1970s, new fault-lines emerged including a surge of support for Celtic separatism, alongside the prospects of a structural crisis of the British state provoking a major realignment of the party system. As Crosland wrote:

> It may be true that, as Robert Nisbet has recently written, 'we live in a kind of twilight age of government, one in which the loss of confidence in political institutions is matched by the erosion of traditional authority in kinship, locality, culture, language, school, and other elements of the social fabric'.[164]

He was alive to the dangers of imposing central government's will on localities and communities insisting in *The Future of Socialism* that the existing structure of schools should not be 'forcibly dismantled'.[165] As Secretary of State despite his wish to abolish grammar schools, Crosland was cautious about his department interfering in the policies of democratically elected

Local Education Authorities (LEAs). He preferred an approach centred on 'persuasion' rather than 'coercion' put into effect in his 1965 circular, insisting that provision in England and Wales should be determined by local rather than national decision-making. Crosland became sceptical of radical institutional reforms mandated by the central state to improve equality of opportunity, as he told an interviewer in 1974: 'There has been a lot of American research which suggests that we were inclined 20 years ago to exaggerate the effect of education taken alone on people's life-chances.'[166]

Another area of controversy was council house sales: the former Head of the Downing Street Policy Unit, Bernard Donoughue, complained that Crosland 'didn't have a sense of what ordinary Labour voters wanted' and was influenced by party views in local government, recalling that 'Anthony Crosland and his advisers (although not most of the regular officials) were disappointing in their reactions' to proposals from Number Ten.[167] Contrary to received wisdom, however, Crosland was not opposed to selling off local authority properties as long as the public sector stock was replenished. This decision was a major weakness of the Thatcher governments' housing policy in the 1980s, the root cause of the current crisis in social housing.[168] He recognised that home ownership 'need not offend socialist principles'.[169] Crosland went further in *The Conservative Enemy* insisting that 'If property is well distributed, a property-owning democracy is a socialist rather than a conservative ideal.'[170] In the 1930s, the Liberal party sought to clarify its doctrine by promoting freedom and self-development through the diffusion of property rights;[171] Crosland eagerly assimilated this position. He was influenced by James Meade who argued that the aim of social democracy was 'to equalise the distribution of private property'.[172]

Crosland was stirred by Tawney's concern with democratising society and improving the quality of life alongside 'the power that people exercised'.[173] This approach was a response to rising affluence: 'Material standards are rising to the point where we can spare more energy, and more resources, for beauty and culture.'[174] Unlike Crosland, Tawney was committed to Christian socialism. Nonetheless, Tawney believed in economic participation and the redistribution of power throughout the workplace and the community, ideas that surfaced in Crosland's writings. He insisted that giving citizens the capacity to influence and shape the local environment was at least as important as income redistribution. Tenants ought to have influence over their local community: 'politicians must lead but they must listen first'.[175] Crosland was a critic of monolithic high-rise tower blocks alongside badly planned urban estates with few public amenities; he lamented the failure of local bureaucrats to 'ask the people what they really wanted'.[176] According to Geoff Gallop: 'Crosland also pointed to the need for voluntary movements to represent the user or the consumer against the producer and bureaucrat...to act as neighbourhood or community associations.'[177]

Crosland's stance has been caricatured as top-down, mechanical socialism, pulling the levers of the state to affect social change.[178] He was influenced by the disposition of the times: the British Left was fundamentally optimistic about what the state could do. Like Keynes and Beveridge, Crosland's approach assumed a primary role for the knowledgeable expert and decision-maker, rather than democratic participation.[179] Mid-twentieth century Britain was governed by an influential Whig–liberal elite, broadly meritocratic in composition but predominantly recruited from the major public schools and the universities of Oxford and Cambridge. This cadre of public service professionals saw their role as one of enlightened public duty. Tensions emerged, nonetheless; liberals became concerned that the burgeoning welfare bureaucracy was stifling social responsibility. The welfare system weakened the incentive for individual and voluntary initiative. The impact of the welfare state in British culture and society was examined in the research of Brian Abel-Smith and Richard Titmuss. They were concerned with how the social service state reinforced passive dependency by its reluctance to acknowledge the reciprocal duties and responsibilities of citizens. As Piachaud has written:

There are two reasons for asserting that citizenship must involve responsibilities as well as rights. First, because this is in tune with the more humane and shared values in society. Second, because any increases in opportunities and power of the poor and disadvantaged in society will always be limited if these are solely provided *for* them, handed down from above. Full rights *of* social citizenship can only be achieved when the government meets its responsibilities and citizens meet theirs.[180]

Such criticisms peppered the speeches of Grimond, leading to a revival in the electoral fortunes of the Liberal party by 1959. Nevertheless, Crosland continued to emphasise the central imperative of freedom, rejecting the statist inheritance of the early Fabians while diverging from the social authoritarianism of New Labour. The tension arises from New Labour's record on civil liberties, 'the war on terror', immigration, criminal justice and localism; alongside constitutional reform in the wake of the Scottish independence referendum. This position reflected the enduring tension since the Labour party's creation between individual liberty and collectivism. Enhancing the rights of the majority of citizens might necessitate diluting the rights of a minority; where the line ought to be drawn was never explicit.[181]

Crosland and liberal social democracy

The previous section demonstrated how Crosland renovated social democracy during the 1950s and 1960s as a strong marriage of individual freedom and social justice. Throughout his work from *The Future of Socialism* to *Socialism Now*, Crosland emphasises four essential themes of liberal progressivism and social democracy: a belief in liberalising legislation so that everyone in Britain can enjoy personal freedom; the legitimacy of a market economy centred on competition rather than state control; the commitment to an enabling state which gives each individual the resources and opportunities to realise their potential; and finally, an open, anti-dogmatic, non-sectarian approach to politics.

Left libertarianism

The first axiom of liberal progressivism was Crosland's belief in libertarianism and social reform. He insisted that state intervention would enhance personal freedom removing constraints on the individual, particularly those lacking material resources; there was an imperative to revoke legislation that unduly curtailed liberty. He was determined to wrestle the mantle of freedom and individualism from the Right in British politics; the Tories by the 1950s supported consumerism but were socially conservative. Crosland's prospectus was a reaction against the austerity, regulations and drab uniformity of post-war British society which sullied Labour's image and reputation. In 1949, the author J.B. Priestley complained: 'The area of our lives under our own control is shrinking rapidly... politicians and senior civil servants are beginning to decide how the rest of us shall live.'[182] Crosland was aware of the dangers for Labour as the party of state collectivism.

In *The Future of Socialism*, he was adamant: 'I should like to see action taken both to widen opportunities for enjoyment and relaxation, and to diminish existing restrictions on personal freedom.'[183] This removal of restrictions should be achieved by changing cultural attitudes alongside government legislation and legislative reform.[184] Socialism must address:

> Socially imposed restrictions on the individual's private life and liberty. There come to mind at once the divorce laws, licensing laws, prehistoric (and flagrantly unfair) abortion laws, obsolete penalties for sexual abnormality, the illiterate censorship of books and plays, and remaining restrictions on the equal rights of women. Most of these are intolerable and should be highly offensive to socialists.[185]

This emphasis on liberty underlines Crosland's disdain for social conservatism, complicit in Britain's post-war decline: restrictions on personal freedom made Britain markedly less innovative.[186] He was influenced by an outpouring of scholarship which sought to explain why Britain's economic performance after 1945 was unimpressive, in particular Michael Shanks' *The Stagnant Society* and Andrew Shonfield's *British Economic Policy Since the War*. These authors focused on structural causes including deficiencies in British society and culture (Shanks), alongside egregious errors in post-war policy-making such as imperial overstretch, excessive overseas military commitments, and the negative impact of the sterling area on Britain's economic performance (Shonfield).[187] In *Britain's Economic Problem*, Crosland emphasised the importance of the sterling area in protecting British industry given the American export surplus and consequent dollar shortage.[188] However, Shonfield saw the sterling area as a cause of post-war stagnation; both he and Shanks emphasised the impact of cultural conservatism on the failure to modernise and renew the economy.

Crosland's Left libertarianism developed in reaction to the sterile Fabianism of the Webbs. He served on the Fabian Society executive for 15 years, including as Chairman; the Fabians mattered inside the Labour party; they were a significant influence on policy-making in the post-war governments. According to Vaizey, Crosland was 'a Fabian in the true tradition – that is…he believed in social enquiry followed by social action'.[189] Yet he had little admiration for the Fabian aesthetic: 'He saw no virtue in sitting on a bed of nails when there was a comfortable chair in the same room.'[190] He insisted: 'For one brought up as a Fabian, in particular, this inevitably means a reaction against the Webb tradition.'[191] Crosland continued:

> I do not wish to be misunderstood. All who knew the Webbs have testified to their personal kindliness, gentleness, tolerance, and humour. But many of their public virtues, so indispensable at the time, may not

be as appropriate today. Reacting as they were against an impractical, Utopian, sentimental, romantic, almost anarchist tradition on the left, they were no doubt right to stress the solid virtues of hard work, self-discipline, efficiency, research and abstinence...But now we surely need a different set of values. Permeation has more than done its job. Today we are all incipient bureaucrats and practical administrators...Now the time has come for a reaction: for a greater emphasis on private life, on freedom and dissent, on culture, beauty, leisure, even frivolity. Total abstinence and a good filing system are not now the right sign-posts to the Socialist Utopia: or at least if they are, some of us will fall by the wayside.[192]

Of course, the Webbs' socialism was not as rudimentary as Crosland depicted: they believed in municipal 'gas and water' socialism, local government and friendly societies, not merely the power of the central state.[193] In reacting against Fabianism, historians of post-war Britain viewed Crosland as among the leading progenitors of the permissive society. His uncompromising commitment to personal freedom and liberty was partly the consequence of his admiration for the United States; at the heart of the American ideal was uninhibited self-expression, the right to lead a life of one's choosing. After decades of restriction, Britain needed a libertarian revolution. Jenkins as Home Secretary between 1965 and 1967 instituted landmark reforms; through *The Future of Socialism*, Crosland provided a compelling justification for the libertarian turn in post-war social democracy. This shift was an improbable but remarkable development given the authoritarian and moralistic influence of the 'Tory-socialist' tradition in the Labour party since the late nineteenth century.

Property rights and the mixed economy

In interpreting social democracy as a partnership of individual freedom and social justice, Crosland emphasised the primacy of property rights within a mixed economy where the private sector and competition played a decisive role. This stance provided an important bridge to liberalism: British Liberals had traditionally emphasised markets and a wider distribution of property 'qualitatively different to socialism'.[194] Crosland believed nationalisation and public ownership were no longer of fundamental importance. Public ownership should be justified pragmatically 'case-by-case'; nationalisation did not necessarily make British society more socialist; socialism would not be achieved by bringing productive assets under state control. The traditional case for nationalisation that emerged after the First World War was outdated.

The justification for public ownership had been, first, the public utility argument that essential services and industries must be protected by the state rather than abandoned to the anarchy of the market; second, nationalisation was necessary to prevent monopolies and private cartels from exploiting consumers, setting artificially high prices; third, the production and supply of raw materials on which the basic industries depended ought to be supervised in the national interest; public ownership, fourth, will generate efficiencies through economies of scale; finally, the profit motive conflicts with a modern industrial economy requiring investment in future productive potential: public ownership guaranteed a high and sustainable level of investment.[195] While these arguments for nationalisation were convincing in theory, the experience of the Attlee governments highlighted practical difficulties. Post-war socialists struggled to create workable management arrangements. Bevin disliked worker's control of nationalised industries which he feared would become 'a series of London transport boards'.[196] Morrison advocated the public corporation model run by experts and business leaders at arm's-length from the workforce and management.[197] Boards created to supervise the nationalised industries were seldom effective, however, and civil servants in Whitehall lacked expertise; Parliament did not have the authority to hold departments or industry boards to account.

While he urged pragmatism, Crosland as the arch-revisionist grew sceptical of public ownership following structural changes in capitalism after the Second World War. He did not believe that nationalisation would 'alter the existing institutional framework in such a way as to give more outlets to existing social motives'.[198] Socialisation through state control would not necessarily instil harmony and co-operation between management and the workforce. The quality of management determined Britain's economic and industrial performance rather than public or private ownership. Crosland was sceptical about industrial democracy insisting that there would always be 'two sides' to industry: management who took decisions and trade unions who asserted the interests of their members.[199] He reached the heretical conclusion that nationalisation might be 'positively bad for industrial relations'. The railways had been brought under state control; as a result, 'a highly centralised and uniform structure' was imposed on 'previous regional traditions and variations'.[200] He was pessimistic about nationalisation in modernising and upgrading Britain's industry and infrastructure: 'There is little reason to expect nationalisation to produce an automatic change for the better.'[201]

The structural changes in capitalism meant nationalisation and public ownership were less appropriate. Full employment as a central pillar of the post-war settlement no longer relied on state control: a high and stable level of employment could be achieved through a mixed economy in which the private sector played a decisive role, as was the case in the Scandinavian countries.[202] More challenging for orthodox socialism was Crosland's claim that a productive economy required incentives for entrepreneurship, promotion of market competition, and sustained improvements in the rate of productivity rather than state ownership. It was essential to defend the claims of political liberty against state interference; competition must be embraced by the Left: 'Not only is there a genuine restriction of freedom involved in forbidding the citizen by law to start producing certain goods...competition is seen to bring greater advantages than post-war socialists realised – in preventing sloth and encouraging initiative, and in increasing the sense of consumer welfare.'[203]

Crosland observed that competition had grown since the Second World War as 'the result of action and pressure by the Left...the absence of competition is...consistent only with a hierarchical caste or feudal society offering no possibility of social mobility'.[204] The suppression of market competition led to ossification, weakening the rights of the individual in a free society.[205] In post-war Britain 'the excesses of competitive individualism have been significantly moderated...competition is seen to have certain compensating advantages'.[206] Samuel Beer writes: 'In revisionist thinking and in the Party documents that reflected it there was...a growing emphasis not only upon the private sector of the economy and the mechanisms of the market but also upon the incentives of gain and competition.'[207] This position fundamentally challenged the traditional view that a socialist economy ought to be collectively owned and planned through the state. Market competition was necessary to improve economic growth and living standards, promoting the ethical claims of equality and social justice. Greater competition meant a higher rate of growth: growth meant increased public expenditure on social services.

The enabling state

The third axis of Crosland's liberal progressivism was his concept of an enabling state. This notion envisaged a middle way between state control and inefficient public monopoly on the one hand, and unfettered market capitalism on the other. The purpose of state action was to tackle material constraints on individual freedom, promoting equal citizenship. This important shift emphasised personal liberty, requiring an active state advancing equality of opportunities and resources. As Marquand attests: 'Positive freedom, of freedom 'to', is not the same as negative freedom, or freedom 'from'. The great Liberal government of 1905–15 curbed the negative freedom of the privileged in order to enhance the positive freedom of the dispossessed.'[208]

Crosland's view was consistent with the New Liberalism of Hobhouse, Trevelyan and Keynes. They believed that political institutions and parliamentary action should improve social welfare and equality in the name of universal citizenship.[209] Crosland drew on the writings of T.H. Marshall arguing that social reforms must be constructed on a platform of civil and political rights, the inevitable consequence of mass democracy and the political inclusion of all classes within the British state.[210] The Attlee governments made significant strides forward:

> The planned full employment welfare state, which has been the outcome of the first successful spell of Labour government, is a society of exceptional merit and quality by historical standards…Poverty and insecurity are in the process of disappearing. Living standards are rising rapidly; the fear of unemployment is steadily weakening; and the ordinary young worker has hopes for the future that would never have entered his father's head.[211]

Crosland envisaged a tripartite model of Keynesian economic management, indicative planning and social welfare inspired by Swedish and German social democracy: 'Keynes-plus-modified-capitalism-plus-welfare-state'.[212] Labour governments should give 'exceptionally high priority to social welfare…[which] received its first great impetus from the Liberal government of 1906' reaching its 'culmination in the Beveridge report and the subsequent Labour legislation'. Crosland acknowledged that the work of Beveridge, a Liberal peer, 'gave the most complete and explicit statement of the philosophy of the national minimum'.[213] The ambition of Beveridge's vision was remarkable:

> The Plan for Social Security is put forward as part of a general programme of social policy. It is one part only of an attack upon five giant evils: upon the physical Want with which it is directly concerned, upon Disease which often causes that Want and brings many other troubles in its train, upon Ignorance which

no democracy can afford among its citizens, upon the Squalor which arises mainly through haphazard distribution of industry and population, and upon the Idleness which destroys wealth and corrupts men, whether they are well fed or not, when they are idle. In seeking security not merely against physical want, but against all these evils in all their forms, and in showing that security can be combined with freedom and enterprise and responsibility of the individual for his own life, the British community and those who in other lands have inherited the British tradition have a vital service to render to human progress.[214]

At the heart of Crosland's programme were universal public services guaranteeing treatment and provision to all free at the point of need. *The Future of Socialism* drew on Wootton's persuasive case for universalism: 'The strongest argument for showering benefits upon rich and poor alike is that nobody need then know who is poor and who is not.' Universalism would strengthen equality of regard and eradicate class differences. Marshall's 'equality of status' was made possible by universal access to state provision:

Even when benefits are paid in cash, this class fusion is outwardly expressed in the form of a new common experience. All learn what it means to have an insurance card that must be regularly stamped, or to collect children's allowances or pensions from the post office. But where the benefit takes the form of a service, the qualitative element enters into the benefit itself, and not only the process by which it is obtained. The extension of such services can therefore have a profound effect on the qualitative aspects of social differentiation.[215]

For Crosland, universal services weakened class and status differences in society, strengthening social security throughout the population. It is striking that the arguments on which he drew owed a significant debt to the radical liberal tradition in British politics.

The values of liberal democracy

Crosland's vision of democratic socialism as a marriage of individual freedom and social justice entailed a commitment to liberal democracy upholding the values of tolerance, freedom of conscience and empiricism in public life. This approach was influenced by the tradition of American liberalism that so enthralled Crosland. His generation of revisionists believed in a 'constructive' approach minimising ideological discord in favour of the systematic resolution of social problems.[216] Progress would be achieved by gradual, evolutionary reform rather than winning the battle of one class, the working class, over another, the bourgeoisie. He argued policy-making ought to be guided by the analysis and appraisal of empirical evidence rather than ideological prejudice.

This revisionist perspective reflected the consensus culture of post-war Britain, mirrored in the Keynesian collectivism dominating the civil service and policy-making establishment, alongside a commitment to the British constitutional settlement.[217] Labour should behave as a future party of power rather than a party of protest. For Crosland 'those who follow the ethic of responsibility…hold themselves accountable for the consequences of their actions. They accept the limitations of political action. They grapple with pragmatic questions of choice and priorities.'[218] This world-view implied 'a purposeful, constructive and discriminating determination to improve an already improving society', in the belief that 'further change will appreciably increase personal freedom, social contentment and justice, constituting the ethical basis for being a socialist'.[219]

Crosland disparaged those in Labour's ranks who remained 'combatively traditional and doctrinal'; the pre-war socialist spirit, 'a lively sense of wrongs crying out for redress' in Cole's words, was outdated in a society of rising affluence:[220]

> Many working-class militants, and still more some middle-class people who have espoused the workers' cause, feel their whole status and psychological security to depend on preserving a traditional, proletarian philosophy of class struggle...For the working-class activist, devoting his entire energies to the socialist movement, both his social status and emotional certainty depend on the conviction that militant struggle is necessary.[221]

In shaping the culture of the labour movement, the dogmatic outlook of 'us and them' was endangering Labour's status as a contender for power. Revisionism aroused controversy, 'casting doubts on the need for militancy...hence the anger with which criticisms of class struggle are often greeted'.[222] Socialism was concerned with 'ethical and emotional ideals'; its purpose was addressing, 'social antagonism and class resentment, visible both in politics and industry, and making society less contented and peaceful than it might be'.[223] Enthusiasm for class conflict was receding as a consequence of the Attlee Government's reforms, widening social security and full employment across the population.

The Left and British liberalism

The consequence of Crosland's assimilation of the radical liberal tradition was a revival of progressivism within social democracy. His writings presciently anticipated the liberal critique of Labour: that liberty was as necessary for progressivism as equality; that property ownership should be distributed within the community rather than controlled by the state; that economic growth and material progress are primarily achieved by private enterprise rather than state intervention and planning.[224] Nonetheless, liberalism in British politics had its detractors. Goodhart avers that British liberalism has been concerned with removing constraints on individual rights. Liberalism is oblivious to the claim that individuals are part of communities with moral connections, long-standing traditions

135

and mutual obligations.[225] The liberal tradition originated in the political thought of Milton and Locke centred on 'the idea of liberty, individual liberty for Englishman primarily, but human liberty ultimately'.[226] Twentieth-century liberalism remained faithful to the English spirit of freedom: the cultural liberalism of the 1960s emphasised claims to equality on behalf of individuals, attacking unjustified restraints on freedom. The economic liberalism of the 1980s denigrated tradition in the name of market forces, taking for granted the 'social glue' and national sentiment which ensured that the United Kingdom remained politically cohesive.[227]

In post-war politics, the New Left apparently won the culture war emphasising the primacy of individual freedom and the merits of diversity, while the New Right triumphed in the battle of economics.[228] But the ascendancy of liberalism allegedly caused irreparable damage to Britain's spirit of community. Locke and Mill's liberalism sought to undermine traditional hierarchies in an emerging industrial society, reforming political institutions with checks and balances that would not restrict individual liberties and interests. This outlook asserted the primacy of the self-interested and atomised individual over communal ties and reciprocal obligations, leading to a 'profound crisis' of liberalism in the wake of Thatcherism.[229] Blair's New Labour and Cameron's Conservatism have entrenched cultural and economic liberalism since the 1990s.[230] This has presaged a turn towards 'relational politics' on Right and Left, rejecting post-war liberal managerialism as too 'hands-on' with the state and too 'hands-off' with the market.[231]

Nonetheless, there has been a misreading of the liberal tradition and too little appreciation of its diversity. The radical tradition of Green and Hobhouse acknowledged that individuals are constituted through their relationships with others; they were circumspect about unfettered free markets as well as non-democratic state control. There was no inherent trade-off between freedom and solidarity. The individual exists in relation to, and through, their interaction with others, an insight captured in Hobhouse's claim: 'Society exists in individuals. Its life is their life, and nothing outside their life.'[232] Crosland emphasised liberty by affirming Mill's 'harm principle': individuals should be free to do as they wish as long as they do not inflict injury on others. Of course, it remains the case that revisionists were largely unaware of concerns about social cohesion and the decline of class solidarities in the 1950s and 1960s. They scarcely anticipated the divisions over political identity and nationalism which emerged, developments Labour struggled to explain within the established class-based narratives of British socialism. Socialism was emotionally committed to the union of the United Kingdom, a position rooted in class affiliation and expressed in support for British welfare institutions, rather than an innate sense of nationhood.

There is a danger of overstating the commitment of post-war Labour governments to liberalism. Addison notes the ambivalence of the British working class towards the permissive society: in 1945, they voted for public housing, social security and a National Health Service, but sought no fundamental breach with the 'Victorian morality' of the inter-war years.[233] Labour's working-class supporters were sceptical of libertarian reform: the Wilson governments' changes 'operated within strict limits'.[234] As Addison points out, despite legislation many homosexual acts remained illegal; there was an increase in prosecutions following the 1967 *Sexual Offences Act* which decriminalised homosexuality for consenting adults over 21. Corporal punishment was retained in schools even though capital punishment and birching were abolished. The institution of marriage grew, despite changing attitudes to pre-marital sexual relationships.[235] The emergence of economic liberalism was similarly nuanced: market liberalism did not arrive in Britain at the behest of the Thatcher governments; Britain retained a laissez-faire policy bias and free trade preference since the mid-nineteenth century that influenced its political institutions, only temporarily altered by the reforms of the post-war governments.[236]

Conclusion

The interchange between the liberal and social democratic traditions continued after Crosland's passing. As Labour faced oblivion in 2010, commentators made the case for a 'Liberal Republic', an antidote to the incipient centralism of the social democratic state. This position emphasised each individual's right to shape a life of their choosing.[237] The focus was on equipping individuals with the 'capabilities' to pursue life-goals, whether individuals can access the resources needed to achieve autonomy and freedom. The contemporary New Liberals attest that they 'care deeply about equality, but in terms of what people can do, rather than what they receive'.[238] Amartya Sen insists that progressive policies should focus not only on income inequality but 'inequality in the distribution of substantive freedoms and capabilities'.[239] Jeremy Fishkin advocates a new 'opportunity-based egalitarianism', where individuals are equipped to lead lives in which they decide how best to live, augmented by public intervention and an active state.[240]

This story is about enriching human capability and freedom, themes at the heart of Crosland's vision. If revisionism eschewed old-fashioned dogmas, radical liberalism offered reformers raw material to fashion a positive ethical and moral appeal which emphasised that socialism was more than 'what a Labour government does'. Gone was the obsession with nationalisation and state control: in its place an emphasis on releasing and nurturing human potential through an enabling state. Sixty years later, the ideological climate relating to collectivism and the state appears markedly less confident in an age of liberalisation and globalisation, alongside the collapse of confidence in the intellectual consensus established by Keynes and Beveridge. According to John Gray, the 'support system' for post-war social democracy and the ideas of moderate socialist intellectuals such as Crosland have been swept away.[241] Marquand identifies major shifts in the framework of ideas, in which the post-war collectivism of Crosland's generation has given way to the neo-liberal age of Thatcher and Blair.[242]

There is a danger of interpreting history as divided into discrete phases where the collectivism of post-war Britain is displaced by the individualism of the Thatcher era. Crosland's optimism about the state's role is less outdated and eccentric than it appears. He understood that the positive freedom integral to radical liberalism entailed active, interventionist government. It was believed in the 1980s and 1990s that any attempt to promote collectivism would fail. Governments should reform institutions to deal with the rising tide of scepticism and taxpayer resistance. The corporatist state together with 'tax and spend' social democracy came under particular attack, prompted by the rise of market liberalism.

It is fashionable to belittle the state in the aftermath of market liberalism's ascendancy. The claim that governments are damaging to economic competiveness and powerless to affect change has, nonetheless, been contested across the rich market democracies. A series of advances have been secured by mobilising the government's powers and resources. These include public investment in the NHS to develop life-saving pharmaceutical drugs and vaccines; public health initiatives to reduce tobacco consumption and improve diet; combined with new medical technologies that have markedly improved life expectancy.[243] The innovation system that generates new products and commercial applications relies on public funding of science, research and infrastructure, particularly 'general purpose technologies' which enabled a sweep of productivity breakthroughs after 1945.[244] In the aftermath of the 2008 crisis, the state stepped in to prevent the meltdown of the banking system from becoming a calamitous depression. Crosland's legacy is that Labour must be a liberal social democratic party giving people greater choice and control over their lives through an enabling state. This perspective emphasises the vitality of the liberal tradition and its importance for social democracy. Developing these ideas is critical to Labour's ability to promote a majoritarian national story, a project that resonates across the nations of the UK.

A further source of conflict in the post-war Labour party was Britain's global role, the moral legitimacy of the Atlantic alliance, the issue of whether to accept closer European integration, and the influence of European social democracies, particularly Sweden, highlighted by Crosland as a society worthy of emulation. These debates related to the existential question of whether Labour should formulate a socialist foreign policy in opposition to the world's leading powers; or accept Britain's position within the alliance of western countries committed to political democracy and the rule of law. Crosland's role in this dispute has, again, been significant; it is the subject of the chapter that follows.

FIVE

America and Europe in post-war social democracy

The United States has more social equality, and less sense of class, than Great Britain...Sweden in other ways comes much nearer to a socialist's idea of the 'good' society with a higher priority to social welfare and the social services. (Anthony Crosland, 1956[1])

Every visitor [to the United States] is struck not only by the lack of glaring objective contrasts between the living standards of different social classes, but also by the general consciousness of equal living standards – the feeling that everything is within reach, and nothing wholly unattainable. This is one of the basic causes of the greater social equality, and the absence of deep class feeling. (Anthony Crosland, 1956[2])

Introduction: Crosland's legacy, Europe and America

This book's central theme is Crosland's influence and legacy as a revisionist theoretician in the post-war Labour party. Social democrats navigating a rapidly changing economic and political landscape latched onto Crosland as the revisionist *par excellence*. As his obituary in *The Times* stated, Crosland's impact was 'greater than the offices he held'.[3] This chapter will step beyond domestic policy to assess the influence of European socialism and American liberalism on the development of Crosland's political thought. It will examine the fractious debate about Britain's role in the world, the political unification of Europe, and the possibilities of a socialist foreign policy in the aftermath of the Second World War. The Labour party viewed Britain's global role after 1945 in terms of the implicit division between American and European models of democratic capitalism. The dilemma of 'America versus Europe' was apparent throughout the twentieth century, referring to the manner in which ideological change on the British Left was inspired by ideas about the market economy, the welfare state and global security derived from continental Europe and the United States.[4] Crosland's prospectus for the future of British social democracy was constructed by assimilating political concepts from America and the European continent.

The chapter begins with consideration of Crosland's admiration for America and the impact of the United States on his view of democratic socialism, especially the emphasis accorded to personal freedom and mass consumption in an age of affluence. Crosland's revisionism was also inspired by regular contact with European socialist parties, in particular the Swedish SAP ('the Social Democratic Workers' Party of Sweden') and the German SPD ('Social Democratic Party of Germany'). He admired the fact that victorious centre-left parties throughout Europe were hastily modernising their appeal, discarding the outdated remnants of Marxist thought. Instead of obsessing about class struggle, those parties focused on how to manage the capitalist economy more efficiently than the Christian Democrats, redistributing the fruits of economic growth to deliver rising living standards for the working class. While Crosland embraced other European social democratic parties, his relationship with the cause of European political unity became increasingly ambivalent. One of the great controversies of his political career was Crosland's stance on British membership of the European Community (EC). The chapter will assess Crosland's perspective on the European question given the impact of European integration on the British Labour party after the Second World War.

Devoting an entire section of a book on Crosland to the world beyond Britain's shores might, to some, appear inappropriate. After all, a common criticism of *The Future of Socialism* was its insularity and parochialism, a refusal to engage with international political developments. According to Anthony Wright: 'Our distance from Crosland is measured by his introductory remark [in *The Future of Socialism*] that he would only write about Britain and ignore the wider world, something impossible in the globalised capitalism of today'.[5] Although Crosland was concerned with the future of *British* social democracy, his ideas were influenced by political practice and sociological change in the United States and Western Europe. His analysis was cognisant of events outside the UK to a greater extent than comparable works, notably Evan Durbin's *Politics of Democratic Socialism* (1940), Douglas Jay's *Socialism in the New Society* (1962), and Bryan Magee's *The New Radicalism* (1962).[6] A distinctive theme was the pressing need to draw on European (predominantly Swedish) and American political experience. The backdrop was the long-standing tension within the Labour party between affiliation with Western Europe and the United States; this was more often perceived as an implicit (or even explicit) choice. The divide is still played out in the aftermath of the Iraq war, alongside growing tensions over Britain's membership of the European Union (EU); while the Conservatives remain divided over Europe, Labour is yet to reconcile itself to an unequivocally European future.

Crosland's admiration for America

Aside from Britain's membership of the EC, Labour's institutional relationship with the continental social democratic parties had never been especially close. There were historical ties to the Social Democrats in Sweden and Germany; Ramsay MacDonald was a personal acquaintance of Bernstein, using his theories to defend robustly the parliamentary road to socialism; Bernstein was an anti-war figure who urged 'an exchange of views...between English and German socialists' to bring the bloodshed to an end;[7] Keir Hardie was an ardent internationalist who hoped that the Second International would prevent the outbreak of war in 1914. And Ernest Bevin cultivated a close relationship with the German trade unions in the 1930s. However, in the decades after 1945, Labour was particularly inspired by progressive reformism in the United States, especially the New Deal liberalism of Franklin Delano Roosevelt and the Great Society programme affirmed by the presidencies of John F. Kennedy and Lyndon Baynes Johnson (LBJ). Crosland had a deep affection for JFK and leading Democrats such as Adlai Stevenson whom he identified as symptomatic of the meritocratic, socially mobile and classless America he so admired.[8]

He maintained a close interest in the Democratic party making frequent fact-finding visits to the United States throughout the 1950s. Late in 1954, for instance, he undertook a study tour of America developing his interest in contemporary sociological theory.[9] Crosland reported in a letter to his mother in 1962: 'Spent a day in Boston campaigning with the President's younger brother [Robert Kennedy].'[10] He noted that American politics was a 'spectacle' of rallies and television broadcasts, although the similarities between Labour and the Democrats were striking: 'Things are much the same, especially the content of the speeches. I often felt I could have got up on the platform and made the Democratic candidate's speeches for him.'[11] The natural empathy with American liberalism enthralled Crosland, as it did other leading revisionists. David Marquand recounts that his experience of America in the 1950s converted him to Crosland's analysis:

> I read *The Future of Socialism* just after I had finished my finals, mostly on a beach in Spain. I could see that it

was a brilliant book, but I didn't like it in a way. If I was anything, I was a Bevanite. There was Crosland putting up a very powerful attack on Bevanite fundamentalism in the Labour party. He was the revisionist *par excellence*. I felt very uneasy about it. Then I went to America for a year as a graduate student at Berkeley. That really converted me to Croslandism. Crosland had been greatly influenced by American sociological writing... he was right that class was nowhere near as prevalent in the United States. Social egalitarianism, equality of regard, did seem to be alive and well in California. Capitalism had changed; this wasn't the capitalism Roosevelt had fought against in the 1930s. America was the future and we could be like that if we tried hard enough. The experience of spending a year in California made me a Croslandite.[12]

Alongside his identification with the Democratic party, Crosland along with leading figures on the Labour Right was strongly committed to the North Atlantic Treaty Organisation (NATO) and the Atlantic alliance. During the 1945–51 Labour governments, Attlee and Bevin pursued a diplomatic policy of persuading the United States to remain engaged in western Europe as a bulwark against the Soviet Union. This position culminated in the formation of NATO in 1949, the cornerstone of British foreign and defence policy.[13] Attlee and Bevin's stance had been possible because of their admiration for America: Bevin and other British trade unionists noted that the Marshall Plan committing significant investment to western Europe was supported by the American trade unions; more important, however, was countering the existential threat of the cold war and the strength of Communist parties in Italy and France, alongside the potential for Germany to turn towards communism. NATO and the Marshall Plan were essential to defend democracy in Europe alongside Britain's national interests.[14] Saving Europe was at the core of Bevin's policy.

Nonetheless, there was a fervent determination on the part of the post-war governments to preserve and strengthen British global influence. Bevin had no doubt that Britain ought to develop its own atomic bomb 'with a Union Jack on it' when the United States terminated wartime nuclear cooperation. The post-war Labour Administration still thought of Britain as one of the 'Big Three' alongside the United States and Russia with global interests to be protected. Attlee told the Labour party conference in May 1945: 'I believe that the British Labour Movement, nurtured in freedom, practised in democracy, devoted to the principles of socialism, can give a lead to the world to free itself from slavery and fear and to establish peace on the sure basis of social justice.'[15]

Bevin was initially committed to the vision of Britain mediating between the United States and the Soviet Union: 'The United States of America is a country which believes in free enterprise. The Soviet Union has socialised her internal economy. Britain stands between the two.'[16] Influential figures on the Left sought to promote the idea of Britain as a 'third force'; they came to regard the European Common Market as an insidious threat to socialist policies of state planning. The concept of a third force was crucial to Bevanite thinking about socialist foreign policy articulated in pamphlets such as *Keep Left*; the aim was 'to hold the balance between Russia and America, but...independent of both. America was regarded as the great stronghold of private enterprise, on which the reforms of the New Deal had made little permanent impression.'[17] Bevan eventually supported the development of a British bomb imploring the Campaign for Nuclear Disarmament (CND) not to send a Labour Prime Minister 'naked into the conference chamber'; an independent deterrent would protect British socialism from 'unwarranted interference' by the United States and Russia.[18]

What was evident by the early 1950s was the crippling economic burden these military commitments imposed: in 1950–51, public expenditure on defence reached more than 8 per cent of national income. Furthermore, American insistence on convertibility as a condition of the loan negotiated by Keynes led immediately to the 1947 crisis, fatally damaging Labour's reputation for economic competence. Bevan's resignation in

1951 and the Bevanite split were triggered by the introduction of NHS charges for teeth and spectacles by Gaitskell. These political divisions might have been avoided were it not for the enormous budgetary strain imposed by Korean rearmament. Foreign policy was a source of bitter confrontation between Gaitskellite Atlanticists and Bevanite 'third force' neutralism, although the differences are exaggerated since both believed that Britain should continue to exercise global leadership.[19] Moreover, the third force strategy was exposed as unworkable by 1947, as France and Italy elected unsympathetic centre-right governments, destroying hopes of an axis of democratic socialist states; in any case, the promise of Marshall Aid for Europe softened the Left's hostility to America despite its support for capitalism and materialist consumerism.[20] Maintaining a global role had been the predominant objective of all twentieth century British governments, only questioned when Wilson withdrew from 'East of Suez' in 1968 and Heath made European Community membership the centrepiece of his foreign policy.[21] This reflex of global leadership continued under Blair's New Labour five decades later.

The belief in the uniqueness of Britain's position in the world remained influential even in the wake of the Suez crisis. The lesson which the Labour leadership drew was not that Britain should retreat from global influence, but that it must exert 'moral leadership' through the authority of the Commonwealth and the United Nations. As the Prime Minister succeeding Eden whose credibility the Suez debacle had destroyed, Macmillan was determined that never again should Britain be separated from Washington; Her Majesty's Government applied to join the Common Market only with the explicit approval of Eisenhower and Kennedy, both of whom supported European integration motivated by geo-politics and global security (Harrison, 2009). Nonetheless, while Labour supported the rundown of Empire, Gaitskell was suspicious of the Common Market because of the damage it might inflict on Britain's Commonwealth ties, alongside fear that Europe meant the end of 'a thousand years of British history'. Crosland adopted the Gaitskellite position on defence, acknowledging the importance of an independent deterrent maintained in co-operation with the United States, while resisting the march of CND through the Campaign for Democratic Socialism (CDS). During 1960–61, Gaitskell won the battle against unilateralism, enabling Labour to retain its credibility as a governing party.

Beyond the imperative of collective security, Crosland was unusual in regarding the United States as offering moral inspiration for British socialism. He was not alone: Durbin described America as, 'one of the great capitalist democracies… founded upon the union of the political system of representative democracy with the economic system of capitalism'.[22] For Durbin, social democracy could not exist without freedom and collective security; the revisionist's view of foreign policy was integral to their political faith. Crosland believed in the emergence of a new economic age in which 'the industrial revolution finally matures into the modern mass production economy, as it has in the United States and is about to do in Britain'.[23] He was influenced by the perceived egalitarianism of American society regarded as much less 'class-bound' than Britain. The weakening of class stratification was captured in a burgeoning literature in which Crosland was immersed through contact with the Harvard sociologist, Daniel Bell.[24] Crosland saw in America 'the absence of deep class feeling'.[25] He insisted that higher living standards and mass consumption created a more egalitarian culture, greater openness to industrial innovation, and a classless society:[26]

> The United States had more social equality, and less sense of class, than Great Britain…social relations are more natural and egalitarian, and less marked by deference, submissiveness, or snobbery…there is much less sense of social stratification.[27]

Crosland was critical of sentimental attitudes towards British working-class life, having little affection for 'class-conscious institutions' and the idea of a 'common culture'.[28] *The Future of Socialism* contained a host of positive references to American society, bursting with adulation for the liberty and freedom that was the centrepiece of America's identity. A.J. Ayer, Crosland's philosophy tutor at Oxford, criticised him for presenting a vision of socialism 'that resembles present day America'.[29] There was suspicion of the United States elsewhere on the British Left; America was, after all, the world's leading capitalist economy. The sociologist and author of the 1945 Labour manifesto, Michael Young, who had been a close friend of Crosland's, reportedly tried to persuade him to tone down the flattering references to America in *The Future of Socialism*; Young's views were rebuffed.[30]

Crosland and European social democracy

Despite long-standing approbation for the United States, Crosland acknowledged that Labour's support for a universal welfare state and National Health Service (NHS) meant that the UK had much in common with continental Europe. Crosland singled out Sweden as the European society worthy of emulation: 'Sweden in other ways comes much nearer to a socialist's idea of the 'good' society', having given 'a higher priority to social welfare and the social services'.[31] Harrison notes that Crosland 'drew upon Labour's long-standing Scandinavian affinity, claiming that Sweden with its welfarist and egalitarian outlook came near to realising the socialist ideal'.[32] Intriguingly, Crosland was largely uninterested in German social democracy, despite the fact that as Donald Sassoon has written, the German SPD was the leading European social democratic party in the twentieth century.[33] The German party was advantaged by electoral strength and intellectual vitality, having achieved an updating of its doctrine at Bad Godesberg in 1959 abandoning class struggle against capitalism in favour of ameliorative social reform.[34] This process of modernisation was captured in the German Chancellor Willy Brandt's aphorism, 'as much market as possible, as much state as necessary': the market economy would continue to achieve the level of social justice desired by social democrats.

Crosland noted that by jettisoning state ownership of the means of production, the Swedish Left had been able to use its powers of economic intervention alongside redistributive taxation to create a fairer society without imperilling personal freedom. The leader of the social democrats, Per Albin Hansson, declared: 'We have had so many victories that we are in a difficult position. A people with political liberty, full employment and social security has lost its dreams.'[35] For Crosland, Swedish social democracy offered an inspiring vision. The revisionist's ideas were in tune with the radical thinking sweeping through other social democratic parties.[36] Denis Healey noted that 'the continental parties have adjusted much better to social and political change than the Labour party'.[3]

The Swedish model attracted interest after the Second World War given its ability to combine sustained economic growth, strong public finances and robust egalitarian outcomes. Gøsta Esping-Andersen has written that Crosland was pursuing a quintessentially Swedish 'Keynes-plus-Beveridge-strategy', but he underestimated the importance of economic institutions such as industrial democracy to Sweden's achievements. The Swedish emphasis on separating ownership from control was similarly downplayed in *The Future of Socialism*.[38] Crosland insisted that capitalism had been transformed in Great Britain as a consequence of the post-war governments' reforms, accompanied by structural changes such as corporatism and Fordism which made capitalism more technocratic and managerially benign. Moreover, Sweden exemplified the strategy of maximising the competitiveness and profitability of the private sector, generating revenues to fund ambitious social programmes. This approach went hand in hand with the development of the post-war settlement, offering a decisive resolution of the social democratic dilemma harnessing profit and enterprise to the advancement of collective provision and social welfare.[39]

Translating policy programmes from one country to another is an unenviable and intricate task. It is probable that Crosland interpreted the rationale of the Swedish social democratic model too literally and exaggerated its achievements; Perry Anderson noted that in Sweden: 'Income distribution is vastly more even than in other western countries, but social mobility is fully as sluggish, and the lived distances between classes probably as great.'[40] Crosland was hardly the first social democratic intellectual to misread the Scandinavian case.[41] The revisionists had not sufficiently appreciated how far the Swedish state was continuously reforming the market economy. The Swedish strategy culminated in the Rein–Meidner plan which sought to replace low-wage, low-productivity firms with high-wage industries and sectors.[42] The social democrats developed a 'market-shaping' strategy which contested the main structures of capitalist production. In Britain, Evan Durbin insisted that planning was 'the indispensable preliminary means for the attainment of the new society'.[43] Labour began to treat planning as a countervailing mechanism against market forces in the 1930s and 1940s; capitalism in the inter-war years led to the paradox of mass unemployment and poverty alongside productive resources remaining idle; but Labour's faith in state planning was increasingly thought to be ill-conceived; the party struggled to develop a viable strategy after the Second World War.[44]

Crosland was instinctively cautious about planning and statutory incomes policies, 'trying to control short-term production decisions from Whitehall through a detailed budget of production'.[45] Lipsey underlines that Crosland remained sceptical of planning agreements and industrial policy: 'He had no faith that civil servants at the Department of Industry would make a better job of running British industry than existing managers.'[46] Since he found it instinctively unattractive, Crosland may have understated the importance of indicative planning in the Swedish model. In fact, interventionist approaches ran into trouble even in Sweden by the mid-1970s following the crisis in the world economy, a succession of oil price shocks, and the long-term process of industrial restructuring. In Britain, planning had been demonised by the Conservatives as belonging to an era of rationing and austerity.[47] Crosland was hardly in a position to update his analysis taking account of the structural pressures on the Swedish model: growing trade union militancy coupled with rising wage inflation and soaring public expenditure threatened even world-renowned Scandinavian social democracy.[48] The Swedish SAP revived the Nordic model during the 1990s by accepting the paradigm of economic openness, liberal globalisation, industrial competitiveness, and a disciplined approach to the public finances.

Despite his reputation for parochialism, Crosland was in touch with the principal developments in major western European states and social democratic parties; having attended an international socialist conference in the Netherlands in 1960, he declared: 'A spectre is haunting Europe – the spectre of revisionism.'[49] Crosland noted that:

> Among the European socialist parties, the British Labour Party is unique in the doctrinal energy which it still devotes to the issue of public ownership. In the comprehensive new draft Programme of the Swedish Social Democratic Party, precisely two brief mentions are made of the extension of collective ownership. In Germany, the SPD abandoned ownership as a major goal as early as 1959 in the famous Bad Godesberg programme...The Austrian party made no mention of nationalisation in its 13 point programme for their recent – and brilliantly successful – election campaign.[50]

He noted that the Dutch Labour party had adopted a programme in which socialism was defined in ethical and moral terms declaring: 'It is desirable for different forms of publicly-owned and privately-owned production to exist side by side.'[51] The socialisation of production should be undertaken where it was necessary to maintain full employment and promote industrial efficiency. The Swedish SAP announced that it favoured public ownership only where state control was required to protect the public interest; otherwise: 'it wants to stimulate private enterprise in those provinces where it shows that it can combine efficiency and progressive thought with responsibility towards consumers, employees, and the community'.[52] Most famously, the German SPD abandoned traditional dogmas at Bad Godesberg in November 1959 insisting that private ownership was acceptable 'where it does not hinder the establishment of social justice'.[53] Public ownership was necessary where alternative means could not be found to control unfettered capitalist forces. By 1960, only the electorally moribund French socialist party in Continental Europe retained the commitment to class struggle and nationalisation.[54]

Sassoon remarks that *The Future of Socialism* made little impact elsewhere in Western Europe;[55] nonetheless, the influence of European social democracy on Crosland was not entirely one-way: his thinking was undoubtedly important in other countries. A Swedish social democrat colleague reported to Crosland in the early 1950s: 'Lately your name has been mentioned rather often in Swedish newspapers and periodicals. The book *New Fabian Essays* has received very favourable reviews in Sweden...it is in particular your essay which has caught the attention of our reviewers.'[56] Drucker noted *The Future of Socialism* was, 'the sole British socialist tract since the Second World War to achieve an international audience'.[57]

Britain's role in Europe

Turning to the vexed issue of British membership of the European Community (EC), Crosland's views have generated much retrospective commentary and analysis. During his early career and at the time of *The Future of Socialism's* publication, he was regarded like other revisionists as an ardent pro-European who believed that Britain's destiny was to play a leading role in a thriving Common Market.[58] Crosland was persuaded by the moral case for unity to avoid the bloodshed which accompanied two major wars in the first half of the twentieth century, consistent with the French diplomat Jean Monnet's founding vision of Europe. This emerging pro-European outlook was articulated by Herbert Morrison, then a member of the House of Lords: 'It is no good for socialists, of whom

I am proud to be one, saying 'workers of all countries unite' and then adding, 'but not with the French under de Gaulle; not with the Germans under Adenauer; not with the United States under their capitalist government'.'[59] Crosland had been a delegate to the Council of Europe as a young parliamentarian in the early 1950s; he was present, 'on the historic day when the doors were thrown open and we watched the German delegates march into the chamber for the first time – a great day of reconciliation which those of us who were present will never forget'.[60]

Throughout the 1950s, Crosland chastised Gaitskell for refusing to seize the opportunities afforded by the European project. The leader's speech promising to safeguard 'a thousand years of British history' caused convulsions within the revisionist camp.[61] In *The Conservative Enemy*, Crosland positioned Europe as the issue of the future: if Britain was to remain a leading economic power, it had to play a decisive role in the emerging Common Market. This analysis was shared with 'One Nation' Conservatives including Macmillan and Heath who sought to make UK membership of the European Community the centrepiece of post-war national strategy. Polling in the early 1960s demonstrated support among British voters for entry, a shift reflected in the climate of elite opinion.[62] The collapse of Labour's economic policy following the devaluation crisis of 1966–67 persuaded Wilson that entry into Europe offered an alternative route to national modernisation. The assumption by 1970 was that Labour would take Britain into the EC as enthusiastically as the Conservatives.[63] In the Wilson era, Britain's global over-reach was curbed by withdrawal 'East of Suez' in the aftermath of devaluation, alongside Wilson's stubborn refusal under American pressure to send British troops to Vietnam. The 1974 government, having questioned the 'Tory terms' of EC membership negotiated by Heath, eventually won the 1975 referendum in favour of staying in.

Getting to that position was, nonetheless, a painful and protracted process with party unity and cohesion under severe pressure. In the 1940s, Bevin advocated, 'European

Unity but not a United States of Europe'.[64] Attlee and Bevin were committed to the ideal of European cooperation, but opposed further steps towards federal integration.[65] In 1950, the Labour Administration decided that Britain should not join the Schuman Plan: having nationalised the coal and steel industries, it did not want them supervised by a supranational authority. While Hardie and MacDonald had been principled internationalists, the working-class rank and file of the labour movement adopted a more nationalistic view of Britain's role in the world associated with the 'Tory-socialist' tradition.[66] The issue of Europe became politically toxic in the Conservative party, but in the post-war years EC membership led to major fissures within the Labour party relating to the role of planning in the economy, and the importance of the transatlantic alliance to post-1945 power politics and world diplomacy.[67] Gaitskell's 1962 speech affirmed the importance of the Commonwealth and Britain's imperial legacy.

The divisions intensified as Labour's defeat in 1970 persuaded Euro-sceptic figures to make their voices heard. Although the party's manifesto had been positive about Europe,[68] Labour remained instinctively cautious about integration: James Callaghan, then a senior Cabinet Minister who had been an enthusiastic supporter of entry, gave a speech in which he underlined his opposition to French being the first language of the EC declaring, 'millions of people have been surprised to hear that the language of Chaucer, Shakespeare and Milton must in future be regarded as an American import from which we must protect ourselves if we are to build a new Europe'; his message, 'non, merci beaucoup', was widely interpreted as a statement of principled opposition to Europe: 'Callaghan attacked the Conservative approach to Europe. He said it would mean a complete rupture of our identity and that monetary union would lead to unemployment.'[69] Two other potential leadership contenders, Healey and, of course, Crosland, gave interviews and speeches in which they outlined their own doubts and misgivings about the European project.[70]

There has been much speculation about Crosland's motives, inseparable from his growing estrangement from Roy Jenkins.

Crosland's controversial speech on Europe to the General Management Committee (GMC) of the Grimsby Labour party was damagingly leaked after he was persuaded to make the case in private.[71] He justified his position by insisting that British entry, as far as he and his constituents were concerned, was a 'second order' issue. During the turbulent months leading up to Crosland's abstention on the Heath Government's legislation, he insisted that Europe was way down his list of priorities given the tasks of ensuring sustainable growth, tackling social inequality, and improving the quality of life. Crosland believed that Europe was 'largely irrelevant to key issues facing ordinary people – growth, inflation, housing, education – and that it would be an act of political folly to allow the [Common] Market to endanger the unity of the Labour party'.[72]

He was accused of tactical expediency by adopting an unprincipled position to court popularity with Labour's grassroots.[73] Much of this criticism is unreasonable: Crosland harboured genuine doubts about whether EC membership would improve Britain's trade position believing the economic impact would be neutral. His stance was mirrored 40 years later by Gordon Brown's decision to rule out UK membership of the European single currency. Crosland would have voted for membership in 1962 had Britain's application not been vetoed by De Gaulle.[74] The revisionists gathered around Jenkins claimed that EC membership would improve the growth potential of the British economy, but they viewed European integration in more idealistic terms: 'Their adherence to the European Community was not so much a policy as a way of life.'[75] Crosland, a natural sceptic, was more cautious: he did not believe that 'blind faith' was a satisfactory basis on which to make major policy decisions. Whatever the strength of the case for membership, it is impossible to explain the battle over Europe in the early 1970s without appreciating the bitter personal conflicts that ensued on the revisionist Right of the Labour party, especially those waged between Crosland and his arch-rival, Jenkins.

By the early 1970s, Crosland came to the view that 'it was absolute folly to break up the party over the issue of Europe'.[76]

Raymond Plant indicates that '[Crosland] didn't share Jenkins' strongly European instincts.'[77] Given that Jenkins had colonised the pro-European position in the party, Crosland believed that he had little to lose by staking out a more 'sceptical' stance. He was 'terribly jealous' of Jenkins' rapid political rise, especially Wilson's decision to appoint his rival as Chancellor in 1967.[78] Crosland never forgave Wilson for giving the Exchequer to Jenkins.[79] According to Dick Leonard: 'Tony was devastated when he didn't get the chancellorship...he was fobbed off with being President of the Board of Trade.'[80] Jenkins and Crosland maintained a 'congenial' relationship 'but there was an obvious rivalry for the future'.[81] By the late 1960s, Jenkins was regarded as the only Cabinet minister who could plausibly replace Wilson: '[Jenkins'] championing of libertarian rights caught the mood of the 1960s...He had developed into a superb House of Commons orator...He had style.'[82] In the early 1980s, Leonard and Jenkins had dinner in Brussels with their wives:

> Roy spoke extremely warmly of Tony. Roy said it was purely by chance that he had got the Chancellorship. Tony had a stronger claim for it. Roy said it was very difficult for Tony to accept this because when they were at Oxford, 'Tony was an absolute star and I was nothing'...Susan once told me that there was a question of Roy's marriage breaking up. Susan said that one day Roy and Caroline Gilmour had turned up hand in hand at their flat in the Boltons and said they were going to leave their partners and set up together. They later thought better of it.[83]

There is a view that had Crosland and Jenkins combined their efforts, they could have dominated the Labour party after Wilson's departure in 1976:[84] Jenkins proposed over dinner to Crosland that he would 'play the second major role in the group' if only he were decisive enough to join the Jenkinsite faction; Crosland's response was curt: 'Their idea of a Labour party is not mine. Roy has come actually to dislike socialism...It is Roy's misfortune that because of his father he's in the wrong Party. As a Liberal or Conservative, he might make a very good leader.'[85] By the time the British Government managed to negotiate Common Market entry, Crosland had abstained on Britain's decision to join. There was a three-line whip on Labour MPs to vote against membership 'on Tory terms'; however, 69 Labour parliamentarians led by Jenkins (including the future leader, John Smith) rebelled and voted in favour. Barbara Castle castigated the Jenkinsites as 'sanctimonious middle-class hypocrites' for refusing to defeat Heath.[86] Leonard recalls that Crosland had wanted to vote against British membership but was eventually persuaded to abstain.[87]

Leading revisionists, notably Bill Rodgers and David Owen were apoplectic at Crosland's 'opportunistic' behaviour. His views on Europe had not substantively changed: in *The Conservative Enemy*, Crosland described himself as 'an instinctive pro-European' and he played a significant role in the 1975 referendum campaign.[88] Susan Crosland recalls that in the wake of the 1971 vote 'there was open hostility from the Jenkinsites for the rest of the parliament'.[89] Like Healey, Crosland was regarded as 'calculating for personal advancement'.[90] He was punished by his own faction: following Jenkins' resignation as Deputy Leader, the former Gaitskellites ('a bullying little clique' according to Susan Crosland)[91] swung behind Ted Short rather than Crosland.[92] His decision to abandon pro-Europeanism proved politically damaging; as a consequence, Crosland's motives have been much debated. His ally in the parliamentary party, Giles Radice, speculates that Crosland was advised by Callaghan to shift position on Europe strengthening his weak political base within the party. By the early 1970s, the majority of the Shadow Cabinet, Labour parliamentarians, and the party's grassroots were hostile to British entry. The activists remained ambivalent about the merits of European membership, fearing the Common Market would morph into a capitalist club constraining the radicalism of future Labour governments. Harold Wilson admitted: 'In all my thirteen years as leader of the party, I had no more difficult task than keeping the party together on the issue.'[93]

It is scarcely surprising that Labour struggled to reconcile itself to any vision of Britain embracing a European future. The intensity of the conflict revealed a growing divide within the party between those articulating a social democratic strategy encompassing moderate reform of the market economy, and those advocating an ideal of nation-state socialism centred on the transformation of the capitalist system. As Sassoon points out, parties on the Left traditionally had a 'stronger national outlook' than Conservative parties: the nation-state had the resources and legislative powers to regulate capitalism. The Left worried that any weakening of national sovereignty would undermine the state's ability to reorganise the British economy around the collective ownership and socialisation of industry.[94] Moreover, the project of an integrated single market in the Treaty of Rome proceeded with relatively little influence from Europe's socialist parties: the Common Market was concerned with removing the barriers to unfettered competition in labour, product and capital markets, giving insufficient priority to social welfare and environmental sustainability (Sassoon, 1996). The Social Chapter was a corrective to the dominance of market efficiency in European integration advanced during Delors' presidency of the European Commission in the 1980s: in the meantime, the Labour party felt its way inch by inch towards conceiving Europe as a way of countering the dominance of Thatcherism. Membership of the EC offered economic stability with the prospect of coordinating monetary policy, alongside a robust model of social protection; the social dimension was continually undermined by the UK Conservative government, however, determined to resist any move towards a European-wide welfare system.[95] By the late 1990s, Blair was adopting a more uncertain position, despite promising to put the UK at the heart of Europe.

Conclusion

This chapter has considered the influence of European socialism and American liberalism on Labour's thinking about Britain's position in the world and the future of social democracy, addressing Crosland's role in the increasingly fractious and volatile debate inside the party. Committed to achieving socialism in one country, Europe and America compelled the labour movement to re-think its ideas at critical junctures in post-war British history. Crosland's status as a socialist theoretician and leading Labour politician ensured that he played a crucial role. The friction between continental European and American influence continues to be played out in today's Labour party. Despite a reputation for insularity, Crosland exposed Labour after 1945 to fresh thinking, notably drawing on the social market philosophy of western Europe and the progressive New Deal liberalism of the United States. This perspective had a critical influence on the nature of the political thought advanced in the post-war party.

New Labour is believed to have been swayed by American ideas and political strategy under Blair and Brown, derived from Clinton's leadership of the 'New' Democrats. Although Blair positioned himself as a committed pro-European, his mission was to fashion the EU in the image of a flexible, deregulated model of American capitalism, allegedly the only viable approach in an age of globalisation. Blair's leadership represented a retreat from the 'unconditional' pro-Europeanism of Kinnock and Smith in the late 1980s and early 1990s, replacing a firm commitment to join the Exchange Rate Mechanism (ERM) with a vague promise to consider future membership of the single currency. Labour fulfilled its promise to sign the Social Chapter but refused to abandon labour market flexibility and industrial relations reforms enacted by the Thatcher governments. Blair saw Britain rather like Attlee and Bevin as a global 'pivot' projecting influence across the world, rekindling Churchill's invocation of British foreign policy as comprising three 'concentric circles' of Europe, the Atlantic and the Mediterranean. As Blair's successor, Brown was unrivalled in his admiration for American liberalism, marvelling at the dynamism of the US model of capitalism and the relative egalitarianism of American society. Like Crosland, Blair and Brown were criticised by the Left for their adoration of the United States.

Ed Miliband, the Labour leader until 2015, sought to lead his party in a more explicitly European direction, away from the free market system tainted by the financial crisis, towards the continental social market economy of Germany and Sweden promising a more 'responsible capitalism'. That said, Miliband sought to harness the economic populism that had given President Obama two consecutive election victories in the United States; although his view of Britain's future remained instinctively pro-European, Miliband continued the tradition of Labour leaders looking across the Atlantic as well as the English Channel. Miliband's position emphasised that for the current party, the instinctive choice between Europe and America continues to define Labour's politics.[96] Underlining these alternative poles were distinctive conceptions of political liberalism: the 'negative freedom' of the United States emphasising freedom from constraint and the liberties attained through free markets, and the 'positive freedom' of advanced European democracies envisaging the state as the bulwark against unfettered market capitalism. Europe and the United States have provoked great battles over principle and doctrine in the Labour party since 1945. The effort to reconcile political ethics with the pursuit of power is the focus of the next chapter: Crosland's legacy as a revisionist theoretician and political strategist in the post-war party.

SIX

Crosland's electoral strategy: 'Can Labour win?'

To refuse to change a slogan or established attitude or ancient shibboleth, merely because it is consecrated by time or possesses sentimental value, is unworthy of a progressive party. (Anthony Crosland, 1962[1])

Middle-class suburbia became increasingly disillusioned with the privations and restrictions of Attlee's 'consensus'. (I. Zweiniger-Barcielowska, 1994)[2]

The need for a restatement of doctrine is hardly surprising. The old doctrines did not spring from a vacuum, or from acts of pure cerebration performed in a monastery cell. Each was the product of a particular kind of society, and of minds reacting to that society... And as society has changed again since before the war, so again a restatement of objectives is called for. The matter can be put quite simply. Traditional socialism was largely concerned with the evils of traditional capitalism, and with the need for its overthrow. But today traditional capitalism has been reformed and modified almost out of existence, and it is with a quite different form of society that socialists must now concern themselves. (Anthony Crosland, 1956[3])

Introduction: Crosland's legacy as revisionist political strategist

Crosland insisted that post-war socialism must abandon consecrated slogans favouring up-to-date sociological investigation and iconoclastic political analysis. Through his numerous organisational activities and writings, Crosland contributed to discussions about the electoral and political strategy of Labour in post-war Britain. This chapter examines his legacy as a political strategist and 'apparatchik' who informed Labour about the imperative of adapting its ideas and programme in the light of economic and social change; he argued 'if socialism is to survive in the modern world, it must undergo a process of modernisation'.[4] The strategy of renovation was paramount in the wake of Labour's electoral annihilation in the 1950s, particularly its third consecutive defeat in 1959. Crosland's objective was not to abandon Labour's values to secure political power but to ensure that social democracy addressed the needs of contemporary society, proposing relevant and practical policies to attract a broad coalition of voters. This approach required reforms of the party machinery to win the battle of organisation and ideas, externally against a resurgent and populist Conservative party, and internally against the Communist-inspired Left. The British Labour party in the aftermath of the bruising Bevanite and Gaitskellite battles of the 1950s was 'a tumultuous alliance of diverse parts'.[5]

The chapter addresses Crosland's role in the fight waged by post-war revisionists to achieve ascendancy in the Labour party. The Conservative enemy that Crosland identified in the wake of the 1951 defeat was not so much the Bevanite Left, but Labour's traditionalism and inertia. The battle to seize control of the party's institutions was accompanied by significant rethinking of Labour's programme in the light of new economic and political realities. This strategy of social democratic revisionism is dealt with in the next section of the chapter. In striving to undermine Labour's 'forces of conservatism', Crosland's approach had similarities with the British New Left, confronting the consequences of class de-alignment and the changing nature of capitalism. Labour could no longer rely on the industrial working class to achieve election victory; it should develop an inclusive appeal understanding the nature of affluence and modernity. The ideological divisions in the party which erupted in the late 1950s, and again in the early 1970s, made this a formidable task. Crosland was adamant that in a socially mobile society, Labour must not choose between principles and power, but see them as interdependent. Without power, principles are meaningless since they can never be enacted; but without principles, power is devoid of ethical purpose. Crosland cited Weber's distinction between 'the ethic of ultimate ends' and 'the ethic of responsibility': socialists must 'grapple with pragmatic questions of choice and priorities, and see the need for reconciliation and compromise...their aim is the best that can be achieved, consistently with their principles, under given circumstances'.[6] The chapter concludes by assessing the relevance of Crosland's revisionism for Labour today, as the old politics of class are displaced by the new politics of identity in an ever more divided United Kingdom.

The 1959 general election defeat

Labour was defeated in the 1959 election by a Conservative party regenerated by Macmillan that many had written off as incompetent and unprincipled in the wake of the Suez debacle. A divisive post-mortem about why Labour had lost again ensued.[7] The 1950s were a traumatic decade: having hoped that the 1945 victory confirmed Labour's ascendancy as the natural governing party, it reacted complacently to the 1951 defeat assuming that the Conservatives would be exposed as a reactionary force intent on dismantling the post-war settlement, permitting a return to the mass unemployment of the inter-war years.[8] The margin of Labour's loss in 1951 was sufficiently narrow (the Conservatives won a parliamentary majority of 17) that any major overhaul of the party's programme and strategic purpose could be avoided. Labour supporters believed their party was on a '50-year march' to socialism: losing the 1951 election was a temporary interruption on a pre-determined path of inevitable social and political progress.[9]

Instead, the 1951 defeat exposed major shortcomings hindering Labour's ability to transform itself into a permanent party of government.[10] As Pugh has written, the Conservatives were able to exploit the suspicion that Labour was obsessed with further nationalisation, exemplified by the commitment to bring sugar refineries into public ownership. This policy demonstrated that only the Tories offered a decisive break from the leviathan of austerity and post-war controls. The late 1940s had been a bleak period of state restriction satirised in George Orwell's novel, *Nineteen Eighty Four*.[11] Working-class hostility towards public ownership was growing. The Conservative recovery by 1951 was the result not only of organisational and policy modernisation but voters' disaffection with rationing and food shortages.[12] Firstly, the Right argued that prolonged austerity was not the inevitable consequence of war, but the result of Labour's incompetence as a party of government.[13] Secondly, the party's campaign was damaged by accusations that it wanted to introduce punitive rises in income tax: Labour suffered a dramatic erosion of support in middle-class suburban constituencies which Morrison had so effectively targeted in the landslide victory of 1945. Crosland himself remarked that in 1951 taxation 'was the most important single issue which caused these people to swing Tory'.[14] The decline in middle-class living standards between 1945 and 1951 was unsustainable; consumption had been squeezed: as a consequence 'the Conservatives became the natural home for middle-class discontent'.[15] Finally, Attlee played his tactical hand poorly, rushing into an election in 1950 and 1951 when the party machinery had not had time to prepare.[16] The redrawing of constituency boundaries in 1950–51 further weakened Labour's prospects, confirming Attlee's reputation as an inept strategist.

Following the defeat of 1951, the party's position deteriorated as it struggled to come to terms with being out of office. By 1955, Labour had 'no new or creative ideas to put before the electorate' and was divided about the priority accorded to nationalisation in its domestic programme: the direction of foreign and defence policy was similarly a cause of rancour.[17] The party was capable at best of uniting around a stultifying commitment to a universal (rather than a selective) welfare state.[18] While Bevanism was concerned with formulating a socialist foreign policy, the intra-party conflict was ascribed to Labour's failure to respond adequately to the growth of affluence. As Lawrence Black remarked of Britain in the 1950s 'affluence had made quality and choice central issues', but Labour found the development of acquisitive materialism unsettling.[19] Michael Young had sought to include legislative measures to empower the consumer in Labour's 1945 manifesto, *Let Us Face the Future*, but they were vetoed by the leadership.[20] Rising real incomes led to a sharp increase in personal consumption from 1951 to 1959. The growth in living standards during the 1950s was greater than that which occurred in the inter-war years from 1918 to 1939. Working-class voters began to identify as 'middle-class' by exhibiting a weaker attachment to Labour as a proletarian party: the rise of new technologies and the growth of the manufacturing and service sector at the expense of traditional industry undermined the significance of manual labour, and with it, a sweep of traditional class identities.[21]

Vernon Bogdanor has written that during the era of affluence, an erosion of class solidarity in Britain depleted the political strength and self-confidence of the labour movement. This was exploited ruthlessly by the Tory leadership of Macmillan and Butler who defined Labour as the opponents of rising consumer affluence; they committed the Conservatives to faster growth alongside the central pillars of the post-war settlement, notably state intervention to maintain full employment and an ambitious programme of house-building.[22] In *The Future of*

Socialism, Crosland warned that his party was 'in grave danger of allowing the Tories to run away with the kudos of being the Party of prosperity and consumption'.[23] After the 1945 defeat, the Conservatives staged a remarkable recovery, reconstructing their electoral majority.[24] The publication of the Industrial Charter in 1947 underlined the party's pragmatic acceptance of public ownership. Labour argued that the Conservatives would provoke industrial conflict at home and turmoil abroad by confronting Soviet Russia, led by 'trigger-happy' Sir Winston Churchill; instead, in domestic and international policy, Macmillan and Butler urged a strategy of 'conciliation' wrong-footing Gaitskell's party.[25] In the aftermath of the Suez debacle, Macmillan adopted a revised national strategy of modernisation which by the early 1960s meant putting Britain at the heart of Europe to avert relative economic decline. In 1959, Labour was beaten in a third consecutive election: the party's share of the vote declined once again, partly a consequence of the rise in support for the Liberal party. The defeat of 1959 was decisive; the *Daily Mail* captured the mood when it argued shortly afterwards:

> Some general elections come and go, like a shower of rain, freshening things up a bit but not changing anything radically, not penetrating to the roots of our political soil. This is not likely to be said of the General Election of October 1959. It will be remembered as a major upheaval, a turning-point, a political watershed. Nothing in politics will ever be quite the same after it was before, either for the three parties, for the trade unions, or for any of us as individuals.[26]

The 1959 result confirmed that Labour was disadvantaged by structural changes in British society: the sociology of the country was apparently less amenable to socialism. Gaitskell sought to galvanise reforming opinion in the party, drawing extensively on Crosland's literary signpost towards *The Future of Socialism*. For Gaitskell, this strategy meant rewriting Clause 4, a course of action which Crosland warned his leader against as it undermined the doctrinal primacy of nationalisation provoking a battle the Left would inevitably win. Crosland and Gaitskell disagreed over tactics: Crosland insisted that a 'cavalier' attitude and scattergun approach was bound to end in disaster, as the party was plunged into civil war.[27] Gaitskell was defeated at the 1960 conference over Labour's position on defence putting a commitment to unilateral nuclear disarmament at the heart of party policy. The price of defeat and discord was making peace with traditionalist forces, particularly the affiliated trade unions, culminating in Gaitskell's infamous speech promising to safeguard 'a thousand years of British history' from European encroachment at the 1962 conference. The speech led to a rapprochement between Gaitskell and the party's activists, but divided revisionist opinion upsetting his closest political allies, as we saw in Chapter Five.[28] The Oxford economist, Andrew Shonfield, insisted in 1960 that Gaitskellite revisionism was guilty not of iconoclastic radicalism, but an absence of creative and novel ideas:

> The result is that the [Labour] party appears to the outside observer to be less prepared in spirit for the many awkward problems which it will have to face as soon as it reaches office that it was even in 1945, when its whole task was enormously simplified by the existence of a comprehensive set of wartime controls and a lot of civil servants sitting ready in their offices with long experience of working them.[29]

This interpretation casts doubt on 'hero-worshiping' accounts of the revisionists, particularly Philip Williams' otherwise flawless work, *Hugh Gaitskell: A Political Biography*.[30] Gaitskell's revisionism was defective since it focused on doctrine but failed to take account of the party's 'ethos': the deeply ingrained beliefs that shaped the institutions and culture of Labour giving voice to 'the exploited and those who sympathise with them'.[31] When Gaitskell and his acolytes proposed to rewrite Clause 4, they were attacking the movement's group loyalty and identity, the notion of a shared past and future that held the party together. The symbolic power of the clause in underlining Labour's opposition to capitalist exploitation was too easily dismissed by the party's middle-class leadership, as Crosland acknowledged.[32] Even arch-revisionists accepted that there were limits as to how far they could explicitly attack the party's doctrine and institutions. The revisionists' dilemma was all too evident by the late 1950s: the leadership was under pressure to update and modernise the party in the face of repeated electoral defeats, but avoided confrontation with Labour's 'proletarian sectionalism'. Shonfield lamented Gaitskell's cautious leadership, a tendency to paper over the cracks of doctrinal disagreement alongside his 'deliberate policy of intellectual self-impoverishment' rather than any indiscriminate assault on the party's identity.[33] Too deferential to traditionalism, Labour was failing to generate ideas that addressed the changing economic and social landscape of Britain in the early 1960s.

The battle for organisational ascendancy

From the beginning, Crosland was a fervent and enthusiastic contributor to debates about his party's electoral strategy; he never behaved as a lonely academic figure closeted in the Ivory Tower. During his early political career, Crosland was viewed as part of an intimate elite circle of intellectuals known as the 'Hampstead set' gathered around Gaitskell. The group, including Jay, Jenkins, Patrick Gordon Walker and Crosland, met regularly at Gaitskell's home in Frognal Gardens, Hampstead: 'what they attempted, together or individually, was to influence the Leader's strategy and tactics'.[34] There has been a tendency to conflate political identities in the post-war Labour party, categorising 'Gaitskellite revisionists' with the Labour Right, and 'Bevanite fundamentalists' with the Left.[35] Crosland was a committed 'Gaitskellite' but he was circumspect about the Right, believing that Morrison and Attlee's generation had few novel ideas to revitalise Labour for the future.

The 1959 election confirmed that nearly 15 years since the end of the Second World War, the Labour party was out of touch with social change. The defeat perplexed and demoralised the labour movement; in its aftermath party activists feared that the Hampstead set were prepared to do anything to regain power, jettisoning the party's most sacred values and traditions. The proposals included changing the party's name, as well as rewriting Clause 4. The revisionists were prepared to seize control of Labour's 'oligarchic institutions', ruthlessly mobilising the block vote to defeat predominantly left-wing constituency parties. In wielding the union's voting power, the revisionists signalled their failure to convert Labour to the cause of social democracy, although the unions were genuinely mass membership organisations in the 1950s. Labour's leaders acknowledged the necessity of electoral pragmatism in a changing society, but the grassroots of the party remained firmly attached to their traditional values and antagonism to economic injustice. This failure to transform the party's base was to haunt the Labour modernisers in the 1990s; they were compelled to accede to traditionalist forces despite successfully rewriting Clause 4.

In the late 1950s, the battle to achieve institutional dominance was of fundamental importance, acknowledging that ideas were insufficient to recast Labour as a viable contender for power. Alongside the intellectual effort to provide a fresh synthesis of social democratic ideas went an intense political struggle to win the case for revisionist thinking. To help the least fortunate in society, Labour had to be a majoritarian party of government rather than a party of futile opposition; Labour had to re-establish itself as a credible governing force in British politics. In the inter-war years, Morrison insisted that Labour must reach out to the English middle classes: 'Labour must attract the black-coated (that is, white-collar) worker', a strategy Morrison put into practice by switching from Hackney South to contest the middle-class constituency of Lewisham South in the 1945 election.[36] In *The Politics of Democratic Socialism*, Durbin noted that the middle class was expanding both numerically and in its influence on society: 'the pre-capitalist classes...are increasingly important as a group...we are living in a society whose class composition is shifting steadily against Marx's proletariat'.[37] Durbin acknowledged the decline of the working-class proletariat and the rise of the managerial middle class, 'the growing army of technicians, white collar workers, and suburban householders'; the party had to appeal beyond its traditional base.[38] Labour must be capable of governing for the whole nation rather than a narrow sectional interest. In a striking passage in *The Conservative Enemy*, Crosland argued: 'There is much talk... of the dangers of sacrificing principle; what is forgotten is the sacrifice of socialist objectives, not to mention human freedom and welfare, involved in a long period of impotent opposition.'[39]

In Crosland's view, political recovery necessitated a broad-based electoral alliance unifying working- and middle-class voters, reconciling Labour's moral purpose with the growth of post-war consumerism and affluence. For the revisionists, electoral recovery would be secured by maximising the leadership's room for manoeuvre, achieving organisational ascendancy by securing the support of union general secretaries.

Following the defeat of the Clause 4 initiative in 1959–60, Crosland was engaged in establishing the Campaign for Democratic Socialism (CDS) as an internal pressure group to win the argument for moderation within the party.[40] The aim was, 'to turn the Labour party into a modern [forward-looking] organisation fit for power'.[41] Gaitskell's biographer, Brian Brivati, writes: 'While Gaitskell was alive and the leader of the party, Crosland was prepared to be a chief of staff and get his hands dirty in the low level business of party factionalism.'[42] Bill Rodgers, future Cabinet minister and founder member of the CDS, recalls Crosland's decisive contribution:

> Throughout the period of preparation before the launching of the campaign Tony Crosland's role was crucial. Not only did he give the intellectual lead reflected in the [CDS] Manifesto: he also showed a single-mindedness of purpose and discipline which

most of us had previously believed he had not possessed. It was he who kept us at it when we met, mainly at his flat, refusing, for example, to let us have a drink until we had done three hours' solid work. He had the authority to keep us together and although he in no way dominated the group, he gave it a lead without which much less would have been done.[43]

Crosland's function was to be the 'ideological inspiration' for the CDS, acting as a key member of its Steering Committee. According to Rodgers, Crosland provided vital leadership refining the case for revisionism.[44] Another key member of the steering committee argued: 'To succeed in politics, you have to have both intellectual inspiration – political stardust – which Crosland's book gave us, and you have to have the power of organisation. We put those together in the CDS.'[45]

Crosland had been appalled by Gaitskell's amateur operation, urging his leader to establish 'a proper system of intelligence and forward planning', including the appointment of a Chief of Staff, a regular process of consultation with union leaders and senior parliamentarians, while radically upgrading the party's communications and opinion research capacity.[46] Crosland was incredulous that in the wake of the 1959 defeat, Transport House had conducted no systematic review of attitudes towards the party.[47] At the end of 1960, the year in which Gaitskell's leadership came under severe pressure as a backlash grew against the initiative to revise Clause 4 alongside the defeat over unilateral nuclear disarmament, Crosland wrote to Gaitskell proposing fresh leadership objectives: 'The crucial task for the next year is to isolate the extreme left and win back or consolidate the left-centre.'[48] He persuaded Gaitskell to re-establish contacts with the principal moderate figures such as Walter Padley of the Union of Shop, Distributive and Allied Workers (USDAW). Crosland was anxious about Gaitskell's position, fearing he was isolated from the working-class base of the party; as he saw it, the 'middle-class leadership' of Labour was perceived as:

Leading from an extreme and rather rigid right-wing position, and has no emotional desire to change any major aspect of the society in which we are living. The element of radicalism and discontent, which even the most moderate left-wing party must possess, seems lacking; even Kennedy sounds more radical than we do...On most other issues of policy, we have long been incredibly conservative...It is Grimond [the Leader of the British Liberal party] and not any of our own leaders, who makes speeches about the public schools, the House of Lords, and social privilege generally.[49]

His ally, Patrick Gordon Walker believed:

Gaitskell has the seeds of self-destruction in him – he almost wants to destroy himself. I said at one point that he had a death wish. He is becoming distrustful and angry with his best friends and wants to take up absolute and categorical positions that will alienate all but a handful.[50]

Crosland sought to persuade Gaitskell to build his leadership around a popular but credible appeal to the party and the wider electorate: 'a radical protest against the terrible conservatism and complacency of British society'.[51] In periods of frustration underlining the futility of opposition, Crosland feared Gaitskell was 'insufficiently radical' for a left-wing leader.[52] Gaitskell and Crosland were engaged in an ill-tempered exchange of letters in which they debated party reform. Gaitskell's replies illuminate the strains in their relationship and his frustration about the practicality of his protégé's proposals; the leader made an irritable request that Crosland produce more original ideas to enable the revisionists to seize the initiative in the party:

We need a much clearer appreciation of how we propose to the party to win the next election. I asked a long time ago that you and your young intellectual friends should work on this – but I can't see the

> results yet. Your pamphlet ['Can Labour Win?] was
> excellent analytically – but is still too vague on practical
> proposals.[53]

Gaitskell continued in a defensive tone:

> I have looked through your earlier letters. The reason
> I did not reply or act on them was that most of the
> proposals were (1) based on ignorance of the facts, (2)
> not sufficiently realistic, (3) too vague and abstract…I
> agree with the starting-point – which implies that by
> going for doctrine we have lost a lot of power.[54]

Following Gaitskell's death in January 1963, the revisionist
Right ceased to organise; the CDS was disbanded. Many of its
leading lights became MPs and ministers in Wilson's 1964–70
administrations; preoccupied with the business of government,
the hold of the moderates over the party weakened leading to
the schism of the late 1970s and early 1980s.[55, 56]

Labour's 'forces of conservatism'

Crosland's political purpose was not just to block the rise of
the extreme Left, but to tackle the party's inexorable drift
towards inertia and conservatism. Labour's tendency to look
nostalgically backwards prevented it from constructing a more
effective challenge to the Conservative party in British politics.
Crosland was troubled by what he perceived to be the 'extreme
conservatism' of the post-war labour movement given the
party's reluctance to adapt and modify its programme. Having
implemented the Attlee Government's 1945 manifesto, caution
and conservatism prevailed by the late 1940s, encapsulated by
figures on the Right such as Morrison, who insisted that the
priority was consolidating the achievements of the Attlee era.

The party continued to uphold the ethos of British
labourism: 'the class-conscious but pragmatic trade unionists
and working-class communities keen to assert themselves
within the existing political system'.[57] Labour's conservatism

had its origins in strategic assumptions that influenced the labour movement's world-view throughout the twentieth century, namely that the displacement of the Liberal party was inevitable since Labour uniquely represented the 'forward march' of the British working class towards democratic socialism. The party's dominant position in British electoral politics was pre-ordained; it saw no need to appeal to a particular group or sectional interest. Also, Labour's 1945 victory encapsulated the conversion of the British people to socialism.[58] This position was captured in an article published by the Labour party in Romford and Brentwood in 1951 predicting that British voters would:

> Return to the Socialist planning now interrupted, which has saved and revived this country, and will turn again with relief to the policy of social justice which is implicit in Labour's principles, and of which Toryism knows nothing…This Tory night can only be brief… they cannot reverse the march of social progress. With the first light of dawn, they and their misdeeds will vanish.[59]

The belief was that support for collectivism, public ownership and state socialism acquired deep roots in British society. As the 1950s progressed, Labour still appealed to pre-war indignities of mass unemployment, poverty and hunger, as society was transformed by the growth of affluence. The playwright Dennis Potter remarked that socialism spoke, 'a language remote from almost everything except the memories of the thirties, meaningless as these might be to the post-war generations'.[60] As Crosland noted, '[T]he youngest one-third of voters in 1959 had no recollection of the Conservatives' pre-war days.' He observed 'traditionalism in Britain is no monopoly of the right'. The Labour party was fast becoming, 'the most conservative and fundamentalist in the world', a position from which it could not hope to win an election.[61]

Crosland's revisionism

The primary challenge to Left conservatism came from Labour's revisionists. Crosland's influence has, quite appropriately, been ascribed to his status as the revisionist *par excellence*. Revisionism had a dual purpose: to make the party's appeal less dogmatic while forging a new identity focused on equality rather than state ownership of the means of production. Radice has written that revisionism was a 'cast of mind' that refocused democratic socialism away from a transformation of the capitalist system towards social reform in the affluent society. Revisionists re-think and adapt their strategies in the light of social change; values were permanent and eternal: policies were addressed towards a particular historical epoch. Crosland insisted that parties of the Left, including British Labour, performed optimally as revisionist parties.

There was nothing inherently socialist about increasing the proportion of British industries under state control, or expanding the level of public expenditure as a share of national income. These strategies were appropriate at particular stages of Britain's post-war development: public ownership to avoid the indignities and insecurities of the inter-war years while escaping the ravages of the war-torn economy; and increasing government expenditure in the 1960s and 1970s to advance public services and the welfare state. As the economy and society evolved, new programmes were necessary to instil socialist values: Stephen Padgett and William Patterson defined social democracy as 'a hybrid political tradition...composed of socialism and liberalism. The social democratic project may be defined as an attempt to reconcile socialism with liberal politics and capitalist society.'[62]

As we have seen, Crosland was inspired by the German reformer, Eduard Bernstein; along with more orthodox figures such as Karl Kautsky and Jean Jaurès, Bernstein sought to reinterpret late nineteenth-century socialism reacting to the Marxist doctrine sweeping through Europe. Bernstein's revisionism departed from orthodoxy and was unusually innovative. Firstly, Bernstein emphasised the need to separate the purposes and ends of democratic socialism from the means of implementation (Berman, 2006). What mattered was achieving practical social reforms, gaining control of the state through the democratic electoral process. Social democrats should immediately discard outdated policies; it was necessary to identify programmes that would realise centre-left values in the light of changing circumstances. In politics, there were few rewards for preserving policies in aspic. Bernstein's second argument acknowledged socialism's dependence on democratic institutions, the 'primacy of politics':[63] social justice had to be achieved through parliamentary democracy rather than political force. This theme was developed in Durbin's *Politics of Democratic Socialism*: parliamentary democracy provided stability in the light of social change; workers and capitalists were bound together by the 'emotional unity' of national belonging, which transcended class divisions.[64] Bernstein accepted the market economy was a permanent feature of European societies instead of plotting capitalism's overthrow and downfall. Finally, Bernstein advocated conciliation between classes rather than the tribal and sectarian traditions immortalised in the infamous refrain from the Labour party's anthem, *The Red Flag*:

> The people's flag is deepest red,
>   It shrouded oft our martyr'd dead
>   And ere their limbs grew stiff and cold,
>   Their hearts' blood dyed its ev'ry fold.
>   Then raise the scarlet standard high,
>   Within its shade we'll live and die,
>   Though cowards flinch and traitors sneer,
>   We'll keep the red flag flying here.[65]

Crosland, like Durbin, conceived democratic socialism as overcoming class divisions rather than ensuring the dominance of the proletariat over the bourgeoisie. The founders of the Labour party, notably Hardie and MacDonald, never construed Labour as an exclusively working-class movement;

they advanced an ethical view of socialism: a moral and humanitarian critique of unjustified wealth and privilege on behalf of all classes in society. For Bernstein, democracy was 'the absence of class rule...a state of society in which no single class enjoys privileges over and against the rest of the community'.[66] He presented a vision of social democracy not as an accommodation between market liberalism on the one hand, and Marxism on the other, but as a distinctive ideology.[67] Bernstein emphasised the pursuit of moral values, insisting that social reform must be achieved on the basis of rational argument and persuasion.

This position ensured an affinity between radical liberalism and social democracy: 'as far as liberalism as a world historical movement is concerned, socialism is not only temporarily but spiritually its legitimate heir'.[68] It was the spirit of 'conscience and reform' that led Leszek Kolakowski to define social democracy as 'an obstinate will to erode by inches the conditions which produce avoidable suffering, oppression, hunger, wars, racial and national hatred, insatiable greed and vindictive envy'.[69] Social democratic parties succeeded where they adopted revisionist programmes. In Britain after 1945, the Attlee governments completed their programme of reform humanising economic arrangements while slaying the 'five giants' of Squalor, Want, Disease, Idleness, and Ignorance.[70] In the era of affluence that followed, Labour had to do more than 'consolidate' wartime initiatives. If socialism's purpose was equality, this should be pursued through effective state intervention rather than public ownership. Britain's post-war settlement had been shaped by Labour's vision: a 'system of beliefs and moral values' which entrenched support for the welfare state and full employment, incorporating the working class within the prevailing consensus.[71] From Bernstein, Crosland gleaned that revisionism was necessary not as an expedient route to victory in a mass democracy, but in forging a credible social democratic programme to have an impact in the real world.

In putting principles into practice, social democrats had to attain power through the ballot-box. *The Future of Socialism* was prepared to acknowledge the electorate's changing aspirations in the Britain of the 1950s instead of reverting backwards; here voters sought not only enhanced social security, but increasing opportunities for personal consumption, higher living standards and self-actualisation. In western Europe, social democratic parties were victorious where they rejected the goal of overthrowing capitalism and prioritised their commitment to practical social improvement in the lives of working people.

Crosland and the rise of the New Left

In attacking the Labour party's conservatism, revisionists exhibited remarkable similarities with the British New Left: the decades of affluence reshaped post-war Britain underlining the inadequacy of 'traditional concepts of socialism'.[72] The New Left was a movement built around the academy seeking to overcome the divisions that traditionally bedevilled socialist politics between theory and practice, bringing together culture and politics.[73] As Michael Kenny has written, the growth of consumer culture and individual prosperity, alongside an erosion of traditional class loyalties meant that British labourism was 'frozen in the past'.[74] The images that had traditionally inspired the British Left, the perception of inevitable capitalist crisis, the trauma of mass unemployment, and the commitment to a class-based politics of 'them and us' appeared threadbare. Crosland and the New Left agreed that socialism had to be rethought, although their analysis inevitably diverged. The New Left assailed Crosland's complacency about inequality alongside his benign view of capitalism.[75] They conceded that capitalism was changing but insisted that Crosland drew all the wrong conclusions: economic power was heavily concentrated; the mixed economy did not constitute a transition towards socialism.[76] In *The Future of Socialism*, Crosland averred: 'The most characteristic features of capitalism have disappeared – the absolute rule of private property, the subjection of all life to market influences, the domination of the profit motive, the neutrality of government, typical laissez-faire division of income and the ideology of individual rights.'[77]

In a subsequent essay, he wrote: 'Post-war full employment appeared to demonstrate that capitalism had solved its inner contradictions. The alleviation of poverty weakened the mood of radical revolt.'[78] According to Crosland, British capitalism had irrevocably changed by the 1950s: 'We would never go back to the capitalism red in tooth and claw that the Labour party had been fighting against since before the end of the Second World War.'[79] In the aftermath of the 2008 crisis, these features of capitalism have evidently not disappeared: the profit motive still dominates, the distribution of income is grossly unequal, and market influences permeate all aspects of society. At the same time, Crosland was scarcely convinced by the New Left's analysis, particularly Raymond Williams' characterisation of a 'common culture' in working-class communities; Crosland objected to the middle-class disdain for consumerism, standing up for the rights of the working class to embrace affluence. He wrote:

> The rich would proceed in a leisurely fashion across Europe to the Mediterranean beauty spots where they would park their Rolls-Royces and take to a boat or a horse-drawn vehicle. As for my constituents who have only a fortnight's holiday, let them eat cake and go back to Blackpool.[8]

The similarities in polemic bridging Crosland and the New Left are, nevertheless, striking. Crosland agreed with Richard Hoggart that the British Left had allowed the Conservatives to define the images of affluence.[81] Black concluded that 'the Labour revisionists and the New Left used an ethical framework to propose ways of building upon affluence rather than opposing it'.[82] As a result, 'the shared territory between the New Left and revisionism was extensive...both the New Left and the revisionists were anxious that Clause 4 and socialism had become associated with the bureaucratic, 'Morrisonian' model of state-owned industry'.[83] Leading figures, notably

Stuart Hall, sought to awaken British socialism to the impact of social change alongside the inadequacy of conventional analysis; Crosland was re-thinking social democracy 'along consumer lines'.[84] Hall admitted to being 'embarrassed' as well as 'stimulated' by Crosland's writings, emphasising the New Left's ambivalence towards revisionism. Another leading figure in the British Marxist tradition, Perry Anderson, acknowledged that Crosland accurately depicted both Left and Right in the Labour party as 'backward-looking', out of step with modernity.[85] The name 'Labour' indicated that the party stood for a narrow sectional interest rather than a new society. The Left's anaemic response to *The Future of Socialism* amounted to an insistence that 'little had changed since the 1950s'; the priority was to defend the achievements of the Attlee era, a preoccupation of the 'lost leader', Nye Bevan. Figures on the New Left were exasperated that the Bevanites offered no serious prospectus for 'socialist renewal'. Anderson bemoaned the Labour Left for failing to 'adjust intellectually to the vast changes in British society':[86] 'Instead of a systematic sociology of British capitalism, the Left tended to rely on a simplistic rhetoric in which 'the common people'...were opposed to 'the interests'. It represented a major failure of nerve and intelligence.'[87] Crosland concurred that labourism's 'anti-theoretical bias' was a major handicap throughout the 1950s.

Labour and the politics of class

Crosland was among a group of revisionist intellectuals who confronted the impact of fundamental change in the class structure for Labour's politics, underlining affinities with the New Left. In the aftermath of the 1959 defeat, Jay admitted: 'The better-off wage earners and numerous salary-earners are tending to regard the Labour party as associated with a class to which they themselves don't belong.'[88] The existential question facing Labour was how it might become a non-doctrinaire party of 'conscience and reform' constructing a broad-based appeal mobilising electoral support throughout British society. Rather like late nineteenth-century ethical socialism, Crosland envisaged a politics of 'universal moral regeneration' tackling exploitation not by overthrowing the ruling class, but promoting an 'egalitarian and harmonious order' that reflected the interests of all in society.[89] These debates are reflected in concerns about Labour's electability and status as a future party of government in British politics. Crossman noted in his diaries in 1953:

> If you give people a bourgeois sense of security, the type of working-class Movement we had forty years ago will no longer appeal to them. The younger people don't feel the same significance in the slogans; on the other hand, the older people won't give up the slogans or the organisation.[90]

The impact of relative affluence on the British working class had been evident in the mid-nineteenth century. Engels' acknowledged in his correspondence with Marx that, 'the masses have got damn lethargic after such long prosperity'.[91] According to Crossman, Labour's electoral base was becoming, 'squashier and squashier and less and less solid, so that one fine day a sudden landslide could take a whole section of it off us'.[92] The decline of class as a determining factor in political life had to be confronted. The previous basis of working-class allegiance to Labour was the sense of belonging to a movement rather than explicit 'agreement' with the party's policies and values, 'at home through occupying a council house in an area of clustered working-class residence, and at work through belonging to a trade union'.[93] Yet as Gaitskell insisted: 'The kind of emotions and behaviours which held the Party together in the past were all based on class...since the war, progress has been such as to weaken these senses of class loyalty upon which the Labour party is based'.[94] The Labour parliamentarian Bessie Braddock made the same point: 'Right now the basic insecurity the workers feel is this: they are haunted by the spectre of the van driving to the door to take away the TV set'.[95] Throughout his career, Crosland 'maintained a consistent interest in the attitudes and behaviour of voters'.[96] He argued that political parties develop an 'image' or 'personality' in the minds of the electorate reinforced through association with symbolic policies and party stereotypes. By the late 1950s, Labour's image was 'steadily less appropriate to changing social conditions'.[9]

Nearly a decade after Attlee's defeat, Labour was regarded as a dreary and austere party of nationalisation and wartime controls. Crosland understood that 'younger voters react especially strongly against both Labour's class image and its identification with the problems and attitudes of a past generation'.[98] By 1959, the party was perceived as no longer capable of promoting prosperity where 'new social forces are at work, gradually breaking down the old barriers between the working and middle classes, and giving birth to new more fluid social groupings'.[99] In reviewing an influential book on the election by David Butler and Richard Rose, Crosland attested that Labour's defeat was not the result of unexpected events or an incompetent campaign. It was the consequence of, 'long-term social forces – forces which, moreover, are by no means yet exhausted'; Crosland was referring to 'the gradual erosion of traditional working-class attitudes'.[100] These changes were leading:

> Almost surreptitiously to weaken the old, proletarian class consciousness of at least the younger and more prosperous workers. We have here a growing group of socially ambivalent, fluid, cross-pressured voters. But the element of ambivalence cannot conceal the one fundamental certainty that the working class is steadily shrinking in size even as judged by the objective tests of income and occupation, and still more rapidly if judged by the subjective tests of social attitudes and aspirations.[101]

Crosland drew on Marx's distinction between 'class for itself' in which a group of class-conscious individuals identify subjectively with a particular identity, and 'class in itself', the objective reality of class position within the social structure.[102]

Much of this analysis had already appeared in the revisionist journal, *Socialist Commentary* in the 1950s. An editorial in 1951 stipulated that Labour had to appeal directly to 'floating voters' if it was to return to government; the 'glaring grievances of the past' had been 'eliminated' and Britain was witnessing 'at least the beginnings of an egalitarian society'; Labour would not win if it merely replayed 'the old gospel' of state control and nationalisation in an era in which traditional class solidarities were waning.[103]

Crosland and Gaitskell extended the analysis provided by *Socialist Commentary*.[104] The growth of affluence and its impact on Britain's class structure were impossible to ignore as the British economy improved its rate of production and consumption: between 1948 and 1958, one-sixth of British families became owner-occupiers and by 1964, half of all families owned their own home; the growth of car ownership went from 2.25 million in 1951 to 8 million by the mid-1960s; 13 million households owned a television set by 1964 compared to one million in 1951.[105] Britain's economic performance under the Conservatives was unimpressive in comparison to continental Europe's recovery, but voters contrasted their situation with the austerity and controls of wartime Britain rather than comparative growth rates with France and Germany.[106] Crosland was obsessed with the implications of the availability of consumer goods and the rise of the affluent society:

> The will to socialism has always been based on the lively sense of wrongs crying for redress, and before the War the wrongs were manifest indeed. But now, instead of glaring and conspicuous evils – squalor and injustice and mass unemployment – we have full employment, the Welfare State and the prospect in 10 years' time of a car to every working-class family. For a party of protest, there is a good deal less to protest about (at least in Britain).[107]

This new affluence perplexed traditional socialists for, '[it] confounded their belief that capitalism was economically inefficient and unjust (which 1931 had confirmed)'.[108] As a precursor to the concept of 'Southern Discomfort' coined by Giles Radice in the early 1990s, 1959 saw the emergence of a stark 'north–south' divide in British politics: Labour improved its electoral position in Scotland and Northern England gaining seats in counties such as Lancashire, but the party went backwards in the South.[109] In the Midlands, the Conservatives achieved a swing of 3.3 per cent and won ten additional seats, but in the North-West where unemployment was higher than average, there was a swing towards Labour of 2.4 per cent.[110] Labour was performing well in regions of Britain where social change was less prevalent, where traditional industries such as mining, textiles, ship-building and industrial manufacturing remained an important source of employment (but were beginning to decline). It was in the new towns and suburbs of England where the Conservatives' electoral advance was strongest, as Crosland noted:[111] 'It is significant that the actual swing during the 1950s was greatest in the South, where the expanding service trades are largely concentrated, and the Midlands, where the newer industries, with their exceptionally high ratio of staff to operatives, are developing most rapidly.'[112]

The defeats of the 1950s were the context in which Crosland attempted to reformulate social democracy; it was a world in which Labour's image had become that of 'a doctrinaire party of unreconstructed nationalisers'.[113] The party's weakness was not only its commitment to state socialism but its growing identification 'in the public mind with a sectional, traditional class appeal'.[114] Structural changes led to an increasing proportion of professional, white collar and technical jobs; as a consequence, fewer voters identified with institutions such as the trade unions. According to Gaitskell, the workforce would be dominated by the 'skilled man in a white overall watching dials in a bright new modern factory [rather] than a badly paid cotton operative working in a dark and obsolete 19th century mill'.[115] In an interview with the *Daily Mail* before the 1959 election, Gaitskell noted: 'When, for instance, a working-class family buys a motorcar I believe it may produce a feeling of a more individual and independent status. Its loyalty ceases to be the simple group loyalty. It begins to function as an independent unit.'[116] When Bevan died relatively young from stomach cancer in 1960, one journalist wrote: 'In the coalfield from which he came, Marx and Engels have been supplanted by Marks & Spencer, and the sound of class war is drowned by the hum of the spin dryer.'[117]

The threat posed by the Conservative party of returning Britain to the inter-war misery of mass unemployment and endemic poverty no longer appeared plausible. The working class was rapidly shedding the old tribal loyalties with devastating consequences for Labour's electoral viability. According to Crosland, the challenge was to confront the long-term implications of social change without surrendering basic political principles:

> A political party is not behaving immorally in studying the wishes of the voters, provided that it wants power not for reasons of personal ambition or prestige but in order to put a programme into effect. There is much talk of…the dangers of sacrificing principle. What is forgotten is the sacrifice of socialist objectives not to mention human freedom and welfare, involved in a long period of impotent opposition.[118]

Improvements in the standard of living and the availability of consumer goods were altering the subjective identity of working-class voters; Roberts observes that 'working-class people were moving from a communally based life to one which was centred more on the home and the nuclear family'.[119] Views of society were changing; such voters were losing their allegiance to political parties.[120] Crosland's analysis verged on sociological determinism: capitalist structures would lead ineluctably towards a more bourgeois society; sociological research, notably Peter Willmott's ground-breaking study of new housing estates, indicated greater continuity in working-class attitudes despite the transition from the inner-city slums: in its predominantly proletarian values, Dagenham was 'the East [of London] reborn'.[121] As Gareth Stedman-Jones indicated 'the objective realities of class discerned by social surveys and sociological analysis do not have any unambiguous bearing upon the fate of class-orientated political parties'.[122]

The consequences of social change for Labour still made sombre reading. Alterations in the class structure did not mean that working-class voters no longer supported the party, but their loyalty could not be taken for granted. Moreover, the structural decline of the working class meant that Labour had to secure votes among the middle-class and 'socially fluid' groups. The party was not the passive victim of social change: consumption and affluence reshaped the class structure and dominant culture, but Labour naively allowed the Conservatives to lay claim to the 'images of affluence'.[123] Crosland insisted that Labour had to make 'a wide radical appeal to broad sections of the population' as a 'progressive, national social democratic party' overcoming 'the oppressive weight of conservatism and inertia'.[124] A series of articles in the aftermath of 1959 concluded: 'all over Europe, certain trends are occurring which threaten the strength of the traditional left'.[125] Crosland contemplated radical measures notably changing Labour's name to 'Social Democratic Party'; he considered severing the party's traditional ties with the unions while forging closer links with the Liberal party.

Those proposals were rejected by Gaitskell, but discussed among so-called Hampstead-set intellectuals in a rare burst of fresh thinking that characterised the period immediately after the 1959 defeat;[126] Crosland's analysis underlines the revisionists' exasperation following Labour's third hammering at the polls; there had to be a change of mind-set throughout the movement if Labour was to win again: 'Above all, we must positively *want* to represent not only the class-conscious miner living in a Scottish mining village, but also the young, un-class-conscious technician owning a car and living in a new Midlands housing estate.'[127] As Bogdanor remarks:

> Whereas in the 1940s, the main worry was insecurity
> – unemployment, poverty, lack of welfare and so on –
> and the watchword of the Labour party was 'fair shares
> for all'…in the 1950s, the issue was 'which party can
> best sustain the new prosperity that we are enjoying?
> That harmed Labour which was associated, as we have
> seen, with austerity and restrictions.[128]

Crosland was developing in embryonic form the modernising platform adopted by Labour under Neil Kinnock's leadership after the 1983 election, advanced under John Smith and Blair in the 1990s. The party's reformers in the 1980s and 1990s concluded that Labour had to update its image and appeal if it was to succeed as a social democratic party: there were inevitably arguments about speed and tactics; after 1992, the young modernisers such as Blair and Brown felt that Smith's approach was too cautious and prudent. There was nonetheless agreement about how far Labour had to travel if it was to be a trusted party of government. Labour modernisers faced a similar predicament to revisionists in the 1950s and 1960s: how to reconcile their loyalty and moral commitment to the labour movement with an understanding of what was required to reconstruct Labour as a credible governing party. This dilemma was never resolved throughout Labour's post-war history.

Labour: a divided party?

It was the failure of the revisionist endeavour that provoked Labour's electoral and political meltdown in the 1970s and early 1980s. Although the split within Labour's ranks did not occur until 1981, the possibility of a break-up was being canvassed among the Labour Right at least a decade before. A prominent parliamentarian, Douglas Bruce-Mann, wrote to Crosland in the mid-1970s:

> Although a public declaration of the extent to which
> the moderate element in the party leadership differs

from the 'militants' would obviously involve a risk of splitting the movement, I am gradually being driven to the view that a split would be less disastrous than a continuation of the present situation. Unless the leadership is agreed on, or capable of enforcing on a Labour Cabinet a statutory incomes policy coupled with an egalitarian fiscal policy, a Labour victory could be more disastrous than defeat. Fear of disturbing party unity is so great that we are sacrificing all credibility with the electorate. It seems to me that the relevant question, in considering what action the 'radical centre' should now take, is not whether the Labour party in its present state could win an election, but whether we could do any good in office.[129]

The mood of despair among Labour's moderate wing was acute; political and personal tensions were never far from the surface. Presenting Crosland with his biography of Herbert Morrison, the arch-revisionist and adviser to the 1974–79 Labour Government, Bernard Donoughue, quipped: 'We thought you might like this study of Herbert since, with all his faults, he did fight to build a democratic socialist party devoted to governing and not just to protesting. Without him, there would not be a mass party for the present lunatics to destroy.'[130] In his early career, Crosland was prepared to adopt a factional position belying his reputation as an armchair intellectual; internal divisions had grown increasingly embittered. Shortly after the publication of *The Future of Socialism*, Crosland's friend, Daniel Bell, reported that he was now a 'hate figure' on the British Left:

I had lunch in London with the editors of the Universities and Left Review ([Charles] Taylor, [Raphael] Samuel etc.). You will be amused to know that they consider the chief enemy to be 'Croslandism'. In the *patois* of the left, you've arrived. Anyone who becomes an 'ism' has achieved historical status indeed.[131]

The *Observer* reported in 1973 that Crosland had 'spearheaded a bid by moderate Labour leaders to swing the party away from doctrinaire nationalisation and anti-private enterprise which they fear might cost them the next election'. There was disagreement within Labour's moderate wing about the most profitable party management tactics to adopt, hindering their efforts to counter the growing influence of the Left:

> Mr Wilson, Mr James Callaghan and Mr Healey will make accommodating sounds to prevent ruptures before the party conference; whereas Mr Crosland from inside the Shadow Cabinet and Mr Roy Jenkins from the sidelines believe the absurdities need to be exposed before they damage the party's fundamental credibility.[132]

By the early 1970s, Crosland was an ardent party loyalist, although he never ceased to point out that if Labour committed itself to the 'absurdities' in *Labour's Programme for Britain* (1973), the party's electoral prospects would be gravely damaged. In entering this fractious debate, post-war revisionists acknowledged Labour's status as an eclectic and diverse coalition of forces combining trade unionism, syndicalism, Christian socialism, municipal socialism, radical liberalism, humanitarianism, and a cadre of middle-class intellectuals all of whom had 'different ideologies and interests'.[133] As Alan Warde has written, the party's union founders sought to attain political power to remove restrictive legislation enabling free collective bargaining on behalf of the working class; the inheritors of radical liberalism saw Labour's purpose in ethical terms as a 'socialist commonwealth' where private profit and greed would be curtailed in the name of social justice and the common good.

The various political traditions bequeathed a party that was irreparably divided in its fundamental doctrine and identity, a breach which the revisionists in the 1950s had sought to heal but could never resolve. The Labour party was an unstable amalgam of competing forces; it remained intact throughout the twentieth century having achieved a fragile accommodation between 'cohesion' and 'division'.[134] The conflict arose because Labour was structurally divided: it was comprised of trade unions diligently asserting their sectional interests; at the same time, the party retained an underlying political cohesion, an ethos of unity and loyalty sustained by antagonism to a common enemy: capitalism and the ruling class. The revision of Clause 4 was disliked precisely because it threatened to weaken the political culture of 'them and us' imperilling the Labour party's shared identity. It is hardly surprising the party has been at odds about its political future, underlining the precarious and problematic nature of the revisionists' undertaking.

In resolving the revisionist's dilemma, reformers appealed to the labour movement's ethic of loyalty and responsibility as Gaitskell faced a sustained challenge to his leadership. The process of self-questioning integral to the revisionist strategy always provokes sectarian conflict, threatening the harmony and accord that has been temporarily brokered. Labour's revisionists antagonised sectional interests who stood to lose out from the reformist programme that Gaitskell, Dalton, Jay and Crosland had been championing in the 1930s and 1940s while appearing to dispel the utopian myth of a 'socialist commonwealth in one country'. Revisionist theoreticians gave the party 'the chance to sheer away from the stultifying doctrines of orthodox Marxism and follow the course of an enlightened social democracy', but Labour scarcely appeared grateful for the opportunity to fight as a prospective party of power in British politics.[135] Revisionist heresies were necessary for Labour to establish itself as a credible governing force after three consecutive defeats, but the revisionists faced the dilemma that divided parties risk undermining their electoral appeal. Wilson's success in the 1964 election was achieved by papering over the cracks opened up during Gaitskell's leadership, projecting a commitment to national modernisation and planning that did not disturb the party's hard-won but fragile unity. Crosland wrestled with this quandary throughout his career; it is striking that by the time of his death, he veered towards prioritising the unity and cohesion of the movement. This situation reflected growing personal animosities among the revisionists: Roy Jenkins was determined to forge a new 'radical centre' in British politics, whereas Crosland saw himself as the keeper of the social democratic flame. Crosland was increasingly dependent on the patronage of James Callaghan, an avowed Labour traditionalist close to the trade unions. In these circumstances, the vitality and dynamism of the revisionist tradition within the Labour party was at risk of disappearing into obsolescent abeyance.

Labour's revisionism today

Labour recovered from the ideological and doctrinal schisms that erupted during the Wilson–Callaghan years, and again in the aftermath of the 1979 defeat. The protracted process of party modernisation discarded a series of electorally unpopular positions on nationalisation and unilateral nuclear disarmament, reaching a new accommodation with the market and reforming the party's structures to make them more 'open' and inclusive. How relevant are these debates about Labour's electoral appeal and legacy as a class party today? The arguments that Crosland was formulating echo throughout the political generations. The 2010 and 2015 results confirm that Labour has lost electoral support across all demographic groups and classes over the last decade; not only the affluent middle classes but among disadvantaged sections of the UK population. According to John Curtice, Labour failed to reverse the decline in its share of the vote among 'C1' (white-collar) and 'C2' (blue-collar manual) voters that occurred between 2005 and 2010.[136] The analysis of fragmentation in Labour's support is complicated by further developments: the changing class composition of Britain's social structure; and the inexorable rise of identity politics across the United Kingdom.

On the class structure, not only is the industrial working class, traditionally the mainstay of trade unionism and organised labour shrinking even further, a process underway in Britain since the 1940s. While class remains subjectively important to an individual's identity, it is no longer as significant in shaping political attitudes and preferences associated with voting behaviour.[137] According to a recent survey:

> Only 39 per cent of the population fit the older stereotypes of middle and working class – those in the Established middle class and the Traditional working class. The majority of the population belongs to one of the other social classes which have not been previously dissected. New affluent workers and Emergent service workers appear to be the children of the Traditional working class, which has been fragmented by de-industrialisation, mass unemployment, immigration and a shift from manufacturing to service-based employment. Generational change and social change intersect in powerful ways.[138]

This analysis does not infer that class has disappeared from the British sociological map. Instead, new structural divisions are emerging associated with the unequal distribution of social, economic and cultural capital according to Michael Savage and Fiona Devine; these are being articulated in British politics such that:

> Changes to Britain's economic and social structure... have pushed to the margins a class of voters who we describe as the 'left behind'; older, working-class, white voters who lack the educational qualifications, incomes and skills that are needed to adapt and thrive amid a modern post-industrial economy.[139]

Robert Ford and Matthew Goodwin indicate there is a generational values shift and growing 'meritocratic cleavage': working-class voters lacking formal educational qualifications are separated from the liberal, university-educated mainstream. They contend that the UK Independence Party's (UKIP) electoral support is:

Heavily concentrated among older, blue-collar workers, with little education and few skills; groups who have been 'left behind' by the economic and social transformation of Britain in recent decades, and pushed to the margins as the main parties have converged in the centre ground. UKIP are not a second home for disgruntled Tories in the shires; they are a first home for angry and disaffected working-class Britons of all political backgrounds, who have lost faith in a political system that ceased to represent them long ago.[140]

In 1964 when Labour returned to power, 70 per cent of voters had no educational qualifications; almost half were employed in manual occupations; by 2010, a third of voters had been to university; 35 per cent of the workforce were in middle-class, professional employment.[141] This change led to a divide in cultural attitudes: in the 2013 British Social Attitudes Survey (BSA), 27 per cent of under-35s said 'they would mind if a close relative married a Muslim'; for those over 65, the figure rose to 66 per cent. 11 per cent of under-35s believe 'same-sex relationships' are 'mostly' or 'always' wrong, compared to 42 per cent among the over-65s.[142] Labour abandoned the pretence that the industrial working class was the natural constituency and heartland of British social democracy in the 1990s, but the political transition was painful: as the party expediently shifted towards the centre-ground, it allegedly abandoned its traditional supporters. Geoffrey Evans and Jon Mellon query the analysis of Labour's defecting working-class base offered by Ford and Goodwin: these voters left the party as it became increasingly centrist in the 1990s, well in advance of UKIP's emergence. Ford and Goodwin fail to address demarcations within the blue-collar working class between traditional manual workers and the self-employed 'petit bourgeoisie' with distinctive preferences in economic policy, taxation and redistribution.[143] British electoral politics was never built around solid blocs of class affiliation: while Labour's identity as a working-class party declined over the last 40 years, Crosland's generation alongside wartime 'greats' such as Morrison and

Attlee grappled with similar developments throughout the 1940s in securing a winning electoral coalition.

The politics of class is complicated by the emergence of identity politics; cultural attitudes to globalisation, multiculturalism and migration are decisive in determining political allegiance: an individual's occupational status within the class structure is not their only salient identity.[144] These developments were scarcely anticipated by revisionists in the 1950s and 1960s; during Crosland's lifetime, Britain made the transition from a predominantly 'mono-cultural' society to a plurality of multicultural communities. Attitudes to economic openness and a multi-ethnic society do not necessarily reflect class identities; the new battleground of British politics is how to manage the divisions arising from an ethnically diverse and culturally heterogeneous society. The traditional conception of national citizenship assumed by writers from T.H. Marshall to Crosland centred on inalienable civil, political and social rights is no longer adequate: providing enough 'cement' for the social democratic state entails treating citizens as part of a national political community with a shared history, underpinned by a common set of cultural values and obligations.[145] Critical debates about national citizenship through the lens of British and English identity have subsequently emerged.

The discussion aroused by the Scottish independence referendum indicates that anxiety about nationhood, identity and territory is capable of superseding the traditional social democratic preoccupation with class, power and the state.[146] The rise of Scottish nationalism was a severe provocation to Labour's 'default unionism' which continued to assume that socialism would transcend national differences mobilising the British working class across the United Kingdom, as it did in the party's 1945 victory. Crosland's generation was sceptical about devolving political power, contributing little new thinking to the question of how to reform the British constitution and parliamentary system. The growth of disengagement and declining public trust in parliamentary democracy were less apparent in Crosland's age; electoral turnouts had remained stable since the Second World War.[147] The decline in the membership of political parties (now temporarily reversed in the Labour party) and formal participation implies that twenty-first century political institutions will need to be reinvented; this was far from evident in Crosland's time.

The changing nature of class and identity politics should not imply that relevant lessons cannot be identified in Crosland's analysis. In understanding the complexity of social change, he insisted a balance had to be struck between principle and power. Crosland instinctively opposed 'opinion-survey driven socialism' which shaped party modernisation throughout the 1990s, insisting that Labour must serve as a forum in which social democratic ideas were debated, rather than becoming an electoral vehicle concerned solely with attaining office. This is reminiscent of the discussion about how Labour should counter the rise of UKIP in its working-class strongholds; Crosland was critical of the 'preference-accommodating' populism which emerged in Labour circles as a response to the Wilson Government's defeat in 1970: 'The restoration of hanging and flogging, a Powellite policy on race, vast reductions in income tax, the withdrawal of family allowances, and an end to student grants and overseas aid...I state flatly that such policies are unacceptable to any social democrat.'[148]

In reviewing a Fabian pamphlet by John Gyford and Stephen Haseler in 1973, Crosland questioned whether the progressive reforms carried out by the Labour governments of the 1960s led to an erosion of working-class support, neglecting the attack on economic inequalities that long preoccupied British socialism. Crosland acknowledged 'Labour needs to pay more attention to issues of popular concern'.[149] In a speech analysing the 1972 US presidential election result, he noted:

> In the US the McGovern debacle shows the disaster which awaits a left-wing party that divorces itself from its central tradition and its natural friends, and seems more concerned with fashionable middle-class issues than with the problems of its traditional supporters. On the other hand, Willy Brandt in Germany, Norman Kirk in New Zealand, and Gough Whitlam

in Australia have shown that social democratic parties with a clear identity and a solid base can win, and win spectacularly.[150]

Crosland went on:

McGovern's nemesis was his failure to win the support of the American worker. That should be our lesson. No doubt we could attract some votes by launching Labour as the party of women's lib. In so doing we would neglect the interests of our natural supporters. Labour in Britain must concentrate, instead, on the real problems facing working people in their day-to-day life.[151]

This debate raised a fundamental issue for the revisionists about whether Labour was actually a 'classless party' appealing to the whole electorate, or whether it should continue to rely on the working class for its core support.[152] Crosland concluded that Labour's position was deteriorating by the early 1970s not because it had forgotten how to appeal to its working-class constituency. The party was adept at attacking the Heath government which ran into serious difficulties over industrial relations, associated with the free market policies in the 1970 'Selsdon manifesto'. The problem was that Labour had 'badly neglected our other task – of looking to the future. The voters know what we are *against*; they do not know what we are *for*. We have no unifying theme in the way that modernising Britain was our theme in the early 1960s.'[153] The Labour party lost momentum as the revisionists, shaken and demoralised by Gaitskell's death, were preoccupied by ministerial office between 1964 and 1970. Wilson's project of national modernisation spurred on by the 'white heat of the technological revolution' was floundering by the late 1960s. The spirit of reform was palpably lost in 'an era of lost innocence, of hopes betrayed...the atmosphere of shabby expediency...hung over the Government like a pall'.[154]

In these circumstances, the revisionist dilemma resurfaced in its most acute form: Crosland's generation would have had to choose between mobilising a fresh burst of intellectual innovation and creative thinking that imperilled the party's traditional values, and maintaining loyalty to 'our people' and the movement paying the price of political sterility. In the end, allegiance to British labourism and 'proletarian sectionalism' won out reinforced by the structure and institutions of the party:

> The central authority within the Labour party was the annual conference, which made policy and elected the National Executive Committee. Within the party conference effective power resided with the trade unions, whose block votes easily overwhelmed the opinions of constituency activists. The culture of the party was nevertheless highly democratic, anti-elitist, as well as vaguely anti-intellectual. Both activists and trade unionists were suspicious of party leaders, who were often more educated and more middle class than the rank and file and who were assumed to be especially vulnerable to the temptations of office-holding and to the corrupting effects of regular mingling with the wealthy and powerful. Again, the memory of Ramsay MacDonald was a potent reminder of the risks involved in giving too much deference to party leaders.[155]

Although Labour remained a relatively open political formation in comparison to the Conservatives, this institutional structure and political culture constrained the range of policy options that would be aired within the party; due deference was paid to the defence of trade union vested interests.[156] The circumstances in which it was hoped revisionism might take root were not exactly propitious. As a consequence, few ideas emerged during the late 1960s and 1970s; the doctrine and institutions of British social democracy appeared to be stagnating despite Labour's precarious electoral victories in 1974. At the end of the 1950s, Crossman, by political instinct on the Bevanite Left of the party acknowledged: 'Gaitskell and his friends are playing the major role, since no one else has anything positive to propose...the fact is that Nye and Harold are not interested in rethinking policy at all.'[157] If the revisionists were not recasting Labour policy after 1970, the party was at risk of ideological torpidity; it was far from clear where the inspiration for programmatic renewal would come from.

Labour's revisionist tradition fragmented in the late 1970s after Crosland's death and the fall of the Callaghan Government; the feebleness of the party's moderate wing and the vicious assault on the post-war settlement imperilled Labour's status as a party of government. The quest for an Alternative Economic Strategy (AES) ignited interest among Labour politicians such as Tony Benn, but the emphasis on state ownership and industrial planning made the strategy too reminiscent of the programme that emerged in the inter-war period. The AES wanted to pick up where Attlee and Bevan left off; the emphasis on import controls and planning agreements seemed implausible given increased exposure to the international economy. There was little evidence by 1974 that the British working class was crying out for more public ownership 'nationalising Marks & Spencer's'.[158] Crosland was adamant that the alternative strategy 'did not stack up politically'; it took no account of the role of the international financial system and the failings of post-war centrally planned economies.[159] The verdict of the New Left organ, *Marxism Today* was that Labour was incapable of attuning itself to the new modernity. By 1997, the party had rediscovered a modernising appeal, but by jettisoning its traditional beliefs enshrined in Clause 4 of the 1918 constitution. The price of electoral recovery was the apparent betrayal of Labour's 'soul': a special issue of *Marxism Today* issued a clear verdict on New Labour's modernisation and early period in power after 1997: 'Wrong'.[160]

Conclusion

Throughout his life, Crosland rejected the claim of Robert Michels and Adam Przeworski that social democratic parties face an incompatible choice between principles and power. He argued Labour could win votes as a majoritarian party while remaining true to its socialist values in a changing world.[161] This strategic insight was a powerful legacy. Nonetheless, under New Labour a crucial question was left unanswered: what was social democracy's purpose in contemporary society? New Labour accepted the disappearance of post-war ideological certainties and the decline of traditional class allegiances, but lacked a distinctive identity having being transformed into a 'catch-all' party of the centre-left. Revisionism gained ascendancy in the 1950s and 1960s not only because it was intellectually dominant and had an election-winning strategy: the revisionists offered a positive ethical and moral framework centred on the cause of a just society less disfigured by class inequalities; this gave involvement in the Labour party a sense of political vocation and meaning (Warde, 1982). Under Blair, the ethical and moral creed became more ambiguous as the party leadership eschewed the language of equality.[162] New Labour's victory over traditional socialism was contingent, reducible to the argument not that it was morally or practically superior, but more likely to succeed electorally. The leadership argued appealing to the median vote was essential in a first-past-the-post, plurality-based electoral system where the Conservatives had won four consecutive elections since 1979. The 'progressive dilemmas' raised for the Labour party over the last 30 years have, nonetheless, been unmistakable.

During the turbulent years of electoral defeat and party factionalism in which the 'glad, confident morning' of Labour's 1945 victory evaporated, Crosland wrestled heroically with disagreements that still bedevil the party today. These debates raise 'progressive dilemmas' for Labour: between idealism and electability; between representation of class interests and an inclusive appeal to all social classes; between national identities rooted in Great Britain as an imagined community creating powerful allegiances towards British socialism (accompanied by a burgeoning sense of Englishness), and a cosmopolitan internationalist outlook combined with the commitment to European integration.[163] A 'progressive dilemma' arises where there is a conflict between the 'ethos' of traditional labourism on the one hand, and the 'doctrine' of modern social democracy on the other centred on ideological pragmatism and modernisation.[164] This discord created a breach within the core identity of Labour which the Blair, Brown and Miliband leaderships were unable to heal. The existential challenge for the party after 1945 was to combine two essential elements: the shared identity and group loyalty of labourism, the adhesive that bound the party together; and revisionist social democracy which had the potential to win elections while constructing a viable governing strategy. Achieving a stable balance between loyalty and the iconoclastic questioning of the party's core beliefs remained highly problematic. This aspiration proved elusive other than at rare moments of victory such as 1964, 1966 and 1997. Forty years since Crosland's death, no-one should pretend that the progressive dilemma is close to resolution.

Having examined Crosland's legacy over the preceding four chapters, the penultimate section of the book addresses the nature of his influence on the Labour party in the four decades since his death. After 1979, the Labour party experienced a 'cultural revolution' and a sharp turn to the Left: it rejected Crosland's political economy centred on reconciling capitalism with social justice, resulting in a historic defeat at the 1983 election. What followed was a period of extensive modernisation under Neil Kinnock and John Smith, culminating in Labour's 1997 victory. Crosland's posthumous impact has been apparent throughout. The next chapter examines his relevance and imprint on the political projects that shaped the party in contemporary times.

SEVEN

Crosland and Labour party modernisation: from Kinnock to Blair

If ideas in politics more than elsewhere are the children of practical needs, nonetheless, it is true that the actual world is the result of men's thoughts. The existing arrangement of political forces is dependent at least as much upon ideas, as it is upon men's perception of their interests. (J.N. Figgis[1])

New Labour in government was defined by the two liberal revolutions of the period. In consequence, it is associated in the public mind with excess – excessive levels of private debt, too much micro-managing government, too much immigration, inflated house prices, too much welfare, and too much money spent for too little return. There is a popular loss of trust in the capacity of the political class to contain this excess and restore a virtuous order. The economic crisis reverberates with a sense of blame, dispossession, and social insecurity as people react to the erosion of the cultural meanings, fidelities, and solidarities that bind them together in society. (J. Rutherford[2])

Introduction

The intellectual vitality and richness of Crosland's political thought, alongside his qualities as a politician, meant that his influence on the Labour party since the 1950s has been pervasive. Crosland's generation drew on the inter-war revisionism of Tawney and Durbin (Warde, 1982), alongside the radical liberal tradition. They insisted that if the British Left emphasised individual rights and freedoms by curtailing its enthusiasm for dogmatic state socialism, radical social democracy had the potential to create a fairer, more equal society. As Tawney wrote in the 1920s: 'A society is free in so far as, within the limits set by nature, knowledge and resources, its institutions and policies are such as to enable all members to grow to their full stature.'[3] By remaining true to its ethical ideals while shaping innovative solutions for new problems, the Labour party had the capacity to win the battle of ideas transforming itself into the natural governing party in British politics. This optimism was nonetheless qualified by the development of post-war Britain, culminating in the watershed event of Labour's 1979 defeat. Since then, Crosland's impact on the party has been contingent and uneven, declining sharply in the late 1970s and early 1980s, while returning to shape the politics of modernisation in the late 1980s and beyond.

This chapter examines the nature of Crosland's legacy since his death. It addresses how far the party's dominant intellectual traditions have been influenced by Croslandite thought. The persistent misrepresentation of Crosland's ideas has been a source of irritation to his followers. Like Keynes, Crosland's thinking has been increasingly misunderstood with the passage of time; carefully argued and nuanced propositions have been transformed into crude shibboleths; like Keynesianism, Croslandism is an amalgam of theories and ideological precepts. As with Keynes, Crosland 'was surrounded by groups of disciples who developed their ideas in directions very different from those envisaged by their masters'.[4] Those who sought to emphasise Crosland's revisionism downplayed his commitment to equality; the focus on his egalitarian credentials created the impression that Crosland regarded strategies such as higher government spending and taxation as axiomatic. Leonard warns: '[I]t is always a hazardous business to guess how a dead person would react to issues which may arise years later and in greatly changed circumstances'.[5] Hattersley has similarly remarked: 'The attribution of posthumous opinions to dead heroes is both intellectually disreputable and personally offensive to their friends.'[6]

The chapter charts the influence of Crosland's ideas on the political and intellectual projects that have shaped contemporary thinking within the party. Neither 'New', 'Blue', nor 'One Nation' Labour is revisionist in the Crosland tradition; none of these approaches draws on Bernstein's analysis, adapting policies to address future challenges while advancing ethical and moral values of equality and social justice. New Labour was electorally pragmatic, principally driven by dynamic shifts in public opinion and electability. Blue Labour repudiated revisionism as part of Labour's liberal heritage. One Nation Labour embraced Crosland's legacy but developed no systematic analysis of the changing sociological and cultural landscape of British society. Crosland argued the British Left had to re-discover its roots in the liberal tradition: this sits uneasily with communitarian visions of socialism, especially Blue Labour given its affinity with Pugh's concept of 'Tory-socialism'. New Labour wanted to draw a line under the past, treating Crosland and the revisionists as embarrassing elderly relatives. Nonetheless, each position engaged with and consequently reworked vital concepts drawn from Crosland's analysis. The Crosland effect has been considerable, leaving a significant mark on the party.

Crosland's influence since 1979

Crosland's appeal and the remarkable imprint he made on Labour are testimony to the clarity and rhetorical force of his writings, as well as his reputation as an outstanding socialist theoretician and minister. Nonetheless, his prescriptions for the party's future encountered hostility and vitriol, especially from the Bevanite Left. Crosland's ideas were principally directed at the Labour party: since the early twentieth century, Labour had a less developed intellectual tradition than its continental counterparts; it was particularly resistant to discussion of a theoretical nature. Following the International Monetary Fund (IMF) crisis in 1975–76 and Labour's catastrophic defeat in 1979, Crosland's vision of social democracy had little currency and prevalence within the party. Among the rank and file, the focus was on the Left's Alternative Economic Strategy (AES) and the rise of Bennite radicalism, rejecting the central tenet of Crosland's analysis that British capitalism no longer required fundamental transformation.

The Cultural Revolution: 1979–83

The efficacy of nationalisation and public ownership re-emerged at the core of the unresolved debate about Labour's doctrine and identity in the wake of the 1979 defeat.[7] This process was accompanied by renewed faith in the party's ability to overhaul central pillars of the capitalist system, socialising production and regaining control of the British economy's commanding heights through import controls, planning agreements and nationalisation.[8] The IMF debacle and the 1978–79 Winter of Discontent sowed the seeds of opposition to the orthodox strategy of which Crosland's political economy was assumed to be symptomatic; since 1976, the Callaghan administration had become 'a conservative monetarist government' according to *Tribune*.[9] The shift to the Left in the unions and the Parliamentary Labour Party (PLP) permitted the resurgence of the Trotskyite Militant Tendency, heightening the mood of atrophy and decay. The structural decline of the British economy and Labour's inability to achieve higher growth or to control inflation paralysed the social democratic project. Income inequality in Britain was lower in the mid-1970s than at any point in the post-war era yet this scarcely produced a society at ease with itself.

Activists were frustrated by the failure of the Labour governments and Labour parliamentarians to enact the party's 1974 manifesto commitment to 'bring about a fundamental and irreversible shift in the balance of power and wealth in favour of working people and their families';[10] the performance of the Wilson-Callaghan governments contrasted unfavourably with the myth of Attlee's heroic achievements. There was an increasing appetite among the party membership 'to participate in a meaningful way in Labour party decision-making. They wanted their elected representatives to be accountable.'[11] A group of influential left-wing economists, principally Stuart Holland, advocated an alternative strategy attacking Crosland's complacency about British capitalism and his belief that 'unfettered market relations' had been replaced by a post-war economy humanised through state intervention.[12] In Holland's view, 'the rise of 'managerial' capitalism has not diluted the power of capitalism as a mode of production'.[13]

Labour's relationship with the unions, which had once been an asset underpinning the party's claim to be a more effective manager of the economy, had by the late 1970s become a liability. Commentators questioned why the country was becoming 'ungovernable', given the failure of the Heath Government to carry through industrial relations reforms. According to Healey, the Labour leadership 'had come to depend on the trade union block vote for protection against extremism in the constituencies…Again and again in the critical years after the 1979 election, incoherence or incompetence in the trade union leadership led us to disaster.'[14] The Callaghan Government fought in vain to make British corporatism function efficiently, but the necessary pay curbs and spending restraints led inevitably to the Winter of Discontent, paving the way for Thatcherism which undermined the social democratic settlement. In the 'cultural revolution' that swept through the party after 1979, Labour came close to extinction as a viable party of government.

It was the defectors to the breakaway Social Democratic Party (SDP) who throughout the period after 1981 were portrayed as the most reliable custodians of Crosland's legacy. As British politics became polarised between Bennism and Thatcherite individualism, Crosland's vision inherited from Hobhouse and Tawney, that equality and liberty were interdependent, came under direct challenge: Thatcherism insisted that liberty should always take precedence over equality and that the state should be rolled back.[15] The British Left countered that equality was the pre-eminent value requiring the assertion of collectivism against the market; Crosland as the revisionist *par excellence* had insisted that equality and liberty were inseparable.[16] The organisational and strategic disintegration of social democracy within the Labour party by 1983 was, nonetheless, to have profound implications for the British Left.

Modernisation under Neil Kinnock and John Smith: 1984– 94

By the late 1980s, however, Crosland's philosophy experienced a revival through Labour's Policy Review launched following its third consecutive defeat. The Policy Review's intellectual underpinning came from the concept of 'positive freedom' discussed in Chapter Four,[17] entailing an activist state that widened access to opportunity, security and welfare. Labour's then Deputy Leader, Roy Hattersley, produced a revisionist tract to inspire the next phase of party modernisation, entitled *Choose Freedom* drawing on Crosland's synthesis of equality and liberty. Hattersley claimed: 'Labour has increasingly allowed itself to be caricatured as the 'we know best party' when we are (or ought to be) the 'we will make you free party'.'[18] The closing lines of the book were taken from a conversation between Crosland and Hattersley, a week before Crosland's death: 'Socialism is all about the pursuit of equality and the protection of freedom – in the knowledge that until we are truly equal we will not be truly free.' The final Policy Review report signalled Labour's attempt to recapture revisionist principles:

> We have, of course, been caricatured as the party that seeks to deny power and choice to the individual and

gather all authority to the state. The reality has always been different. To us the state is an instrument, no more, no less: a means, not an end. Collective action has always been designed to create opportunities and advance the freedom of the individual and, cumulatively, of the whole community.[19]

The Policy Review encouraged a 'second wave' of revisionism culminating eventually in Labour's 1997 victory.[20] The party embarked on a decade long process of revising its ideology and programme, having stared into the abyss in 1983. Attention focused on Kinnock's struggle to rid the party of far left entryism. He engineered significant departures from policies that Labour had adopted after 1980, reversing the commitment to withdrawal from the European Community, to unilateral nuclear disarmament, and to sweeping state intervention in the economy. The more demanding task was devising alternative governing principles following the collapse of the Keynesian consensus while attuning the Labour party to the realities of market liberalism, privatisation and the weakening of union power that had occurred after 1979. Labour embraced the new constitutional agenda including devolution to Wales and Scotland, House of Lords reform, freedom of information legislation, and reform of the UK electoral system. Nonetheless, the party had no convincing answer to the massive rise in unemployment and the unprecedented growth of inequality during the 1980s; traditional working-class Labour supporters increasingly accepted that 'there was no alternative' to Thatcherism. These voters often responded enthusiastically to the Thatcher Government's message of individual aspiration and rising prosperity, symbolised by the popularity of council house sales: in the 1987 election, for example, the Conservatives finished 18 per cent ahead of Labour among manual 'C2' workers in Southern England.

Thatcherism faltered in the wake of its third victory. Broad public antipathy to the Poll Tax and an increasingly flawed leadership style contributed to Margaret Thatcher's removal from office in November 1990. Moreover, a prolonged recession exposed the hollowness of her Chancellor, Nigel Lawson's claim to have brought on a British 'economic miracle'. Catastrophically, Labour still lost the 1992 election to the relatively inexperienced John Major. Polls showed deep mistrust of the Labour leadership, particularly on economic competence and tax. Labour's defeat underlined the precarious nature of the modernisation project. Blame was heaped on John Smith's 'Shadow Budget' which had promised an increase in the value of the state pension and child benefit, financed by a rise in National Insurance. Bryan Gould, a prominent and highly effective member of the Labour Shadow Cabinet, wrote that the party's tax proposals threatened 'to place a cap on the aspirations of those voters, particularly in the south of England, who had found Mrs Thatcher's appeal so irresistible precisely because she offered them new horizons'.[21] As a consequence, Smith who defeated Gould to succeed Kinnock in 1992 launched the Social Justice Commission with a mandate to review the party's social policy; the aim was to provide, 'a comprehensive assessment and re-appraisal of the social condition of our nation'.[22]

Despite successive defeats, the rapid erosion of the manual working-class, and Labour's retreat into its traditional 'heartlands', there had been countervailing structural changes since the 1980s which flowed definitively in the party's favour. The end of the cold war and imminent collapse of the Soviet Union aided Labour's modernisation. The potential for right-wing scaremongering about the Left's willingness to stand up to Communism was markedly reduced; the fall of Communism discredited traditional demands for a centrally planned economy. The European social model became the object of admiration and emulation on the British Left, rather than suspicion and disdain. Until then, Labour undertook almost no analysis of what European integration meant for the party's focus on Westminster politics. Labour benefited from the growing prominence of 'post-materialist' causes including environmentalism, feminism, multiculturalism and gay rights championed by revisionists in the 1960s. Many sympathisers from the generation of university educated radicals remained outside party politics; those who had been drawn into Labour during the 'cultural revolution' were amenable to the project of Left modernisation articulated in journals such as *Marxism Today*. New progressive movements emerged in opposition to Thatcherism demanding constitutional reform, including Charter 88, the campaign for Fair Votes, and the Scottish Constitutional Convention. Their programmes were largely incorporated by Smith into Labour party policy following his election as leader.

Nevertheless, Labour's modernisation according to some commentators was not an updating of the social democratic tradition; it was a defensive accommodation with the politics of Thatcherism.[23] Gould, who eventually departed British politics, insisted: 'The position taken by Labour's leaders in the late 1980s and into the 1990s was a position of surrender...an acknowledgement that really we had lost the argument, that a Thatcherite agenda had been established to which we could only accommodate, [one that we] couldn't change.'[24]

Colin Hay claimed that through the Policy Review under Kinnock and Smith, Labour severed its ties with post-war social democracy, internalising the ideological dominance of globalisation and free markets while abandoning the goal of a developmental state; the aim of this 'preference-accommodating' strategy was to win back lost voters overcoming the electorate's fear of Labour by endorsing the agenda of the Thatcher governments, despite structural contradictions in the New Right's political economy. Similarly, Richard Heffernan states that New Labour's commitment to modernisation entailed 'a wholesale re-evaluation of past Labour practice'.[25] What emerged was a definitively 'post-Croslandite' agenda: whereas Crosland argued that markets and capitalism had to be constrained by government intervention, Blair's party allowed the market to dominate state and society. Using a 'spatial model of ideological comparison', Heffernan concludes that 'Blair stands far closer to Margaret Thatcher than he does to Tony Crosland'; Crosland's revisionism was about re-casting Labour's identity to secure 'age-old' Labour objectives, whereas New Labour redefined the party's ends away from equality.[26]

Other authors emphasised continuities: post-war politicians from Attlee to Crosland were mostly pragmatic, accepting that social justice would be achieved through a mixed economy with the private sector made fairer by state intervention.[27] The 1989 Policy Review drew heavily on the doctrine of post-war social democracy emphasising the indivisible relationship between equality and liberty:

> It is in order to provide the largest number of real choices for the largest number of people that socialists believe in the redistribution of wealth and the power that goes with it. For the sum of freedom within a society is bound to be increased as the resources, which now enable the very rich to exercise an infinity of choices, are used to enable the rest of society to choose the basic necessities of life.[28]

Martin Smith has emphasised that substantive differences between the Conservatives and the Labour party over the relationship between the market and the state were still in place at the end of the Policy Review process. Labour's shift to the right after 1983 was not an accommodation with Thatcherism; it marked a return to the policies of the post-war settlement, acknowledging the constraints imposed by the international economy and the equivocal success of state intervention after 1945 (Smith, 1994). This development paved the way for New Labour under Blair and Brown. New Labour is said to have abandoned the primacy of equality as the goal of social democracy; but as Chapter Three demonstrated, even the revisionists struggled to define their galitarian commitment. They acknowledged 'equality of opportunity is not enough', but accepted that there were limits to how far those on high incomes would accept punitive tax rises; growth was central to any viable strategy of redistribution in mature capitalist democracies. Moreover, in emphasising differences over equality, Heffernan underplays a source of affinity between

Crosland and Blair, namely the importance of personal freedom and individualism in a mass consumption society. New Labour went further than the revisionists of the 1950s and 1960s in accepting the virtues of markets, but Crosland acknowledged that the profit motive was necessary for individual liberty and sought the removal of all unnecessary legislative restraints on freedom. The spatial model that Heffernan employs reduces ideological change to particular 'Left/Right' dimensions, rather than examining the complex and fluid conceptual structures underpinning the historical development of ideas in British politics.[29] The world that Blair confronted in the 1990s was fundamentally altered from the post-war economy and society that was the backdrop to Crosland's *Future of Socialism*; Left and Right are not fixed ideological categories but remain socially and politically malleable.

Labour after Crosland: from 'New' to 'Blue' to 'One Nation' Labour

Crosland and New Labour

Nevertheless, despite Crosland's influence within the party, under New Labour his legacy was frequently ignored. Whereas a teleological interpretation would conceive Crosland as the progenitor of New Labour, the relationship between the modernised Labour party and Crosland is ambiguous and contested. New Labour was the product of several 'critical junctures': a response to Conservative electoral domination; acknowledging the perceived efficiency of modernised capitalism and globalisation; and in the light of this, the necessity of discarding outdated shibboleths.[30] New Labour stimulated the debate about the third way for social democracy in an era of globalisation, influenced by New Times gurus including the social theorist, Anthony Giddens, and the German sociologist, Ulrich Beck. They dismissed as old-fashioned 'tax and spend' Keynesianism and statist social democratic institutions, emphasising the need to embrace the global knowledge economy and markets. The rejection

213

of Crosland's strategy compelled New Labour, in their view, to reinvent social democracy, abandoning the belief that state, society and the economy should be modernised by government intervention. The emphasis on devolution, constitutional change, and reform of public services led to new developments, not least the weakening of the unitary British state, perceived in the 1940s as the central agent of socialist transformation.[31] The fascination of these thinkers with New Times, the emergence of the 'risk society', and the service-based economy centred on the 'thin air' of knowledge production rather than industry distanced New Labour from its social democratic heritage. New Times thinkers discarded Crosland's legacy, dismissing the efficacy of traditional models of social democratic governance and economic management.

If New Labour's record in government after 1997 is scrutinised, however, the divergence with revisionism is less clear-cut. The Blair and Brown governments achieved an expansion of public spending more ambitious than any previous Labour government, aided by the rapidly growing economy.[32] Blair and Brown were reluctant to adopt the language of egalitarian reform drawn from revisionist social democracy, eschewing the discourse of equality.[33] Whereas Kinnock and Smith sought to move Labour towards the centre-ground by discarding unpopular policies and reaching an accommodation with markets, Blair and Brown embraced the market wholeheartedly.[34] New Labour's aim was to transform the party into an election-winning machine. Labour had to come to terms with a new electoral landscape in which traditional class identities and allegiances were declining in the face of structural change. Thatcherism had reshaped British society after 1979; the party had to address the implications of the Conservative Government's legacy without abandoning Labour's age-old commitment to social justice. This legacy included the growth of tax resistance, increasing resentment towards welfare recipients, alongside the decline of the labour movement pointing towards the fracturing of social democracy and the halting of Labour's 'forward march'.[35] The collectivist institutions of the post-1945 settlement from Keynesian demand management to nationalisation could not be recreated in the 1990s. No wonder as one historian presciently observed: 'The ghosts and collective memory of Labour party history rest heavily on the shoulders and social democratic legitimacy of the modernisers of New Labour.'[36]

Unlike the Attlee governments which drew on Beveridge and Keynes, New Labour had no pre-conceived centre-left settlement on which to build. In 1945, Labour could enact the programme developed by the wartime coalition in favour of the welfare state, the National Health Service, alongside the 1944 Education Act.[37] The post-war agenda of social security was implemented in an age when the labour movement was a significant force in British society. By the 1990s, confidence in the ideology of state intervention and planning had evaporated; membership of the party and the trade unions was in rapid decline. Facing these constraints, Labour sought to fashion a political vehicle capable of winning power. New Labour's mission was to overcome the electoral dominance the Conservative party enjoyed in British politics after the First World War. The twentieth century had been a Conservative century; if Labour did not radically overhaul its image and appeal, the same fate awaited the party in the twenty-first century.

New Labour's third way was tailored to post-industrial Britain. The Labour governments enabled Britain to escape the legacy of relative decline that dominated political debate from the 1950s to the 1990s.[38] Blair and Brown stressed the importance of economic competitiveness in a globalised economy, achieved through a social investment state promoting human capital and innovation. The aim was to achieve what Marxists prophesied was impossible under capitalism: to reconcile economic efficiency with social justice. New Labour sought to reinvent Britain as a pioneer of scientific and creative innovation within a dynamic, service-based economy. The UK's exposure to the financial crisis undermined this goal: the service sector in practice meant greater reliance on financial services as a source of employment and national income. In the late 1940s, British industry (notably manufacturing, raw materials and utilities) comprised 41 per cent of GDP; by 2013 it was 14 per cent; services had increased from 46 to 79 per cent while financial services accounted for 10 per cent of GDP by 2009.[39] The debate about British capitalism's virtues examined 60 years previously in *The Future of Socialism* resurfaced in the wake of the crash.

The Blair and Brown governments combined Thatcherism's emphasis on competitive markets with the aim of a fairer, more inclusive society. New Labour combined policy innovation and radicalism on the one hand with orthodoxy and deference to the political establishment on the other; in this respect the post-1997 governments were remarkably similar to the Attlee years. New Labour achieved the historic goal of full employment that defined the 'golden age' of Keynesianism from 1945 to 1973; but the Blair–Brown governments were committed to a conventional monetary policy, notably low inflation and low interest rates. After 1997, a statutory minimum wage was enacted to protect the low paid; on the other hand, reform of employment regulation and industrial relations legislation was modest; there was a determination to preserve labour market flexibility. New Labour put forward ambitious policies to eliminate child poverty raising family incomes and promoting employment participation; however, a regime of 'conditionality' was imposed on the long-term unemployed; so-called 'problem families' were targeted as the rights and responsibilities of the welfare contract were re-written. There was a willingness to address the structural causes of crime and disorder, but the Blair–Brown years witnessed a cumulative increase in the prison population leading to the growing criminalisation of young people. New Labour introduced a multitude of liberal reforms including an equal age of consent for gay people and enforcement of equal pay for women; however, civil liberties were jeopardised by the rise of the surveillance and security state following the 9/11 attacks. Blair was committed to Britain playing a leading role in the European Union (EU) signing up to the principle of a single currency; yet in foreign affairs, New Labour strengthened

Britain's alignment with the United States through military intervention in Afghanistan and Iraq.

New Labour was determined to draw a line under the electoral and political defeats that bedevilled post-war social democracy. Only in 1945 and 1966 had Labour secured decisive majorities. Labour governments in 1947, 1949, 1967 and 1976 were derailed by economic and financial crises destroying their reputation for economic competence (Gamble, 2003). The growth of an embittered industrial relations climate eroded the unity and strength of the labour movement. The party was beset by acrimonious disagreement between 'revisionists' and 'fundamentalists', which Wilson's astute party management skills only temporarily suspended in the mid-1960s. The party after 1951 had been paralysed by intellectual sterility and ideological vacuity, the only basis on which Labour would remain united. The Attlee governments had been the apotheosis of socialist achievement but ran out of steam. No alternative social democratic strategy emerged other than Crosland's revisionism. New Labour preferred to bury the party's unpromising past, allowing only for deferential paeans of praise to the long forgotten Attlee years.

Roy Hattersley subsequently claimed Blair and Brown had forsaken the egalitarian politics of Crosland's era. New Labour's legacy was growing income inequality: a failure to reverse the extreme wealth and income divide emerging under the Thatcher governments. As Gaitskell's biographer Brian Brivati attests, Blair cynically abandoned Labour's commitment to equality, eschewing traditional social democratic beliefs. The modernisers were uncomfortable with Gaitskell and Crosland whose old-style egalitarianism meant 'levelling-down' alongside toxic policies of redistribution. New Labour was determined to discard the electoral millstone of Old Labour: the modernisers' heirs were consigned to the 'dustbin of history' so desperate was New Labour to proclaim the end of 'tax and spend' socialism. In Blair's campaign to rewrite Clause 4, Martin Francis noted 'one figure was conspicuous by his absence: that of Anthony Crosland'.[40] As a consequence, the debate about a third way for the Left entailed little engagement with revisionism. The world was being redefined by disruptive forces: globalisation, liberalisation and financialisation beyond the comprehension of post-war social democracy.[41]

This view of an irreconcilable divide between Old and New Labour is, nonetheless, questionable. It reinforces the demarcation between Old and New Labour which was to the modernisers' advantage, implying that New Labour was poles apart from the traditional party in its aims and values. This claim is disputed regardless of the rhetoric of New Labour politicians. There was already an ideological transition underway in British politics before Margaret Thatcher's victory. Hugh Pemberton has shown how the response of the Callaghan Government to the crises of the 1970s anticipated New Labour's key preoccupations. The Prime Minister sought to emphasise civic duties alongside equal citizenship, tackling producer interests in the public sector while devising initiatives to make social security benefits conditional on actively seeking employment.[42] His speech at Ruskin College in October 1976 underlined the importance of rigour in school standards, addressing the concerns of aspirational parents about quality in public services. Labour's emphasis on equality and education in the 1960s shifted to focusing on preparing young people for the world of work.[43] Moreover, Donoughue recalls that Callaghan and Healey assumed the Keynesian model of demand management was in serious difficulty by the mid-1970s. It was Callaghan who pointedly told the 1976 conference that governments were no longer able to spend their way out of recession and maintain full employment:[44]

The cosy world we were told would go on forever, where full employment would be guaranteed by a stroke of the Chancellor's pen, cutting taxes, deficit spending – that sort of cosy world is gone... Now we must get back to fundamentals. First, overcoming unemployment now unambiguously depends on our labour costs being at least comparable with those of our major competitors. Second, we can only become competitive by having the right kind of investment at

the right kind of level, and by significantly improving
the productivity both of labour and capital.

British social democracy was undergoing a turbulent shift
before Blair and Brown arrived on the political scene. Crosland
advised a conference of local authority leaders in 1975 that 'the
party's over'; public expenditure would be tightly controlled,
falling as a proportion of national income.[45] By acceding
to the IMF loan in 1976 after the oil price shocks and the
collapse of confidence in sterling, the Labour Government
chose integration into the world economic system rather than
a siege economy: a socialist commonwealth 'in one country'.[46]
Callaghan's 1976 speech did not claim that the state no longer
had any role to play in the economy; governments would
continue to take action against unemployment, as they did
under Brown in the late 1990s.[47] It was the post-war strategy
of Keynesian demand management and the commitment
to maintaining full employment through countercyclical
government spending that was no longer viable.[48]

The Labour governments after 1997 were not as far removed
from the Attlee and Wilson administrations in politics and
policy as is often assumed. Having initially accepted the
spending limits imposed by their Conservative predecessors,
New Labour ministers dramatically increased public
expenditure arresting the declining quality of public services.[49]
They emphasised the importance of access to public provision
and the contribution of public services to a civilised society.
The post-1997 governments addressed child and pensioner
poverty through targeted increases in benefits and tax credits.
The aim was to narrow the gap between the bottom and
middle of the distribution; this strategy was flawed, however:
income inequality continued to rise as top incomes soared.
Nonetheless, the sincerity of the government's intentions
is hard to doubt. There are continuities between 'Old' and
'New' Labour governments. The New Labour administrations
removed legislative restraints on freedom, creating an equal
age of consent and incorporating the European Convention
on Human Rights into UK law; Britain became more socially

liberal. Blair's support for the Atlantic Alliance marks a point of connection with Old Labour although it cannot be assumed that Attlee or Wilson would have supported President Bush in pursuing the global 'war on terror', invading Iraq in 2003 (after all, Wilson avoided committing British troops in Vietnam). In fact, all Labour Prime Ministers since 1945 have ascribed importance to the special relationship. The divergence between Old and New Labour is not as stark as it initially appears.[50] The similarities are, in many ways, striking.

The assumption that Crosland would have shunned the policies adopted by modernisers following the election defeats of the 1980s and 1990s is problematic. Crosland sought to address inequalities aggravating the 'distance factors' between social classes. Unlike New Labour, he recognised the importance of an ethical critique of the market, according as much importance to human dignity as the narrow pursuit of material wealth. Tawney, a decisive influence on Crosland, developed the concept of ethical socialism emphasising the importance of the moral economy. E.P. Thompson's influential analysis of industrialisation similarly criticised the excesses of market capitalism.[51] Gaitskell claimed 'the pursuit of material wealth by and for itself' was 'empty and barren' echoing the New Liberals such as Green and Hobhouse; Labour must eschew the 'selfish, acquisitive doctrines of capitalism' building a 'socialist community based on fellowship, co-operation and service'.[52] In the light of this, other commentators have concluded: 'New Labour threw out the baby with the bathwater. It got rid of all sorts of stupidities like Clause 4, but we lost the Crosland view that socialism is about equality.'[53] There was a marked contrast between New Labour's third way and the revisionist social democracy of the post-1945 era. New Labour was circumspect about how far national governments could reverse economic inequalities; it was enthusiastic about the imperatives of wealth creation accepting the absolute dominance of market forces.

We cannot know exactly what Crosland would make of these developments. Revisionism acknowledged the reality of a changing economy and society, while recognising that 'means' have to adapt as the world is altered. The scale of the structural changes underway in Britain by the late 1980s and early 1990s makes it inconceivable that a public intellectual of Crosland's stature would have resorted to passively defending the post-war settlement. Social democracy cannot succeed by searching for 'a better yesterday' as Ralph Darendorf once described its traditional adherents.[54] To claim Crosland as a New Labour moderniser before his time is misleading; it is similarly wrong to assume that he would have condemned all of New Labour's strategies as unprincipled or expedient.[55] Those familiar with Crosland's thinking such as Dick Leonard question how far New Labour repudiated the revisionist legacy.[56] On taxation, for example, Crosland in the 1950s favoured a standard income tax rate of 35 per cent and a higher rate of 83 per cent; as a practising politician, however, 'he would have appreciated the enormous pressure on Tony Blair – in the light of the 1992 election defeat – to pledge not to increase the 40 per cent maximum rate bequeathed by the Tories'.[57] Crosland might have acknowledged the political necessity of Brown's 'stealth taxes' given the growth of tax resistance among voters; and he would probably have admired Brown's efforts to target resources on the least advantaged. New Labour's record 'ranked well against most of Crosland's criteria for building a socialist society'.[58]

Crosland and Blue Labour

The economic crisis ending 13 years of Labour rule has been judged to comprehensively invalidate Crosland's analysis. John Gray insists: 'Crosland's thinking is no longer applicable'; it assumes robust growth in economies which had been crippled by the financial crash.[59] The goal of an egalitarian society constructed through the surplus generated from dynamic capitalist markets was destroyed: western economies have entered a phase of low growth, secular stagnation and rising inequality. The social democracy that flourished in Britain after 1945 was underpinned by rising employment and living standards accompanied by redistribution towards the needy.

New Labour's demise in the wake of the financial crash has initiated a new and distinctive strand of political thought in the party: 'Blue' Labour.[60]

Blue Labour is noticeably eclectic, drawing on the tradition of syndicalism, alongside the guild socialism of G.D.H. Cole and Harold Laski. Equally important has been the emphasis of ethical socialism on community, fellowship and the co-operative spirit. That said, Blue Labour can evidently be located in the party's 'Tory-socialist' tradition depicted as:

> The many typical politicians who played a central role in the movement combining left-wing and right-wing values in a consistent and coherent fashion, championing their class and socialism on the one hand along with class collaboration, patriotism, imperialism, and authoritarianism on the other. In fact, this thread runs through Labour history from Edwardians like Will Thorne to interwar figures such as Ernest Bevin, to James Callaghan and George Brown in the post-1945 generation and to more recent leaders including David Blunkett, John Reid and Hazel Blears who have upheld the working-class authoritarian tradition as distinct from the movement's liberal tradition.[61]

Pugh's formulation alludes to a divide between the party's authoritarian wing and its liberal tradition, with revisionists in the 1950s and 1960s encamped on the libertarian side of British politics. The tension between these traditions had led to numerous 'ideological and cultural divisions within the movement' concerning the role of religion in schools, reforms to restrict the sale of alcohol on licensed premises, regulation of gambling, as well as the perennial issues of free trade and national defence; the 'Tory-Socialists' argued for conscription in the build up to the First World War given widespread fears of German invasion, anathema to the Labour–Liberal leadership.[62] Nonetheless, whether a firm demarcation between the authoritarian and liberal traditions existed throughout the twentieth century is less clear. David Lipsey attests that despite his commitment to the permissive society, Crosland would have been sympathetic to Blue Labour's concerns identified with his working-class constituents in Grimsby.[63]

The Blue Labour agenda represents a departure from orthodox thinking in the light of the crisis engendered by recent electoral defeats. In charting a new vision for socialism, Blue Labour acknowledged Crosland's imprint on the political thought of the party but insisted that it was New Labour's similarity to revisionism that explained the party's paralysis. As one commentator remarked:

> Critics of Labour's time in government are often heard describing new Labour as Croslandite, and they don't mean it as a compliment. The argument goes that the 1997–2010 government embodied three failings that came straight from Tony Crosland: the pursuit of equality as a statistical abstraction over meaning and relationships in the lives people really live; a belief that the market should largely be left to its own devices; and the proposition that the main engine of egalitarian politics is redistribution through tax and spending.[64]

It is believed that New Labour sought to reform state and society through top-down bureaucratic institutions, using the levers of government to restructure the welfare system and public services. Labour was an uneasy marriage between an ethical socialist and co-operative vision on the one hand, and the Fabian tradition of officious, overbearing management on the other.[65] The predominance of centralised Fabianism undermined the success of post-war socialism according to Blue Labour, explaining the unfulfilled premierships of Attlee, Wilson, Blair and Brown. The belief that the state should act to promote the public good while the market was left to its own devices led inevitably to rising inequality, despite increasing public expenditure and a structural deficit by the time of the crash. The rate of public investment was barely sustainable given that the financial system was vulnerable to severe shocks: 'The crash of 2008 is the defining moment for articulating the limits of both state and market approaches.'[66] New Labour's strategy was flawed, just as the Attlee and Wilson governments mistakenly combined economic orthodoxy with insipid government interventionism.

Blue Labour's critique of the revisionist legacy appears intellectually persuasive. The argument that post-war egalitarianism was bedevilled by middle-class liberal intellectuals whose abstract political theories distanced the party from the realities and lived experiences of British working-class life is compelling. Crosland's associate, Michael Young, had made this point in the 1950s, welcoming the revisionist's emphasis on an open society embracing the new middle class, but voicing concern that Labour should not lose its connection with traditional working-class communities.[67] The influence of logical positivism on the revisionists was regarded as unhelpful, promoting empirical rationalism over the 'common-sense' instincts and sentiments of families, workplaces and neighbourhoods. Maurice Glasman, one of Blue Labour's renowned thinkers, is a 'virtue-theorist' vehemently hostile to liberalism.[68] The imposition of universal liberal values such as equality and justice through state institutions, formal rules and bureaucratic procedures makes it less likely that communities will speak to one another advancing the common good.[69] Revisionism imposes a separation between ethical and moral values, the 'ends' of politics; and institutional and policy changes, the 'means' required to bring the ends about; as a result, Crosland never developed a vision which secured the allegiance of citizens connecting egalitarian policies with the values of society at large.[70]

Blue Labour attacked the legacy of the post-war Fabian managerial state, reclaiming the 'exiled traditions' of nineteenth century co-operation, mutual aid and ethical socialism.[71] The success of Attlee's ministers in implementing the 1945 manifesto embedded the primacy of the central state in the political thought of the British Left.[72] For Blue Labour, the party's strategy for social reform was too narrow, wedded to the orthodox twentieth-century liberalism of Keynes and T. H. Marshall. Blue Labour exhibited 'a deep antipathy towards liberalism' dominating all the mainstream parties in British politics.[73] It rejected New Labour's synthesis of 'social with economic liberalisation under the joint aegis of the central bureaucratic state and the global free market'.[74]

The social revolution of the 1960s promoted emancipation under the guise of freedom; the economic revolution of the 1980s created new forms of consumerism and acquisitive materialism.[75] The global integration of the economy encouraged 'a post-national cosmopolitanism which tended to valorise novelty, the global and change over the ordinary, the local and belonging'.[76] Commodification in which workers are treated as material objects to be bought and sold on the market was actively encouraged, reflecting the unprecedented decline of the labour movement and falling trade union density. The labour market flexibility promoted by the Thatcher governments did enable the achievement of full employment under New Labour, but at the price of degrading human capital: many individuals were working beneath their productive potential. Guild Socialism understood work as a social good only where individuals had control over the productive process; Blue Labour promotes workers' guilds and industrial democracy giving employees additional decision-making power.[77] In so doing, Blue Labour articulates a moral economy akin to guild socialism: 'a politics of the common good...through civic institutions that promote virtue rather than vice'.[78]

In contrast, contemporary liberalism refuses to confront financial capitalism and the dominance of global markets.[79] New Labour accepts acquisitive consumerism and global market forces as a fact of life: there is no attempt to harness institutions and traditions to counter the ascendancy of markets. Liberals are obsessed with abstract reforms that nominally set individuals free, rather than practical action that promotes the public interest.[80] The British Left of the 1960s and 1970s alongside New Labour in the 1990s focused on emancipation rather than solidarity.[81] While the 1945 settlement was undermined by the crisis of national identity and the collapse of corporatism, the post-1979 consensus was threatened by rising inequality; both arose from the deficiencies of twentieth-century liberalism.[82] British identity fractured in the face of a declining ethic of nationhood and growing individualism; economic inequality attenuated the structural divisions between classes. Liberalism and the permissive society further destabilised working-class communities making them vulnerable to the economic dislocation of the 1980s and 1990s while bequeathing a legacy of polarisation and social breakdown.[83] The dominant strain of liberalism governing all the major parties viewed individuals as self-interested and atomistic: as unable to see beyond their immediate desires.[84]

Blue Labour appeals to 'the radical tradition of British romanticism' with its roots in High Toryism and the co-operative movement rejecting the legacy of liberalism.[85] It recaptures the inner force of early socialism drawing on: 'A long line of working-class Toryism: a rollicking, rambunctious, fiercely patriotic and earthy tradition, at odds both with the preachy nonconformist conscience that saturated the culture of provincial liberalism and with the patronising, 'we-know-best' preconceptions of metropolitan intellectuals.'[86]

Liberalism can never provide an answer to 'Britain's most entrenched problems: its imbalanced economy, its atomised society, its lack of common identity'.[87] Blue Labour offers a comprehensive critique of New Labour's legacy in office; Blair and Brown's indifference to the insecurities generated by globalisation and their complacency towards the alienation experienced by working-class voters were their Achilles heel.[88] Blue Labour echoes the romanticism which became influential in European socialism before the First World War, especially in Germany. This view of socialism was nationalistic emphasising, 'a *Gemeinschaft*, a rebirth of the nation...a vague mystical enthusiasm for leadership and comradeship, expressed opposition to rationalism and "bourgeois liberalism".'[89]

Through its excoriating critique, Blue Labour's analysis emphasises the extent of Crosland's impact on the Labour party, underlining the destructive influence of liberalism on British social democracy. Frank Field bemoans the waging of a liberal 'culture war' against his working-class constituents.

Blue-collar working-class electors are hostile to Labour's view of society: they no longer perceive the party as proud of Britain, willing to defend its borders by controlling immigration while promoting a welfare state where rights have to be earned.[90] Blue Labour emphasises that working-class traditions, cultures and institutions which earned people's respect ought to be nurtured. In its former radical strongholds in Northern England and Scotland, the liberal tradition is retreating.[91] Britain's heritage of political liberalism cannot address the vexed politics of territory, identity and power. The Left is losing elections across Europe not only because it lacks economic credibility, but it has so little to say about national identity. Working-class voters are troubled by the erosion of national borders and allegiances: uneasiness about ethnic and cultural diversity is rising.[92] In Mair's words, mainstream centre-left parties are 'disconnected from the wider society'.[93] To map a path back to power, social democratic parties have to emphasise the collective attachments that give meaning to citizen's lives in a world of insecurity.[94] In particular, national identities mitigate the economic divisions created by market liberalism, revitalising support for redistributive programmes that promote social justice.[95]

The interpretation of British socialism offered by Blue Labour and its appraisal of Croslandite social democracy has enlivened debate: Blue Labour offers 'a thought-provoking yet controversial critique of the economic and cultural liberalism within the Labour elite'.[96] Yet Blue Labour's position is hardly flawless. The attack on New Labour's bureaucratic centralism is noteworthy: the claim that localism is always the answer to political disengagement and declining confidence in public services, a position shared with the authors of New Labour's *Purple Book*, remains controversial.[97] Moreover, Blue Labour never confronts the dilemma that all democratically elected politicians face in managing the state: governments may divest themselves of responsibility by giving managerial and financial autonomy to local institutions, but ministers in Whitehall get blamed when things go wrong. Citizens remain uneasy about the growth of 'postcode lotteries', excessive local variation and inequality in service standards, especially in sensitive arenas such as the National Health Service.[98]

At the same time, where Crosland looked to Sweden, Blue Labour emulates Germany with its tradition of workers' councils, representation on company boards and regional banking overseen by a federal political system built on subsidiarity. Yet Germany's economic performance since the 1990s has not been unequivocally successful; inequality has been growing as rising employment participation is accompanied by declining real wages.[99] The German banking system was affected by the 2008 crisis, not only financial institutions in the Anglo-Liberal countries. There is the question of whether German institutions could be exported to the United Kingdom given the divergent legacies of the two countries. New Labour struggled in vain to incorporate structural reforms from the Nordic welfare states after 1997.

Blue Labour has too little to say about how national communities ought to work together in the modern world.[100] As David Runciman notes, Blue Labour is vulnerable to the charge of parochialism and insularity levelled at Crosland: Britain's relationship with the European Union and the rest of the world is barely considered. Another point relates to the ethic of fellowship and fraternity in British socialism. Crosland did not denigrate the Christian socialist tradition; he wrote in *The Future of Socialism*:

> The aims of the Christian socialist bore a close resemblance to those of Owenism, though of course the inspiration was different – in the one case a Benthamite belief in universal happiness, in the other a concern with Christian ethics. But for both the essential evil was the competitive pursuit of private gain, and the objective of a co-operative society of communal ownership, in which mutual love and brotherhood would replace the selfish antagonisms inevitably bred by competitive capitalism.[101]

Despite the attractive language of Christian socialism, revisionists had doubts about the efficacy of a 'co-operative social purpose'. Christian socialism emphasised kinship and mutual association but Crosland was unenthusiastic about giving primacy to community life. His central purpose in *The Future of Socialism* was to highlight the ethical value of equality rather than nationalisation. Crosland feared that in an age of individualism, 'an excess of community spirit led to busy bodying invasions of privacy and personal freedom'.[102] Moreover, as Chapter Three demonstrated, the revisionists could not foresee how communitarian values might be translated into practical political action, foreshadowing difficulties confronting New Labour in the 1990s.[103] Having emphasised that 'by the strength of our common endeavour we achieve more than we achieve alone', Blair's ministers struggled to give those values expression in government policy. After abandoning the 'old' Clause 4 in 1995, they discarded doctrine altogether. Community regeneration was an area of particular weakness under New Labour; resources were squandered, creating ineffective public 'quangos' with too little grassroots involvement.[104] New concerns arose about the extent of ethnic and religious conflict in communities, amid fears that Britain was 'sleep-walking towards segregation'. Blue Labour wants to revive the ethic of fellowship and belonging but struggles to spell out how this should be achieved.

Blue Labour's definition of liberalism and its influence on British politics since the Second World War is contested. The discussion of the radical tradition in Chapter Four highlighted the varied nature of liberalism. The parliamentarian David Lammy tells us:

> Labour is not a liberal party. Unlike the Liberal Democrats, we do not see people simply as free-floating individuals. Our politics is not orientated towards an unrealisable version of freedom where we can each do whatever we please. Instead Labour politics is built on the idea that people are social beings, dependent on one another.[105]

Blue Labour is right to emphasise that certain aspects of political liberalism are not well equipped to deal with small 'c' conservatism in British national life, especially anxiety about immigration and national identity. Lammy aims to reposition the Liberal Democrats as pivotal to the centre-right, free market 'Orange Book coalition' negotiated with the Conservative party in 2010. However, his argument involves a questionable interpretation of the Liberal tradition, failing to address liberalism's development in the late nineteenth century; the New Liberalism explicitly acknowledged the limitations of atomistic individualism while recognising the social nature of individuals and their mutual dependence on one another: 'liberalism relies quite heavily on certain moral norms, especially tolerance and responsibility'.[106] Positive freedom entails active intervention by the state to regulate the economy and secure equal access to public provision. As Mill emphasised in his later writings:

> The prophet of social liberalism is rightly seen as the champion of individual freedom. But the freedom he prized was not freedom to accumulate or exploit, but freedom to grow through arduous practice in civil associations and local bodies, and in so doing to contribute to the worth of society.[107]

Of course, a strain of radical liberalism emerged in the late twentieth century in the United States and Britain that did contest the role of collectivism, urging the rolling back of the state: market liberalism, referred to ubiquitously as 'neo-liberalism'.[108] But market liberalism is a strand in a diverse political tradition: it is misleading to assume a 'false dichotomy' between the liberal and social democratic traditions; in fact 'the social democratic and liberal traditions substantially overlap'.[109] The New Liberalism retained an organic conception of the common good expressed in the work of Green and Hobhouse; ethical socialism emphasised the importance of community and fraternity over a central bureaucratic state.[110] Although Glasman is determined to assail liberalism as the enemy of a revived ethical socialism, there are affinities between liberalism and Blue Labour, notably the emphasis on mutualism, localism and associationalism (Jackson, 2009). Blue Labour's assault on liberalism is too indiscriminate to deliver a knock-out blow.

The same applies to the historic division between the 'authoritarian' and 'liberal' traditions in the Labour party. This divide was captured in the electoral dilemma of how Labour retains its traditional working-class constituency while winning the support of the middle-class intelligentsia; at first glance, the rift appears unbridgeable. In reality, however, Labour's strategy in opposition and in government has always been:

> [T]o try to satisfy both groups and find ways of maintaining the party's traditional liberalism while dealing with voters' fears on issues of crime, immigration, asylum, and most recently, terrorism. It is a delicate balance and probably the best a party like Labour can do is to adopt a series of compromises.[111]

New Labour under Blair and Brown 'contained elements that were simultaneously metropolitan liberal and communitarian, patriotic and internationalist, Fabian and devolutionist'; the Labour governments emphasised the importance of social obligations and duties, adopting a robust approach to crime, anti-social behaviour, and abuse of the welfare system, alongside the restoration of 'respect' in communities.[112] Blue Labour by rejecting Croslandite social democracy propels the party towards an illiberal position that is antithetical to Labour's plural political traditions, making its appeal narrower and more exclusive. In contrast to both New and Blue Labour, Ed Miliband's One Nation project positively embraced Crosland's legacy.

Crosland and One Nation Labour

Prior to his leadership victory, Miliband eschewed New Labour's ambivalence towards revisionism, paying close attention to Crosland's political thought. In the wake of the 2008 financial crisis, egalitarianism became once again intellectually fashionable, as well as politically credible. The crash undermined global capitalism, allegedly presaging a shift to the Left in the advanced market democracies. Miliband's concept of 'One Nation' Labour repositioned his party emphasising vital components of Crosland's inheritance. According to Dick Leonard, before becoming leader Miliband 'spoke most enthusiastically in private as well as public, obviously regarding Crosland as a major intellectual influence'.[113] During a sabbatical year at Harvard University, Miliband intended to produce a contemporary updating of *The Future of Socialism*.[114] He also planned to publish an edited volume on Crosland's legacy with Roy Hattersley, an ambition put on hold after winning the party leadership.[115]

One Nation Labour demonstrated an affinity with Crosland's ideas, particularly *The Future of Socialism*'s emphasis on eradicating inequality. According to one leading Labour figure: 'Crosland's political vision has a striking 'one nation' quality: 'the purpose of socialism is quite simply to eradicate this sense of class and to create in its place a sense of common interest and equal status'.'[116] Crosland emphasised the importance of citizens leading shared lives through public institutions: what was notable about comprehensive schools and the welfare state was that in theory they brought individuals together irrespective of class background. One Nation was defined by Miliband as: '[a] country where everyone has a stake, where prosperity is fairly shared and where we have a shared destiny, a sense of shared endeavour and a common life that we lead together.'[117] On the face of it, One Nation was little more than a presentational device, but it served as an umbrella for Miliband's putative rejuvenation of the party. The One Nation project rejected New Labour's deferential approach to markets, advocating reform of Britain's dysfunctional model of capitalism.[118] The aim was to develop a 'supply-side socialism of the Left' driving the British economy to pursue a high-wage, high-productivity strategy. Like Blue Labour, One Nation Labour was also 'conservative in valuing relationships, family and community as the basis of social order and as sources of reciprocity and well-being'.[119]

Crosland's influence on Miliband's One Nation project culminated in the publication of Peter Hain's recent monograph, *Back to the Future of Socialism*.[120] Hain was an ally of Miliband's having supported him for the party leadership in 2010. *Back to the Future of Socialism* attempts to give substance to Miliband's One Nation vision. The book examines the party's doctrine and programme in the aftermath of the financial crisis, drawing on Crosland's political and economic analysis. Hain described *The Future of Socialism* as 'Crosland's most lasting significance to the Labour party'.[121]

Hain insists that Labour should offer a genuine alternative to austerity drawing on Crosland's legacy as a socialist theoretician. He emphasises that Crosland resisted attempts to cut public expenditure and scale back growth throughout his career, although his message was too rarely heeded. However, Crosland's legacy in relation to economic management is contentious as Labour struggled to establish credibility throughout the 1960s and 1970s. The Wilson Administration defied pressures to devalue sterling but finally capitulated in 1967; it was forced to deflate the economy to correct the balance of payments deficit and retain international confidence in the pound. In the aftermath of the oil price shock and world recession, the Callaghan Government in 1976 was again compelled to accede to public expenditure cuts, negotiating a $3.9 billion loan from the International Monetary Fund (IMF). The Treasury's argument was that the economy was in danger of 'overheating' and should be squeezed creating 'a hole for expansion'; however, the Treasury's view that the British economy was growing too quickly was implausible given the severity of the world recession; the issue for Crosland was how to finance public debt ensuring higher levels of government spending while maintaining confidence in sterling.[122]

The predicament the Labour Government faced in 1975–6 was unenviable: alongside the pressure on the pound, the Public Sector Borrowing Requirement (PSBR) was running out of control; this meant either higher long-term interest rates to attract overseas investors, or printing money leading to escalating inflation which had already reached 30 per cent in 1975.[123] The only viable alternative was drastic cuts in public spending. Crosland initially opposed the terms of the IMF agreement when negotiators demanded a fiscal contraction equivalent to 20 per cent of the budget deficit, insisting 'there is no economic case for further deflationary cuts':

> No one seriously suggests that, given the prospective level of unemployment and spare capacity under existing policies, we need still more deflation to make room for exports and investment...Far from improving matters, further cuts would by their probable effect on rents and on relations with the Trade Union Congress (TUC) seriously threaten the Social Contract and the prospects for wage stability next year.[124]

Despite his opposition in Cabinet, Crosland eventually conceded following a damaging run on the pound which investors were convinced was still overvalued.[125] According to Tony Benn, the IMF package involved 'cuts into public services so deep as to endanger their basic function, and cuts in social benefits that would put at risk the Social Contract'.[126] Although the situation initially improved with falling interest rates and a strengthening pound, the scale of the cuts and the imposition of a 5 per cent pay norm in September 1978 brought the Callaghan Administration to political breaking-point: the post-war priority of full employment and social welfare was imperilled by the control of inflation and public spending.[127]

After 2010, the Coalition government imposed austerity measures in the wake of the financial crash, securing assent from senior Labour figures including Miliband and Ed Balls about the necessity of fiscal retrenchment. In contrast, Hain demanded that the Labour party rediscover its Keynesian convictions, upholding Crosland's vision of what social democracy was apparently for: a high and stable level of public expenditure. Hain accepted quasi-Keynesian demand management could not be resurrected 40 years after the IMF crisis. Maintaining aggregate demand is hard, to say the least, in a globalised economy. The UK depends on overseas lenders to fund its trade deficit which means retaining the confidence of the financial markets, as Crosland reluctantly accepted in 1976. Yet Crosland's resistance to government spending cuts was not matched by any comprehensive analysis of the structural weaknesses of British economic performance. By the 1970s, the UK economy was plagued by major imbalances; social democrats preferred to castigate Tory mismanagement but had no plausible alternative strategy. Britain in the 2010s still has one of the highest current account deficits in the industrialised world, and is particularly exposed to global shocks. Critics argue that the British economy is still not productive enough, overly dependent on the financial sector and the City of London; the UK's skills base is anaemic with too many school leavers lacking qualifications; wage inequalities continue to spiral; Britain is losing out in the global development of new technologies; the UK produces too few exports to pay its way in the world.[128] Domestic policies have limited purchase given Britain's membership of the European Union and integration into the world economy, a point which Miliband (and Crosland) were slow to acknowledge.

Both Crosland and One Nation Labour have a positive view of Scandinavian social democracy, regarding Sweden as a country worthy of emulation given its acceptance of globalisation tempered by its commitment to equal citizenship and social welfare. One Nation Labour showed interest in the co-ordinated social market capitalism of Germany with its regional banks, its federal political system, alongside its mandatory worker representation on company boards and federal political system. In the 1952 *New Fabian Essays*, Crosland advocated similar changes in British industry akin to the John Lewis model: 'To alter the legal structure of company ownership as to substitute for shareholders' sole control, a constitution which explicitly defines the responsibilities of the firm to worker, consumer and community; workers would become members of the company, and have their representatives on the board of directors.'[129]

Crosland was broadly positive about the manner in which structural changes in British capitalism were developing in the 1950s; One Nation Labour has been noticeably more critical. The starting-point is the reaction against financial capitalism. Citing the former American President, Theodore Roosevelt, Miliband wanted to tackle the 'crony capitalism' of monopolies and price-fixing; Miliband sought to define his leadership by standing up to elite interests notably the energy companies, tax avoiders and the Murdoch press.[130] The Labour party had been through three major crises in its history: the collapse of Ramsay MacDonald's Government in 1931; Margaret Thatcher's victory in 1979; and Labour's 2010 election defeat, the second worst since universal suffrage.[131] One Nation Labour was intrigued by how Thatcherism exploited the collapse of the post-war settlement, accompanied by the breakdown of corporatism and the emergence of an alternative model of monetarist economics. The crisis underlined that market liberalism was failing; Labour had to devise a new governing prospectus. Miliband's adviser, Stewart Wood, argued: 'This moment is like the late 1970s in one important way: it is a time that calls for spotting the exhaustion of an old settlement, this time the one established by the Thatcher government, and for politicians who are bold enough to argue for big change.'[132] Miliband himself claimed: 'In every generation, there comes a moment when the existing way of doing things is challenged. It happened in 1979 and again in 1997. This is another of those moments.'[133] Jon Cruddas and Jonathan Rutherford insist that since 1945, 'social renewal and active democracy' have been, 'squeezed out of national debate by orthodox Marxism and the social democracy of Anthony Crosland'.[134]

Although Miliband paid tribute to Crosland's vision emphasising the ethical importance of equality, One Nation Labour was also circumspect about the revisionist tradition. The aim was to identify a left of centre position distinct from Blair and Brown, overturning the established New Labour orthodoxies of the 1990s. But this scarcely entailed a fundamental reassessment of British social democracy in a changing political landscape. One Nation Labour displayed remarkably little curiosity about the sociology of the United Kingdom: there is no analysis of the new class structure of Britain, for example, as distinct from Crosland's writing in the 1950s and 1960s. Issues of national identity and culture were avoided. The Institute for Public Policy Research (IPPR) report on 'The Condition of Britain' provided a coherent framework, but the findings were ignored by Miliband's team.[135]

More surprisingly, Miliband's rhetorical support for a more equal society was qualified by his willingness to take few political risks. David Lipsey observed: 'Labour today remains tentative and nervous about measures to tackle the sumptuary wealth of the successful.'[136] Helen Thompson has noted:

> Miliband's political language is the discourse of crisis and the desperate need for structural reform of the economy to reduce inequality...Yet there is nothing in the policies he has thus far offered, from the mansion tax to freezing energy prices that would remotely amount to a radical economic programme aimed at addressing what is purportedly so badly wrong.[137]

One Nation Labour acknowledged the weakness of the revisionist strategy in the 1950s and 1960s, too complacent about the productive potential of the British economy; having abandoned state ownership and nationalisation, insufficient attention was paid to formulating a modern industrial strategy while reforming the financial system. Nonetheless, Miliband's team similarly ignored the case for reforming the state, lapsing into old style bureaucratic Fabianism by proposing to abolish 'free' schools and academies; artificially control energy prices; impose state regulation of the media; and resist moves to break up public sector monopolies in public service delivery.[138] This position envisaged a relationship between states and markets of 'public good, private bad': the vital point that market forces had to be managed and where necessary restrained by regulation was undermined by the careless language of 'predators and producers'. Labour was exposed as the Chancellor, George

Osborne, re-set the terms of political engagement on the economy: Brown's dividing-lines of 'investment' versus 'cuts' were superseded by the Conservative message of 'sound finances' versus 'bankruptcy', redefining Britain's economic problem as the public deficit and debt.[139] One Nation Labour's electoral strategy was predicated on a narrow coalition of traditional Labour supporters, left-leaning Liberal Democrats, and assorted Greens and former Nationalist voters. In 2015 this approach led to one of Labour's worst defeats since the First World War. Miliband failed to confront the political and economic reality facing British social democracy: a vigorous and dynamic private sector was necessary to improve living standards and provide resources to fulfil the party's social ambitions. If the revisionism of Crosland was about applying an original 'cast of mind' developing a broad-based appeal in an affluent society, his political instincts were far removed from the defensive caution of One Nation Labour.

Conclusion

Crosland's revisionism provided the starting-point for Labour's revival in the past; this helps to explain the ongoing fascination with his ideas. New Labour has been defined as a revisionist project, aiming to adapt and modify the party's programme in the light of changing circumstances: Clause 4 was re-written to emphasise enduring values rather than a doctrinal commitment to nationalisation; the party made a distinctive appeal to the affluent voters of Southern England.[140] This strategy emphasised the importance of winning a reputation for economic competence: only through growing national income was investment in public services feasible. Superficially at least, Labour's revisionism bore fruit leading to three consecutive parliamentary majorities in 1997, 2001 and 2005. More fundamentally, however, New Labour's revisionism was at best superficial and half-hearted. Blair and Brown had ambitions to transform Labour into the natural party of government, but the process was never completed. This hesitancy is the story of revisionism stretching back to even Crosland and Bernstein.

Whereas Bernstein and Crosland wrestled with the competing imperatives of loyalty and fidelity to the movement on the one hand, and tackling outdated shibboleths on the other, New Labour appeared relaxed about abandoning social democracy's intellectual heritage. Either way, the most recent phase of Labour's revisionism was plainly an 'unfinished revolution'.

There is little to be gained by returning to the New Labour model. The challenges that confront social democracy underline the redundant nature of the third way shaping New Labour two decades ago.[141] Then, economic growth was expected to remain high and stable; breakthrough technologies epitomised by the rise of the Internet hinted the era of boom and bust bedevilling post-war British economic history was over. The world has moved on: the 'NICE' decade of 'non-inflationary constant expansion' has given way to a 'GRIM' decade of depressed real wages and declining living standards; the threat of secular stagnation hangs over the western economic powers.[142] Parties must relate to an electorate in which fears about rising immigration and 'free-riding' in the welfare state have grown markedly. New Labour was convinced that globalisation could be managed in the public interest, but the gulf between 'cosmopolitan' voters who gained from globalisation, and 'left behind' voters who feared open borders and free markets, has widened ominously. The promise of investment in education and human capital as the next frontier of egalitarian strategy failed to ensure a 'rising tide would lift all boats'. Economic mobility has been declining in advanced market democracies; social pessimism grows as parents' fear that their children will be worse off. Rising economic inequality has sparked panic inside the global institutions of market liberalism, notably the IMF. The IMF is concerned that global capitalism will become politically unsustainable.

These anxieties are more potent where the sense of solidarity, communal belonging and mutual attachment is threatened: the culprit may be less the ethnic and religious diversity prompted by successive waves of immigration, but the weakening of group loyalty and identity centred on class and community in

Britain during the 1960s and 1970s.[143] Our societies have been shaped by a conception of political liberalism which protects and enhances individual rights. The increase in disengagement from representative democracy and the growth of distrust undermine established party systems, exacerbated by the rise of populist parties. New Labour's third way ascribed importance to European integration, with Britain playing a leading role in the EU. But structural divergences and crisis 'aftershocks' are creating new divisions across Europe. The EU's rationale as an engine of convergence and unification appears questionable. In this context, social democrats must launch a new revisionism of the Left, adapting policies to changing circumstances in a post-industrial economy and society.

Crosland recognised that Labour had to change with the times if it was to remain a social democratic party providing a signpost for the future. The purpose of an ideology is not to outline a social democratic Utopia; it is to demonstrate how a better society will be practically brought about. Revisionists have exercised influence since the creation of the Labour party: Crosland was not the only twentieth-century revisionist. The inter-war generation of Tawney, Durbin, Dalton and Gaitskell developed the revisionist method as Labour struggled to establish its governing credibility following the party's ignominious departure from office in 1931. Since Crosland's era, practising thinkers such as Bryan Gould in *A Future for Socialism* and Roy Hattersley in *Choose Freedom* sought to articulate a new social democratic vision.[144] Rather than interpreting Labour's revisionist tradition in terms of two waves of post-war and then post-Thatcherite reform,[145] revisionism has a diverse history stretching back to late nineteenth-century radical liberalism. Revisionists have been reshaping the party for changing times throughout the twentieth century, including during the 'dark days' of the early 1930s and the early 1980s.[146] The claim that 'Labour's revisionist tradition is a rich and strong one' is still convincing although it should not blind us to revisionism's limitations and inadequacies.[147]

This chapter assessed Crosland's influence on the party since his death, in particular on three major political projects that have developed since the 1990s. The relationship of his posthumous legacy to each has been strained: Blue Labour defines Croslandite social democracy as the enemy of enlightened ethical socialism. One Nation Labour discerns virtues in Crosland's egalitarianism, but the language of 'predatory' capitalism is a departure from the optimistic account of capitalist development adumbrated in *The Future of Socialism*. New Labour kept its distance from the party's revisionists, despite similarities once the record of the 1997–2010 governments has been appraised. Crosland left a significant and lasting mark on the Labour party, but he was a contentious figure who provoked disagreement and discord. He insisted that for Labour to have a viable future, the party must redefine social democracy as a marriage of individual freedom and social justice rediscovering its roots in the liberal tradition. This was a controversial step for a party with an authoritarian 'Tory-socialist' tradition, revealing an antipathy to liberalism going back to the early twentieth century. It made Crosland's revisionism highly contingent: he struggled to reconcile his status as a loyalist claiming deep roots in the labour movement, with his reputation as the revisionist *par excellence* ruthlessly attacking outdated ideological dogmas.

The chapter that follows addresses the future of the Labour party and social democracy as the Left struggles to come to terms with the 2008 crisis, alongside receding faith in the political system and growing antipathy towards representative democracy. Having examined Crosland's influence on past ideological projects, it is important to assess what his inheritance offers today's Labour party. Labour ought to remain a revisionist party addressing the economic and social landscape of a changing Britain, adapting its policies to new circumstances. The party needs to develop a political identity drawing on liberal social democracy: advancing individual freedom within a national political community where we have reciprocal responsibilities and duties; where restraints on individual liberty arising from the operation of unfettered market forces and an overbearing central state are gradually eroded. As Crosland argued in 1960: 'We want issues which make not a narrow class or sectional appeal, but a wide, radical appeal to broad sections of the population, including the newly emerging social groups.'[148] Liberal social democracy is focused on the inclusive ethic of 'conscience and reform' rather than militant class struggle.

EIGHT

The future of social democracy and the British Left

If there is to be such a thing as Liberal Socialism –
and whether there be still a subject for inquiry – it
must be…democratic. It must come from below, not
above…it must engage the efforts and respond to the
genuine desires not of a handful of superior beings but
of great masses of men. (Leonard Hobhouse[1])

The dynamic of any living movement is to be found,
not merely in interests, but in principles, which unite
men whose personal interests may be poles asunder,
and that if principles are to exercise their appeal, they
must be frankly stated. (R.H. Tawney[2])

Introduction

Crosland's radical 'cast of mind' would recommend a revisionist
social democratic strategy for twenty-first century Britain. The
starting-point of revisionism is to comprehensively assess New
Labour's legacy, just as *The Future of Socialism* was informed by
rigorous and granular analysis of Attlee's achievements. While
Attlee's ministers presided over a war-torn economy on the

243

verge of bankruptcy, the situation confronting New Labour was seemingly propitious. Throughout the late 1990s and 2000s, the UK economy was stable with growth aided by the boom in financial services. Buoyant tax receipts flowing into the Exchequer ensured a record public sector surplus, enabling redistribution and public investment without antagonising the middle classes. As Crosland envisaged, growth made it possible to increase discretionary consumption and living standards across the income distribution, while delivering additional funding to public services. After the structural aftershocks of the 1970s and 1980s, a model of capitalism emerged in the western economies: higher growth meant governments no longer had to choose between 'private affluence' and 'public squalor'. This mood of relative affluence suited New Labour's electoral strategy which was centred on a shift towards, as well as a reconstruction of, the centre ground appealing to the median voter as well as the party's traditional working-class supporters.[3]

The Conservatives, for so long the natural governing party in British politics, were in disarray having lost three consecutive elections for the first time in modern political history. Thirteen out of 15 countries in Western Europe were governed by social democratic parties, heralding a new era in which the centre-left dominated the electoral scene. New Labour's legacy is nevertheless a mixed picture as we saw in the previous chapter: on the one hand, it is hard to avoid the conclusion that the Blair and Brown governments missed an opportunity to recast the landscape of British politics, bequeathing a more long-lasting inheritance. On the other hand, New Labour faced severe constraints despite the booming economy, while initiating changes in economic and social policy which differed from their Conservative predecessors and previous Labour governments: 'The effect of this curious conjuncture is that not only voters, but also scholars, political leaders, analysts and activists might well forget the numerous and largely significant innovations to which New Labour can rightly claim.'[4]

This chapter begins by assessing Labour's record, particularly on the social democratic priorities of equality and economic growth. It deals with the major structural challenges confronting centre-left politics in a post-industrial society and then defines the core governing questions for social democracy in relation to public services and the state; redistribution; and economic management. Finally, the chapter addresses the implications of Crosland's analysis for Labour's contemporary doctrine and programme. *The Future of Socialism*'s relevance has inevitably faded, but Crosland's insurgent 'cast of mind' provides inspiration for generating new political ideas and governing programmes. As a starting point, Crosland's account of the fundamental socialist aspirations still has relevance:

1. an over-riding concern with social welfare, and a determination to accord a first priority to the relief not merely of material poverty, but of social distress or misfortune from whatever cause;
2. a much more equal distribution of wealth, and in particular a compression of that part of the total which derives from property income and inheritance;
3. a socially 'classless' society, and in particular a non-elite system of education which offers equal opportunities to all children;
4. the primacy of social over private interests, and an allocation of resources (notably in the fields of social investment and town and country planning) determined by the public need and not solely by profit considerations:
5. the diffusion of economic power, and in particular a transfer of power from the large corporation (whether public or private) both to workers (either directly or through their unions) and through consumers (through the Co-operative movement);
6. generally, the substitution of cooperative for competitive and self-regarding social and economic relations;
7. in foreign affairs, the substitution of disarmament, international action and the rule of law for nationalism and power politics;
8. racial equality (both at home and abroad), the right of colonial peoples to freedom and self-government, and the

duty of richer nations to give aid and support to smaller ones;

9. an increase in the rate of economic growth, both for the sake of a higher standard of living and a pre-condition of achieving other objectives;

10. a belief, not merely in Parliamentary democracy, but in the rights and liberty of the individual as against the state, the police, private or public bureaucracy, and organised intolerance of any kind.[5]

Crosland defined such principles as the centrepiece of a modern social democratic strategy. Then as now, we might disagree about the best means of realising these goals. Since revisionists reassess policies in the light of changing circumstances, the fiscal and institutional mechanisms required will be distinct from those of Crosland's era in the 1950s to the 1970s. Given fundamental shifts in the structure of capitalism over the last three decades, social democracy should focus on the spectre of rising wealth inequality alongside growing disparity of life-chances, as the ownership of capital, assets and property has been concentrated in fewer hands. This inequity not only diminishes social justice: a vastly unequal distribution of wealth curtails human freedom, weakening aggregate demand and economic efficiency. That raises the question of what can be done: a central proposal in this chapter is a universal capital endowment bestowed onto every citizen on reaching adulthood, funded through a reformed inheritance and wealth tax that would enrich individual freedom and make progress towards a more equal society. This idea along with other proposals draws imaginatively on the radical liberal tradition, re-energising Labour's politics as Crosland did 60 years ago.

A fairer and more equal society

Despite the auspicious context of a healthy and growing economy, New Labour's legacy has not been one of unequivocal success in building a fairer, more equal society. Thirteen years in power gave Labour for the first time in its history an unprecedented opportunity to reshape British society and its institutions, but the UK remained profoundly unequal. It was not just that the distribution of income and wealth resulted in a growing gap between rich and poor. Opportunities in Britain were still overwhelmingly determined by 'social inheritance' and circumstances of birth.[6] Hills has shown that despite fluidity in household incomes, family circumstances and class background continue to powerfully shape an individual's life-chances.[7] Class is less important in shaping political attitudes than in post-war Britain: but class heavily conditions educational achievement, occupational destinations and performance on the main indicators of economic success. The legacy of inequality was not only the result of the Thatcher governments but repeated policy failures after 1945 when Britain was unable to overcome structural decline leading to an erosion of public investment. The largest rise in post-war inequality was in the 1980s and 1990s, which Labour in government halted but did not reverse.

Britain became materially wealthier after 1945: as the former minister John Vaizey noted, by the late 1970s the standard of living was 'emphatically higher' than 'when the guns stopped firing in 1945'.[8] This apparent prosperity was reflected in rising real wages, improvements in public infrastructure, and better housing. Social reforms duly advanced personal freedom; popular culture was transforming Britain's class structure and markedly reducing social differentiation.[9] Participation in higher education increased following Crosland's tenure at the Department of Education and Science, with twice as many part-time students and growing numbers of women and students from ethnic minority backgrounds admitted to university.[10] However, enduring post-war problems soon resurfaced: throughout the 1950s and 1960s, Labour had been unable to constrain the sectional demands of the trade unions: it could not devise a satisfactory mechanism for containing wage costs which led to a stop–go cycle of growth followed by bouts of deflation; moreover, the determination to protect wage differentials weakened the position of the low paid in non-unionised sectors. Throughout the 1980s, the

Thatcher governments exacerbated inequality by attacking the generosity and coverage of state benefits, while allowing the polarisation between 'working' and 'workless' households to grow. That was the context that New Labour inherited in 1997.

The levels of poverty and inequality were unprecedented in post-war history given one in four children was living in poverty by 1997 compared to one in eight in 1979. Post-tax income inequality had more than doubled, while the incomes of the poorest were lower in real terms in 1995–96 than they had been when Margaret Thatcher came to office.[11] The increase in inequality was driven not only by reductions in marginal tax rates and lower benefit levels, but growing polarisation in the labour market: by the late 1990s, a fifth of working age households had no one in work compared to 8 per cent in 1975, a consequence of deindustralisation and the disappearance of jobs in manufacturing and the nationalised industries.[12] Inequality increased further because of disparities in wage growth, as Paul Gregg points out: real wages for median workers rose by 23 per cent between 1979 and 1995, but in the highest percentile, wage growth was more than 40 per cent. Declining investment since the 1980s also had an effect: net public sector investment fell from 5.9 per cent in the 1960s and 1970s to 3.1 per cent between 1985 and 1995 (Hills, 2005).

New Labour sought to discard poorly targeted spending commitments, prioritising the alleviation of structural disadvantage. In particular, the party abandoned a 'generalised attack' on income inequality, targeting relative poverty among families with children and pensioners. The Social Justice Commission established by John Smith had recommended a move away from universal cash benefits, the hallmark of Labour's 'Shadow Budget' in the 1992 election. The Conservatives had been able to claim that Labour's plans contained a hidden 'bombshell' that would lead to tax rises for middle income earners. New Labour was determined not to make ambitious spending pledges that would undermine hard-won trust on tax. The party's priorities were improving socio-economic outcomes and narrowing differences throughout the population, as illustrated in Table 8.1:[13]

Table 8.1: Labour's goals in social policy

Policy area	Policy goals
Poverty and inequality	To end child poverty by 2020, halving it by 2010. To eradicate pensioner poverty.
The under-fives	Ensure an equal starting-point for all children, 'an inclusive society where everyone has an equal chance to achieve their full potential', according to the 1997 Labour manifesto.
Health	To improve the overall health of the UK population, while reducing health inequalities.
Education	To raise levels of educational equality giving all pupils the opportunity to realise their potential creating a strong economy and a fairer society.
Deprived neighbourhoods and spatial inequalities	By 2020, no-one should be subject to serious disadvantage because of the neighbourhood in which they live.

The broad principles of Labour's approach outlined by John Hills were as follows:

- selective universalism and a targeted assault on poverty, especially child and pensioner poverty; Blair announced an ambitious goal to halve, and finally to end, child poverty by 2020;
- no across the board benefit rises: for example, the relative value of Job Seekers Allowance (JSA) fell as earnings rose;
- social security was defined as 'spending on failure';
- a 'work-first' strategy for helping the unemployed meant downward pressure on benefits for adults of working age;
- greater conditionality in the welfare state included tougher eligibility criteria for working-age benefits;

- no recourse to direct redistribution: Labour pledged in 1997, 2001 and 2005 that the basic and higher rate of income tax would not rise;
- there was, as a result, a general lack of concern about inequality at the top. [14]

What were the consequences of Labour's reforms for living standards and inequality in the UK? Growth in real incomes during the New Labour years divided into distinct periods: between 1996–67 and 2001–02, household incomes grew by more than 3 per cent; between 2001–02 and 2007–08, growth slowed dramatically to 1 per cent (with consumption driven by increased household borrowing); after 2007–08, average disposable incomes increased as a result of lower inflation, lower interest rates, higher state benefits, and the temporary stimulus provided by the reduction in VAT.[15] Wage inequality grew under Labour, but at a slower pace than in the Conservative years between 1979–80 and 1996–97;[16] the wage differential between the highest and lowest paid had increased by 1.4 per cent per annum, but after 1997 it rose by only 0.6 per cent for men, and 0.3 per cent for women. The surge in wage inequality slowed: membership of trade unions began to increase modestly; the introduction of the National Minimum Wage (NMW) in April 1999 markedly improved the position of low paid workers.

Having witnessed a dramatic rise in income inequality throughout the 1980s, the changes after 1997 were modest: the Gini co-efficient which measures the extent of household income inequality on a scale from 0 to 100 rose slightly in Labour's first term to 0.35, but fell again after 2001; it increased during the initial phase of the financial crisis: this led to cumulative growth in inequality from 0.33 in 1996–7 to 0.36 by 2010–11.[17] Overall, inequality did not fall despite the fact that as Joyce and Sibieta demonstrate, income growth was highest in the second and third poorest income deciles, and lowest in the seventh, eighth and ninth richest deciles: inequality rose cumulatively because the top 10 per cent of earners experienced the fastest growth in incomes, while the poorest 10 per cent witnessed the slowest growth. Income inequality was influenced by changes at the very top and bottom of the distribution. In the final year of the government, inequality fell substantially: 'the largest 1-year fall for at least 50 years', as the result of the new 50 per cent marginal tax rate combined with the impact of the financial crash on top incomes.[18] Inequality was falling across the income distribution as Labour left office.

Despite Crosland's optimism in the 1950s, there was no 'immutable law' guaranteeing Britain's advance towards equality: the Institute for Fiscal Studies reported that the UK had become far more unequal during the 1980s and 1990s, 'a parade of dwarfs and a few giants'.[19] After 2011, austerity policies and cuts disproportionately hit the poorest households; in contrast, high income groups benefited from rising asset prices and interest rates reaching record lows as the result of Quantitative Easing. According to the Organisation for Economic Co-operation and Development (OECD), income inequality since the mid-1970s among working-age households had risen faster in the UK than in any other industrialised country: 'From a peak in 2000 and subsequent fall, it has been rising again since 2005 and is now well above the OECD average.'[20] Before taxes and benefits in 2012–13, the richest fifth of households had an average income of £81,300, 15 times greater than the poorest fifth.[21] The tax and benefits system has a progressive impact on income distribution while the welfare state is relatively efficient: the ratio of average incomes between the top and bottom fifth of households falls to four to one.[22] Nonetheless, the UK Gini coefficient increased markedly during the 1980s, fell slowly in the early 1990s, rose in the early 2000s, and has remained broadly flat since the financial crisis.[23]

The growth of wage inequality and the polarisation of the income distribution since the 1970s have been unprecedented. A child in the UK is significantly more likely to grow up in poverty than in other Northern European countries: the percentage of households with children in poverty has risen dramatically since the 1970s and is among the highest in the

OECD.[24] Britain has lower earnings mobility than in other advanced economies; children are more likely to inherit the economic position of their parents than in Canada, Australia and the Nordic states; the intergenerational transmission of inequality is reflected in the educational achievement of children.[25] In 2012–13, 38.7 per cent of pupils eligible for free school meals (FSM) attained an A*–C grade in English and Mathematics GCSE in English schools, compared to 65.3 per cent among 'non-FSM' pupils. The class divide in educational achievement is growing. Poor parental employment prospects and lack of educational qualifications contribute to the transmission of poverty across generations.[26]

The rise in income inequality was fuelled by the growing share going to the top 1 per cent of earners: from 7.1 per cent in 1970 to 14.3 per cent by 2005; in 2008, 0.1 per cent of the population were earning 5 per cent of all total pre-tax incomes.[27] Other factors implicated in rising inequality include the highest paid experiencing an increase in average working hours; the expansion of self-employment to around one in seven of the UK workforce leading to a growing division in earnings; and more people marrying within their own 'earning class', as underlined by the gap between the wives of 'rich' and 'poor' husbands rising from £3,900 in 1987 to £10,200 by 2004.[28] In the background are structural forces that have widened the dispersion in wages and incomes across all advanced economies since the 1970s: new technologies and automation have led to higher wage differentials; deregulation of labour market institutions has accentuated pay inequalities while global trade integration has exacerbated wage polarisation; this has been further affected by the increasing supply of skilled workers in the global labour-force.[29]

The increase in UK income inequality is exacerbated by the decline of 'jobs for wages'. As the share of returns from growth distributed to capital rather than labour has grown since the 1970s, fewer workers can maintain their living standards through wages earned in the labour market. Nearly 50 per cent of global wealth goes to the top 1 per cent, increasing dramatically since the crisis.[30] As Hills and Glennerster point out, while 'far more attention is paid to the flow of income to individuals and households than to their stock of assets' the growth of wealth inequality is even more perturbing.[31] The focus on the income distribution and the incidence of poverty is unsurprising.[32] Yet it is wealth inequality which is soaring in the UK: by 2010, the top 10 per cent of households in Britain had net assets of more than £970,000, but the bottom 10 per cent had less than £13,000.[33] The richest 1 per cent of households own 20 per cent of all marketable wealth.[34] The ability to access wealth shapes choices for individuals and households: whether to purchase a home, take time off work to retrain or care for family members, acquire an asset such as a small business, or enjoy a financially secure retirement.[35] The net wealth of the top 10 per cent is 850 times greater than the bottom 10 per cent; there are gaps within generations as well as between them: the top 10 per cent of households aged 55–64 have assets of more than £1.46 million accumulating significant property and pension wealth.[36] The bottom 10 per cent had assets of less than £29,000. Younger generations are least likely to gain from rising property prices, as they are more liable to carry debts from higher education: 'In this way, inheritance tends to reinforce advantage and widen differences in wealth.'[37]

As a result, income and wealth inequality is more egregious than Crosland anticipated in *The Future of Socialism*; President Obama recently declared economic inequality is 'the defining challenge of our time'.[38] The OECD has shown that UK spending on public services helps to alleviate inequality, but the welfare system has become less redistributive despite the growth of targeting towards poorer groups: poverty continues to cast a long shadow; social divisions stretch back across generations.[39] Moreover, higher levels of inequality negatively affect the long-term growth rate. The International Monetary Fund (IMF) has demonstrated using recent data that 'lower net inequality is robustly correlated with faster and more durable growth'.[40] Inequality is not only 'ethically undesirable': it weakens the economy's productive potential exacerbating structural imbalances.[41] Since the liberalising reforms of the 1980s and 1990s, 'GDP and productivity have grown more slowly than over previous decades, contrary to widespread belief. The volatility of economic growth has also been much greater.'[42] Britain's weak post-war performance is a consequence of an entrenched social divide. Crosland pointed out in the 1950s that class-based inequalities breed 'social resentment', increasing industrial conflict and undermining innovation. The negative impact of class inequalities has been borne out in Britain's political and economic history since 1945.[43]

New Labour embraced the concept of 'radical meritocracy' aiming to improve social mobility. Evidently too few children had their life-chances transformed due to the persistence of structural disadvantage in under-performing regions, undermining incentives to acquire educational qualifications and employment. It related to the dominant culture and social attitudes in Britain: the persistence of hierarchy, snobbery and class status reinforced by bastions of social privilege, notably the public schools and the House of Lords. The gender pay gap narrowed slowly in the New Labour years while progress went into reverse after 2008. Outcomes improved for ethnic minority communities with additional measures to outlaw discrimination and promote equality, but the education and employment prospects of Afro-Caribbean males and the Bangladeshi community barely altered. The life-chances of young people in white working-class communities in the former industrial regions continued to decline. Britain after 13 years of New Labour was scarcely a more equal or classless society.

Too few ideas emerged to constructively address inequality. A concerted effort to tackle social and economic inequalities required the Labour governments to construct new social and economic institutions, reallocating property rights and redistributing capital, wealth and assets on a scale matching the creation of the privatised industries, the National Lottery, council house ownership, and the saving schemes championed by Conservative governments in the 1980s and 1990s. This approach relates to New Labour's unsatisfactory restructuring and reform of public services. At the heart of the Attlee Government's political settlement was the commitment to a universal welfare state: social security through contributory benefits and services free to all at the point of need. The welfare state created 'an island of altruism' in a 'sea' of markets and private capitalist greed.[44] As Labour abandoned state ownership and came to terms with the market in the 1980s and 1990s, its resolve to defend the traditional public sector hardened. The Blair governments' reforms were fiercely resisted, promoting damaging competitive forces that commercialised the public sector, imperilling the traditional social democratic ethos of altruism and the public interest.[45] The Private Finance Initiative (PFI) and Public Private Partnerships (PPPs) imported private capital into the public sector, allowing public resources to be used for private gain as the state absorbed increasing commercial risk. This process corroded the public sphere blurring the distinction 'between it and the private domain'. Marquand writes that: 'incessant marketisation... has done even more damage to the public domain than low taxation and resource starvation'.[46]

This confusion over the public sphere highlights the ambiguous nature of British socialism and the Labour party. In the 1920s, Labour was committed to the aspirations contained in Clause 4. Electoral success followed quickly; the industrial working class rallied to 'their' party and movement: but Labour entered government in 1924 and 1929 without a clear doctrine or well-developed programme, and was subsequently engulfed by financial crises. The party spent the late 1930s battling to formulate a credible strategy drawing haphazardly on quasi-Keynesian theories. In the 1940s, Labour was able to use the experience gained from Churchill's wartime coalition to its advantage. The party sought to confront the social and economic problems besieging post-war Britain: a commitment to nationalisation and state ownership of productive assets provided Labour with an unmistakable sense of purpose, offering a temporary truce in its doctrinal battles (Marquand, 2004). By the late 1950s, however, the ideological ceasefire was over: the revisionists argued that the unequivocal commitment to nationalisation was electorally damaging and had to be discarded. An alternative governing strategy emerged in the 1960s emphasising the 'ends' of equality and social welfare achieved through the 'means' of progressive taxation and an interventionist state. Rather than promising state ownership, economic growth would ensure rising public expenditure and working-class living standards, thereby forging a new social democratic society.

Following the bitter disputes provoked by Labour's catastrophic 1983 defeat, New Labour fashioned a model of British social democracy which redefined the role of the state for an age of globalisation. The commitment to universalism and treatment 'free at the point of need' remained, but a role for the private sector in the delivery of publicly funded services was embraced. Free markets meant an acceptance of labour market flexibility, alongside deregulation in product and capital markets beyond the structural reforms of the Thatcher governments'. There was a further disposal of state assets; the previous governments' programme of liberalisation was maintained. New Labour's agenda was inspired by Clinton's Democrats in the United States. Not surprisingly, a debate erupted over whether the modernised party's ideology was compatible with socialism as it has been historically understood. Blair welcomed the view that Labour had become a post-ideological party, embracing a new relationship between state and market. In the late nineteenth century, socialists under Fabian influence devised a strategy known as 'socialism in capitalism', in which an enlarged public sector would steadily permeate the entire capitalist system, increasing the size and influence of socialist institutions and 'communal action'.[47] Fabian 'gas and water socialism' was one model encompassing this approach. But New Labour's reforms acknowledged that the strategy of permeation was over: the public and private sectors were deployed interchangeably; there was no presumption that services should be publicly provided; the purpose was to deliver public goods efficiently to citizens, not to permeate capitalism. The reforms led to fierce disagreement, however; by the time of Labour's defeat in 2010, it had come full circle from where the party started in the early twentieth century: it proved impossible to resolve a coherent position on the relationship between states and markets and the provision of public services that commanded assent across the labour movement.

At the same time, the ethos of equality can never be reduced to what governments do: as Crosland acknowledged, equality of regard is about how individuals relate to one another. G.A. Cohen remarked: 'I now believe that a change in social ethos, a change in the attitudes people sustain toward each other in the thick of daily life, is necessary for producing equality.'[48] Transforming values and attitudes had been a central preoccupation of early twentieth-century ethical socialism and the New Liberalism, but it was sidelined at the end of the Second World War by bureaucratic Fabianism. In the intervening decades, attitudes grew markedly less propitious. John Curtice writes that 'Britain is seemingly less concerned now about equality and fairness than it was during the last recession of the early 1990s...the British public continue to adhere to a relatively inegalitarian mood.'[49] The 'thermostatic' model of public opinion indicates that preferences for policy change among voters decline as governments alter the policy framework to take account of previous concerns: the adoption of redistributive fiscal policies is likely to lead to an erosion of support for redistribution over time, as it did with Blair and Brown.[50] New Labour's failure to promote a positive case for equality would still have disappointed Crosland. In government, Labour underestimated the severity and scale of economic inequality; there was insufficient analysis of the underlying causes and triggers of structural disadvantage in the income and wealth distribution. Issues left unaddressed included: what should be done about the declining position of the unskilled and the weak labour market prospects of those with few qualifications? What determines inter-generational inequalities between the so-called 'baby-boomers', and the pressures and insecurities faced by younger cohorts? What should be done to avert new 'social risks' transferring inequality from one generation of excluded families and deprived children to the next? These are 'policy puzzles' that a new generation of social democratic revisionists in Britain must confront.

New Labour: a new economic model?

Blair and Brown's Labour party sought to develop an economic model acknowledging the failures of previous Labour governments. The weakness of *The Future of Socialism* was the absence of a credible growth strategy; Crosland insisted that the problem of growth had largely been solved. The inability of Conservative governments to resolve Britain's weak performance was then ruthlessly exploited by Harold Wilson.[51] The lack of a credible plan for production bedevilled social democracy throughout the 1960s and 1970s; Wilson's 'white heat of technology' fizzled out. The failure to combine 'science with socialism' underlined that social democracy had no magic elixir. By the early 1960s, there was agreement across the political parties as to the necessary modernisation measures, influenced by French experience and the creation of a planning commission in the aftermath of the Second World War: a Conservative politician such as Macmillan had been a supporter of 'middle way' 'capitalist planning' in the 1930s;[52] the problem was implementing those initiatives in the British context given external constraints, namely the balance of payments deficit, overseas military commitments, and the defence of sterling.[53] George Brown's National Plan was not based on any fundamental assessment of Britain's relative decline, despite the opportunities presented for a modernising social democratic party. The Wilson governments failed to address the causes of post-war stagnation: the perpetuation of the class divide; 'them and us' attitudes in industrial relations; the failure of European-style social partnership to flourish in Britain; an elite distaste for industry and enterprise; aside from decades of neglect of high-quality vocational and technical training.[54]

The inability to develop a convincing growth strategy was a lacuna in post-war social democracy: it had not been resolved as the party returned to government in 1997. New

Labour briefly flirted with stakeholder capitalism: the idea was that Britain should emulate the social market economies of Germany and the Nordic countries by emphasising a long-term partnership between the state, the private sector and the trade unions 'based upon an expansionist economic policy within a broad quasi-Keynesian framework'.[55] But the party soon abandoned any attempt to offer an alternative to the dominant model of liberal political economy; stakeholding was dismissed as too radical by Blair and Brown since it implied that corporate firms have responsibilities to the consumer and the trade unions.[56] The New Labour leadership feared social partnership would be misinterpreted as an 'Old' Labour agenda conceding new powers to the trade unions. Moreover, Labour did not want to undermine the liberal growth model which at first glance appeared to provide the necessary resources to fund its social vision. New Labour broke decisively with the economic management approach of previous Labour governments, promising neither to tax and spend, nor to use public borrowing and state intervention to deliver growth and jobs.[57]

Labour under Blair and Brown did preside over the longest period of sustained growth in British economic history, with the United Kingdom outperforming its major competitors.[58] Brown's decision to surrender Treasury control over interest rates, making the Bank of England operationally independent, enhanced economic stability. Nor was growth egregiously unbalanced: economists' report the financial sector accounted for only 0.4 per cent of the 2.8 per cent annual expansion in the economy after 1997. Improvements in human capital and new technologies led to rapid productivity growth: 'the gains in productivity were real rather than a statistical artefact'.[59] During the 1980s, improvements in productivity had been generated by increased flexibility in the employment market and were accompanied by rising wage inequality; productivity growth after 1997 was the consequence of ICT innovation and a growing pool of human capital.[60] Improvements in competition policy, more efficient market regulation, investment in higher education, alongside rising immigration all contributed towards growth. Public investment in education increased from 5 per cent of national income in 1997 to 5.4 per cent in 2007, higher than Germany (4.5 per cent) and the United States (5.3 per cent). There was a marked increase in the number of university educated workers from 23 to 33 per cent, although Britain's weakness in apprenticeships compared to Germany and Switzerland was not addressed.[61] UK economic performance contrasted starkly with the previous 25 years where Britain had been 'characterised by a lack of resilience to external shocks and a higher level of macro-economic instability than in other G7 economies: unemployment, inflation and real interest rates were greater than comparable economies, while per capita incomes were markedly lower'.[62]

Labour's strategy after 1997 was heavily influenced by the New Democrats. This approach to economic policy associated with Clinton 'gurus' such as Larry Summers, Bob Rubin and Gene Sperling viewed globalisation and technological change, particularly the Internet, as opening up a new frontier of economic growth. Their economic strategy emphasised three pillars: fiscal discipline to keep interest rates low and to stimulate private investment; public investment in human capital and technology; alongside expanded trade and open markets.[63] There were weaknesses in the New Democrat framework, however. Firstly, there was complacency about regulating financial services, together with the need for increased public and private sector investment. The role of institutions and culture alongside the normative values of the economy were downplayed, yet it is evident that 'capitalism is a socio-economic system where institutions are key'.[64] Secondly, globalisation and new technologies failed to stimulate an economic miracle: the tendency towards 'boom and bust' alongside inequality in the income distribution continued. The Labour governments accepted the advice of reputable economists that growth rates achieved in the recovery of the late 1990s were sustainable; as a consequence, the expansion of public spending after 2000 continued for longer than should have normally been the case.[65]

Similarly to Clinton's Democrats, New Labour embraced the virtues of global liberalisation; on the surface, financialisation promoted unprecedented prosperity. The City of London was celebrated as a major financial centre with a global comparative advantage relative to New York and Singapore, attracting unprecedented foreign investment. But there were clearly consequences that should have been foreseen but were not. Increasing innovation in banking and new financial instruments meant a growing volume of inadequately regulated transactions, accompanied by a consumer and house price boom with rising levels of public and private sector debt: the household debt to income ratio had increased from 100 per cent in 1999 to 180 per cent by 2008.[66] In order to incentivise risk-taking and profitability, rewards and bonuses rose dramatically regardless of long-term improvements in institutional performance. During the credit boom, the bonuses earned by bankers soared, further inflating asset prices: in 2007, five banks in the United States paid their staff a total of $66 billion, of which $39 billion was bonuses. In the UK financial sector, bonuses reached a total of £19 billion by 2008. The profits proved unsustainable; the collapse of property values resulted in massive bank losses, requiring taxpayer bailouts of £124.9 billion.[67] Fundamental weaknesses in New Labour's strategy were exposed. The expedient focus on reassurance made the party cautious about intervening in markets. The legacy was under-investment in infrastructure, notably transport and housing; growing regional inequalities reflected in the disparity between the South-East, Northern England and the devolved nations; an economy too dependent on financial speculation and an unsustainable property and construction boom; and the financing of public and private consumption through debt: a strategy of 'privatised Keynesianism'.[68] Inadequate regulation was the New Labour governments' most serious error in economic policy-making.

A further weakness was the British economy's productive potential. Having been sanguine in the 1950s, Crosland grew concerned about Britain's future growth prospects. In the 1990s, Britain's economic position appeared favourable; there was a decade of rising productivity, employment and living standards. Until the crisis, UK growth outstripped France and Germany, inflation averaged 1.5 per cent, the unemployment rate was half the Eurozone average, and the rise in per capita GDP meant that Britain leapt from last to third place in the G7.[69] This apparent success contrasted markedly with previous Labour governments which ran into serious difficulties within months of gaining office. These governments struggled to develop effective strategies to manage the short-term cycle and to address the long-term challenge of industrial stagnation. Thatcherism rejected the inevitability of decline, emboldened by changes in the global economy.[70] Reforms were introduced that compelled economic restructuring, accelerating the transformation from an industrial economy to a service-based economy while creating a long tail of inequality and polarisation.[71] The agenda of privatisation and market deregulation was designed to cultivate a renewed spirit of British prosperity and affluence, the centrepiece of four consecutive victories for the Conservative party after 1979. British social democracy was unable to resolve whether to embrace the goal of economic modernisation or to undertake a futile defence of declining sectors and regions in which the labour movement's base was sharply falling. New Labour accepted many Thatcherite reforms, but the post-1997 boom was punctuated by the biggest slump since the 1930s, tarnishing its economic legacy.

Challenges for the next decade

The party's cautious instincts under Blair and Brown meant that New Labour was unable to match the structural transformations instigated by the Thatcher administrations. All governments from Lloyd George and Attlee to Thatcher and Blair are defined by their legacy of creating landmark institutions. New Labour introduced the National Minimum Wage and the devolved bodies in Scotland, Wales and Northern Ireland; it breathed new life into the National Health Service. By the 2005 election, however, the party had lost momentum: it was visibly running out of steam. The Blair and Brown governments having implemented their 1997 and 2001 manifestos were unable to revitalise themselves in office. This sense of exhaustion was the mirror-image of the Attlee Government's failure to develop a fresh prospectus in the 1940s, as Labour's manifesto, *Let Us Face the Future*, had been implemented by 1949. The task of re-energising Labour in government was a novel problem since never before had the party won two, let alone three, consecutive terms of office. Departmental ministers had become increasingly managerial and technocratic. The leadership was insensitive to undercurrents of change in society and the economy: from employment and the labour market to the new class structures, it continued to rely on *Marxism Today*'s analysis from the 1980s and the sociology of Beck and Giddens.[72] The challenge of transforming public services acquired importance to the detriment of other social democratic objectives. The focus on using the private sector to improve the quality of public goods was consistent with Labour's pragmatic view of the relationship between states and markets; nevertheless, the inference that private providers are always preferable put ideological principle before 'what works'. The fractious debate over the 'means' of delivering public services ensured that the ethical and moral 'ends' of Labour's politics were obscured. British social democracy cannot turn back to the modernising New Labour project of the 1990s; revisionism is concerned with applying moral and ethical values to a changing economy and society. There have been important and far-reaching changes in Britain since Blair and Brown's governments took office. The financial crisis undermined market liberalism, raising new concerns about structural imbalances fuelled by income and wealth inequality. The incomes of the richest are projected to rise 11 times faster than those on the lowest incomes as a consequence of earnings disparities and changes in social security.[73] Blue-collar, manufacturing and agricultural labour once accounting for more than half of all jobs now constitutes less than a fifth of employment.[74] Self-employment is at its highest point for 40 years;[75] there are more than five million small- and medium-sized enterprises (SMEs) in the UK.[76] The proportion of UK workers who were trade union members fell to 25 per cent in 2014; only 14 per cent of the private sector workforce join a union; members are likely to be older and employed in professional occupations.[77] The ongoing revolution in the labour market and gender roles has thrown open the future of work and family life. There has been an increase in the number of households where women are the principal breadwinner from 18 to 31 per cent.[78] These workers are more likely to be educated to university level, but the rise of 'dual earner' households reflects increasing pressure on family incomes due to the inadequacy of wages, underlined by the persistence of the gender pay gap. The erosion in the social base of the labour movement and the collectivist values that held the party in thrall for much of the twentieth century has continued. The centre-left will have to engage with the social forces reshaping the politics of the next decade, applying Crosland's rigorous 'cast of mind' and modernising impulse.

The first challenge relates to underlying structural changes in the UK economy.[79] Social democracy was historically concerned with how to humanise capitalism, a theme addressed at length in *The Future of Socialism*. Crosland's analysis was attacked for its complacency about the market economy; similarly, much of the Left's critique of capitalism in the 1950s and 1960s lacked sophistication. There was then a failure to understand that the globalised financial system had an impact on the economic management regimes of national governments. A new analysis of contemporary capitalism is needed, recognising the significant transformation in production and distribution associated with the rise of an information and service-based economy.[80] The centre-left will need to recognise that societies which have become materially wealthier have to focus on new sources of wellbeing and contentment, notably the quality of relationships and social trust; at the same time, future growth and prosperity means distributing the capacity for innovation and wealth generation throughout society, rather than it being hoarded by the privileged few.[81] This effort includes greater devolution in England after 70 years of centralisation, reviving local government at the city-region and neighbourhood level, as well as the traditional institutions of 'gas and water' municipal socialism and the Town Hall.

The economy has been further restructured: it is more exposed to international market forces; increasingly geared towards the high- and low-skilled service sectors; and more prone to divisions between rich and poor households. In 2025, Britain will be more prosperous than it was in 1997, but its workforce will be competing against the global supply of labour; technology and automation are transforming supply-chains while reconfiguring traditional middle-class occupations such as public administration, law and accountancy that drove social mobility in the 1950s and 1960s.[82] The long-term decline of heavy industry made Labour's cloth cap image counterproductive even in the 1970s and 1980s. The expansion of global trade and the rise of China and India enabled UK companies to enter rapidly growing markets including electronics, pharmaceuticals, aerospace, biotechnology, as well as high-value business consultancy and the creative industries.[83] The consolidation of the European Single Market creates new opportunities to expand export markets while economic restructuring has produced a more unbalanced economy: growth and productivity are driven by England's affluent South-East; many former industrial areas have been locked into a 40-year spiral of cumulative decline. The UK will have to fight to ensure that it can 'pay its way in the world', while preventing low income households and poorer regions from being left further behind in the 'global race' for competitiveness (Mulgan, 2005).

The risk of polarisation has increased as technological change transforms the nature of skills and education: the growth of job insecurity has been accompanied by deterioration in the prospects of the low-skilled.[84] The world economy is entering a 'second machine age' driven by digital technologies rather than mechanisation and manufacturing processes: this requires new capabilities and learning across the workforce, an education revolution more far-reaching than Crosland's creation of comprehensive schools in the 1960s.[85] High-skilled jobs in science, technology and the professions are vulnerable to competition from emerging markets.[86] The rise of e-commerce ensures that firms search globally for the cheapest services and suppliers: the UK is a net beneficiary of globalisation since the increase in British-based businesses off-shoring services and products is small relative to the rise in total output.[87] More than half of the employment created in Britain since the 1990s has come from business services: information technology, accountancy, research, advertising and consultancy, as labour productivity has caught up with the leading G7 economies; while rising productivity in manufacturing from the 1970s led to an overall reduction in employment, productivity growth has driven job creation in the UK services sector.[88]

The increase in 'lovely' and 'lousy' jobs has polarised the UK's 'hour-glass' labour market. Incomes at the top have raced ahead; the CEO of a FTSE 100 company is paid 66 times the average wage of a shop floor worker: the ratio is 98:1 when stock options and bonuses are included.[89] The globalised labour market means greater wage competition, holding inflation in check but exacerbating the squeeze on living standards; automation and computers were emerging in Crosland's era, but are now slowing the pace of job creation in major sectors.[90] Since 2008, productivity growth in the British economy has collapsed. Market economies such as the United States and Britain might become 'jobless societies', in which human workers are retained only where the wealthy seek exclusive services or where labour is cheaper than new technologies.[91] Rising cost pressures mean that outsourcing and off-shoring will continue despite opposition from the labour force and trade unions; the 'jobs for life' model that was the backbone of post-war Britain's affluence and prosperity is under threat.[92] The material gains of new technologies will need to be spread widely rather than monopolised among the elite: even sustained productivity growth is unlikely to close the gap; the alternative is to democratise access to capital and assets, as Dani Rodrick proposes. The 'social innovation dividend' ensures that workers receive an additional income to their earnings in the labour market, sharing profits from public equity stakes in the application of new commercial technologies.[93]

Another feature of structural change is the 'resource crunch'. Growing scarcity will drive up commodity prices in the long-run, notably the cost of food and fuel (Mulgan, 2005). Despite recent volatility in commodity markets and uncertainties about the Chinese growth model, the pace of climate change is likely to accelerate: there will be rising energy and commodity prices for consumers, against the backdrop of a relative decline in oil production and an anticipated rise in coal and natural gas generation; the danger is reduced access to stable supplies of water, in particular for countries with high population densities adding to migratory pressures; the demand for food is likely to rise across the world by 2030, as new patterns of demand emerge driven by the growth of the global middle class.[94] The expanded use of nuclear fuels will be limited by the low supply of uranium; the uncertainty about energy prices will benefit relatively low-consuming, service-based economies notably the UK.[95] Social democratic governments will have to manage resource limits, using levers at their disposal from taxation and regulation to industrial policy in order to incentivise behavioural change.

The second long-term issue confronting centre-left politics is the transformation of the state and public services. The pressures and demands on elected governments have continued to accelerate beyond anything anticipated in 1945. Insouciant as always, Crosland insisted that the resource requirements of post-war collective provision would be met through economic growth; this would also allow for growing consumption. But an increasingly affluent population has rising expectations: as citizens become richer, they want to spend more of their income on 'merit goods', especially health and education. The public sector is being restructured by technological innovation, an increasing focus on prevention and lifestyles, alongside the impact of behavioural change; long-term costs have risen as delivery remains labour-intensive: in relation to conventional measures of productivity, health and social care are 'stagnant sectors'.[96] Nevertheless, education is being transformed away from the 'one size fits all' curriculum of the mass production industrial age, encouraged by digital technologies. Labour's education reforms in the 1960s and 1970s addressed the structure of schooling but scarcely considered what young people needed to succeed in work and life. Today, educational performance is declining in economically marginalised regions of the UK, as gaps widen risking the entrenchment of inter-generational disadvantage.[97]

The west is facing an 'obesity crisis': diet and physical inactivity contribute to 47 per cent of diseases, and 60 per cent of deaths globally; there has been a significant growth in childhood obesity over the last 30 years, especially in Britain and America.[98] In the UK and the United States, the rate of health improvement has slowed since the 1990s as the result of smoking prevalence, infant mortality, inequality and higher premature death rates.[99] There has been an improvement in 'health consciousness': the public are willing to invest in healthy lifestyles, marked by a general decline in smoking, while older citizens are conscious of the importance of physical wellbeing which may reduce the long-term cost of healthcare.[100] During Crosland's career in the 1960s and 1970s, 'male and female life expectancy at birth' in the UK was 71: today, it is more than 80; in all probability, attention will shift to developing countries that are likely to experience a major increase in lifestyle conditions associated with the spread of western diets, smoking and excessive alcohol consumption.[101]

The third related shift affecting social democracy is demographic change and the ageing society, a legacy of the social changes unleashed by the post-war governments. The proportion of the UK population living to at least 100 is likely to increase significantly over the next 50 years. When *The Future of Socialism* was published, the major social policy issue was pensioner poverty and material deprivation among the elderly. Today, it is the inadequacy of social care enabling older people to live fulfilling and independent lives. The engagement of the 'active retired' will be vital for addressing the cost pressures in public services. The traditional age of retirement is more and more irrelevant, as growing numbers of workers return to the labour market; the pattern of 'non-retirement' results from a wish to remain physically active, together with affordability anxieties given the inadequacy of pensions.[102] Medical advances are slowing the ageing process significantly: living a long life is likely to be routine by 2030; it is possible that deaths from cancer, heart disease and Alzheimer's will be greatly reduced, leading to lower health demand but a major long-term rise in the elderly population.[103]

It is not just society's capacity to cope with dependency on public provision that is important, but the ability of 'baby boomer' generations to use their electoral strength in preserving existing entitlements at the expense of the young. Across the EU post-2008, 'there was redistribution from families and children towards pensioners. Spending on education was significantly reduced in the most vulnerable countries, which also affects the young generation'.[104] The risk is a 'lost generation' in European societies permanently scarred by the absence of job-ready skills and loss of contact with the labour market. Equally, within the baby-boomer population there are groups that are vulnerable to poverty and exclusion in old age; the size of the working-age population has reached its peak, and will in all probability decline: the working-age population in the west (aged 16–64) is at its highest point ever.[105] By 2030, the ratio of pensioners to the working-age population will be 1:3.[106] Moreover, age structures will continue to diverge: Europe is composed of ageing countries, while Africa and the Middle-East are dominated by younger societies where at least 60 per cent of the population are under the age of 30; the proportion of the global population living in western states will decline from 24 per cent in 1980 to 16 per cent by 2025: there are likely to be more jobs than people in the next 30 years in Britain, necessitating a controversial revision of retirement policy as well as attitudes to migration.[107] These were not questions that troubled Labour's revisionists in the 1950s, nor indeed Blair's modernisers in the 1990s.

The rapid pace of population change means that western countries are likely to need more rather than fewer immigrants; to sustain the working-age population at current levels will require higher net immigration: a declining population will constrain GDP growth in rich market democracies.[108] The risk is that Europe becomes less attractive to prospective immigrants; the continent is currently an attractive destination, but the focus of migration flows could shift to more stable Latin American and Asian countries.[109] Britain may face the prospect of having to compete for immigrant labour against the backdrop of rising community tensions. Integration needs to be managed to ensure that Britain remains a hospitable and attractive environment with adequate social cohesion. The Internet has promoted long-distance links between immigrant communities and the homogenisation of global culture through mass communications; nonetheless, anxieties about Islamicisation and extremism are rife in western societies: a global society exacerbates resentment.[110] Minority groups can have increasing influence on national agendas while there has been a counter-reaction with the growth of far right populist parties since Enoch Powell's infamous 'rivers of blood' speech in 1968. An important issue for public and private institutions will be how to nurture a committed, high productivity workforce amid growing ethnic diversity and cultural heterogeneity.

The fourth major challenge confronting the centre-left is global interdependence. Crosland's generation was concerned with the deadly certainties of cold war nuclear conflict. Today's generation face a multiplicity of threats from 'conventional' and 'unconventional' non-state actors; terrorism has developed rapidly making use of advanced technologies and social networks.[111] In Crosland's time, the dominant position of the west in global geo-politics was taken for granted. Today, European Union (EU) member-states face the prospect of dramatically reduced global influence; the EU has so far failed to emerge as a serious actor on the world-stage: there has been a shift of geo-political power from the west as the international system pivots towards emerging markets.[112] The European continent will experience the shrinkage of global power unless the EU is reformed; when security crises occur, the EU often fails to act unless shielded by American military might.[113]

The erosion of the international role and significance of the dollar means that it will rapidly lose its status as the primary global reserve currency, another indication of the 'decline of the west'.[114] However, the dominance of China and India should by no means be taken for granted: there are significant hurdles, growing social pressures, and lack of adequate safety nets which constrain economic development.[115] As a consequence, per capita GDP may not increase much up to 2030; Russia wants to increase its global influence, but is hampered by weak infrastructure, declining investment in education and public health, alongside endemic problems of crime and corruption; other emerging powers include Turkey, Iran and Indonesia underlining the growing influence of the Muslim world on the global stage.[116]

The final structural shift for the centre-left is addressing declining trust in political institutions. In *The Future of Socialism*, the citizen's confidence in Parliament and established political structures was taken for granted. Since the 1950s, disengagement from the political system has risen, although citizens have become increasingly involved in 'non-traditional' political activity epitomised by the rise of new social movements. Membership of voluntary and charitable organisations has continued to increase, alongside the growth of social and consumer activism.[117] Confidence in the media, parliament and the political system has plummeted to new lows; according to a recent *British Social Attitudes Survey*, less than one in ten people in the UK trust politicians, although they have more confidence in their local Member of Parliament.[118]

The growth in inequality and the freezing of social mobility will result in greater resentment towards political and corporate elites.[119] The tide of inequality is the result of growing market disparities and weaker redistribution in the face of increased tax resistance. Since 2008, the rich were perceived as 'immune' from austerity. There has been a growing debate about the future of market capitalism since the crash; long-term reforms of the financial system are needed but governments appear incapable of decisive action. Disquiet about capitalism may encourage a shift from the narrow focus on growth to a new

271

debate about the quality of GDP; materialism and acquisitive consumerism could lose their influence in affluent societies.[120] Democracy's future will be affected by the transformative power of the Internet as the traditional political elite, no longer viewed as the custodian of the public interest, is destabilised by the rise of social media; the decline of political parties is accompanied by the growth of corporate power and lobbying, in particular the influence of corporate interests on national governments.[121]

These structural developments, largely unanticipated in Crosland's time, are radically altering the political and policy landscape that social democracy in Britain is confronting. Effective strategies will require a break with the dominant institutions and policy instruments of the post-war era. For instance, widening opportunity and social mobility require a focus not only on reducing child poverty, but addressing the impact of the neighbourhood and school on educational performance,[122] drawing on intangible assets such as networks and cultural capital. Curriculum reform is needed to ensure that young people are prepared for the new economy, rather than prioritising anachronistic concepts of academic excellence. Improving health requires an agenda that takes account of diet, fitness and chronic disease, the wider impact of the physical environment, as well as social factors notably inequality and mental illness. Throughout western health systems, the priority is to integrate services through collaboration, while promoting self-care and mutual support. Labour has to address these debates through its political traditions derived from social liberalism and social democracy, alongside the ideas bequeathed by the revisionist generation through tracts such as *The Future of Socialism*.

Where next for Labour?

The indelible mark left by Crosland on the British centre-left since the 1950s has been remarkable and is traced throughout this book. However, each generation has to define for itself what liberal progressivism and social democracy means in their times. Revisionism has been predominantly concerned with economic issues, especially Britain's unsatisfactory post-war performance. This focus on the economy is hardly surprising: after all, Crosland, Jay, Dalton and Gaitskell were university-trained economists. Nonetheless, Crosland insisted that Labour and the centre-left should address the broader public agenda including quality of life, personal fulfilment and wellbeing. A social democratic party had to consider what kind of growth is now viable: whether faster growth is plausible given intensive global competition, and whether it is desirable given the environmental limits imposed by climate change? The nature of economic growth relates to the debate about subjective well-being and life satisfaction; material progress does not necessarily improve happiness; indeed, mental illness and social stress have been rising in the western industrialised countries:

> Amidst the satisfaction people feel with their material progress, there is a spirit of unhappiness and depression haunting advanced market democracies throughout the world, a spirit that mocks the idea that markets maximise well-being…The current unhappiness and malaise are not marked by revolutionary sentiments, for the ethos of modern market democracies is characterised by strong beliefs in the legitimacy, if not the practices, of its institutions. But in subterranean ways the modern era may be languishing while another is struggling to be born.[123]

Robert E. Lane points to the paradox that as real incomes increase and individuals experience improvements in economic security, material comfort, education and life expectancy, their subjective wellbeing declines. Similarly, Avner Offer argues that well-being has failed to keep pace with affluence in western societies, as consumerism erodes the personal and social commitment that individuals require for self-fulfilment.[124] Consumers are caught in a 'hedonistic treadmill' denying them real choice while contributing to social and psychological maladies. As a consequence, higher monetary incomes do not necessarily increase happiness and contentment.[125] Keynes wrote in 1930 in *The Economic Possibilities for our Grandchildren*:

> For the first time since his creation, man will be faced with his real, his permanent problem – how to use his freedom from pressing economic cares, how to occupy the leisure, which science and compound interest will have won for him, to live wisely and agreeably and well.[126]

The question of how to lead a flourishing life in capitalist democracies frequently surfaced in Crosland's political thought. Equality was not just about where an individual is located on the income distribution, but how well they relate to others: there should be areas of life governed by principles of human need and equal worth rather than the calculus of market exchange. For Crosland, equality of regard was achieved by creating public institutions that bring citizens together across the income and class divide, at least as important as economic equality and the distribution of material resources.[127] This relates to the availability of public services, as well as the provision of amenities, cafes, parks, accessible countryside, open urban spaces and the quality of the public realm. And it alludes to the question of power: not only giving people a chance to shape lives of their choosing, but ensuring that power is exercised as close as possible to citizens and localities, breaking down unaccountable concentrations of privilege.

Crosland's legacy remains pertinent: in a changing Britain, social democrats must be revisionists applying an original 'cast of mind' to present-day conditions, revising their programmes in the light of altered circumstances.[128] The New Labour agenda of the 1990s was a product of its times. A revisionist programme has to secure individual freedom, economic efficiency and social justice in the new political context. Social democracy has to ensure that the plight of the disadvantaged resonates with the affluent if a more just distribution of income, wealth and assets is to be achieved, emphasising the fundamental importance of bringing citizens together across class demarcations.

The central tasks of British social democracy

Crosland acknowledged that no social democratic party could replicate the ideological prospectus of a past generation. Croslandite social democracy was forged as the age of Attlee and austerity gave way to an era of affluence. Labour must now shape a political project relevant to the twenty-first century: the task is not so much to formulate a detailed prospectus, as to identify a central organising principle providing centre-left parties with an electoral strategy, a governing approach, and in due course, a coherent programme.[129] Crosland's 'cast of mind', his 'modernising impulse' and revisionist spirit, should continue to influence the Left's vision. Changes in the economic and social environment necessitate rigorous differentiation between 'ends' and 'means', the *sine qua non* of revisionism. The new revisionism should be rooted in egalitarian values; it has to learn from the rest of the world while integrating the political traditions of social democracy and social liberalism; and today's revisionism must develop a credible alternative to Conservatism in British politics. Centre-left parties still face three principal strategic tasks in government, as they did in Crosland's time:[130]

- to secure macro-economic stability alongside sustainable and fair growth, to oversee discretionary rules that minimise risk, and to protect the British economy from external shocks;
- to ensure that there are high-quality public services and a social service state available to every citizen;
- to undertake redistribution by smoothing out economic inequalities as a countervailing force against unfettered market capitalism, while redistributing resources and risks more equitably across the life-cycle.

This mission is by no means straightforward in a harsh economic climate; social democratic parties must govern despite the constraints imposed by the 'new hard times'. The Labour party will have to reconcile its moral values and ethical ideals with what Tawney once called 'a little cold realism'; following two painful election defeats, it will require 'an interval in which to meditate its errors'.[131]

Macro-economic stability and economic reform

Social democrats ought to carefully reflect on the experience of past Labour governments. The Attlee administrations were propelled to power committed to the virtues of a planned economy. Not only had central planning helped to win the Second World War: the misery and deprivation created by mass unemployment in the 1930s would be avoided by introducing a regime of state intervention. The British economy had been on the verge of liquidation when the guns stopped firing in 1945; Labour faced innumerable constraints and its economic strategy developed haphazardly. Dalton's reliance on regional planning and investment controls was superseded by Keynesian demand management after 1947 under Cripps and Gaitskell.[132] What Crosland termed 'the traditional socialist case for planning' was rejected on the grounds that 'the price mechanism is now a reasonably satisfactory method of distributing the great bulk of consumer goods and industrial-capital goods'.[133] The use of quasi-Keynesian automatic stabilisers to maintain full employment was the centrepiece of the macroeconomic framework. By the mid-1950s, Crosland concluded that British capitalism had been transformed by the 'managerial revolution'. The 'greedy capitalists' were marginalised as the ownership of companies was separated from their control: private sector enterprises were run by a benign managerial elite committed to a partnership with unions and the state.

By 1997 when New Labour was elected, the world had changed fundamentally. Large companies were global rather than national; they were trading in fiercely competitive internationalised labour, product and capital markets. British capitalism was dominated by the financial services sector; manufacturing industry was experiencing a long-term relative decline. Globalisation and markets were embraced as a fact of life. During the 1970s, Crosland was 'criticised for failing to understand that national polities can be constrained by the power of international capitalism'.[134] New Labour accommodated itself to the economic and political realities of globalised markets, along with centre-left parties across the advanced capitalist countries.

Well in advance of the financial crisis, however, it was clear that a more volatile and financialised capitalism was emerging. The 2008 crash underlined the inherently unstable characteristics of markets. Firstly, markets have an inherent tendency towards crises, shocks reverberating beyond national economies to afflict the international system. Furthermore, imperfect information leads governments to adjust policy incorrectly, exaggerating cyclical trends in the economy.[135] Secondly, international financial markets reward the owners of capital rather than wage-earners, compressing the incomes of the intermediate and low skilled: the wage share has declined markedly since the early 1990s. Thirdly, if economic interdependence is not matched by international institutions overseeing financial markets and addressing the shifting global power balance, instability is bound to wreak havoc. The appetite for returning to an anti-globalisation and protectionist strategy of 'British socialism in one country' is limited, but social democracy has to demonstrate that it can address growing volatility and inequality. This approach entails new models of public intervention and political action which harness local, regional, national, European and global institutions.

For social democracy, the logical response to the crash was to rebuild political support for the interventionist state. In the aftermath of the crisis, apprehensive voters directed their resentment not only towards irresponsible financial institutions and avaricious bankers, but incompetent elites, including Labour ministers, who failed to regulate markets and protect the public finances from 'boom and bust'. The party's task is to rebuild confidence in government's capacity to protect the public interest against global market forces. This draws on the distinction made by Keynes between the agenda and non-agenda of governments: the state's focus should be 'those functions which fall outside the sphere of the individual'.[136] Davis writes: 'such policies, for Keynes, in effect function as public goods. They enable attainment of desired results through collective action, which the disaggregated results of individual behaviour are unlikely to achieve.'[137] The state's responsibilities are to guarantee the supply of public goods ensuring a functioning capitalist economy alongside ecological sustainability and social justice. This framework goes beyond the New Democrat's supply-side agenda centred on fiscal discipline and strategic public investment in human capital and science. Such public investment is necessary, but on its own will never alleviate fundamental imbalances between consumption and investment alongside manufacturing industry and services, as well as the growing UK regional divide. Britain is world-leading in technological innovation but still has relatively few high-tech companies among the best globally. While France, Germany and the Nordic countries do whatever is necessary to nurture world-class companies, British governments make a virtue of standing aside.

This more sustainable and productive model of capitalism does not oppose private enterprise and competitive markets: it harnesses the virtues of entrepreneurialism and markets to the public good. It is not 'anti-business' to object to a 'race to the bottom' in the global economy; short-termism in an economy geared towards investment in infrastructure, skills and technology is counterproductive damaging long-term performance; the state and market have to collaborate, encouraging new forms of wealth creation and enterprise.[138] This claim relates to the theme of a stakeholder economy, adumbrated in Will Hutton's work, *The State We're In*, updated more recently by John Kay, John Plender and Marianna Mazzucato[139] who each examine the weakness of free markets and the vital role of public institutions. In *A Firm Commitment*, Colin Mayer similarly focuses on corporations and institutions that build trust in a sustainable market economy.[140] In the *Harvard Business Review*, Mark Porter and Mark Kramer write:

'A big part of the problem lies with companies themselves, which remain trapped in an outdated approach to value creation that has emerged over the past few decades.'[141] Under shareholder capitalism, the goal is optimising short-term performance, missing important customer needs while neglecting innovation and investment that determines long-term success. Porter and Kramer insist: 'companies must take the lead in bringing business and society back together'. In the stakeholder economy, companies serve the interests of workers and the community, not only shareholders, encouraging strategies for business development and growth that recognise the obligations and responsibilities of business to society. This vision is consistent with the structural trends shaping today's capitalism based on collaboration, a new technological frontier, and a 'sharing economy'.

The government's agenda in forging an inclusive capitalism has to be coherent. Firstly, it means ensuring a resilient economy where firms and institutions have the confidence to plan ahead; where banking and financial institutions support wealth creation by limiting undesirable speculative activities. Secondly: tackling inequalities in the distribution of income and assets that weaken broad-based consumption as a stimulus to long-term innovation. Thirdly: cultivating sustainable growth through public–private sector collaboration, ensuring continuing improvements in the quality of public services and infrastructure. This model foresees a virtuous cycle in which higher growth is derived from public investment combined with greater international competitiveness; investment entails economic stability and growing tax revenues which limit inequalities in the income distribution; stability and growth in turn enable long-term investment in public services and public goods. That policy equilibrium has been the hallmark of successful social democracies throughout Europe.

There is an additional responsibility on governments, however: active measures to break up concentrated economic power, dispersing ownership of capital and assets. Social democracy must promote a 'property-owning' democracy: the redistribution of property and assets aims to disperse control over wealth. The reform of property ownership means a more affordable supply of land to households and businesses, adjusting the beneficial tax regime. The tax system in the UK transfers wealth from 'productive' to 'unproductive' sectors with negative repercussions for growth and prosperity.[142] The revenue from a property levy and new council tax bands for high value properties should be invested in shared ownership schemes and affordable housing, so more families gain a foothold on the housing ladder. Profit-sharing schemes improve workers' capacity to build a capital base, while social ownership can disperse wealth more widely. The aim is to create resilience safeguarding wealth-generating sectors, without dampening the pluralism and experimentation necessary for a vibrant capitalist economy. Joseph Schumpeter spoke of creative destruction as 'the essential fact about capitalism': productivity growth is generated by new production models replacing old systems leading to an ongoing turnover in jobs, as well as cycles of recession and expansion; economies that limit creative destruction by imposing regulatory and institutional restraints run the risk of lower growth, productivity and living standards.[143] Governments cannot regain control of the economy through state ownership and planning, but they can use levers to develop rules and regulations that alter long-term incentives and behaviour, in so doing reconstructing the supply-chain.

In the aftermath of the financial crisis, the British Left has turned against capitalism. Social democracy's historic purpose is to protect citizens from the instability and disorder of markets.[144] It was Marx who anticipated that under capitalism 'all that is solid melts into air' as the production process entails waves of restructuring. Having accommodated itself to the market, the purpose of European social democracy was to save capitalism from itself rather than replacing capitalism with an alternative economic system. Reform was the aim of early twentieth-century radical liberals including Hobhouse and Lloyd George, as well as Keynes. In principle, social democrats are strategically well positioned to manage the mixed economy since they are prepared to intervene in the public interest, rather than to be deluded by unjustified faith in market forces. For the market is not a natural, self-correcting system. Neither can financial interests be allowed to dominate democratic decision-making, regardless of the modern tax state's dependence on capitalist growth: any change in Britain's political economy is unlikely 'without serious engagement with the ways in which the state itself has been captured by, and made itself dependent on, an array of private, corporate interests tied to the financial sector'.[145] The political elite must resolve how the flow of international capital into the UK, particularly London and the South-East, distorts the housing market especially when property is treated as a 'risk-free' investment asset.[146]

Public services and the role of the state

There has been vigorous debate within European social democracy since the 1950s about the role and purpose of the state, alongside the relationship between the state and its citizens. After the Second World War, the Swedish Social Democrats sought to define the state as 'the people's home'. The German SPD qualified its view of state socialism at Bad Godesberg in 1959, emphasising a thriving market economy. British social democracy has remained attached to the structures and institutions of the British state. For much of the last century, Labour was as reluctant as the Conservative party to reform the state, despite the hostility of early socialists to the established political system. The growth in the capacities and responsibilities of government after the First World War marked a new phase of British political development: state institutions were associated with the ideals of collectivism and socialism. After 1940, the organised working class was integrated into the British state, symbolised by Ernest Bevin's appointment as a minister in the wartime coalition. The acceptance of indicative planning and Keynesian demand management within the civil service and policy-making establishment allowed Britain to avoid the social and economic turmoil that marked the inter-war years, maintaining full employment and promoting social security.

Nonetheless, the centre-left has been compelled to update and 'modernise' its view of the state. Vernon Bogdanor attests that a 'golden straightjacket' has been imposed on British social democracy, weakened by two countervailing political forces: territorial devolution and globalisation. Globalisation and devolution undermine the power of the nation-state as conceived by the Westminster model, curtailing government's ability to achieve social justice. The relationship between territory and the welfare state is increasingly fluid: citizens are less likely to identify the social security afforded by welfare institutions with the United Kingdom as a multinational state.[147] Post-war social democracy had taken the British state's cohesion for granted despite the emergence of Celtic nationalism in the late 1960s. More recently, attention has focused on 'active citizenship': strengthening bonds within neighbourhoods and communities, alongside the vertical relationship between citizens and government; support for an active state depends on sustaining the sense of 'we': the ethic of belonging, shared identity and national community.[148] The attempt to redefine 'Britishness' proved elusive following devolution to Scotland, Wales and Northern Ireland in the late 1990s. The pace of mass migration, alongside the emergence of new divisions between religious communities and a predominantly secular society, have further weakened social cohesion.[149]

The state's ability to invest in public services is under pressure. Before the First World War, Britain devoted 12 per cent of national income to funding the emerging welfare system;[150] under Labour after 1997, it reached 43 per cent (48 per in the wake of the financial crisis); it is set to fall to 36 per cent by 2019–20 in the aftermath of austerity. The combination of secular stagnation in which growth remains anaemic, alongside continuing demographic pressure, will heavily constrain spending. The sense of foreboding about future spending constraints brings to mind Keynes' remarks in *Economic Possibilities for our Grandchildren*:

> We are suffering just now from a bad attack of economic pessimism. It is common to hear people say that the epoch of enormous economic progress... is over. That the rapid improvement in the standard of life is now going to slow down – at any rate in Great Britain; that a decline in prosperity is more likely than an improvement in the decade which lies ahead of us.[151]

State funding has been squeezed as the tax base is depleted due to a high rate of tax evasion and avoidance; behavioural changes in which citizens consume fewer 'harmful' goods, notably alcohol, tobacco and petrol; and the compression of real wages further depleting tax revenues: the lack of resilience in the tax base was a major contributor to the post-2008 fiscal crisis.[152] The cuts in the basic rate of tax were excessive, while an expensive system of pension tax relief disproportionately favouring the better-off was entrenched. Britain requires major tax reform: James Meade's principle that taxes ought to be levied at a similar rate for income, capital, wealth and inheritance is significant.[153] This policy would improve the reliability of revenues, removing anomalies and distortions that protect current privileges and encourage unproductive investment. There is a case for shifting the tax burden from income to property and wealth, alongside hypothecation of funding: creating an explicit link between taxes, National Insurance contributions, and levels of investment in services such as the NHS. Crosland recognised the importance of maintaining the legitimacy of collective provision in an affluent society where tax resistance was growing.

The social democratic state has to incentivise improvements in public sector productivity, particularly in the NHS and social care that are capable of squaring the circle of rising costs and expectations. Social productivity focuses on how the quality of public services can be improved by harnessing the capabilities of citizens.[154] In a society where individuals are more knowledgeable and better educated, the structure and organisation of public services can be redesigned. The paternalism of post-1945 provision is untenable. There should be far less reliance on formal structures and institutions; a greater focus on shared value and social productivity; and increased scope for 'co-creation' of services through healthier lifestyles and improvements in mental health. There is a growing emphasis on preventative treatment: for example, US insurance providers are cutting premiums for individuals with fewer health risks. In the English health system, patients who do not curb behaviours such as smoking and poor diet are at risk of being denied life-saving treatments.

Disruptive reorganisation remains unpopular with the public sector professions; institutional reforms, notably quasi-markets and New Public Management, that separate commissioning from provision are seldom viewed positively. The centre-left ought to build on what already exists, adapting policies inherited from previous governments into progressive institutions: for instance, in education, targeting investment in academies and free schools towards the most deprived areas. Public interest and equity principles have to be strengthened given the diverse mixed economy of English schools, very different to Crosland's vision of comprehensive education. Primary care and GP access in the NHS are another area where equity has been threatened by growing diversity of provision. The integration of services is crucial for future health and social care, yet this has been an ambition since the 1960s. The obstacles to integration locally are not merely internal market reforms, but a predominantly centralised system of healthcare planning and provision.

The sustainability of public provision leads to the vexed question of how to distribute costs equitably between the citizen and the state given scarce resources: co-payment of university tuition fees and social care have established a precedent for innovative funding mechanisms. As public services have developed since the Second World War serving an increasingly affluent population, the centre-left must confront how the taxpayer-funded system ought to evolve. It will be necessary to devise new funding systems while protecting social democratic principles of universalism and inclusivity.

Redistribution across the life-cycle

The Attlee Government's vision of equality focused on 'fair shares' for wage-earners, alongside equal opportunities for the working class. Beyond the 1944 Education Act, schools nonetheless played a limited role in Labour's thinking given the importance attached to state ownership and nationalisation. The party's purpose was not to transform the class structure of British society, as the authors of the *New Fabian Essays* complained in 1952. Crosland's strategy for comprehensive schools was spelt out in *The Future of Socialism*, and enacted after his appointment to Education in 1965: equality was tied to a revolution in educational provision. The revisionists were determined to address the fundamental causes of class stratification, combining an assault on privilege through taxation of inheritance and capital with comprehensivisation. It was hoped that post-war affluence would create a more classless society, but it was evident by the 1970s that relative poverty and structural inequality had become entrenched. Crosland was disappointed by the slow pace of progress, a setback he lamented in his 1974 collection, *Socialism Now*.[155]

New Labour inherited the long-term consequences of Thatcherism's reforms. Labour sought to combat structural disadvantage, especially the one in five households where no-one was working, channelling welfare support to encourage employment participation while increasing benefits for children and pensioners. Social policy was designed to sustain public support but, inevitably, criticisms emerged as we saw in the previous chapter: the party was judged not to have made sufficient progress in reducing poverty; Labour's impact on income inequality was insignificant; the Blair governments were unconcerned about the riches amassed by the wealthy. The party's programme left major questions unanswered: for instance, how does the state ensure those with few qualifications are able to access the labour market earning a living wage? How far does discrimination, on the basis of characteristics such as gender, ethnicity and disability, cause poverty? Is it legitimate for the state to make moral judgements that, for the able-bodied, paid employment is the best route out of poverty (even if that restricts an individual's ability to be a good parent or carer)? Work has not always proved to be a sustainable route out of poverty; the national minimum wage, even combined with tax credits, is not a 'living wage' in a two-adult household where only one adult is working.[156]

The labour market needs reform to protect the interests of workers in non-unionised sectors ensuring employees have greater flexibility, not only firms and management: this is essential to increase employment participation particularly among parents with children, those who have been economically inactive, and workers with disabilities. At the same time, employment regulation that re-balances security and flexibility must be tailored to a competitive economy with a high proportion of SMEs that are exposed to international markets: it has to be non-bureaucratic and 'light touch'.

Centre-left parties face invidious choices over redistribution across the advanced democracies. Health, education and social care have absorbed a growing share of spending since the 1980s: as citizens get richer, they want to consume public goods of quality and excellence; demography and technological change create additional pressures. Social democratic governments prioritised universal provision ensuring that rich and poor alike gain equal access to services, reducing the distance between classes and maintaining the consensus for state financing. The evidence from the Nordic countries is that universalism generates greater equality. If the priority is spending on services, however, the danger is that income redistribution that narrows the gap between the wealthy and poor will be emphasised less. Voters' growing scepticism about contributing a greater share of their income to the tax state imposes a trade-off between income redistribution and investment in public services. The squeeze on public resources has been accentuated since the 2008 crisis by huge banking sector bail-outs.

A further quandary in a world of limited resources relates to equality of outcome versus opportunity: if governments are focused on equalising the income distribution 'here and now', investment that alters the long-term allocation of human and financial capital from early education to asset redistribution is inevitably less of a priority. An equal opportunity society is, of course, harder to achieve where the gap between rich and poor is growing: opportunity and outcomes are mutually reinforcing, but there is a question of priorities. This relates to the theme of why inequality matters: individuals can survive on low incomes where their situation is transient; they may be able to escape poverty relatively easily, for example young people with good educational qualifications; however, some individuals are trapped in structural disadvantage throughout their lives, particularly those without job-ready education and training.[157] This perspective relates to Amartya Sen's claim that access to material resources matters in so far as it shapes an individual's capabilities: what they can do and be.[158] Social democracy's purpose must be to distribute incomes efficiently across the income distribution and between the generations, while ensuring a more egalitarian distribution of primary incomes through reform of labour, product and capital markets. Beveridge's welfare state was designed to insure citizens against the 'five giants' of unemployment, lack of adequate housing, poor education, poverty and ill-health. Crosland foresaw the limitations of that strategy; like the New Liberals, he advocated measures to tackle wealth inequalities while encouraging a property-owning democracy that equalised the distribution of marketable assets.[159] The reform of property ownership remains a crucial task in the new century.

The stakeholder society

The vision of positive liberty centred on more 'equal opportunities for self-development' promoted by Green and Hobhouse in the early twentieth century and advanced by Crosland in *The Future of Socialism* remains highly pertinent.[160] Crosland's writings drew together vital principles at the heart of the liberal enlightenment: 'equality', a just allocation of resources, opportunities and public goods, and 'freedom': the ability to use resources according to the individual's priorities and values to maximise human flourishing.[161] This approach is what Philippe Van Parijs[162] defines as real freedom: individuals should have the resources to realise their talents and shape a life of their own imagining.[163] Social democracy must tackle disparities in life-chances; society is weaker if market forces are allowed to dominate and the wealthy 'super-rich' detach themselves.[164] Real freedom implies 'starting-gate opportunities', egalitarianism rooted in an ethic of personal responsibility as well as individual rights. Whether we succeed or fail is influenced by the individual's choices and motivation; but undeniably, the unequal concentration of wealth and class inequalities threatens freedom:[165] all of us should have the opportunity to develop ourselves by accessing collective goods.

How can a new social democratic egalitarianism be advanced in contemporary circumstances? There are numerous proposals to move towards greater equality: a higher national 'living' wage; tougher regulation of executive pay; incentivising unionisation to protect workers in low wage sectors; increasing the supply of social housing; a higher marginal tax rate on those earning over £250,000 a year; improvements in the state education system; an expansion of childcare; increasing the value of child benefit; alongside restoring universality in the welfare system.[166] These interventions are undoubtedly worthy of consideration; however, the gains will in all likelihood be transient and incremental. For instance, measures to protect low wage earners are essential; but the 'jobs for wages' model has produced declining returns since the 1970s. The state ought to use regulatory and legislative mechanisms to lean against the tide of inequality, but fundamentally reversing the downward pressure on wages will be arduous and in any case, insufficient. Social democratic governments in Northern Europe have focused on paid work and the labour market, offering social protection conditional on taking up employment opportunities.[167] Even those who have found work usually remain dependent on the state: low wages mean that they require an ongoing income subsidy through tax credits to survive; as a consequence, the low paid have less effective freedom.[168] This inequity is unacceptable to egalitarian social democrats.

The radical policy strategy is *a universal capital endowment, a stakeholder grant initially set at the level of £20,000 bestowed on every citizen at the age of 21.* It would be funded by an annual 2 per cent levy on all unearned income from assets, property, wealth, inheritance and capital gains.[169] Among the advocates of a public endowment was the philosopher, Thomas Paine, who articulated proposals for 'a national fund, out of which there shall be paid to every person, when arrived at the age of 21 years, the sum of 15 pounds sterling'.[170] The eighteenth century American republicans believed that equality of property ownership was necessary for a 'self-governing society' where individual citizens are independent and self-reliant; British socialists such as Tawney and Cole similarly advocated social ownership of assets rather than wholesale nationalisation.[171] The capital endowment would be available to every young adult in Britain for investment in a deposit to purchase a home, to fund their higher education, to undertake an apprenticeship, or to start a new business. The grant acknowledges the legitimate claim of every individual to a stake in the nation's wealth.[172] The endowment is funded by a levy on the unequal distribution of unearned wealth rather than income tax, underlining 'the expressive power of taxation': greater equality in the allocation of wealth for the next generation is secured by taxing inequalities in the current generation.[173]

Taxing wealth and asset-holding to fund a universal endowment constitutes a bold social democratic strategy. It depends on maintaining a vibrant market economy in which wealth is widely dispersed, where rewards flow to productive sectors. Western societies, notably the United Kingdom and the United States, have traditionally taxed property, housing and land at lower rates than income, advantaging those who rely on unproductive assets: a new political economy should focus on democratising access to capital, housing, land and education.[174] The taxation system is less efficient at generating revenues from asset-holding, wealth and property. The New Liberalism incorporated an essential distinction derived from Mill between legitimate earned income and inefficient unearned income.[175] A wealth levy is a lifetime accessions tax affecting the recipient rather than the giver, encouraging the diffusion and spreading of inheritance.[176] New mechanisms of wealth taxation inevitably create losers; political parties have been reluctant to create electoral hostages to fortune by interfering with inheritance tax, more often reducing liabilities.[177] British social attitude surveys indicate voters are far from convinced about the argument for wealth and inheritance taxes. Nonetheless, politicians have a responsibility to make an ethical case: taxing earned incomes is less efficient; the proceeds of a wealth levy would go directly into a universal endowment; reforms can help to make the system fairer encouraging the rich to spread their wealth.[178] Other taxation reforms should include capping the tax-free sum for pensions, as well as abolishing higher rate tax relief, neither of which are justified on equity and efficiency grounds.[179]

The debate about inheritance has to be reframed given the scale of inequality and social privilege in Britain. Inheritance remains unequally distributed: between 1995 and 2005, one in five individuals inherited wealth; half of all inheritance went to the top 10 per cent (estates valued at more than £0.5 million).[180] In the tradition of civic republicanism, Paine insisted inheritance should never be a function of family background, but is our right by virtue of citizenship. We each have a legitimate claim to a share of society's resources; this should not be dependent on the brute luck of being born into a wealthy family:[181] 'The earth, in its natural uncultivated state was, and ever would have continued to be, the common property of the human race...the system of landed property...has absorbed the property of all those whom it dispossessed, without providing, as ought to have been done, an indemnification for that loss.'[182]

At present, young people from wealthy families have private endowments to buy a privileged education, claim a stake in the housing market, and establish their own business without incurring major risk. According to Hills, there are 'long lasting advantages for children from wealthier family backgrounds and for those who are able to accumulate assets in early childhood'.[183] There have been stark warnings about the emergence of a 'hereditary meritocracy', echoing Young's *Rise of the Meritocracy*. Educated parents use selective schools, enrichment for their children, along with social networks and cultural capital to transmit advantages to the next generation.[184] Those with less wealth and fewer assets struggle to access opportunities.[185] The danger is a 'lost generation' of young people lacking qualifications while losing contact with employment, trapped in a cycle of financial hardship and despair. Not surprisingly, wealth inequality and the decline of income mobility have led to increasing resentment against elites.[186] In contrast to the post-war years where rising prosperity dispersed wealth across the generations, parents fear that their children's living standards and life-chances are being curtailed. A universal endowment rebalances the distribution of opportunities, enabling young adults to adopt a long-term perspective on what they want to achieve, avoiding decades of hopelessness and 'quiet desperation'.[187] The endowment appeals to 'small-c conservative voters', a vital element of Labour's electoral coalition, emphasising reciprocity, a 'something for something' culture, while enabling young people to get their foot on the ladder. In reality, the endowment proposal is a stepping-stone towards a 'participation income' requiring individuals to demonstrate that they are engaged in economically and socially useful activity for which they receive a basic subsistence income from the state (Atkinson, 2015); this ensures that citizens are no longer dependent on paid employment, enabling simplification of the welfare and social insurance system. The universal endowment should be accompanied by further measures that assist individuals to share in the nation's wealth:

Firstly, the shortage of affordable housing markedly increases social resentment and is a major barrier to families fulfilling their aspirations. Young people are compelled to rent for longer, particularly in London and the South-East. *Social democracy needs an agenda to extend home ownership introducing more sustainable forms of finance and credit, while expanding the availability of land to increase the supply of housing.* The UK's dysfunctional housing market has meant that buy-to-let investment significantly outperforms the construction of new homes; 45 per cent of land with planning permission in London is owned by those with little or no intention of undertaking development.[188] More flexible planning laws are insufficient: it has to become more profitable to build homes; the 1961 Land Compensation Act ought to be reformed allowing 'city region authorities to acquire land at closer to existing use value in conjunction with their own land in dedicated housing zones. This will make the market more efficient, ensuring that the rewards of innovation and hard work flow to all firms and workers in a city region rather than to those who own property assets.'[189] As well as building more homes, there ought to be statutory regulation of the private rented sector, curbing excessive rent rises and improving the security of tenure.

Secondly, there should be more social ownership and incentives to create mutualised businesses. There ought to be greater profit-sharing and employee share ownership: enabling the majority to share in rising prosperity means diffusing wealth and asset ownership through the promotion of profit-sharing arrangements, as envisaged by the John Lewis Partnership where every employee receives an annual dividend payment in addition to their salary. An additional proposal is that employees should have the right to request up to 5 per cent of the share capital of a company, with an obligation on employers to consider and respond to all requests.[190]

Thirdly, in technologically advanced economies, a growing share of productivity growth accrues to the owners of capital; *to off-set this, governments should establish public venture capital funds that take equity stakes in new technology businesses* making periodic 'social dividend payments' to low and middle income households, supplementing wages rather than allowing the gains to be swallowed by private investors; funds would be raised by governments issuing bonds in the financial markets.[191]

Fourthly, wherever possible government should set an example in democratising asset ownership: rather than selling all of the shares in the publicly owned Royal Bank of Scotland (RBS) to private investors, one-third should have gone to a trust managed on behalf of customers, and a further third to employees of the bank.[192] This approach would have spread the benefits of dividend payments more widely than current investors in the stock market; the structures of ownership in the British economy have to be reformed.

Fifthly, inequality should be addressed by *focusing on the primary distribution of income through labour market and public procurement regulations that promote a living wage and curtail exploitation*; this means investing in measures such as affordable childcare that increase labour market participation; promoting flexible working to engage 'hard to reach groups' more efficiently in employment; using competition policy to prevent consumer exploitation in purchasing essential commodities such as food and energy; and expanding the coverage of occupational pensions to make them affordable for those on low incomes.[193]

Sixthly, *the centre-left's goal should be to allow people to keep as much of their hard-won income as possible, instead taxing the proceeds of unearned wealth, capital and property.* The Mirrlees Review of Taxation proposed a shift from direct to indirect taxes, replacing regressive taxes such as stamp duty and council tax with new levies on property. An annual property tax on the most expensive homes would enable governments to give additional tax relief to low- and middle-income tax payers. Reforming tax allowances and moving people out of the tax system altogether is intuitively appealing; but the most efficient way to raise family incomes and reduce child poverty beyond the national minimum wage has been targeted tax credits. The system of tax credits has to be reviewed, however, emphasising that they are primarily about supporting those in work, particularly families; tax credits are 'earned', while there is a need to strip out wasteful administrative complexity and bureaucracy.

Seventhly, *the emphasis of social democracy has to be on production and growth, not only redistribution of the existing stock of wealth and assets.* The state can play a constructive role in fostering innovation and domestic expansion, as Mazzucato argues in *The Entrepreneurial State*; by investing in physical infrastructure and R&D in an era when borrowing costs have reached record lows, governments can incentivise higher education institutions and venture capitalists to work together developing new products and services expanding the productive potential of the economy and in turn reconstructing the supply-chain towards high-value growth.[194]

The Left should criticise an economy too often failing those on low and middle incomes; but focusing on 'zero-hours contracts' and the living wage will not appeal to the relatively affluent workers, the skilled working-class and white-collar occupational groups who do not believe that social democracy has anything to offer aspiring, upwardly mobile voters. If forthcoming elections are fought against the backdrop of a modest recovery in real wages and, in comparison to the previous decade, a mood of relative affluence and prosperity, the centre-left must demonstrate that it can support the desire for rising personal consumption, as well as decent public services. High income taxes on ordinary wage-earners were never part of Labour's core programme: in 1945, only 12 million families in Britain paid income tax after an extension of the tax system during the war; by the end of the 1990s, the figure had reached 26.9 million.[195] The burden of income tax should be as low as practicable, while supporting low-paid families in work through the living wage, targeted efforts to improve skills and earning power, alongside extra measures such as subsidised childcare. To entrench the consensus for taxpayer funding, the Left has to demonstrate that standards in public health and education will be at least as high as in the private sector.

Conclusion

This chapter addressed the future of the Labour party and British social democracy: it began by assessing the record of New Labour in government in relation to inequality and economic policy. The Blair and Brown governments undertook significant innovations, enabling them to avoid the errors of previous Labour administrations; on the other hand, there was a clear regulatory failure in financial markets, alongside complacency about the scale of inequality and the underlying weakness of British economic performance. To succeed in the next century, Labour should remain an intellectually dynamic party committed to the politics of 'conscience and reform'. This mantle of 'conscience and reform' rejects the politics of class struggle and class antagonism, forging a broad-based progressive alliance between social democracy and social liberalism. The next generation has an unparalleled opportunity to establish a new phase of social democratic dominance in British politics.

This political strategy should be accompanied by a renovation of the liberal and progressive tradition on the centre-left, linking the New Liberals, the inter-war economists of the New Fabian Research Bureau, the post-war revisionists together with contemporary social democrats. The emphasis on economic egalitarianism traditionally located within social democracy ought to be combined with a commitment to individual freedom and human flourishing integral to social liberalism.[196] New Labour sought to engineer this marriage in the 1990s but succeeded in alienating many liberal progressives. Crosland emphasised the ethical and moral ideals animating social democracy, obscured by the mid-twentieth century preoccupation with state ownership. Like his close friend Michael Young, he believed, 'by concentrating so heavily on the development of the state, the party...was neglecting the moral heart of socialism'.[197]

New Labour, in contrast, was focused on electoral strategy, winning the allegiance of the median voter and establishing the party's reputation for economic competence.[198] Only by pursuing realistic but radical reforms that address contemporary problems can Labour fulfil its destiny as a progressive force in British politics. The challenge is not to produce an array of new policies, but to delineate a central organising idea for social democracy: in the 1940s and 1950s, it was planning and public ownership; in the 1960s and 1970s, equality and government spending; as a signpost to 2030, social democracy has to stand for a more productive as well as a more equal society where disparities in life-chances are eroded by an attack on inherited wealth and privilege. Labour will lack the energy and drive to govern in a cold climate for social democracy unless it can re-discover not only the party's radical 'cast of mind', but also its soul.[199]

NINE

Conclusion: a future for socialism?

British society – slow-moving, rigid, class-ridden –
has proved much harder to change than we supposed.
Looking back with hindsight, the early revisionist
writings were too complacent in tone; they proposed
the right reforms, but under-rated the difficulty
of achieving them in a British context. (Anthony
Crosland[1])

Mr Callaghan just isn't in your class. He does not have
the first class intelligence for the job, he does not have
a really sure grasp of economics, as you have, he does
not represent any fresh radical outlook which you can
offer. We need someone like you. (Letter from Mr
Kevin Kavanagh[2])

The conventional view serves to protect us from the
painful business of thinking. (John Kenneth Galbraith,
American economist[3])

Great changes are not caused by ideas alone; but they
are not affected without ideas. (Leonard Hobhouse[4])

Introduction

This book sought to trace the impact of Crosland's revisionist analysis on the Labour party since the publication of *The Future of Socialism* in 1956. It examined, in particular, his emphasis on equality in contradistinction to state ownership; the legacy of Crosland's liberal progressivism in a traditionalist party of sectional interests and ambiguously socialist aspirations; the influence of continental Europe and the United States on Crosland's reformulation of social democracy; and his view of electoral strategy in an affluent Britain characterised by rising consumption and individualism. The theme throughout is Crosland's inheritance and the debate about ideas in the party and across the British Left over the last 60 years. The Crosland effect was a reflection of his personality and character, his charisma and profound intelligence, alongside his ability to speak audaciously to the mood and circumstances of the times. His impact was a reflection of Crosland's outstanding political and intellectual qualities, but also a consequence of the existential crisis afflicting Labour in the late 1950s. This turmoil gave him the opportunity to play a decisive role in remaking the party. Improbably for a post-war socialist raised in the Exclusive Brethren and the Fabian tradition, Crosland was a 'bon viveur' who relished hedonism and the pursuit of the good life.[5] In *The Future of Socialism*, he envisaged a civilised, tolerant and enlightened Britain in which people could conceivably enjoy living. Kenneth O. Morgan has written that 'Crosland is surely to be commended for setting his face against the Puritanism which disfigures so much of the labour movement'.[6] This Croslandite New Jerusalem combined American ingenuity and classlessness with Scandinavian egalitarianism and tranquillity. His optimistic reinterpretation of social democracy contrasted starkly with the negative disposition that David Marquand characterised as Labour's 'strange, inward-looking proletarianism'.[7]

While he was praised and acclaimed among British social democrats, liberals and public intellectuals, the endorsement of Crosland's work was far from unanimous. This book sought to highlight deficiencies and limitations in his analysis of society, economy and state, as well as its strengths. For all its iconoclasm and eloquence, *The Future of Socialism* was a controversial text generating heated debate long after its publication. As a socialist theoretician facing up to changing political realities, Crosland's writings inevitably attracted disapproval. After all, his analysis was designed to contest and reshape the dominant political narrative in the Labour party. The imperfections, nonetheless, arise from two familiar but interwoven sources: Crosland's background in the British policy-making establishment after the Second World War; and the inherent weaknesses of his intellectual outlook.

Croslandism: a critique

At the outset, Crosland's experience made him too sanguine about the British political system and machinery of government. This contentment was ironic given that early socialists had been motivated by an innate suspicion of the state, and a desire to preserve the political and economic freedoms of the working class and their trade union institutions (Morgan, 2008). Crosland exhibited a naiveté about the ability of Britain's political institutions to enact social reforms. He later acknowledged unease about the efficacy of the Westminster model; in an article published in *Socialist Commentary* entitled 'Equality in Hard Times', he advocated 'a wider sharing of political power within the nation' through radical devolution.[8] Nonetheless, Crosland's complacency about existing governing arrangements is difficult to discount. The sentiment of quiet self-satisfaction ran deep within the post-war liberal mandarinate, and was actively promoted throughout the civil service and the universities of Oxford and Cambridge. It was argued that British political institutions had survived two world wars and would now serve as the apparatus for implementing the post-war settlement. Crosland's father had been a high-ranking civil servant;[9] his son had little sympathy with the view of the Labour Left, notably Tony Benn, that the civil service was inherently opposed to a radical socialist programme.

Marquand concurs that Crosland's work lacked an overarching view of the political and constitutional structure of the state. These criticisms resonated more strongly during the crises of the 1970s and 1980s; labourism had remarkably little to say about the predicament facing British democracy. The revisionists assumed that they were in full control of the state once power was achieved through the democratic electoral process; they never faced up to the question of how they would achieve the outcomes specified in Labour's programme: the essential issue of implementation in the governing process.[10] The political class avoided reforming a predominantly centralised and bureaucratic state refusing to concede greater local autonomy.[11] In fairness, Crosland presented his 1970 Local Government White Paper as granting financial freedom to local authorities. But the post-war revisionists were indifferent to the declining legitimacy of local intermediate institutions and the growing resonance of national identities within the United Kingdom. Reforming parliamentarians including Marquand and John Mackintosh highlighted the inadequacies of Crosland's strategy in failing to address the weaknesses of the state and the paralysis of the English ancien regime reinforced by relative national decline. They drew on a burgeoning literature relating the deterioration of the British economy to the inherent weaknesses of Britain's governing institutions, and the failure to create a developmental state in contrast to post-war continental Europe.[12]

In addition, strong criticisms were made of Crosland's egalitarian policies. His social mission in the 1960s was comprehensive education; he famously promised 'to destroy every fucking grammar school in England'; the dream was never realised: in some areas of England, grammar schools survived.[13] Labour failed to develop a vision of post-selective education which acknowledged the talents and abilities of every pupil, a weakness undermining Crosland's legacy. Robert Skidelsky believes that Crosland's hostility to grammar schools was excessive, leading to tolerance of mediocrity while unintentionally entrenching elitism by reinforcing the popularity of public schools.[14] The Head of Wilson's Policy Unit, Bernard Donoughue contends:

> You needed to be clearer what you put in its place. Vast factory comprehensives were not necessarily better. I didn't think it was necessary to abolish grammar schools. You could have a more pluralistic system. There was something Stalinist about comprehensives. Crosland like too many people in the Labour party wasn't interested in quality, he was interested in ideology.[15]

Research has indicated that comprehensive schools have outperformed selective grammars since the 1960s.[16] That said, Crosland's analysis of education policy was inadequate; he had little to say about the curriculum and teaching, issues eventually addressed by James Callaghan in his 1976 Ruskin speech.[17]

Moreover, currents of intellectual energy that infected the New Left and consequently shaped New Labour in the 1990s such as gender and feminist politics, alongside concerns with legitimacy and identity in British society, scarcely arose in Crosland's writings. Rita Desai contends that post-war revisionism exhibited the 'sociological deficiency of British culture' focusing predominantly on economic questions while ignoring issues of political authority and power.[18] American behavioural science sustained its hold over British academics and intellectuals, promoting a technocratic managerialism in an age defined by Daniel Bell as 'the end of ideology'.

The Future of Socialism, Crosland's most seminal and authoritative contribution to social democratic thought, was naturally a product of the intellectual and political climate of the 1950s. His early writings were inspired by a belief that following Churchill's devastating election defeat in 1945, the Conservatives had accepted major planks of the post-war settlement. Crosland insisted the 'One Nation' party of Macmillan and Butler posed no existential threat to social democracy:

> Economic prosperity and social security have softened
> the acerbities of political conflict. Under the impact of
> democratic pressure and a changed climate of opinion,
> Conservatives have come to accept a large measure of
> liberal reforms; and much of what the Left preached
> forty years ago is now non-controversial. Under these
> circumstances, the militant language of class war, the
> terminology of revolt and counter-revolt, is (slowly)
> passing out of usage.[19]

Crosland argued that the Conservatives would struggle to
maintain their reputation as the natural governing party: they
had proved less effective at maintaining full employment,
and had no coherent strategy for expanding social security
and the public services. Labour in 1945–51 demonstrated
that it could manage post-war Britain at least as efficiently;
the Right were swimming against the tide of ideas flowing
irreversibly towards collectivism. Nonetheless, Crosland's
optimism was confounded by successive electoral defeats in
the 1950s, followed by the neo-liberal 'counter-revolution' of
the 1970s and 1980s.[2]

In the wake of Crosland's death, British social democracy
was manifestly operating in a cold climate. While his analysis
influenced the debate about ideas in the Labour party,
the revisionist undertaking could scarcely be regarded as
unambiguously successful: Crosland's generation had been
unwilling to confront the party's dominant sectional interests.
As middle-class intellectuals who felt instinctively ill at ease in
a proletarian party, they came to hero-worship the organised
working class together with the myths embodied in British
labourism. The revisionists never overcame the 'progressive
dilemma' identified by Marquand: radical intellectuals will
naturally be reluctant to work within the Labour party given
its emphasis on group loyalty and intolerance of dissent, but
if they do not, the consequence is permanent Tory rule.[21]
The 'lingering unease' between intellectuals and the labour
movement is captured in Crossman's diaries following an
exchange with Gaitskell:

Of Roy Jenkins, he said, 'He is very much in the social swim these days and I am sometimes anxious about him and young Tony [Crosland]. We, as middle-class socialists, have got to have a profound humility. Though it's a funny way of putting it, we've got to know that we lead them because they can't do it without us, with our abilities, and yet we must feel humble to working people. Now that's alright for us in the upper middle class, but Tony and Roy are not upper and I sometimes feel that they don't have a proper humility to ordinary working people.'[22]

Crosland survived by eventually subordinating himself to the conservative ethos of the labour movement: 'the exclusive attitudes of labourism, its denial of legitimacy to other progressive forces, and its assumption that the 'working class' (by which is meant the trade-unionised working class) has a special virtue, and a special claim on society'.[23] It was this mind-set that alienated progressive intellectuals such as Hobhouse and Keynes. As a politician, Crosland:

Ostentatiously became not just a party man but one of the boys, in a way he never had been before...This man who had acquired a unique reputation for austerity of intellect and integrity of argument, and for personal behaviour that showed indifference to the approval of others, had started to compromise in pursuit of his ambition...It was as if he had turned into a different person. Even his appearance changed. Over a few years his face altered from being lean, light-skinned and well defined to becoming heavy, puffy, and leather-skinned, with a mottled reddish colour. ('The colour of raw sausage meat', said Bernard Williams, who referred to the new Tony witheringly as 'sausage-face'.)[24]

The accommodation with labourist orthodoxy, 'the embodiment of the working class and its institutions',[25] stabilised Crosland's position given his reputation as the arch-revisionist, but the project to remake the party for an age of affluence and modernity was imperilled. The enthusiasm for speaking truth to power was undermined by rediscovered affection for, and loyalty towards, the movement's values and institutions. This allegiance limited the scope for interrogation of the party's doctrine and Labour's troubled relationship with the post-war electorate. By the early 1970s, Crosland was more than willing to compromise with traditionalism in return for personal advancement, embracing the politics of the Social Contract espoused by the Wilson–Callaghan governments. His response to the 1970 defeat was to reiterate central themes from *The Future of Socialism*, namely the overriding importance of equality; now in a leadership position, Crosland appeared increasingly cautious and circumspect.[26] Where there had been radicalism there was now an absence of fresh thinking; he failed to revitalise social democracy in the light of economic paralysis, industrial stagnation, the rise of Celtic nationalism and the fragmentation of the British state.

The revisionists' compliance with labourism was rational in political terms, but prevented Labour from developing into an effective social democratic party. The implicit conflict between devotion and faithfulness to the movement on the one side, and the willingness to be a dissenting voice against its prejudices on the other, is the paradox of the revisionist tradition embodied in Crosland's personal life and political career. His friend and political rival, Roy Jenkins, resolved the conundrum by leaving the Labour party altogether, dividing the centre-left of British politics; the result was predictably Conservative electoral dominance, as Keynes foresaw in the early twentieth century.

Turning to the flaws in Crosland's intellectual outlook, this book highlighted four central criticisms: his failure to specify what sort of equality the Left should pursue; Crosland's disregard of Britain's structural economic problems and their international context; the inability to confront trade union interests in British politics; and the distraction created by the revisionists' appetite for internal party conflict, neglecting the national interest and Britain's role in the world. Crosland may have influenced Labour's thinking, but his approach had inadequacies symptomatic of the party's long-standing 'anti-theoretical bias'. It was not just the Bevanites and the *New Left Review* that focused on the limitations of Croslandism. A potent critique emerged from within the Labour Right, among those instinctively sympathetic to the revisionist tradition.

Crosland and equality

Equality naturally assumes importance in Crosland's writings: it provided the ethical and moral inspiration for a revised conception of socialism, discarding the traditional obsession with nationalisation and state control of the 'commanding heights' of industry. But in the 1960s and 1970s, Crosland was increasingly unable to defend his view of egalitarianism against a resurgent market liberalism: if equality was an emotional value that individuals were free to reject according to their moral preferences, did equality offer an ethical ideal to justify a fairer distribution of resources throughout society?[27] Crosland's analysis makes it no easier to resolve the question bedevilling social democratic doctrine for half a century: equality of what? Equality of opportunity? Equality of outcome? Equality of regard? Crosland was never committed to developing a moral conception of equality: as a 'passive hedonist', he was sceptical that the values of individual citizens could be changed through persuasion, and saw his role as that of an 'economic technician' rather than a moralist.[28] In any case, he believed that British society was moving decisively towards equality: share ownership was dispersed; capitalism 'red in tooth and claw' had been tamed; the welfare state was slaying Beveridge's 'five giants'; class differentiation was ostensibly diminishing. The weakness in Crosland's analysis, however, was that in so far as inequality had narrowed in the 1950s and 1960s, it proved an aberration in twentieth-century history. Since the 1980s, inequality in the UK has markedly increased.

In the 1950s, it had been tempting for the revisionists to dismiss Bevan's tract, *In Place of Fear*. Bevan, nonetheless, had a point: post-war affluence had not abolished material deprivation. Absolute poverty, unemployment and social inequality remained. Crosland was never able to determine how Labour should define equality, concluding merely that equality of opportunity was 'not enough'. Douglas Jay's measure of 'the minimum practicable inequality' was the most precise formulation provided. Crosland's turn to Rawls in the early 1970s scarcely afforded an original justification for his egalitarianism. The governing circumstances and adversities of the 1960s and 1970s strained the social democratic commitment to equality. In the 1980s and 1990s, the Thatcher governments encouraged a shift away from the egalitarian principles of the post-war settlement towards a new individualism.[29] Crosland had been too optimistic about Britain's conversion to the egalitarian ideal as the years of post-war reconstruction faded into the distance. New Labour was accused by Crosland's supporters of abandoning the party's commitment to equality motivated by electoral expediency; in truth, Labour's egalitarian values appeared increasingly threadbare by the late 1970s.

Britain's economic problem

On Crosland's views of capitalism and growth, he overstated the resilience of the market economy and its future growth potential. His claim that economic growth was no longer 'on a long view of primary importance to socialism' was alarmingly complacent.[30] Convinced that long-standing problems had been resolved, he insisted: 'We should not now judge a Labour government's performance primarily by its record in the economic field.'[31] But it was precisely the weak performance of post-war Labour governments in financial management that threatened the party's status as a contender for power. There was a lack of attention to the external problems bedevilling the British economy after the Second World War. The 1965 Gaitskell Memorial Lecture was the most comprehensive account Crosland offered of how to improve economic growth: the key was raising the productivity of investment by improving technical knowledge and removing restrictive practices; using deflation to solve periodic balance of payments crises merely dampened employer's expectations, depressing future investment.[32] In his preface to *The Future of Socialism*, Crosland breezily declared that he would not consider the world beyond British shores, an admission unimaginable in more recent appraisals of social democracy. He failed to anticipate that market capitalism might become more financialised and global, increasingly avaricious and unstable.

His complacency about Britain's long-term economic problem calls into question the relevance of Crosland's analysis for contemporary society. The failure to comprehend the economy's exposure to international forces meant that he underemphasised the balance of payments, alongside the challenge of sterling parity which constrained post-war growth, forcing governments to adopt 'stop–go' policies.[33] According to critics, there was a recurring tendency in Crosland's work to downplay supply-side factors. There is little doubt that as an Oxford economist he was aware of Britain's weakness in the aftermath of the Second World War. Responding to one of Crosland's papers, a colleague highlighted the danger of inflation and the wage spiral:

> I think you minimise unduly the danger of a continued inflationary trend at home, or...minimise the extent to which this danger arises from a state of excess demand. I can't see how an indefinitely continuing increase in British costs of production can be stopped (as contrasted with slowed down) so long as we maintain a strong sellers' labour market. And if British prices cease again to be perfectly competitive, the dilemma between another dose of devaluation or belated deflation will not admit of any satisfactory solution.[34]

This lack of attention to the British economy's deficiencies was evident in Crosland's dispute with Wilson about devaluation.[35] Wilson's fixation with maintaining the value of sterling has been criticised;[36] nonetheless, senior figures in the 1964–70 governments vehemently opposed devaluation.[37] The Prime

Minister believed that devaluation involved significant economic and political risks, having been persuaded by his economic adviser, Thomas Balogh, that socialist planning policies would resolve Britain's balance of payments deficit; Callaghan promised the US Treasury Secretary that Britain would not devalue and saw this as a matter of personal honour; George Brown feared that devaluation would reduce the real wages of his working-class constituents, although he had changed his mind by July 1966; all the Ministers who opposed devaluation were afraid that the Conservatives would attack Labour as the party of devaluation after Stafford Cripps' decision to devalue in 1949, undermining Labour's reputation for economic competence.[38] Nevertheless, Crossman was incredulous that 'James Callaghan and Harold Wilson are personally committed to the defence of the pound to a quite extraordinary degree.'[39] Left-wing economists including Nicholas Kaldor, Robert Neild and Ian Little advocated devaluation to restore growth and competitiveness while tackling the balance of payments crisis.[40] Along with members of the Cabinet including Crosland, Crossman, Jenkins and Castle, they opposed blindly defending the pound on the foreign exchange markets; in November 1967 the Wilson government was forced to devalue, depleting the party's economic credibility.[41] Callaghan remarked years later: 'The man in the street felt let down because he had been led to believe that if devaluation took place, it would be a consequence of the Labour government's incompetence.'[42]

Nonetheless, while Crosland's stance has been admired in the Labour party, devaluation was treated as a magical elixir; this overestimated the ability of Keynesian demand management to strengthen production and growth, while downplaying the persistent structural problems afflicting Britain's industrial base. The belief that the long-standing and deep-rooted problems of the British economy would be solved merely by an adjustment of the exchange rate was mistaken. Among those advocating a quasi-Keynesian approach, there was a tendency to exaggerate the importance of macro-economic policy.[43] Under pressure from his party, Wilson insisted that fundamental weaknesses would not have been addressed by an early decision to devalue. The July 1966 sterling crisis had already led to a severe deflationary programme, including spending cuts and a wage freeze.[44] The economy was operating at close to full capacity by 1967, with 3 per cent growth and falling unemployment. Expanding exports and investment inevitably meant cutting public and private consumption, the logic of Jenkins' 1968 budget, raising taxes cumulatively by £923 billion.[45] Devaluation had been rejected by Wilson on firmly political grounds: it required deflation to ensure that resources were driven into export industries, which meant curtailing working-class living standards after the long years of Conservative affluence under Macmillan and Butler.[46]

The principle of holding down consumption to increase investment had been emphasised in Labour's programme since the 1920s, but this was likely to have damaging electoral consequences in an affluent society.[47] Any alteration in exchange rate policy ought to be a 'last resort' since 'it could provoke retaliation and trigger a return to 1930s-style economic nationalism'; the defence of the pound in 1964–65 had not compelled the Wilson Government to abandon full employment since the availability of credit from the International Monetary Fund (IMF) and Group of Ten countries allowed the continuation of expansionary domestic policies.[48] That said, the 1967 devaluation confirmed that the balance of economic power was shifting irreversibly from the nation-state to the international monetary system as capital flowed effortlessly between financial centres: the strategic choice for social democratic governments was between a siege economy, and accommodation with 'resurgent neo-liberalism'.[49] British politics became polarised between the Left's national protectionism and the Right's market liberalism.[50] *The Future of Socialism* epitomised the limitations of post-war social democracy, developing a strategy for redistribution without any corresponding model of production and growth. The abandonment of central planning as the instrument to generate economic growth in a market economy exposed an intellectual vacuum at the heart of British social democracy.[51]

This assessment of the inadequacies of Crosland's ideas was taken up by revisionist sympathisers, notably his fellow parliamentarian, Brian Walden, who observed in the 1970s that Crosland's enthusiasm for libertarianism undermined his economic analysis:

> So anxious is he to welcome the era when economics is no longer the science of scarcity that he is inclined to announce the impending demise of poverty and exploitation a little prematurely. He wants to pass on to more exciting cultural and environmental issues and is forever tugging against the chains that hold him earthbound to the production obsessions of the Labour party.[52]

British industry was underperforming in world markets. The national strategy widely canvassed within the political class was to subject Britain's industrial base to international competition, removing the legacy of imperial protection, joining the European Common Market, and pursuing free trade with the United States.[53] Britain experienced rapid globalisation and financialisation, as structural reforms promoted untrammelled competition and liberalisation. From the late 1960s, the UK experienced a contraction of its industrial base, undermining the potential for growth leading to a significant increase in unemployment throughout the former industrialised areas during the Thatcher governments. Despite the impact of structural changes on traditional working-class industries, Crosland retained a commitment to open markets, unsympathetic towards the Left's alternative strategy.[54] Nonetheless, he opposed the public expenditure cuts imposed by the IMF's negotiators in 1975–76, arguing that Labour would pay the price for continuing deflation. Cuts would lead to: '(a) demoralisation of the decent rank and file; (b) strain on trade union loyalty…(c) breeding of an illiterate and reactionary attitude to public expenditure; (d) and the collapse of the strategy I proposed last year…Now no sense of direction and no priorities: only pragmatism, empiricism, safety first.'[55]

He was convinced that the IMF agreement was 'wrong economically and socially, destructive of what he had believed in all his life'.[56] Crosland subsequently withdrew his opposition, having been convinced by Callaghan and Healey that there was no alternative to deflation given the pressures exerted by the financial markets.[57] According to Hattersley:

> There was never much chance of Denis Healey's IMF proposals being defeated. Tony Crosland fought a dashing rear-guard action and won whenever the battle turned into hand to hand combat. But the Chancellor had reserves…The silent minority were waiting to follow the Prime Minister's lead.[58]

Crosland's special adviser, David Lipsey, remarked: 'Crosland never really took on board the question of international confidence…we were only just getting used to being an economy in a global financial system'.[59] Crosland's view of the IMF agreement was 'this is nonsense but we must do it. He knew it meant the abandonment of his position as a revisionist theorist.'[60]

The trade union question

By 1975, the economy's performance was deteriorating further; the centrepiece of the revisionist strategy was equality through government spending, redistributive taxation and the welfare state. This approach was called into question casting doubt on the credibility of Crosland's intellectual framework. Peter Jenkins believed there was an intractable dilemma undermining social democracy: advancing the universal welfare state of Keynes and Beveridge and prioritising full employment was in fundamental conflict with the regime of free collective bargaining.[61] The revisionists had long neglected the trade union question: social democrats could only finance the welfare state and sustain economic growth if the unions were willing to moderate wage claims, an expectation that was implausible due to escalating industrial militancy from the 1960s; the number of working days lost due to 'official' and 'unofficial' strike action rose dramatically between 1960 and 1980.[62]

The unions remained influential in their ability to win pay disputes and stoke wage inflation but struggled to enforce discipline after an escalation of 'wild-cat' strikes. The trade unions acceded to the revisionist strategy in the 1950s, supporting Gaitskell's right-wing candidacy against Bevan because the revisionists upheld the fundamental right of the unions to engage in free collective bargaining.[63] Crosland and Gaitskell sought to avoid statutory intervention, putting their faith in voluntarism. In the adversarial culture of industrial conflict, there was a risk that real wages would outstrip improvements in productivity where organised labour had the greatest strength. The solution was an incomes policy, but this proved unworkable in the British context given the absence of institutions designed to ensure coordination between employers and the state characterising the Swedish and German models of social market capitalism.

The trade unions were ill-equipped to pursue constructive relations with employers at plant and company level; the poor quality of management was similarly corrosive. The attempt to resolve the social democratic dilemma through the imposition of a mandatory incomes policy was undermined, first by the defeat of the *In Place of Strife* White Paper in 1969, then by the collapse of the Social Contract after the Winter of Discontent. As Daniel Bell foresaw, in a post-industrial society class divisions based on the opposition between capital and labour give way to more disaggregated conflict between 'group interests' and the 'public interest'.[64] Britain required a system for regulating wage settlements that led to a fairer distribution of income without producing a sharp spike in price inflation. Labour governments were compelled to confront the sectional demands of the unions, but, in failing to do so, the party sacrificed its ethical claim as the party of equality despite investing heavily in egalitarian programmes, especially during the 1974–79 governments. Labour had to construct an electoral majority that went 'beyond the narrow bounds of proletarian sectionalism'.[65]

Sympathetic critics of Crosland such as Jenkins and Walden did not disagree with his vision of a more humane and just society. The problem was that while 'the ends are clear, it is the means which are not'.[66] Labour was unable in Tawney's words 'to subordinate the claims of this section of the movement or that to the progress of the whole'.[67] *The Future of Socialism* and *Socialism Now* failed to confront the crisis of British industrial relations. The belated attempt to impose a statutory incomes policy amid rising inflation led to political paralysis, as the union movement shifted further to the Left. As a consequence, the post-war social democratic vision of growth and expansion without price inflation no longer appeared tenable.

Ideology before national interest

Crosland's revisionism can therefore be seen as incapable of resolving the social democratic dilemma. Samuel Beer noted the tendency towards 'compulsive ideologism' in the post-war Labour party.[68] 'Revisionists' and 'fundamentalists' were both embroiled in a protracted ideological conflict which gave only a passing glance to Britain's national problems. The long-term questions confronting Britain were viewed through the prism of party factionalism rather than the national interest; the disagreement about state ownership of industry and the mixed economy dragged on throughout the twentieth century.[69] As a consequence, Labour lacked the ideological subtlety required to become an effective reforming government, symbolised by its estrangement from Keynes. The party adopted aspects of Keynesian economic theory, but failed to embrace his intellectual vision; Keynes believed that economic policy entailed creativity and improvisation rather than rigid adherence to dogmatic ideas about the state and the economy: 'Keynes' economic radicalism dictated a particular style of politics which proved to be beyond the comprehension of the Labour party'.[70]

Labour politicians wrestled with Keynes' ideas: Dalton, Durbin and Meade sought to fashion a post-1931 economic policy through the *New Fabian Research Bureau* (NFRB). The aim was 'to apply the new Keynesian economic thought to the woolly socialism of the Ramsay MacDonald era'.[71] Keynesianism offered theoretical underpinning: it 'legitimised the doctrine of equality...it demonstrated that economic expansion depended on broadening the base of consumption through a diffuse distribution of income and wealth'.[72] In his review of Roy Harrod's biography of 'the master', Crosland points out that Keynes was a member of the Liberal party estranged from socialism despite his connections to the Fabian society. Keynes acknowledged that British progressivism was unhelpfully divided in the twentieth century between Labour and the Liberal party. Keynes would never countenance joining the Labour party, however, since it would compel him 'to pay lip-service to trade unionist tyrannies, to the beauties of the class war, or to doctrinaire State Socialism – in none of which he believes'.[73] He concluded 'the predominant element of the Labour party is old-fashioned and even anti-intellectual'. The party struggled to develop a reputation for economic competence after the First World War adopting programmes which 'in their hearts they have believed to be economically unsound'.[74] Keynes acknowledged that social reform would increasingly depend on Labour, replacing the Liberals as the major opposition to the Conservative party in advancing 'three political goals of economic efficiency, social justice, and individual liberty'.[75] There is an overlap between Keynes' social liberalism, and the revisionist social democracy that emerged from Crosland:

> Keynes' views could never have been labelled socialist. He did not believe in nationalisation, which he thought was a silly irrelevance in present-day conditions. Indeed, he went further, and maintained that there was, 'a profound connection between personal and

political liberty and the rights of private property and private enterprise'.[76]

Ben Pimlott concluded that 'Keynesianism was a hard doctrine for the Labour party to swallow'.[77] Keynes provided an intellectual rationale for public intervention and fiscal redistribution that assisted the British Left in the wake of the 1931 crisis, but ultimately 'Keynes was indifferent to the moral claims of socialism'.[78] By seeking to reform markets, Keynesians attempted to preserve the existing system rather than striving to attain a new, post-capitalist economic order. Throughout its history, Labour struggled to resolve whether a commitment to ameliorative social reform was adequate for a socialist party. For all its eloquence and audacity, Croslandite revisionism scarcely confronted the fundamental weakness of post-war social democracy. The tendency was to take for granted prevailing assumptions about Britain's place in the world; Attlee and Bevin set the tone after 1945, sticking rigidly to the belief that Britain must protect its great power status by acquiring an independent deterrent in the wake of the Second World War.[79] Too little attention was paid to the long-term national interest: 'the questions vital to Britain's future could not be discussed within the confines of the party system and the political conventions which surround it'.[80] Labour's civil war over party doctrine and the battle to control its institutions preoccupied the revisionists, weakening their effort to transform Labour into a radical governing force.

Crosland in retrospect

By the year of his death in 1977, Crosland's benign characterisation of post-war Britain had been confounded: discord between employers and the workforce had intensified; the industries that had been nationalised after the Second World War performed erratically; sustained growth could no longer be assumed as the industrialised countries experienced prolonged stagnation. Social democracy offered few answers, paving the way for neo-liberal domination in the 1980s and 1990s. The New Liberalism of Green and Hobhouse which envisaged a vital role for the state in removing the barriers to human flourishing was swept aside by the market liberalism of Hayek and Friedman. Ever since the Callaghan Government negotiated the IMF loan in 1976, the party has wrestled with the same fundamental question: what was Labour's answer to neo-liberalism in a global, footloose, internationalised economy?[81] The Left of the party argued that the remedy was greater state involvement alongside increased public expenditure; the Labour Right retorted that they had effectively managed the crisis unleashed by the 1973–74 oil price shock and that the economy was now improving; what neither offered was a compelling signpost to the future as the party's relationship with the unions deteriorated amid bitter divisions between the political and industrial wings of the movement.[82]

New Labour's third way, like Croslandite revisionism, proved deficient, assuming that capitalist economies were becoming knowledge-based while permanently eradicating the structural antagonism between workers and management. Global capitalism was becoming harder to control; the diversification of production into global supply chains made regulation through the nation-state less effective; technological change meant that returns to labour were declining especially for the low-skilled; high-quality knowledge economy employment went hand in hand with an expansion of low wage service jobs: the gap between the wealthy and poor intensified.[83] In the aftermath of the financial crisis, the pragmatic Labour Right was exposed: just as a social democratic critique of the market was necessary, the moderate Left was 'asleep at the wheel' having sanctioned decades of light-touch regulation, celebrating the exuberance of markets when it suited them; Labour had become a victim of this 'Faustian pact'. Social liberalism and social democracy were predicated on a critique of the market, but as progressives sought to reclaim the market in the 1990s, this critical perspective was lost. It ought to be remembered that markets are inherently 'prone to instability, excess and abuse'.[84]

The prospects for social democracy 40 years after Crosland's death do not appear propitious. John Gray and Vernon Bogdanor insist that globalisation is destroying social democracy by undermining the state, although nation-states are devising new means of exercising power and sharing sovereignty. As Geoff Mulgan writes: 'the basic powers of governments have not diminished...the idea that governments have become impotent is an illusion, albeit one that can provide a useful alibi': states retain their capacity to raise taxes and spend public resources; they can resolve collective problems from organised crime to environmental degradation; states are enhancing their role in relation to new challenges from early childhood disadvantage to the demographic pressures of population ageing.[85] The New Labour administrations provide evidence of how social democratic governments pursue their aims in the face of structural constraints, as they do in Northern Europe and the Nordic countries. In fact, New Labour underestimated its room for manoeuvre: despite securing unprecedented parliamentary majorities, Blair and Brown were terrified that Britain remained a fundamentally Conservative country.

Others conclude the importance of Crosland's critique of state socialism has been oversold. *The Future of Socialism* was neither visionary nor path-breaking.[86] Jeremy Nuttall is convinced that the book 'is neither a masterpiece nor a work rendered wholly obsolete by advancing decades'.[87] Similarly, John Campbell writes: 'Crosland's [*The Future of Socialism*] was not in fact strikingly original.'[88] The revisionist assault on Marxism was undertaken by Bernstein in the 1890s, a point Crosland acknowledged. It is certainly tempting to dismiss Crosland as a throwback to a bygone age. There was no successor generation of 'Croslandites' who emerged after his death: numerous figures who had once claimed the revisionist mantle including David Marquand, Shirley Williams and Bill Rodgers defected to the Social Democratic Party (SDP) in 1981. Those who remained in the Labour party, notably Roy Hattersley and Giles Radice, had found Crosland increasingly arrogant and aloof, unwilling to cultivate a new generation of revisionists; he 'gave them little encouragement in their own efforts to think out new strategies…Crosland said at one point that he was "too bloody busy" to rethink his whole philosophy'.[89] Rodgers recounts that many social democrats in the party shifted their allegiance to Jenkins: 'Tony was our hero, but stage by stage we transferred our loyalty, support and affections [to Roy Jenkins], because Tony had no loyalty to his own friends.'[90]

It is claimed that the significance of revisionism has been exaggerated by the hero-worshiping Croslandites. The neo-Marxist Left was declining by the mid-1950s, without the need for Crosland's intellectual tirade. Crossman acknowledged the weakness of the Labour Left's position. The Bevanites were distracted by their pursuit of a socialist foreign policy, having no domestic programme to revitalise the party. Bevan's eulogy to democratic socialism, *In Place of Fear*, was widely read but insubstantial in comparison to *The Future of Socialism*.[91] In his speech to the 1959 conference, Bevan implored: 'Are we going to send a message from this great Labour movement, which is the father and mother of modern democracy and modern socialism, that we in Blackpool in 1959 have turned our backs on our principles because of temporary unpopularity in a temporarily affluent society?'[92]

Such analysis hardly seemed equal to the scale of the electoral and policy challenge that Labour faced by the late 1950s. Brian Harrison ventures that 'Crosland's book is almost twice as long as Bevan's, far more tightly argued, better documented, and far better briefed on recent social-science ideas.'[93] The Left never produced a convincing riposte. Crossman's *Labour in the Affluent Society* insisted that Labour would return to power when capitalism's internal contradictions had been exposed: 'We must give warning of the crisis ahead and condemn the Affluent Society as incapable of coping with it.'[94] This view had little traction in the post-war party; the Left had no serious alternative strategy.[95] Crosland's *Encounter* review condemned Crossman's 'repugnant' over-emphasis on economic issues at the expense of, 'personal freedom, equality of incomes, the rights of the consumer, and the greatest possible diffusion of power'.[96] The rebuke was memorable: 'The left are not the only people who can claim a socialist theory while the rest of us are thought to be mere pragmatists and administrators.'[97] Nonetheless, the party turned to Wilson after Gaitskell's death, offering reconciliation in the name of national modernisation, rather than the uncompromising reformist ethic of revisionism.

While the influence of post-war revisionism might have been exaggerated, this book has shown that Crosland's marriage of social justice through collective action with personal liberty through legislative reform offered a distinctive prospectus for post-war social democracy. Successive 'waves' of revisionism attempted to seize the initiative by putting freedom at the heart of centre-left ideology.[98] Instead of imperilling liberty, collectivism's advance was made compatible with the age of personal freedom.[99] This reconciliation was achieved through Crosland's support for comprehensive reform of the laws governing personal behaviour, measures implemented by Jenkins as Home Secretary (the case had been persuasively articulated a decade before in *The Future of Socialism*); Britain became a more libertarian and 'permissive' society. Crosland's view of political economy accepted the primacy of property rights and the profit motive. The aim of replacing capitalism with an alternative economic system was futile: social democracy must reform markets, not strive to abolish them. As such, Crosland's vision of the enabling state aimed to guarantee that each individual had access to opportunities and material resources, narrowing the class divide while minimising inequalities in the distribution of wealth, income and power. Finally, Crosland's approach was embedded in a commitment to political liberalism: social problems should be resolved through rational analysis rather than prejudice. Labour must be a party receptive to a diversity of traditions; constitutional politics and parliamentary institutions had served Britain well; public service and duty was the fundamental purpose of politics.

What Crosland bequeathed, above all, was a methodology for practising social democratic politics in a new society. He emphasised not only the separation of institutional means from ideological ends, the sine qua non of revisionism. His political outlook was shaped by powerful intellectual impulses of relevance today. Firstly, Labour would never win as a 'class-based, socialist party'; it had to build support as a national party in the name of a truly classless society. Secondly, socialism was a moral enterprise that was about more than the production and distribution of material goods; it emphasised the quality of life and a public realm that broke down the 'distance factors' between classes. Instead of preaching 'abstinence and a good filing system', social democracy must enhance the right to private enjoyment and self-fulfilment. Thirdly, Croslandite revisionism was fiercely anti-paternalistic: the role of collective institutions was to equip individuals with the 'capabilities' to lead flourishing lives. His egalitarianism constituted an attack on 'the indefensible differences of status and income that disfigure our society'.[100] Fourthly, the Left had to apply its 'sociological imagination' to understand the complexity of social and cultural change in Britain; instead of mourning the loss of traditional institutions and political identities, socialism had to embrace positively the post-war world. Fifthly, Crosland eschewed narrow liberal cosmopolitanism, acknowledging the importance of national and communal attachments that enabled citizens to experience a sense of belonging (reinforced by contact with his Grimsby constituents), while rejecting jingoistic chauvinism: Crosland had no time for 'reviving old dreams of empire';[101] he was an internationalist who 'believed we should link our destinies with a dynamic and resurgent Europe'.[102] These are powerful legacies to bestow on British social democracy.

Revisionism: hope betrayed?

For all its inadequacies, Crosland's liberal progressivism stood the test of time rather than crumbling to dust. As Peter Jenkins reminds us 'Social democracy has had a knack of proving its obituarists premature.'[103] It is true that by 1979, Labour had manifestly thrown away its economic credibility: the collapse of post-war corporatism paved the way for successive

Conservative victories triggering a profound crisis of British labourism. Thatcherism's ethos of individualism undermined the electoral viability of social democracy. The long-term consequences, however, were not as predictable as they first appeared. Even as real incomes grew, middle-class voters instinctively valued public services, reacting against the 'private good, public bad' obsessions of the New Right. Neither did the majority of the electorate wish to see the legislative reforms of the permissive society reversed. They saw Britain's future lying with an integrated Europe, as much as with Anglo-America and the Atlantic alliance.

The 'declinist' narrative where the dominance of social democracy gives way to disappointment and decay (mirrored in Crosland's career) is misplaced.[104] To interpret the 1940s and 1960s as unique moments of unparalleled progressive reform destroyed by the crises and upheavals of subsequent decades misunderstands the past. The British electorate in the immediate aftermath of the Second World War was not universally radicalised; the post-war Labour governments faced severe constraints; as the 1950s progressed, the party struggled to come to terms with mass prosperity: Lawrence Black writes that Labour politicians 'to a large extent brought upon themselves their alienation from popular affluence'.[105] Moreover, the 1970s was not quite the 'crisis decade' portrayed in popular history. Nick Tiratsoo argues: 'We have come to see the decade in a way which magnifies the bad and neglects the good.' Historians have revised dominant interpretations of British society and politics in those years.[106] As Hugh Pemberton reminds us 'the 1970s was also a decade of progressive politics...given the economic and political challenges they faced, policy-makers of that decade coped reasonably well'.[107]

The subtle shift towards a new social democratic settlement paved the way for New Labour's political dominance, sparking a rupture within contemporary Conservatism which suffered a protracted period of political marginalisation. Social democracy 'lost the battle' to defend the post-war settlement, but 'won the war' of long-term values.[108] Social liberalism was the most enduring ideology in Britain's political culture, despite voters last electing a Liberal government in 1915:[109] Crosland battled to adapt the Labour party to the changes in state, society and economy that enveloped late twentieth century Britain. His revisionism offered more than arid pragmatism and economic efficiency: Crosland's account of socialism inspired subsequent generations since it was grounded in a distinctive ethical and moral framework. Gaitskell was believed to be the typical English upper-class rationalist, dismissed by Bevan as 'a desiccated calculating machine'. Yet Gaitskell had moral passion and courage: he believed in the application of logic to social problems combined with a deep, spiritual commitment to the cause of social justice.[110] The same could be said of Crosland.

His optimism about social reform in British society was matched by a willingness to contest 'the rhetoric of reaction' in British politics, laying out a radical alternative drawing on economics, sociology and political theory.[111] It is misleading to pretend that Crosland would have endorsed the programme of the post-1997 governments; indeed, it is impossible to know how he would have responded to structural changes that New Labour encountered in the wake of Thatcherism. Crosland may well have found the Blair and Brown governments insufficiently egalitarian, as well as too complacent about the threat to personal liberty, particularly that implied by the security state. Nonetheless, Labour's ability to secure three consecutive parliamentary majorities for the first time in its history would undoubtedly have delighted him. Whatever Crosland's misgivings about Labour's complacency in regulating financial capitalism and global markets, he would have acknowledged that Gordon Brown's government prevented a serious financial crash from sliding into a catastrophic depression.

Crosland's biographer, Kevin Jeffreys, asks poignantly whether Crosland would have died a disappointed man, a 'tragic figure' whose ideas had been discredited, whose social democratic governing project lay in tatters, a personality who had left little significant mark on British politics.[112] As Jeffreys' points out, Labour's problems really began following the party's defeat in 1979: had Callaghan called an election in the autumn of 1978, Labour may have secured a further term of office. The contours of contemporary British political history would have been different.

The leading disciples of Crosland, Lipsey and Leonard, stress that: 'Croslandism' didn't fail: it was never carried out in Britain.[113] The Crosland prospectus avoided the excesses of doctrinaire Marxism and the limitations of Fabian traditionalism: 'Crosland gave the Labour party the chance to remain a party ideologically committed to a certain kind of change without at the same time being committed to an ideology no longer rooted in reality.'[114] While the Wilson–Callaghan governments introduced landmark legislative reforms, they never succeeded in rebuilding Labour's reputation as an economically competent party. No coherent solution to the post-war malaise of sluggish growth and rising inequality was discovered. Crosland's liberal egalitarianism was marginalised in the Labour party, with little impetus coming either from parliamentarians or the trade unions. Having never been properly carried out in the 1960s and 1970s, Croslandism can hardly be said to have failed.

The argument can be made that Crosland had a more substantive impact on his party than many who led Labour after the Second World War. His leadership prospects were not always as bleak as has been implied.[115] Crosland had little interest in the day to day mechanics and organisational machinery required to hold the party together.[116] But according to Donoughue, Wilson told him in 1975: 'Roy Jenkins is finished. Crosland is much better now...Healey won't get it when I go'; Wilson for a brief period saw Crosland as his natural 'heir'.[117] Leonard concedes that Crosland would have made fundamental errors if he had won 'but he would have been a much more inspiring leader than Jim Callaghan'.[118] Michael Young duly praised Crosland as uniquely 'the sort of leader open to new ideas'.[119] He was 'by far the best Prime Minister the Labour Party never had'.[120] As the result of his outstanding gifts as a socialist theoretician and captivating political personality, Croslandism retains its 'enhanced appeal' on the British Left.[121]

Summary

Crosland's message to today's Labour party in all likelihood would be this. By adopting an insurgent 'cast of mind', the party must apply its values to Britain in 2030, rather than facing backwards to the 1970s and 1980s. Countless reports and surveys demonstrate that the life-chances of too many citizens are limited by deep structural disadvantage: poverty and deprivation cast a long shadow, transmitting inequality across generations. British society is bedevilled by significant disparities in the distribution of wealth, assets and property. Tawney noted at the turn of the twentieth century: 'What thoughtful rich people call the problem of poverty, thoughtful poor people call with equal justice a problem of riches.'[122] Despite major social changes since the Second World War, Britain remains a country riddled with class-based inequalities.

Labour's purpose must be to unlock opportunity, to release and to nurture human potential bestowing individuals with the power to lead lives they have reason to value. The most successful progressive governments in history have been those that set the terms by which future generations live: Asquith and Lloyd George's 1906–15 Liberal governments; Roosevelt's New Deal; the 1945 Attlee Government. These administrations redrew the parameters of legitimate political action, defining a popular 'common sense' for their age. Social democrats in the twenty-first century must advance progressive reforms combining individual freedom, economic efficiency and social justice. Recent developments in egalitarian theory focus on enabling individuals to lead flourishing lives by opening new paths to fulfilment: tackling 'bottlenecks' that constrain opportunity while valuing diverse pathways to success, instead of focusing on narrow achievement such as academic selection at age 11 or entry into a restricted range of professional occupations.[123] The focus of policy should be encouraging individuals to pursue their goals by developing capabilities, in Sen's terms 'the freedom that a person actually has to do this or be that'.[124] An enabling state must fashion a new society committed to 'pluralism of opportunity';[125] liberal egalitarianism bestows resources onto individuals so that they are able to choose from a range of lifestyles.[126] However, this flowering of human capabilities will not be viable unless individuals are protected from the unrestrained forces of unfettered market capitalism; the differences in class, wealth and income must be progressively narrowed. This emphasises the obligation of citizens to participate in politics and democracy: 'without participating in the common life that defines them and in the decision-making that shapes their social habitat, women and men cannot become individuals.' [127]

Despite five years of Conservative–Liberal coalition government, the Labour party should not abandon the liberal tradition in British politics. It is necessary to work across boundaries of party interest and political traditions to fight for progressive causes: defending Britain's role in the European Union and projecting the United Kingdom as a multi-ethnic, cosmopolitan state. If Great Britain isolates itself from the European Union, it will be harder to win the argument for regulating global capitalism and entrenching social protection. The question of Britain's future role in the world will hardly be resolved if the political and territorial identity of the UK is in flux.[128] The disintegration of the Union of England, Wales, Scotland and Northern Ireland would represent a historic defeat for the centre-left, undermining the national institutions and political relationships that the UK has made possible. British social democracy has to address the rising tide of English identity and interests.[129] In cultivating common ground between the social democratic and liberal traditions, Labour has an historic opportunity to forge a revitalised progressive alliance reaching across a sweep of constituencies on the radical centre-left, reconnecting the politics of principle with the politics of power.

Crosland's revisionism equipped the Labour party with a narrative and governing programme to fight the intellectual and political battles of the post-war era. His warning was that

Labour would never succeed in British politics as a conservative party: social democracy had to be reformist, countering the inertia that bedevilled post-war Britain. The party must overcome the inadequacies of its threadbare doctrine and ambiguous strategy, ensuring that the ethic of radical humanitarianism, social justice and personal freedom could flourish. *The Future of Socialism* was an eloquent affirmation of Labour's libertarian tradition. It is hard to disagree with Pimlott that 'to describe yourself as a 'Crosland socialist' still carries meaning...if much of the Crosland canon still seems dated, there remains a core which has increased in relevance with the passage of time.'[130]

Jeremy Corbyn's rise to the Labour leadership was portrayed as a repudiation of reformist social democracy and a rejection of the Croslandite tradition; the forces propelling Corbyn's ascendancy are antipathy to global capitalism and disillusionment with bourgeois representative democracy.[131] Yet Corbyn's aim is to build a socialist society centred on the renationalisation of industry and public ownership; he lacks a convincing strategy. Labour's challenge will remain to create a credible alternative to the Conservative party, capable of making lasting change in British society while expanding opportunities to those denied them. Crosland's thought remains apposite: he followed a critical and questioning approach rooted in substantive ethical beliefs, refusing to pay attention to whatever passes as conventional wisdom.[132] The Labour party's mission remains 'to abolish all advantages and disabilities which have their source, not in differences of personal quality, but in disparities of wealth, opportunity, social position and economic power'.[133]

Sixty years since *The Future of Socialism*, Crosland's analysis is still the benchmark against which Labour's political thought is assessed.[134] His strategies and politics remain a critical reference point by which the quality of the party's ideas and leadership are judged. As Morgan attests, 'There has been no significant statement of socialist doctrine in this country – perhaps in any country – since Crosland in the mid-1950s.'[135] That emphasises the durability of the inheritance bequeathed by Crosland to the Labour party and the British Left since the Second World War. This is an extraordinary achievement: whatever the travails afflicting British social democracy, there is every reason to expect that Crosland's insurgent 'cast of mind' and modernising impulse will live on. The question that remains is whether the Labour party can still be a satisfactory vehicle for revisionism, or whether a fundamental realignment of the centre-left in British politics is now inevitable.

References

Works by C.A.R. Crosland

Crosland, C.A.R. 'A Social Democratic Britain', Tract 4, London: Fabian Society, 1971.

Crosland, C.A.R. *Britain's Economic Problem*, London: Jonathan Cape, 1953.

Crosland, C.A.R. 'Can Labour Win?', London: The Fabian Society, 1960.

Crosland, C.A.R. 'Equality in Hard Times', *Socialist Commentary*, October 1976.

Crosland, C.A.R. 'How Labour Can Kill the Image that Haunts its Future', *Daily Herald*, 1959.

Crosland, C.A.R. 'Policies for the People, by the People', *Socialist Commentary*, November 1971.

Crosland, C.A.R. 'Social Democracy in Europe', Tract 438, London: Fabian Society, 1975.

Crosland, C.A.R. *Socialism Now and Other Essays*, London: Jonathan Cape, 1974.

Crosland, C.A.R. *The Conservative Enemy*, London: Jonathan Cape, 1962.

Crosland, C.A.R. *The Future of Socialism*, London: Jonathan Cape, 1956.

Crosland, C.A.R. 'The Future of the Left', *Encounter*, March 1960.

Crosland, C.A.R. 'The Hugh Gaitskell Memorial Lecture', University of Nottingham, April 1965.

Crosland, C.A.R. 'The Transition from Capitalism', in R.H.S. Crossman (ed.), *New Fabian Essays*, London: Turnstile Press, 1952.

Crosland, C.A.R. 'Towards a Labour Housing Policy: The Herbert Morrison Memorial Lecture', Tract 410, London: Fabian Society, 1971.

Crosland, C.A.R. 'Why Labour Lost the Vote: A Review of the British General Election of 1959 by D.E. Butler and Richard Rose', *Observer*, 12 June 1960, Crosland archive 13/20 (150), LSE.

General references

Abramovsky, L., Griffith, S. and Sako, M. *Off-shoring of Business Services and its Impact on the UK Economy*, London: Advanced Institute of Management Research, November 2004.

Ackerman, B. and Alsott, A. *The Stakeholder Society*, New Haven, CT: Yale University Press, 2001.

Addison, P. *The Road to 1945: British Politics and the Second World War*, London: Jonathan Cape, 1977.

Addison, P. *No Turning Back: The Peacetime Revolutions of Post-War Britain*, Oxford: Oxford University Press, 2010.

Anderson, P. 'Sweden: Study in Social Democracy', *New Left Review*, Volume I (9), May–June 1961.

Anderson, P. 'The Left in the Fifties', *New Left Review*, Volume I (29), January–February 1965.

Annan, N. *Our Age: The Generation That Made Post-War Britain*, London: HarperCollins, 1990.

Ansell, B. and Gingrich, J. 'A Tale of Two Trilemmas', in A. Wren *The Service Economy in Transition*, Oxford: Oxford University Press, 2014.

Arblaster, A. 'Anthony Crosland: Labour's Last 'Revisionist'', *Political Quarterly*, Volume 48 (4), October 1977.

Arthur Lewis, A. *The Principles of Economic Planning*, London: Allen and Unwin, 1950.

Atkinson, A.B. *Public Economics in an Age of Austerity*, London: Routledge, 2014.

Atkinson, A.B. *Inequality: What Can be Done?*, Princeton, NJ: Princeton University Press, 2015.

Ayer, A.J. *Language, Truth and Logic*, London: Dover Publications, 1952.

Bale, T. 'Dynamics of a Non-Decision: The "Failure" to Devalue the Pound, 1964–67', *Contemporary British History*, Volume 10 (2), 1999.

Bale, T. *Sacred Cows and Common Sense: The Symbolic Statecraft and Political Culture of the British Labour Party*, London: Ashgate, 1999.

Barker, R. *Political Ideas in Modern Britain*, London: Routledge, 1978.

Beech, M. *The Political Philosophy of New Labour*, London: IB Tauris, 2006.

Beech, M. and Hickson, K. 'Blue or Purple? Reflections on the Future of the Labour Party', *Political Studies Review*, Volume 12, pp. 75–87, 2014.

Beer, S. *British Politics in the Collectivist Age*, New York: Knopf, 1965.

Behrens, R. 'The Centre: Social Democracy and Liberalism', in L. Tivey and A. Wright (eds), *Party Ideology in Britain*, Basingstoke: Macmillan, 1989.

Beland, D. *What is Social Policy? Understanding the Welfare State*, Cambridge: Polity, 2006.

Berman, S. *The Primacy of Politics: Social Democracy and the Making of Europe's Twentieth Century*, Cambridge: Cambridge University Press, 2006.

Benn, T. *Years of Hope: Diaries, Letters and Papers, 1940–1962*, London: Hutchinson, 1994.

Beveridge, W. Cmd 6404, 'Social Insurance and the Allied Services', London: HMSO, 1942.

Birch, A.H. *Responsible and Representative Government*, London: Allen and Unwin, 1964.

Black, L. 'Coming to Terms with Affluence: Socialism and Social Change in 1950s Britain', Conference on 'Consensus or Coercion? The State, the People and Social Cohesion in Post-war Britain', London: University College London, 13 March 1999.

Black, L. *The Political Culture of the Left in Affluent Britain 1951–64*, Basingstoke: Palgrave Macmillan, 2002.

Black, L. *Redefining British Politics: Culture, Consumerism and Participation 1954–70*, Basingstoke: Palgrave Macmillan, 2010.

Black, L., Pemberton, H. and Thane, P. *Britain in the 1970s*, Manchester: Manchester University Press, 2014.

Blanden, J., Gregg, P. and Machin, S. 'Social Mobility in Britain: Low and Falling', *Centre Piece*, pp. 18–20, London: London School of Economics, Spring 2005.

Bogdanor, V. 'Entry into the European Community 1971–73', Gresham College Lecture, 11 March 2014.

Bogdanor, V. 'General Election 2015', Gresham College Lecture, 29 July 2015.

Bogdanor, V. 'Labour in Opposition 1951–64', in V. Bogdanor and R. Skidelsky (eds), *The Age of Affluence*, London: Penguin, 1970.

Bogdanor, V 'Social Democracy', in A. Seldon (ed.), *Blair's Britain*, Cambridge: Cambridge University Press, 2007.

Bogdanor, V. 'The General Election 1959', Gresham College Lecture, 11 November 2014.

Boliver, V. and Swift, A. 'Do Comprehensive Schools Reduce Social Mobility?', *British Journal of Sociology*, Volume 62 (1), 2011.

Bosanquet, N. and Townsend, P., *Labour and Inequality: Sixteen Fabian Essays*, London: Fabian Society, 1982.

Briggs, A. 'The Labour Party as Crucible', in G. Dench (ed.), *The Rise and Rise of Meritocracy*, Oxford: Political Quarterly/Blackwell Publishing, 2006.

British Social Attitudes 31, London: National Centre for Social Research, 2014.

Brivati, B. 'Crosland as Apparatchik', in D. Leonard (ed.), *Crosland and New Labour*, Basingstoke: Macmillan, 1997.

Brivati, B. *Hugh Gaitskell*, London: Politicos Publishing, 2006.

Brivati, B. *The End of Decline: Blair and Brown in Power*, London: Politicos, 2007.

Brivati, B. and Bale, T. (eds), *New Labour in Power*, London: Routledge, 1997.

Brogan, D.W. 'The Future is Behind Us? On the North Atlantic Left', *Encounter*, Issue 1, 1960.

Brown, G. 'Foreword', in A. Crosland, *The Future of Socialism: Fiftieth Anniversary Edition*, London: Constable and Robinson, 2006.

Brown, G. 'A Modern Agenda for Prosperity and Social Reform', London: Social Market Foundation, 3 February 2003.

Brynjolfsson, E. and McFee, A. *The Second Machine Age: Work, Progress and Prosperity in a Time of Brilliant Technologies*, New York: W.W. Norton, 2014.

Cairncross, A. *The British Economy Since 1945*, Oxford: Blackwells, 1992.

Callaghan, J., Fielding, S. and Ludlum, S. (eds) *Interpreting the Labour Party*, Manchester: Manchester University Press, 2004.

Campbell, J. *Roy Jenkins: A Well-Rounded Life*, London: Jonathan Cape, 2014.

Carlin, W. and Soskice, D. *Macroeconomics: Institutions, Instability and the Financial System*, Oxford: Oxford University Press, 2013.

Clark, T. and Dilnot, A. *Long-Term Trends in British Taxation and Spending*, London: Institute for Fiscal Studies, 2002.

Clarke, P. *A Question of Leadership: From Gladstone to Thatcher*, London: Penguin, 1991.

Clarke, P. 'Crossman and Social Democracy', *London Review of Books*, March 1981.

Clarke, P. *Keynes: The Twentieth Century's Most Influential Economist*, London: Bloomsbury, 2009.

Clarke, P. *Liberals and Social Democrats*, Cambridge: Cambridge University Press, 1978.

Clarke, P. 'The Progressive Movement in England', *Transactions of the Royal Historical Society*, Volume 24, 1974.

Cobham, D., Adam, C. and Mayhew, K. 'The Economic Record of the 1997–2010 Labour Government: An Assessment', *Oxford Review of Economic Policy*, Volume 29 (1), 2013.

Cole, G.D.H. *Great Britain in the Post-War World*, London: Gollancz, 1942.

Collini, S. *Liberalism and Sociology: L.T. Hobhouse and Political Argument in England 1880–1914*, Cambridge: Cambridge University Press, 1979.

Collins, P. 'Labour needs something Blue and something New', *Prospect*, 26 March 2015.

Collins, P. and Reeves, R. *The Liberal Republic*, London: Demos, 2009.

Cooke, G. *Society of Equals*, London: Demos, 2009.

Cooke, G. Lawton, K and Pearce, N., *The Condition of Britain: Strategies for Social Renewal*, London: Institute for Public Policy Research, 2014.

Corry, D. 'Labour and the Economy 1997–2010: More than a Faustian Pact', in P. Diamond and M. Kenny (eds), *Reassessing New Labour: State, Society and Economy Under Blair and Brown*, London: Political Quarterly, 2011.

Corry, D., Valero, A. and Van Reenan, J. 'UK Economic Performance', *London School of Economics Discussion Paper*, March 2011.

Coutts, K. and Gufdgin, G. 'The Macroeconomic Impact of Liberal Economic Policies in the UK', Centre for Business Research, Judge Business School: University of Cambridge, April 2015.

Cronin, J. *New Labour's Pasts: The Labour Party and its Discontents*, Harlow: Pearson Education, 2004.

Cronin, J. 'The Ironies of New Labour', Paper presented to 'What's Left of the Left Conference', Center for European Studies, Harvard University, 9–10 May 2010.

Crosland, S. *Tony Crosland*, London: Jonathan Cape, 1982.

Crossman, R. *The Diaries of a Cabinet Minister Volume I*, London: Mandarin, 1991.

Crossman, R.H. 'Towards a Philosophy of Socialism', in R.H. Crossman, *New Fabian Essays*, London: Turnstile, 1952.

Crouch, C. *The Strange Non-Death of Neo-Liberalism*, Cambridge: Polity Press, 2011.

Cruddas, J. and Rutherford, J. *One Nation: Labour's Political Renewal*, London: The Labour Party, 2014.

Curtice, J. 'A Defeat to Reckon With: On Scotland, Economic Competence, and the Complexity of Labour's Losses, *Juncture*, 17 June 2015.

Curtice, J. 'The Uphill Battle for "Responsible Capitalism"', *Public Policy Research*, Volume 19 (2), pp. 129–30, 2012.

Dalton, H. *Practical Socialism for Britain*, London: George Routledge and Sons, 1935.

Davenport, N. *Memoirs of a City Radical*, London: Weidenfeld and Nicolson, 1974.

Davis, J.B. *The State of Interpretation of Keynes*, New York: Springer Science, 1994.

Davis, M. 'Arguing Affluence: New Left Contributions to the Socialist Debate 1957–63', *Twentieth Century British History*, Volume 23 (4), 2012.

Dell, E. *A Strange Eventful History: Democratic Socialism in Britain*, London: HarperCollins, 2000.

Dench, G. 'Reviewing Meritocracy', in G. Dench (ed.), *The Rise and Rise of Meritocracy*, Oxford: Political Quarterly/Blackwell Publishing, 2006.

Desai, R. *Intellectuals and Socialism*, London: Lawrence and Wishart, 1991.

Diamond, P. and Liddle, R. *Beyond New Labour: The Future of Social Democracy*, London: Methuen Politicos, 2008.

Donoughue, B. *Downing Street Diary*, London: Politicos, 2006.

Donoughue, B. *Prime Minister: The Conduct of Policy under Harold Wilson and James Callaghan*, London: Jonathan Cape, 1987.

Dow, J.C.R. and Saville, I.D. *A Critique of Monetary Policy: Theory and British Experience*, Oxford: Oxford University Press, 1990.

Driver, S. and Martell, L. *New Labour*, Cambridge: Polity Press, 2006.

Drucker, H.M. 'All the King's Horses', in W. Patterson and A. Thomas (eds), *The Future of Social Democracy*, Oxford: Clarendon Press, 1988.

Drucker, H.M. *Doctrine and Ethos in the Labour Party*, Edinburgh: Mainstream Press, 1978.

Durbin, E. *The Politics of Democratic Socialism*, London: Labour Book Service, 1940.

Emy, H.V. *Radicals, Liberals and Social Politics 1892–1914*, Cambridge: Cambridge University Press, 1973.

Esping-Andersen, G. *Politics versus Markets*, Cambridge: Polity, 1999.

Esping-Andersen, G. *The Three Worlds of Welfare Capitalism*, Princeton, NJ: Princeton University Press, 1990.

Evans, G. and Mellon, J. 'Working Class Votes and Conservative Losses: Solving the UKIP Puzzle', *Parliamentary Affairs*, pp. 1–16, Advanced Access, 17 April 2015.

Faucher-King, F. and Le Gales, P. *The New Labour Experiment*, Redwood City, CA: Stanford University Press, 2010.

Field, F. 'A Blue Labour Vision of the Common Good', in I. Geary and A. Pabst (eds), *Blue Labour: Forging a New Politics*, London: IB Tauris, 2014.

Fielding, S. 'Hell, No! Labour's Campaign: The Correct Diagnosis but the Wrong Doctor', in A. Geddes and J. Tonge, *Britain Votes 2015*, Oxford: Oxford University Press/ Hansard Society, 2015.

Fielding, S. *The Labour Governments 1964–70: Labour and Cultural Change*, Manchester: Manchester University Press, 2003.

Fielding, S. *The Labour Party: Socialism and Society Since 1951*, Manchester: Manchester University Press, 1997.

Figgis, J.N. *Studies of Political Thought from Gerson to Grotius*, Cambridge: Cambridge University Press, 1916.

Financial Times, 'Labour needs an honest debate about Tony Blair', 10 June 2015.

Finlayson, A. 'Should the Left go Blue? Making Sense of Maurice Glasman', Open Democracy, 27 May 2011.

Fishkin, J. *Bottlenecks: A New Theory of Equal Opportunity*, Oxford: Oxford University Press, 2014.

Foote, G. *The Labour Party's Political Thought*, Basingstoke: Macmillan, 1985.

Ford, R. and Goodwin, M. *Revolt on the Right: Explaining Support for the Radical Right in Britain*, London: Routledge, 2014.

Ford, R. and Goodwin, M. 'Understanding UKIP: Identity, Social Change and the Left Behind', *Political Quarterly*, Volume 85 (3), 2014.

Francis, M. 'Mr Gaitskell's Ganymede: Reassessing Crosland's *The Future of Socialism*', *Contemporary British History*, Volume 11 (2), 1997.

Freeden, M. *The New Liberalism: An Ideology of Social Reform*, Oxford: Clarendon Press, 1978.

From, A. *The New Democrats and the Return to Power*, New York: St Martin's Press, 2013.

Gaffney, J. and Lahel, A. 'The Morphology of the Labour Party's One Nation Narrative: Story, Plot and Authorship', *Political Quarterly*, Volume 84 (3), November–December 2013.

Gaitskell, H. 'Socialism and Nationalisation', Tract 300, London: Fabian Society, 1956.

Gamble, A. 'A Review of Britain's Place in the World: A Historical Inquiry into Import Controls by A.S. Milward and G. Brennan', Institute of Historical Research, July 1997.

Gamble, A. *Between Europe and America: The Future of British Politics*, Basingstoke: Palgrave Macmillan, 2003.

Gamble, A. *Britain in Decline*, Basingstoke: Macmillan, 1983.

Gamble, A. *Crisis Without End? The Unravelling of Western Prosperity*, Basingstoke: Palgrave Macmillan, 2014.

Gamble, A. 'Progressive Politics: A New Beginning', *Policy Network*, 23 September 2015.

Gamble, A. 'The Economy', in A. Geddes and J. Tonge (eds), *Britain Votes 2015*, Oxford: Oxford University Press/Hansard Society, 2015.

Gamble, A. *The Free Economy and the Strong State*, Basingstoke: Palgrave Macmillan, 1994.

Gamble, A. *The Spectre at the Feast*, Basingstoke: Palgrave Macmillan, 2009.

Gamble, A. and Prabhakar, R. 'The New Assets Agenda', in G. Dench (ed.), *The Rise and Rise of Meritocracy*, Oxford: Political Quarterly/Blackwell Publishing, 2006.

Gamble, A. and Wright, A. 'The New Social Democracy', *Political Quarterly*, London: 2004.

Gay, P. *The Dilemma of Democratic Socialism*, New York: Collier Books, 1970.

Glasman, M. 'The Good Society, Catholic Social Thought, and the Politics of the Common Good', in I. Geary and A. Pabst (eds), *Blue Labour: Forging a New Politics*, London: IB Tauris, 2014.

Goldthorpe, J. 'Understanding – and Misunderstanding – Social Mobility in Britain. The Entry of the Economists, the Confusion of Politicians and the Limits of Educational Policy', *Barnett Papers in Social Research*, Oxford: Oxford University Department of Social Policy and Intervention, 2012.

Goodhart, D. *A Post-Liberal Future*, London: Demos, 2012.

Gordon Walker, P., *Political Diaries 1932–1971*, London: The Historian's Press, 1991.

Gould, B. *A Future for Socialism*, London: Jonathan Cape, 1989.

Gould, B. *Goodbye to All That*, Basingstoke: Macmillan, 1995.

Gray, J. *After Social Democracy*, London: Demos, 1996.

Gray, J. *Post-Liberalism: Studies in Political Thought*, London: Routledge, 1993.

Gray, J. 'Ralph Miliband and Sons', *Guardian*, 4 September 2010.

Green, T.H. *Works: Volume III*, London: Longmans and Green, 1885.

Greenleaf, W.H. *The British Political Tradition Volume I: The Rise of Collectivism*, London: Routledge, 1983.

Greenleaf, W.H. *The British Political Tradition Volume II: The Ideological Heritage*, London: Routledge, 1983.

Gregg, P. 'Pre-distribution as a new set of policy tools', Discussion Paper, London: Policy Network, 2012.

Griffiths, S. 'New Labour, New Liberalism and Revisionism's Second Wave', in S. Griffiths and K. Hickson (eds), *British Party Politics and Ideology After New Labour*, Basingstoke: Palgrave Macmillan, 2009.

Grimes, A. 'Introduction', in L.T. Hobhouse, *Liberalism*, Oxford/New York: Oxford University Press, 1964.

Hacker, J. 'What's Predistribution Got To Do With It?: Assessing New New Labour', *New Statesman*, 21 April 2015.

Haddon, C. 'The Commission on Social Justice 1992–94', London: Institute of Government, July 2014.

Hain, P. *Back to the Future of Socialism*, Bristol: Policy Press, 2015.

Hall, S. 'Crosland Territory', *New Left Review*, I/2, March–April 1960.

Harris, J. 'Social Policy, Saving, and Sound Money', in P. Clarke and C. Trebilcock (eds), *Understanding Decline: Perceptions and Realities of British Economic Performance*, Cambridge: Cambridge University Press, 1997.

Harris, J. *William Beveridge: A Biography*, Oxford: Oxford University Press, 1977.

Harrison, B. *Seeking a Role: The United Kingdom 1951–70*, Oxford: Oxford University Press, 2009.

Harrop, A. 'Crosland and One Nation Labour', *The Fabian Review*, London: Fabian Society, October 2013.

Harrop, A. and Reed, H. 'Inequality 2030', Fabian Policy Report, London: Fabian Society, 2015.

Hatherley, O. 'Lower than Vermin: Nye: The Political Life of Aneurin Bevan', *London Review of Books*, 7 May 2015.

Hattersley, R. *Who Goes Home? Scenes from a Political Life*, London: Little Brown, 1995.

Hattersley, R. *Choose Freedom*, London: Michael Joseph, 1987.

Hay, C. 'Labour's Thatcherite Revisionism: Playing the "Politics of Catch-up"', *Political Studies*, pp. 700–7, XLII, 1994.

Healey, D. *The Time of My Life*, London: Politicos Publishing, 2006.

Hennessy, P. *Establishment and Meritocracy*, London: Haus Publishing, 2015.

Hennessy, P. *Having it So Good: Britain in the Fifties*, London: Penguin, 2007.

Heffernan, R. *New Labour and Thatcherism: Political Change in Britain*, Basingstoke: Palgrave Macmillan, 1999.

Hickson, K. 'Social Democracy and Happiness', in S. Griffiths (ed.), *Happiness*, London: Social Market Foundation, 2008.

Hickson, K. *The IMF Crisis of 1976 and British Politics*, London: IB Tauris, 2005.

Hickson, K. and Griffiths, S. *British Party Politics and Ideology after New Labour*, Basingstoke: Palgrave Macmillan, 2014.

Hills, J. *Good Times, Bad Times: The Welfare Myth of Them and Us*, Bristol: Policy Press, 2014.

Hills, J. *Towards a More Equal Society*, Bristol: Policy Press, 2005.

Hills, J. and Glennerster, H. 'Why the Left Need to Take Wealth Seriously Again', *Juncture*, Volume 20 (1), Summer 2013.

Hills, J., Bastagli, F., Cowell, F., Glennerster, H., Karagiannaki, E. and McKnight, A., *Wealth in the United Kingdom*, Oxford: Oxford University Press, 2014.

Hindmoor, A. *Constructing Political Space: New Labour at the Centre*, Oxford: Oxford University Press, 2005.

Hobhouse, L.T. *Liberalism*, Oxford/New York: Oxford University Press, 1964.

Hobhouse, L.T. *The Elements of Social Justice*, New York: Holt and Company, 1922.

Hobsbawm, E. 'The Forward March of Labour Halted?', *Marxism Today*, September 1978.

Hobson, J. *The Crisis of Liberalism: New Issues of Democracy*, London: P.S. King, 1920.

Hodgson, G. *Labour at the Crossroads*, Oxford: Martin Robertson, 1981.

Hofstadter, R. *The American Political Tradition and the Men Who Made It*, New York: Anchor Press, 1948.

Holland, S. *The Socialist Challenge*, London: Quartet Books, 1978.

Homer-Dixon, T., Maynard, J.L., Mildenberger, M., Milkoreit, M., Mock, S.J., Quilley, S., Schröder, T. and Thagard, P., 'A Complex Systems Approach to the Study of Ideology: Cognitive–Affective Structures and the Dynamics of Belief Systems', *Journal of Social and Political Psychology*, Volume 1, 2013.

Howell, D. *British Social Democracy: A Study in Development and Decay*, London: Croom Helm, 1976.

Hunt, T. 'Reviving our Sense of Mission: Designing a New Political Economy', in R. Philpot (ed.), *The Purple Book: A Progressive Future for Labour*, London: Biteback Books, 2011.

Hutton, W. *The State We're In*, London: Vintage, 1996.

Jackson, B. *Equality and the British Left*, Manchester: Manchester University Press, 2006.

Jackson, B. 'Revisionism Reconsidered: "Property-Owning Democracy" and Egalitarian Strategy in Post-War Britain', *Twentieth Century British History*, Volume 16 (4), 2005.

Jackson, B. 'Socialism and the New Liberalism', in B. Jackson and M. Stears (eds), *Liberalism as Ideology: Essays in Honour of Michael Freeden*, Oxford: Oxford University Press, 2012.

Jackson, B. 'We Are All Social Democrats Now', in G. Cooke and J. Purnell, *We Mean Power*, London: Demos, 2009.

Jay, D. *The socialist case*, London: Faber and Faber, 1937.

Jay, D. *Socialism in the New Society*, London: St Martin's Press, 1962.

Jeffreys, K. *Anthony Crosland: A New Biography*, London: John Blake, 1999.

Jeffreys, K. 'The Old Right', in R. Plant, M. Beech and K. Hickson (eds), *The Struggle for Labour's Soul: Understanding Labour's Political Thought Since 1945*, London: Routledge, 2004.

Jones, P. *America and the British Labour Party: The Special Relationship at Work*, London: IB Tauris, 1997.

Jones, T. *Remaking the Labour Party: From Gaitskell to Blair*, London: Routledge, 1996.

Joyce, R. and Sibieta, L. 'An Assessment of Labour's Record on Income Inequality and Poverty', *Oxford Review of Economic Policy*, Volume 29 (1), pp. 178–202, 2013.

Kaufman, G. 'Power Failure: A review of *Friends and Rivals* by Giles Radice', *Guardian*, 14 September 2002.

Kaus, M. *The End of Equality*, New York: Basic Books, 1992.

Keating, M. *Rescaling the State: The Making of Territory and the Rise of the Meso*, Oxford: Oxford University Press, 2014.

Kenny, M. *The First New Left*, London: Lawrence and Wishart, 1995.

Kenny, M. *The Politics of English Nationhood*, Oxford: Oxford University Press, 2014.

Kenny, M. 'Ideological Politics', in *Developments in British Politics 10*, Basingstoke: Palgrave Macmillan, 2016

Kenny, M. and Pearce, N. 'What National Story Does the Left Need to Tell', *Juncture*, London: Institute for Public Policy Research, 21 May 2015.

Keynes, J.M. 'Am I a Liberal?', London: Royal Economic Society, 1925.

Keynes, J.M. 'Liberalism and Labour', *The New Republic*, 3 March 1926.

Keynes, J.M. 'The Dilemma of Modern Socialism', *Political Quarterly*, Volume 3 (3), July–September 1932.

Keynes, J.M. 'The Economic Possibilities for our Grandchildren', in L. Pecchi and G. Piga, *Revisiting Keynes*, Cambridge: MIT Press, 2010.

Keynes, J.M. *The End of Laissez-Faire: The Economic Consequences of the Peace*, pp. 26, London: BN Publishing, 2009.

Keynes, J.M. *The General Theory of Employment, Interest and Money*, New York: Kessenger Publishing, 1936.

Kippin, H. and Lucas, B. 'From Big Society to Social Productivity', London: Royal Society of the Arts, 2011.

Kitschelt, H. *The Transformation of European Social Democracy*, Cambridge: Cambridge University Press, 1994.

Kogan, M. 'Anthony Crosland: Intellectual and Politician', *Oxford Review of Education*, Volume 32 (1), pp. 71–86, 2006.

Kogan, M. *The Politics of Education: Edward Boyle and Anthony Crosland in conversation with Maurice Kogan*, London: Penguin, 1971.

Kohn, H. *Political Ideologies of the Twentieth Century*, New York: Harper Torchbooks, 1966.

Labour Party, *Labour's Programme for Britain*, London: The Labour Party, 1973.

Labour Party, *Meet the Challenge, Make the Change: A New Agenda for Britain*, London: The Labour Party, 1989.

Labour Party Manifesto, 'Let Us Work Together – Labour's Way Out of the Crisis', London: The Labour Party, 1974.

Lammy, D. 'A Politics Centred on Relationships', in I. Geary and A. Pabst (eds), *Blue Labour: Forging a New Politics*, London: IB Tauris, 2014.

Lane, R.E. *The Loss of Happiness in Market Democracies*, New Haven, CT: Yale University Press, 2000.

Lawton, D. *Education and Labour Party Ideologies 1900–2001*, London: Routledge, 2005.

Le Grand, J. *The Strategy of Equality: Redistribution and the Social Services*, London: Allen and Unwin, 1982.

Leonard, D. (ed.) *Crosland and New Labour*, Basingstoke: Macmillan, 1999.

Leonard, D. 'What Would Tony Crosland make of New Labour?', *Guardian*, 17 February 2002.

Liddle, R. 'Can the Idea of a United Europe be Revived as a Progressive Left Project? The British Labour Perspective', London: Policy Network, February 2014.

Lindley, J. and Machin, S. 'Wage Inequality in the Labour Years', *Oxford Review of Economic Policy*, Volume 29 (1), pp. 165–77, 2013.

Lipsey, D. 'The Meritocracy Myth – Whatever Happened to the Old Dream of a Classless Society?', *New Statesman*, 26 February 2015.

Lipsey, D. 'Revisionists Revise', in D. Leonard (ed.), *Crosland and New Labour*, Basingstoke: Macmillan, 1997.

Lipsey, D. and Leonard, D. (eds), *The Socialist Agenda: Crosland's Legacy*, Basingstoke: Macmillan, 1981.

Lister, R. 'Ladder of Opportunity or Engine of Inequality', in G. Dench (ed.), *The Rise and Rise of Meritocracy*, Oxford: Political Quarterly/Blackwell Publishing, 2006.

Lonergan, T. and Blyth, M. 'Radical but Credible Policies are Available to the Labour Party', *The Financial Times*, 10 September 2015.

Lowes, N. and Painter, A. 'Identity Politics', London: Searchlight Report, 2011.

Luard, L. *Socialism without the State*, Basingstoke: Macmillan, 1978.

Lukes, S. 'The Future of British Socialism', in B. Pimlott (ed.), *Fabian Essays in Socialist Thought*, London: Heinemann, 1984.

Lupton, R., Hills, J., Stewart, K. and Vizard, P. 'Labour's Social Policy Record: Policy, Spending and Outcomes 1997–2010', Research Report 1, Centre for the Analysis of Social Exclusion/LSE, June 2013.

MacDougall, D. *Don and Mandarin: Memoirs of an Economist*, London: John Murray, 1987.

McKibbin, R. 'The economic policy of the second Labour Government 1929–1931', *Past and Present*, Volume 68, 1975.

McKibbin, R. *The Ideologies of Class*, Oxford: Clarendon Press, 1990.

McKibbin, R. 'With or Without the Workers', *London Review of Books*, 25 April 1991.

Mackintosh, J.P. 'Has Social Democracy Failed in Britain?', *Political Quarterly*, Volume 49 (3), August–October, 1978.

Mackintosh, J.P. 'Socialism or Social Democracy? The Choice for the Labour Party', *Political Quarterly*, Volume 43 (4), 1972.

Magee, B. *The New Radicalism*, London: Secker and Warburg, 1962.

Magee, B. 'Tony Crosland As I Knew Him', *Political Quarterly*, Volume 81 (2), April–June 2010.

Mair, P. *Ruling the Void*, London: Verso Books, 2013.

Marquand, D. *Ramsay MacDonald*, London: Jonathan Cape, 1977.

Marquand, D. *The Unprincipled Society: New Demands and Old Politics*, London: Jonathan Cape, 1988.

Marquand, D. *The Progressive Dilemma: From Lloyd George to Kinnock*, London: Heinemann, 1991.

Marquand, D. 'Moralists and Hedonists', in A. Seldon and D. Marquand (eds), *The Ideas That Shaped Post-War Britain*, London: Fontana, 1996.

Marquand, D. *Decline of the Public: The Hollowing-Out of Citizenship*, Cambridge: Polity Press, 2004.

Marquand, D. 'Review of Speak for England! A New History of the Labour Party by Martin Pugh', *New Statesman*, 2 April 2010.

Marquand, D. 'Towards a Realignment of the Mind', London Commonwealth Club, Compass Lecture, 10 February 2011.

Marquand, D. 'How Liberalism Lost its Way', *New Statesman*, 12–18 September 2014.

Marris, P. 'Just Rewards: Meritocracy Fifty Years Later', in G. Dench (ed.), *The Rise and Rise of Meritocracy*, Oxford: Political Quarterly/Blackwell Publishing, 2006.

Marshall, T.H. *Social Citizenship*, Cambridge: Cambridge University Press, 1950.

Marx, K. and Engels, F. *Collected Works. Volume 6: 1845–48*, London: Harmondsworth, 1970.

Mason, P. 'Keynes and Our Grandchildren: Recapturing an Alternative Vision of Economic Progress', *Juncture/IPPR*, 21 July 2015.

Mason, P. *Post-Capitalism: A Guide to Our Future*, London: Allen Lane, 2015.

Mayer, C. *A Firm Commitment: Why the Corporation is Failing and How to Restore Trust In It*, Oxford: Oxford University Press, 2014.

Mazzucato, M. *The Entrepreneurial State: Debunking Public Versus Private Sector Myths*, Anthem Press, 2013.

Meade, J. *Efficiency, Equality, and the Ownership of Property*, London: Routledge, 1964.

Meredith, S. 'Mr Crosland's Nightmare? New Labour and Equality in Historical Perspective', *British Journal of Politics and International Relations*, Volume 8(2), pp. 238–255, 2006.

Milbank, J. 'The Blue Labour Dream', in I. Geary and A. Pabst (eds), *Blue Labour: Forging a New Politics*, p. 29, London: IB Tauris, 2014.

Miliband, D. 'Political Quarterly Annual Lecture', London School of Economics, 2012.

Miliband, E. 'Speech to the Labour Party Conference', September 2012.

Miliband, R. 'Socialist Advance in Britain', in R. Miliband and J. Saville (eds), *The Socialist Register 1983*, London: Merlin Press.

Milburn, A. and Coats, D. 'Why Trade Unions Need a "Clause 4 Moment"', *The Financial Times*, 2 March 2006.

Miller, D. *Citizenship and National Identity*, Cambridge: Polity Press, 2000.

Milward, A. *The United Kingdom and the European Community, Volume I: The Rise and Fall of a National Strategy, 1945–1963*, London: Frank Cass, 2003.

Morgan, K.O. *Ages of Reform: Dawns and Downfalls of the British Left*, London: IB Tauris, 2008.

Morgan, K.O. *Labour in Power 1945–51*, Oxford: Clarendon Press, 1984.

Morton, A.R. 'After Socialism? The Future of Radical Christianity', *University of Edinburgh Centre for Theology and Public Issues, Occasional Paper 32*, Edinburgh: University of Edinburgh, 1994.

Mulgan, G. 'Labour Britain', *Fabian Review*, London: The Fabian Society, Summer 2005.

Mulgan, G. 'Lessons of Power', *Prospect*, August 2005.

Mullard, M. and Swaray, R. 'New Labour Legacy: Comparing the Labour Governments of Blair and Brown to Labour Governments since 1945', Volume 81 (4), *Political Quarterly*, 2010.

Musgrave, R. 'The Voluntary Exchange Theory of Public Economy', *Quarterly Journal of Economics*, Volume 53, pp. 213–38, 1939.

Naim, M. *End of Power: From Boardrooms to Battlefields, and Churches to States, Why Being in Charge isn't What it Used to Be*, New York: Basic Books, 2013.

Newman, M. *Ralph Miliband and the Politics of the New Left*, London: The Merlin Press, 2002.

Newton, S. 'The Sterling Devaluation of 1967, the International Economy and Post-War Social Democracy', *English Historical Review*, CXXV, pp. 912–45, 2010.

Nicholls, D. 'Positive Liberty 1880–1914', *The American Political Science Review*, Volume 56 (1), March 1962.

Nuttall, J. 'Tony Crosland and the Many Falls and Rises of British Social Democracy', *Contemporary British History*, Volume 18 (4), pp. 52–79, 2004.

Offer, A. *The Challenge of Affluence: Self-Control and Well-Being in the United States and Britain Since 1950*, Oxford: Oxford University Press, 2006.

O'Hara, G. *Governing Post-War Britain: The Paradoxes of Progress 1951–73*, Basingstoke: Palgrave Macmillan, 2012.

O'Leary, D. 'Something New and Something Blue: The Key to Labour's Future', *New Statesman*, 21 May 2015.

Office for National Statistics, 'The Effects of Taxes and Benefits on Household Income 2012–13', *Statistical Bulletin*, 26 June 2014, London: Office for National Statistics.

Office for National Statistics, 'UK Earnings Mobility', London: Office for National Statistics, 23 September 2014.

Organisation for Economic Co-operation and Development (OECD), 'Divided We Stand: Why Inequality Keeps Rising, Country Note – United Kingdom', 5 December 2011, Paris: OECD.

Ostry, J., Berg, A. and Tsangarides, C. 'Redistribution, Inequality and Growth', Washington: International Monetary Fund, April 2014.

Pabst, A. 'Introduction', in I. Geary and A. Pabst (eds), *Blue Labour: Forging a New Politics*, London: IB Tauris, 2014.

Padgett, S. and Patterson, W. *A History of Social Democracy in Post-War Europe*, London: Longman, 1991.

Paine, T. *The Rights of Man*, London: Wordsworth Publishing, 1996.

Parr, H. *Britain's Policy towards the European Community: Harold Wilson and Britain's World Role 1964–67*, London: Routledge, 2006.

Pelling, H. *A Short History of the Labour Party*, London: Macmillan, 1961.

Pelling, H. *America and the British Left: From Bright to Bevan*, London: Adam and Charles Black, 1956.

Pemberton, H., Black, L. and Thane, P. (eds), *Reassessing 1970s Britain*, Manchester: Manchester University Press, 2013.

Pemberton, H. 'Relative Decline and British Economic Policy in the 1960s', *The Historical Journal*, Volume 47 (4), 2004.

Pemberton, H. 'Strange Days Indeed: British Politics in the 1970s', *Contemporary British History*, Volume 23 (4), 2009.

Philpot, R. (ed.), *The Purple Book*, London: Biteback, 2011.

Piachaud, D. 'Revitalising Social Policy', *Political Quarterly*, Volume 62 (2), 1991.

Piketty, T. *Capital in the Twenty-First Century*, Cambridge, MA: Harvard University Press, 2014.

Pimlott, B. *Labour and the Left in the 1930s*, Cambridge: Cambridge University Press, 1978.

Pimlott, B. 'Hugh Was That? Review of Hugh Gaitskell by Brian Brivati', *Independent on Sunday*, 29 September 1996.

Pimlott, B. 'Uber-Tony', *London Review of Books*, 3 September 1998.

Pimlott, B., Kavanagh, D. and Morris, P. 'Is the 'Postwar Consensus' a Myth?' *Contemporary British History*, Volume 2(6), pp. 12–15, 1989.

Plant, R. 'Democratic Socialism and Equality', in D. Lipsey and D. Leonard (eds), *The Socialist Agenda: Crosland's Legacy*, London: Jonathan Cape, 1981.

Pollard, S. *Britain's Pride and Britain's Decline: The British Economy 1870–1914*, London: Edward Arnold, 1989.

Porter, M. and Kramer, M. R. 'Creating Shared Value', *Harvard Business Review*, January–February 2011.

Potter, D. *The Times*, 27 April, 1959.

Potter, D. *The Glittering Coffin*, London: Gollancz, 1960.

Power, A. *Estates on the Edge*, Basingstoke: Palgrave Macmillan, 1999.

Pugh, M. *Speak for Britain! A New History of the Labour Party*, London: Vintage, 2011.

Radice, G. *Friends and Rivals: Crosland, Jenkins and Healey*, London: Abacus, 2003.

Radice, G. 'In Praise of Revisionism: The Social Democratic Challenge Today', Lecture at Policy Network, 14 May 2007.

Radice, G. *Labour's Path to Power: The New Revisionism*, London: Macmillan, 1989.

Radice, G. *The Tortoise and the Hares: Attlee, Bevin, Cripps, Dalton, Morrison*, London: I.B. Tauris, 2008.

Reeves, R. 'Flee Your Tents, Oh Israel', in G. Cooke and J. Purnell (eds), *We Mean Freedom*, London: Demos, 2009.

Reid, A.J. and Pelling, H. *A Short History of the Labour Party*, Basingstoke: Palgrave Macmillan, 2005.

Reisman, D. *Anthony Crosland: Opportunity and Outcome*, Basingstoke: Macmillan, 1997.

Reisman, D. *Anthony Crosland: The Mixed Economy*, Basingstoke: Macmillan, 1997.

Richards, P. 'Back to the Future: The Decentralised Tradition and Labour's Way Forward', in R. Philpot (ed.), *The Purple Book: A Progressive Future for Labour*, London: Biteback Books, 2011.

Roberts, E. cited in Ramsden, S. 'Remaking Working-Class Community: Sociability, Belonging and "Affluence" in a Small Town, 1930–80, *Contemporary British History*, Volume 29 (1), 2014.

Robinson, E. and Twyman, J. 'Speaking at Cross Purposes? The Rhetorical Problems of Progressive Politics', *Political Studies Review*, Volume 12, 2014.

Rodgers, W.T. *Hugh Gaitskell 1906–1963*, London: Thames and Hudson, 1964.

de Ruggiero, G. *The History of European Liberalism*, London: Oxford University Press, 1927.

Runciman, D. 'Has the Age of Political Giants Passed? *Juncture*, Volume 21 (2), 2014.

Runciman, D. 'Socialism in One Country', *London Review of Books*, Volume 33 (15), 11 July 2011.

Rutherford, J. 'The First New Left, Blue Labour, and English Modernity', *Renewal*, Volume 21 (1), 2013.

Saggar, S. *Pariah Politics: Understanding Western Radical Islam and What Should be Done*, Oxford: Oxford University Press, 2008.

Sainsbury, D. *Progressive Capitalism*, London: Biteback Books, 2013.

Sassoon, D. *One Hundred Years of Socialism*, New York: The New Press, 1996.

Sassoon, D. 'Reflections on the Labour Party's Programme for the 1990s', *Political Quarterly*, Volume 62 (2), 1991.

Savage, M. and Devine, E. 'A New Model of Social Class? Findings from the BBC's Great British Class Survey Experiment', *Sociology*, doi: 10.1177/0038038513481128, 2013.

Schlesinger, A., Jr. 'Crosland's Socialism: A Review of *The Conservative Enemy*', *The New York Review of Books*, 1 June 1963.

Schumpeter, J. *Capitalism, Socialism, and Democracy*, New York: Harper and Bros, 1942.

Sen, A. *Development as Freedom*, Oxford: Oxford University Press, 1999.

Sen, A. *The Idea of Justice*, London: Allen Lane, 2009.

Shanks, M. *The Stagnant Society*, London: Harmondsworth, 1961.

Shaw, E. Losing Labour's Soul? New Labour and the Blair Government 1997–2007, London: Routledge, 2008.

Shaw, E. *The Labour Party Since 1979: Crisis and Transformation*, London: Routledge, 1996.

Shonfield, A. 'A Deadlock on the Left', pp. 12–13, *Encounter*, Issue 5, 1960.

Shonfield, A. *British Economic Policy since the War*, London: Harmondsworth, 1958.

Skidelsky, R. *Britain since 1900: A Success Story?*, London: Vintage Books, 2014.

Sloman, P. 'Partners in Progress? British Liberals and the Labour Party Since 1918', *Political Studies Review*, Volume 12, 2014.

Sloman, P. 'Rethinking a Progressive Moment: The Liberal and Labour Parties in the 1945 General Election', *Historical Research*, Volume 84, pp. 722–44, 2011.

Sloman, P. *The Liberal Party and the Economy 1929–64*, Oxford: Oxford University Press, 2015.

Smith, M. 'Understanding the "Politics of Catch Up": The Modernisation of the Labour Party', *Political Studies*, pp. 708–15, XLII, 1994.

Soroka, S. and Wlezien, C. 'On the Limits to Inequality in Representation', pp. 319–27, *Political Science and Politics*, 41 (2), 2008.

Soroka, S. and Wlezien, C. 'Political Institutions and the Opinion–Policy Link', paper presented at the European Consortium for Political Research Joint Sessions of Workshops, St. Gallen, Switzerland, 12–17 April 2011.

Stedman-Jones, G. *Languages of Class: Studies in English Working-Class History 1832–1982*, Cambridge: Cambridge University Press, 1984.

Steinmo, S. 'The Political Economy of Swedish Success', in W. Schafer and W. Streek, *Politics in the Age of Austerity*, Cambridge: Polity Press, 2014.

Tawney, R.H. *Equality*, London: Harper Collins, 1965.

Tawney, R.H. 'Lecture: Poverty as an Industrial Problem', London: London School of Economics, 1913.

Tawney, R.H. *The Acquisitive Society*, London: Penguin, 1921.

Tawney, R.H. *The Attack and Other Papers*, London: Allen and Unwin, 1953.

Tawney, R.H. 'The Choice Before the Labour Party', *Political Quarterly*, Volume 3, 1932.

Tatchell, P. *The Battle for Bermondsey*, London: Gay Men's Press, 1994.

Thorpe, R.A. *Super-Mac: The Life of Harold Macmillan*, London: Pimlico Press, 2011.

Thomas-Symonds, N. *Nye: The Political Life of Aneurin Bevan*, London: IB Tauris, 2014.

Thompson, E.P. *The Making of the English Working-Class*, London: Penguin Classics, 2013.

Thompson, H. 'Post-Crisis, Post-Devolution Politics and the Mansion Tax', *Political Quarterly*, Volume 86 (1), January–March 2015.

Thompson, N. *Political Economy and the Labour Party*, London: Routledge, 2006.

Thomson, D. 'The Idea of Equality', in D. Thomson (ed.), *Political Ideas*, London: Penguin Books, 1966.

Tiratsoo, N. 'Popular Politics, Affluence and the Labour Party in the 1950s', in A. Gorst, L. Johnman and Scott Lucas (eds), W. *Contemporary British History 1931–61: Politics and the Limits of Policy*, London and New York: Pinter Press, 1991.

Tiratsoo, N. 'Reconstruction, Affluence and Labour Politics', in N. Tiratsoo (ed.), *The Attlee Years*, London: Continuum, 1991.

Tomlinson, J. *The Politics of Decline*, London: Routledge, 2000.

Tomlinson, J. 'The Decline of the Empire and the Economic 'Decline' of Britain', *Twentieth Century British History*, Volume 14 (3), 2003.

Tomlinson, J. *The Labour Governments 1964–70: Economic Policy*, Manchester: Manchester University Press, 2004.

Toye, R. 'The Forgotten Revisionist: Douglas Jay and Britain's Transition to Affluence 1951–1964', in L. Black and H. Pemberton (eds) *An Affluent Society? Britain's Post-War 'Golden age' Revisited*, London: Ashgate, 2004.

Tudor, H. *The Preconditions of Socialism*, Cambridge: Cambridge University Press, 1993.

Wall, S. *The Official History of Britain and the European Community Volume II: From rejection to referendum 1963–75*, London: Routledge, 2013.

Warde, A. *Consensus and Beyond: The Development of Labour Party Strategy Since the Second World War*, Manchester: Manchester University Press, 1982.

Weber, M. 'Politics as a Vocation', in M. Weber, *The Vocation Lectures: Science as a Vocation, Politics as a Vocation*, Indianapolis, IN/Cambridge: Hackett Publishing, 2004.

West, E. 'Civil Economy: Blue Labour's Alternative to Capitalism', in I. Geary and A. Pabst (eds), *Blue Labour: Forging a New Politics*, London: IB Tauris, 2014.

Wicks, R. 'Revisionism in the 1950s: The Ideas of Anthony Crosland', in C. Navari (ed.), *British Politics and the Spirit of the Age*, Keele: Keele University Press, 1996.

Wickham-Jones, M. 'The Future of Socialism and New Labour: An Appraisal', *Political Quarterly*, Volume 78 (2), 2007.

Wiener, M. *English Culture and the Decline of the Industrial Spirit 1850–1980*, Cambridge: Cambridge University Press, 1985.

Williams, F. *Fifty Years' March: The Rise of the Labour Party*, London: Odhams Press, 1949.

Williams, P. *Hugh Gaitskell: A Political Biography*, London: Jonathan Cape, 1979.

Wilkinson, R. and Pickett, K. *The Spirit Level: Why Equality is Better for Everyone*, London: Penguin, 2010.

Willmott, P. *The Evolution of a Community*, London: Routledge and Kegan Paul, 1963.

Wincott, D. 'European Social Democracy', in D. Leonard (ed.), *Crosland and New Labour*, Basingstoke, Macmillan, 1999.

Winter, J.M. *Socialism and the Challenge of War: Ideas and Politics in Britain 1912–18*, London: Routledge and Kegan Paul, 1974.

Wood, S. 'One Nation Labour: Remarks to One Nation Labour Conference', Queen Mary University of London, April 2013.

Wootton, B. *Plan or No Plan*, London: Gollancz, 1934.

Wright, A. 'Whither Labour: Seeking Reinvention and a Realistic Radicalism', *Juncture*, London: Institute of Public Policy Research, 2015.

Wright, A. *British Politics: A Very Short Introduction*, Oxford: Oxford University Press, 2013.

Wright, A. 'New Labour, Old Crosland?', in D. Leonard (ed.), *Crosland and New Labour*, Basingstoke Macmillan, 1999.

Young, M. 'Interview with Geoff Dench', in G. Dench (ed.), *The Rise and Rise of Meritocracy*, Oxford: Political Quarterly/ Blackwell Publishing, 2006.

Young, M. *The Rise of the Meritocracy*, London: Penguin, 1958.

Zweiniger-Barcielowska, I. 'Rationing, Austerity and the Conservative Party Recovery After 1945', *The Historical Journal*, Volume 37 (1), 1994.

Notes

Preface

[1] There are certain similarities with the reformist wing of the German Social Democrats, as Peter Gay outlines in his book, *The Dilemma of Democratic Socialism* (New York: Collier Press, 1970). Gay argues that Bernstein's strain of reformist socialism in Germany failed because the revisionists were unwilling to tackle the traditional centres of power in German socialist politics; as a consequence, their opponents rallied and eventually gained a position of 'insuperable strength' in the labour movement.

[2] M. Smith, 'Understanding the "Politics of Catch Up": The Modernisation of the Labour Party', *Political Studies*, pp. 708–15, XLII, 1994.

[3] R. Miliband, 'Socialist advance in Britain', in R. Miliband and J. Saville (eds), *The Socialist Register 1983*, pp. 117, London: Merlin Press.

[4] A. Gamble, 'Progressive Politics: A New Beginning', *Policy Network*, 23 September 2015.

[5] G. Radice, 'In Praise of Revisionism: The Social Democratic Challenge Today', Lecture at Policy Network, 14 May 2007.

[6] S. Crosland, *Tony Crosland*, London: Jonathan Cape, 1982; K. Jeffreys, *Anthony Crosland: A New Biography*, London: John Blake, 1999.

[7] D. Leonard and D. Lipsey (eds), *The Socialist Agenda: Crosland's Legacy*, London: Jonathan Cape, 1981.

[8] D. Leonard (ed.), *Crosland and New Labour*, London: Macmillan, 1999.

[9] M. Francis, 'Mr Gaitskell's Ganymede: Reassessing Crosland's *The Future of Socialism*', *Contemporary British History*, 11 (2), 1997; Wickham-Jones, M. 'The Future of Socialism and New Labour: An Appraisal', *The Political Quarterly*, 78 (2), 2007.

[10] K. Hickson and S. Griffiths, *British Party Politics and Ideology after New Labour*, Basingstoke: Palgrave Macmillan, 2014.

[11] D. Riesman, *Anthony Crosland: Opportunity and Outcome*, Basingstoke: Macmillan, 1997.

[12] Peter Hain, *Back to the Future of Socialism*, Bristol: Policy Press, 2015.

[13] Notable exceptions include R. Desai, *Intellectuals and Socialism*, London: Lawrence & Wishart, 1991; D. Marquand, 'Moralists and Hedonists', in D. Marquand and A. Seldon, *The Ideas That Shaped Post-War Britain*, London: Fontana, 1996.

[14] S. Fielding, *The Labour Party: Socialism and Society Since 1951*, pp. 20, Manchester: Manchester University Press, 1997.

[15] J. Callaghan, S. Fielding and S. Ludlum (eds), *Interpreting the Labour Party*, pp. 1, Manchester: Manchester University Press, 2004.

Chapter One

[1] A. Crosland, Selection Speech to the South Gloucestershire Constituency Labour Party Selection Meeting, Crosland archive 13/21 (65), LSE.

[2] Cited in W.T. Rodgers (ed.), *Hugh Gaitskell 1906–1963*, p. 14, London: Thames and Hudson, 1964. The quotation refers to Gaitskell's close friend, Evan Durbin.

[3] This description was used by none other than the Marxist scholar Ralph Miliband in an otherwise coruscating review of Crosland's treatise.

[4] R. Crossman, *The Diaries of a Cabinet Minister Volume I*, London: Mandarin, 1991.

[5] G.D.H. Cole cited in R. Hattersley: www.newstatesman.com/node/146848.

[6] Cited in B. Harrison, *Seeking a Role: The United Kingdom 1951–70*, pp. 445–6, Oxford: Oxford University Press, 2009.

[7] Cited in A. Crosland, *The Future of Socialism*, p. 44, London: Jonathan Cape, 1956.

[8] A. Crosland, *The Future of Socialism*, p. 44.

[9] M. Kogan, 'Anthony Crosland: Intellectual and Politician', *Oxford Review of Education*, Volume 32 (1), pp. 71–86, 2006.

[10] Interview with D. Lipsey, House of Lords, 2 March 2015.

[11] Although both Roy Hattersley and Gordon Brown originally hailed from the Labour 'right', Hattersley was perceived to have shifted leftwards in his reaction to the policies of the New Labour governments after 1997.

[12] G. Brown, 'Foreword', in A. Crosland, *The Future of Socialism: Fiftieth Anniversary Edition*, London: Constable and Robinson, 2006.

[13] M. Wickham-Jones, 'The Future of Socialism and New Labour: An Appraisal', *Political Quarterly*, Volume 78 (2), p. 224, 2007.

[14] A. Gamble, *Between Europe and America: The Future of British Politics*, Basingstoke: Palgrave Macmillan, 2003.

[15] J. Tomlinson, *The Labour Governments 1964–70: Economic Policy*, Manchester: Manchester University Press, 2004.

[16] *The Financial Times*, 'Labour needs an honest debate about Tony Blair', 10 June 2015.

[17] A. Milburn and David Coats, 'Why Trade Unions Need a "Clause 4 Moment"', *The Financial Times*, 2 March 2006.

[18] A.J. Reid and H. Pelling, *A Short History of the Labour Party*, Basingstoke: Palgrave Macmillan, 2005.

[19] A.J. Reid and H. Pelling, *A Short History of the Labour Party*, p. 203.

[20] H. Kitschelt, *The Transformation of European Social Democracy*, p. 156, Cambridge: Cambridge University Press, 1994.

[21] S. Beer, *British Politics in the Collectivist Age*, p. 403, New York: Knopf, 1965.

[22] S. Berman, *The Primacy of Politics: Social Democracy and the Making of Europe's Twentieth Century*, Cambridge University Press, 2006.

[23] D. Marquand, 'Moralists and Hedonists', in A. Seldon and D. Marquand (eds), *The Ideas That Shaped Post-War Britain*, London: Fontana, 1996.

[24] D. Beland, *What is Social Policy? Understanding the Welfare State*, p. 12, Cambridge: Polity.

[25] S. Berman, *The Primacy of Politics*, p. 202.

[26] S. Berman, *The Primacy of Politics*; G. Stedman-Jones, *Languages of Class: Studies in English Working-Class History 1832–1982*, Cambridge: Cambridge University Press, 1984.

[27] Quoted in R. Behrens, 'The Centre: Social Democracy and Liberalism', in L. Tivey and A. Wright (eds), *Party Ideology in Britain*, Basingstoke: Macmillan, p. 74, 1989; L.T. Hobhouse, *Liberalism*, New York: Henry Holt, 1911.

[28] D. Beland, *What is Social Policy? Understanding the Welfare State*, p. 12, Cambridge: Polity.

[29] Cited in A. Wright, *British Politics: A Very Short Introduction*, p. 35, Oxford: Oxford University Press, 2013.

[30] Interview with R. Plant, House of Lords, 23 February 2015.

[31] D. Leonard, 'Introduction', in D. Lipsey and D. Leonard (eds), *The Socialist Agenda: Crosland's Legacy*, p. 1, 1981.

[32] D. Sainsbury, *Progressive Capitalism*, p. 101, London: Biteback Books, 2013; cited in P. Hain, *Back to the Future of Socialism*, p. 9, Bristol: Policy Press, 2014.

[33] http://news.bbc.co.uk/1/hi/uk_politics/8393746.stm.

[34] K. Hickson, 'Social Democracy and Happiness', in S. Griffiths (ed.), *Happiness*, London: Social Market Foundation, 2008.

[35] The idea of a post-war 'consensus' in British politics has been strongly contested as the debate between Ben Pimlott and Dennis Kavanagh has testified; Pimlott, B., Kavanagh, D. and Morris, P., 'Is the Postwar consensus a myth?'. The concept of a post-war 'settlement' refers more loosely to a set of domestic policies focused on maintaining full employment through Keynesian demand management, alongside the commitment to a universal welfare state and the National Health Service (NHS).

[36] A. Arblaster, 'Anthony Crosland: Labour's Last "Revisionist"', *Political Quarterly*, Volume 48 (4), p. 416, October 1977.

[37] Interview with B. Donoughue, 26 February 2015.

[38] M. Freeden, *The New Liberalism: An Ideology of Social Reform*, Oxford: Clarendon Press, 1978.

[39] www.newstatesman.com/node/146848.

[40] J.A. Hobson, *The Crisis of Liberalism: New Issues of Democracy*, p. xii, London: P.S. King, 1920.

[41] A. Gamble and A. Wright, 'The New Social Democracy', *Political Quarterly*, London, 2004.

[42] A. Warde, *Consensus and Beyond: The Development of Labour Party Strategy Since the Second World War*, Manchester: Manchester University Press, 1982.

[43] H. Pelling, *A Short History of the Labour Party*, London: Macmillan, 1961.

[44] S. Berman, *The Primacy of Politics*, p. 7.

[45] S. Berman, *The Primacy of Politics*, p. 202; S. Crosland, *Tony Crosland*, London: Jonathan Cape, 1982.

[46] D. Marquand, *The Progressive Dilemma: From Lloyd George to Kinnock*, London: Heinemann, 1991.

[47] A. Crosland, Speech to the South Gloucestershire Constituency Labour Party Selection Meeting, Crosland archives 13/21 (65), LSE.

[48] A. Crosland, 'Can Labour Win?', p. 9, London: The Fabian Society, 1960.

[49] T. Jones, *Remaking the Labour Party: From Gaitskell to Blair*, London: Routledge, 1996.

[50] T. Jones, *Remaking the Labour Party: From Gaitskell to Blair*.

[51] A. Gamble, *The Spectre at the Feast*, Basingstoke: Palgrave Macmillan, 2009.

[52] V. Bogdanor, 'General Election 2015', Gresham College Lecture.

[53] Cited in S. Crosland, *Tony Crosland*, p. 57.

[54] A. Howard, 'Exciting Friend', *New Statesman*, 3 May 1999.

[55] S. Crosland, *Tony Crosland*, p. 64–5.

[56] Cited in G. Williams, 'Anthony Crosland: The Forgotten Man in Labour Politics?', Trinity College Oxford Report 2010–11, www.darkoptimism. org/TrinityReport2010-11.pdf.

[57] G. Radice, *Labour's Path to Power: The New Revisionism*, London: Macmillan, 1989; A. Wright, 'Postscript', in D. Leonard (ed.), *Crosland and New Labour*, Basingstoke: Macmillan, 1999.

[58] H.M. Drucker, *Doctrine and Ethos in the Labour Party*, Edinburgh: Mainstream Press, 1978.

[59] N. Annan, *Our Age: The Generation That Made Post-War Britain*, p. 561, London: HarperCollins, 1990.

Chapter Two

[1] J.M. Keynes, *The General Theory of Employment, Interest and Money*, Cambridge: Cambridge University Press/Royal Economic Society, 1936.

[2] A. Shonfield, 'A Deadlock on the Left', pp. 12–13, *Encounter*, Issue 5, 1960.

[3] B. Harrison, *Seeking a Role: The United Kingdom 1951–70*, pp. 443–4, Oxford: Oxford University Press, 2009.

[4] A. Howard, 'Exciting Friend', *The New Statesman*, 3 May 1999.

[5] G. Williams, 'Anthony Crosland: The Forgotten Man in Labour Politics?', Trinity College Oxford Report 2010–11, www.darkoptimism.org/TrinityReport2010-11.pdf.

[6] This biographical account draws on S. Crosland, *Tony Crosland*, 1982; K. Jeffreys, *Anthony Crosland: A New Biography*, 1999.

[7] G. Williams, 'Anthony Crosland: The Forgotten Man in Labour Politics?', Trinity College Oxford Report 2010–11.

[8] G. Williams, 'Anthony Crosland: The Forgotten Man in Labour Politics?', Trinity College Oxford Report 2010–11.

[9] Interview with W.T. Rodgers, 2 March 2015.

[10] N. Davenport, *Memoirs of a City Radical*, p. 171, London: Weidenfeld and Nicolson, 1974.

[11] J. Callaghan, 'Mr Anthony Crosland Tributes', *Hansard*, Volume 926, pp. 1034–41, 21 February 1977.

[12] D. Lipsey and D. Leonard, *The Socialist Agenda: Crosland's Legacy*, London: Jonathan Cape, p. 7.

[13] Giles Radice, 'Speech to the Fabian Society Crosland Memorial Conference', Grimsby, 16 September 2006.

[14] 'Labour's Jubilee: Mr Crosland Recites Achievements', *Bristol Evening News*, 1950, the Crosland archive 7/3, LSE.

[15] Interview with D. Leonard, February 2015; 'Test Case', Labour Party Election Literature 1955, the Crosland archive 7/3, LSE.

[16] S. Crosland, *Tony Crosland*, p. 88.

[17] L. Black, *Redefining British Politics: Culture, Consumerism and Participation 1954–70*, p. 66, Basingstoke, Palgrave Macmillan, 2010.

[18] Cited in L. Black, *Redefining British Politics: Culture, Consumerism and Participation 1954–70*, p. 66.

[19] S. Crosland, *Tony Crosland*, p. 53.

[20] S. Crosland, *Tony Crosland*, p. 65.

[21] M. Kogan, *The Politics of Education: Edward Boyle and Anthony Crosland in Conversation with Maurice Kogan*, p. 150, London: Penguin, 1971.

[22] T. Benn, *Years of Hope: Diaries, Papers and Letters*, p. 237, London: Hutchinson, 1994.

[23] Interview with R. Hattersley, 6 March 2015.

[24] B. Harrison, *Seeking a Role: The United Kingdom 1951–70*, p. 482.

[25] Interview with D. Leonard, 11 February 2015.

[26] S. Crosland, *Tony Crosland*, p. 86.

[27] Interview with W.T. Rodgers, 2 March 2015.

[28] B. Magee, 'Tony Crosland as I knew him', *Political Quarterly*, Volume 81 (2), April–June 2010.

[29] N. Annan, *Our Age: The Generation That Made Post-War Britain*, p. 561, London: HarperCollins, 1990.

[30] M. Kogan, *The Politics of Education: Edward Boyle and Anthony Crosland in conversation with Maurice Kogan*, p. 150.

[31] S. Crosland, *Tony Crosland*, p. 86.

[32] S. Crosland, *Tony Crosland*, p. 67.

[33] M. Francis, 'Mr Gaitskell's Ganymede'.

[34] Interview with D. Leonard, 11 February 2015.

[35] Interview with D. Leonard, 11 February 2015.

[36] G. Williams, 'Anthony Crosland: The Forgotten Man in Labour Politics?', Trinity College Oxford Report 2010–11.

[37] Interview with Dick Leonard, 11 February 2015.

[38] J. Callaghan, 'Mr Anthony Crosland Tributes', *Hansard*, Volume 926, pp. 1034–41, 21 February 1977.

[39] S. Crosland, *Tony Crosland*, p. 273.

[40] B. Magee, 'Tony Crosland as I knew him', *Political Quarterly*, p. 181.

[41] Interview with R. Hattersley, 6 March 2015.

[42] P. Williams, *Hugh Gaitskell: A Political Biography*, London: Jonathan Cape, 1979.

[43] R. Desai, *Intellectuals and Socialism*, p. 117, London: Lawrence and Wishart, 1991; R. Skidelsky, *Britain Since 1900: A Success Story?* London: Vintage Books, 2014.

[44] Interview with G. Radice, House of Lords, 16 December 2014.

[45] Cited in S. Crosland, *Tony Crosland*, p. 372.

[46] B. Pimlott, 'Uber-Tony', *The London Review of Books*, September 1998.

[47] D. Leonard, 'What would Tony Crosland make of New Labour?', *Guardian* 17 February 2002.

[48] D. Leonard, 'Introduction', in D. Lipsey and D. Leonard (eds), *The Socialist Agenda: Crosland's Legacy*, p. 13.

[49] D. Reisman, *Anthony Crosland: The Mixed Economy*, p. 46, Basingstoke: Macmillan, 1997.

[50] B. Donoughue, *Prime Minister: The Conduct of Policy under Harold Wilson and James Callaghan*, p. 105, London: Jonathan Cape, 1987.

[51] Interview with D. Lipsey, House of Lords, 2 March 2015.

[52] B. Donoughue, *Downing Street Diary*, London: Politicos, 2006.

[53] R. Crossman, *The Diaries of a Cabinet Minister Volume I*, p. 138, London: Mandarin, 1991.

[54] R. Crossman, *The Diaries of a Cabinet Minister Volume I*, p. 433.

[55] R. Crossman, *The Diaries of a Cabinet Minister Volume II*, p. 614.

[56] Interview with D. Leonard, 11 February 2015.

[57] Interview with W.T. Rodgers, 2 March 2015.

[58] Crosland secured 17 votes on the first ballot compared to 90 for Michael Foot, 84 for Jim Callaghan, 56 for Roy Jenkins, 37 for Tony Benn, and 30 for Denis Healey (Jeffreys, 1999). S. Crosland, *Tony Crosland*, p. 318.

[59] G. Kaufman, 'Power Failure: A Review of *Friends and Rivals* by Giles Radice', *Guardian*, 14 September 2002.

[60] B. Donoughue, *Downing Street Diary*, p. 414.

[61] B. Donoughue, *Downing Street Diary*, p. 702.

[62] Interview with D. Lipsey, House of Lords, 2 March 2015.

[63] Interview with B. Grocott, House of Lords, 15 December 2015.

[64] An opinion poll conducted in 1976 to assess the credentials of the leadership contenders only demonstrated how far behind Crosland was as a serious candidate to be Labour leader. Comparing Crosland with Jim Callaghan, the eventual victor, 78 per cent thought Callaghan 'capable' of being the leader, but only 25 per cent said so of Crosland; 76 per cent rated Callaghan as 'strong' against 30 per cent for Crosland. Crosland scored little better on measures of 'honesty' and 'likeability'; he was in fact a long way behind Healey, Jenkins and Foot: Crosland archive 13/20 (178), LSE.

[65] Giles Radice, 'Speech to the Fabian Society Crosland Memorial Conference', Grimsby, 16 September 2006.

[66] Interview with G. Radice, 2 December 2014.

[67] This biographical account draws on S. Crosland, *Tony Crosland*, 1982; K. Jeffreys, *Anthony Crosland: A New Biography*,1999.

[68] S. Crosland, *Tony Crosland*, p. 63.

[69] S. Crosland, *Tony Crosland*, p. 64.

[70] R. Plant, 'Democratic Socialism and Equality', in D. Lipsey and D. Leonard (eds), *The Socialist Agenda: Crosland's Legacy*, London: Jonathan Cape, 1981.71 A. Crosland, *The Future of Socialism*, back cover, London: Jonathan Cape, 1956.

[72] www.newstatesman.com/uk-politics/2010/08/labour-party-miliband-2.

[73] H. Drucker, 'All the King's Horses', in W. Patterson and A. Thomas, *The Future of Social Democracy*, p. 109, Oxford: Clarendon Press, 1988.

[74] Interview with R. Hattersley, 6 March 2015.

[75] J. Ganesh, 'Conservatives Should be Pro-market, Not Pro-business', *The Financial Times*, 15 April 2013.

[76] B. Harrison, *Seeking a Role: The United Kingdom 1951–70*, p. 446.

[77] G. Radice, 'Speech to the Fabian Society Crosland Memorial Conference', Grimsby, 16 September 2006.

[78] S. Crosland, *Tony Crosland*, p. 68.

[79] G. Radice, *The Tortoise and the Hares: Attlee, Bevin, Cripps, Dalton, Morrison*, London: I.B. Tauris, 2008.

[80] Interview with Lord Giles Radice, House of Lords, 16 December 2014.

[81] Cited in P. Clarke, *A Question of Leadership: From Gladstone to Thatcher*, p. 143, London: Penguin, 1991.

[82] M. Pugh, *Speak for Britain: A New History of the Labour Party*, p. 308, London: Vintage, 2011.

[83] Interview with D. Marquand, 24 July 2015.

[84] B. Magee, 'Tony Crosland as I knew him', *Political Quarterly*.

[85] M. Pugh, *Speak for Britain: A New History of the Labour Party*, p. 308.

[86] G. Radice, 'Speech to the Fabian Society Crosland Memorial Conference', Grimsby, 16 September 2006.

[87] H. Tudor, *The Preconditions of Socialism*, p. xxiv, Cambridge: Cambridge University Press, 1993.

[88] R.H. Tawney, 'The Choice Before the Labour Party', *Political Quarterly*, Volume 3, p. 327, 1932.

[89] A. Crosland, *The Future of Socialism*, p. 113.

[90] R. Wicks, 'Revisionism in the 1950s – the Ideas of Anthony Crosland', in C. Navari (ed.), *British Politics and the Spirit of the Age*, Keele: Keele University Press, 1996.

[91] S. Crosland, *Tony Crosland*, p. 68.

[92] Cited in D. Reisman, *Anthony Crosland: Opportunity and Outcome*, p. 126, Basingstoke: Macmillan, 1997.

[93] T. Jones, *Remaking the Labour Party: From Gaitskell to Blair*, London: Routledge, 1996; H.M. Drucker, *Doctrine and Ethos in the Labour Party*, Edinburgh: Mainstream Press, 1978.

[94] E. Shaw, *The Labour Party Since 1979: Crisis and Transformation*, p. 5, London: Routledge.

[95] D. Reisman, *Anthony Crosland: Opportunity and Outcome*.

[96] Interview with Lord Giles Radice, House of Lords, 16 December 2014.

[97] B. Castle, 'Review of the Conservative Enemy by C.A.R. Crosland', *Tribune*, 30 November 1962.

[98] K. Jeffreys, *Anthony Crosland: A New Biography*.

[99] K. Jeffreys, *Anthony Crosland: A New Biography*, p. 63.

[100] S. Hall, 'Crosland Territory', *New Left Review*, I/2, March–April 1960.

[101] A. Wright, 'New Labour, Old Crosland?', in D. Leonard (ed.), *Crosland and New Labour*, Basingstoke: Macmillan, 1999.

[102] H.M. Drucker, *Doctrine and Ethos in the Labour Party*.

[103] E. Shaw, *The Labour Party Since 1979: Crisis and Transformation*, p. 6.

[104] D. Leonard, 'What would Tony Crosland make of New Labour?', *Guardian*, 17 February 2002.

[105] D. Marquand, *The Progressive Dilemma: From Lloyd George to Kinnock*, p. 177, London: Heinemann, 1991.

[106] J. Nuttall, 'Tony Crosland and the Many Falls and Rises of British Social Democracy', *Contemporary British History*, Volume 18 (4), pp. 52–79.

[107] S. Crosland, *Tony Crosland*; K. Jeffreys, *Anthony Crosland: A New Biography*; J. Nuttall, 'Tony Crosland and the Many Falls and Rises of British Social Democracy'.

[108] W.T. Rodgers (ed), *Hugh Gaitskell 1906–1963*, pp. 11–12, London: Thames and Hudson, 1964.

[109] 'Anthony Crosland: The Man Who Never Was', Profile, *New Statesman*, 28 September 1973.

[110] A. Howard, 'Exciting Friend'.

[111] D. Reisman, *Anthony Crosland: The Mixed Economy*, p. 12.

[112] M. Weber, 'Politics as a Vocation' in M. Weber, *The Vocation Lectures: Science as a Vocation, Politics as a Vocation*, Indianapolis, IN/Cambridge: Hackett Publishing, 2004.

[113] S. Crosland, *Tony Crosland*, p. 154.

[114] A. Howard, 'Exciting Friend'.

[115] D. Reisman, *Anthony Crosland: The Mixed Economy*, p. 225.

[116] D. Runciman, 'Has the age of political giants passed?, *Juncture*, Volume 21 (2), p. 104, 2014.

[117] P. Clarke, 'A Question of Leadership: Gladstone to Thatcher', p. 3.

[118] P. Clarke, 'A Question of Leadership: Gladstone to Thatcher', p. 3.

[119] A. Crosland, *The Future of Socialism*, p. 361.

[120] D. Marquand, *The Progressive Dilemma: From Lloyd George to Kinnock*, p. 177.

[121] Interview with D. Leonard, 11 February 2015.

[122] J. Vaizey, 'Anthony Crosland: A Profile', *Encounter*, p. 87, August 1977.

[123] Interview with R. Plant, House of Lords, 23 February 2015.

[124] B. Magee, 'Tony Crosland as I knew him', *Political Quarterly*, p. 178.

[125] P. Williams, *Hugh Gaitskell*.

[126] B. Pimlott, 'Uber-Tony', *The London Review of Books*.

[127] www.newstatesman.com/uk-politics/2010/08/labour-party-miliband-2.

Chapter Three

[1] A. Crosland, *The Future of Socialism*, p. 169, London: Jonathan Cape, 1956.

[2] A. Crosland, *The Future of Socialism*, p. 169.

[3] D. Leonard (ed.), *Crosland and New Labour*, Basingstoke: Macmillan, 1999.

[4] Interview with R. Hattersley, 6 March 2015.

[5] M. Young, Interview with Geoff Dench, p. 77, in G. Dench (ed.), *The Rise and Rise of Meritocracy*, Oxford: Political Quarterly/Blackwell Publishing, 2006.

[6] R. Lister, 'Ladder of Opportunity or Engine of Inequality', p. 233, in G. Dench (ed.), *The Rise and Rise of Meritocracy*, Oxford: Political Quarterly/Blackwell Publishing, 2006.

[7] W. Arthur Lewis, *The Principles of Economic Planning*, p. 10, London: Allen and Unwin, 1950.

[8] S. Padgett and W. Patterson, *A History of Social Democracy in Post-War Europe*, London: Longman, 1991.

[9] P. Clarke, *Keynes: The Twentieth Century's Most Influential Economist*, p. 67, London: Bloomsbury, 2009.

[10] J. Rawls, *A Theory of Justice*, Cambridge: Harvard University Press, 1971.

[11] R. Plant, 'Democratic Socialism and Equality', in D. Lipsey and D. Leonard (eds), *The Socialist Agenda: Crosland's Legacy*, London: Jonathan Cape, 1981.

[12] A. Crosland, *The Future of Socialism*, p. 44.

[13] R. Plant, 'Democratic Socialism and Equality', p. 138.

[14] A. Crosland, *The Future of Socialism*, p. 123.

[15] K.O. Morgan, *Labour in Power 1945–51*, p. 506, Oxford: Clarendon Press, 1984.

[16] Cited in P. Addison, *No Turning Back: The Peacetime Revolutions of Post-War Britain*, p. 9, Oxford: Oxford University Press, 2010.

17 Cited in E. Shaw, *The Labour Party Since 1979: Crisis and Transformation*, p. 3, London: Routledge, 1996.

18 P. Clarke, *A Question of Leadership: From Gladstone to Thatcher*, London: Penguin, 1991.

19 A. Warde, *Consensus and Beyond: The Development of Labour Party Strategy Since the Second World War*, pp. 24–5, Manchester: Manchester University Press, 1982.

20 R.H. Crossman, 'Towards a Philosophy of Socialism', p. 1, in R.H. Crossman, *New Fabian Essays*, London: Turnstile, 1952; and cited in A. Warde, *Consensus and Beyond: The Development of Labour party Strategy Since the Second World War*, p. 26.

21 Cited in A. Warde, *Consensus and Beyond: The Development of Labour party Strategy Since the Second World War*, p. 26.

22 A. Crosland, *The Future of Socialism*, p. 58.

23 A. Warde, *Consensus and Beyond: The Development of Labour Party Strategy Since the Second World War*.

24 R. McKibbin, 'The Economic Policy of the Second Labour Government 1929–1931', *Past and Present*, Volume 68, pp. 121–3, 1975.

25 Cited in N. Davenport, *Memoirs of a City Radical*, p. 180, London: Weidenfeld and Nicolson, 1974.

26 A. Warde, *Consensus and Beyond: The Development of Labour Party Strategy Since the Second World War*, pp. 24–5.

27 G. Radice, *The Tortoise and the Hares: Attlee, Bevin, Cripps, Dalton, Morrison*, London: I.B. Tauris, 2008.

28 A. Briggs, The Labour Party as Crucible', p. 22, in G. Dench (ed.), *The Rise and Rise of Meritocracy*, Oxford: Political Quarterly/Blackwell Publishing, 2006.

29 J. Harris, *William Beveridge: A Biography*, p. 378, Oxford: Oxford University Press, 1977.

30 A. Crosland, 'Can Labour Win?', p. 16, London: The Fabian Society, 1960.

31 R. Plant, 'Democratic Socialism and Equality', p. 139; A. Crosland, *The Future of Socialism*, p. 138.

32 A. Crosland, *The Future of Socialism*, p. 138.

33 Plant, 'Democratic Socialism and Equality', p. 139.

34 R. Wicks, 'Revisionism in the 1950s: The Ideas of Anthony Crosland', in C. Navari (ed.), *British Politics and the Spirit of the Age*, Keele: Keele University Press, 1996.

35 R.H. Tawney, *Equality*, p. 47, London: Allen and Unwin, 1928.

36 A. Crosland, *The Future of Socialism*. These are set out in K. Hickson, 'Crosland and Happiness', in S. Griffiths (ed.), *Well-Being*, pp. 60–2, London: The Social Market Foundation, 2007.

37 A. Crosland, *The Future of Socialism*, p. 147.

38 A.B. Atkinson, *Inequality: What Can be Done?* Princeton, NJ: Princeton University Press, 2015.

39 A. Crosland, *The Future of Socialism*, p. 141.

[40] A. Crosland, *The Future of Socialism*, p. 142.

[41] R. Wilkinson and K. Pickett, *The Spirit Level*, p. 264, London: Penguin, 2011; A.B. Atkinson, *Inequality: What Can be Done?*

[42] www.oecd.org/eco/growth/InequalityMobility.pdf.

[43] A. Crosland, *The Future of Socialism*, p. 140.

[44] A. Crosland, *The Future of Socialism*, p. 140.

[45] K. Hickson, 'Crosland and Happiness', in S. Griffiths (ed.), *Well-Being*, pp. 62–2; A. Crosland, *The Future of Socialism*, p. 125.

[46] Cited in D. Reisman, *Anthony Crosland: The Mixed Economy*, p. 113, Basingstoke: Macmillan, 1997.

[47] A. Crosland, *The Future of Socialism*, p. 147.

[48] R. Wicks, 'Revisionism in the 1950s: The Ideas of Anthony Crosland'.

[49] M. Kogan, 'Anthony Crosland: Intellectual and Politician', *Oxford Review of Education*, Volume 32 (1), p. 74, 2006.

[50] A. Crosland, *The Future of Socialism*, p. 191.

[51] M. Kogan, 'Anthony Crosland: Intellectual and Politician', *Oxford Review of Education*, p. 76.

[52] A. Crosland, *The Future of Socialism*, p. 202.

[53] S. Fielding, *The Labour Governments 1964–70: Labour and Cultural Change*, Manchester: Manchester University Press, 2003.

[54] Memorandum by the Secretary of State for Education and Science, 'Public Schools', Cabinet C (65) 155, p. 3, 19 November 1965.

[55] Memorandum by the Secretary of State for Education and Science, 'Public Schools', pp. 4–5.

[56] M. Kogan, 'Anthony Crosland: Intellectual and Politician', *Oxford Review of Education*, p. 78.

[57] M. Kogan, 'Anthony Crosland: Intellectual and Politician', *Oxford Review of Education*, p. 81. Crosland moved to the Board of Trade before the proposal to raise the school leaving age to 16 was considered; the plan was defeated due to public expenditure cuts following devaluation (B. Brivati and T. Bale (eds), *New Labour in Power*, London: Routledge, 1997).

[58] H.M. Drucker, *The Doctrine and Ethos of the Labour Party*, Edinburgh: Mainstream Press, 1978.; G. Cooke, *Society of Equals*, London: Demos, 2009.

[59] A. Crosland, *The Future of Socialism*, p. 231.

[60] D. Lipsey, 'The Meritocracy Myth – Whatever Happened to the Old Dream of a Classless Society?', *New Statesman*, 26 February 2015.

[61] A. Crosland, *Socialism Now*, p. 15, London: Jonathan Cape, 1974.

[62] D. Lipsey, 'The Meritocracy Myth – Whatever Happened to the Old Dream of a Classless Society?', *New Statesman*.

[63] J. Blanden, P. Gregg and S. Machin, 'Social Mobility in Britain: Low and Falling', *Centre Piece*, pp. 18–20, London School of Economics, Spring 2005.

[64] J. Blanden, P. Gregg and S. Machin, 'Social Mobility in Britain: Low and Falling', *Centre Piece*, pp. 18–20.

[65] J. Goldthorpe, 'Understanding – and Misunderstanding – Social Mobility in Britain. The Entry of the Economists, the Confusion of Politicians and the Limits of Educational Policy', *Barnett Papers in Social Research*, Oxford University Department of Social Policy and Intervention, 2012.

[66] www.cipd.co.uk/binaries/britain-at-work-in-the-reign-of-queen-elizabeth-ii_2012.pdf

[67] B. Harrison, *Seeking a Role: The United Kingdom 1951–70*, p. 205 , Oxford: Oxford University Press, 2009.

[68] A. Crosland, *The Future of Socialism*, p. 286.

[69] J. Goldthorpe, 'Understanding – and Misunderstanding – Social Mobility in Britain. The Entry of the Economists, the Confusion of Politicians and the Limits of Educational Policy'.

[70] V. Boliver and A. Swift, 'Do Comprehensive Schools Reduce Social Mobility?', *British Journal of Sociology*, Volume 62 (1), 2011.

[71] J. Goldthorpe, 'Understanding – and Misunderstanding – Social Mobility in Britain. The Entry of the Economists, the Confusion of Politicians and the Limits of Educational Policy'.

[72] 'An Hereditary Meritocracy', *The Economist*, 24 January 2015.

[73] www.brookings.edu/blogs/social-mobility-memos/posts/2014/02/10-opposites-dont-attract-assortative-mating-reeves.

[74] P. Hennessy, *Establishment and Meritocracy*, London: Haus Publishing, 2015.

[75] D. Lipsey, 'The Meritocracy Myth – Whatever Happened to the Old Dream of a Classless Society?', *New Statesman*.

[76] M. Young, *The Rise of the Meritocracy*, London: Penguin, 1958.

[77] A. Crosland, *The Future of Socialism*, p. 54.

[78] A. Crosland, *The Future of Socialism*, p. 54.

[79] J. Goldthorpe, 'Understanding – and Misunderstanding – Social Mobility in Britain. The Entry of the Economists, the Confusion of Politicians and the Limits of Educational Policy'.

[80] R.H. Tawney, *The Acquisitive Society*, London, 1930; H.M. Drucker, *Doctrine and Ethos in the Labour Party*, p. 52.

[81] B. Jackson, *Equality and the British Left*, p. 175, Manchester: Manchester University Press, 2006.

[82] Interview with R. Plant, House of Lords, 23 February 2015.

[83] http://scholarship.law.upenn.edu/cgi/viewcontent.cgi?article=4040&context=penn_law_review

[84] H. M. Drucker, *Doctrine and Ethos in the Labour Party*.

[85] R. Skidelsky, *Britain Since 1900: A Success Story?*, London: Vintage Books, 2014.

[86] H. M. Drucker, *Doctrine and Ethos in the Labour Party*.

[87] Interview with R. Plant, House of Lords, 23 February 2015.

[88] A. Schlesinger, Jr., 'Crosland's Socialism: A Review of *The Conservative Enemy*', *The New York Review of Books*, 1 June 1963.

[89] Cited in A. Schlesinger, Jr., 'Crosland's Socialism: A Review of *The Conservative Enemy*', *The New York Review of Books*.

[90] A. Crosland, *The Conservative Enemy*, p. 156, London: Jonathan Cape, 1962; and cited in A. Schlesinger, Jr., 'Crosland's Socialism: A Review of *The Conservative Enemy*', *The New York Review of Books*.

[91] Cited in D. Lawton, *Education and Labour Party Ideologies 1900–2001*, p. 68, London: Routledge, 2005.

[92] A. Crosland, *The Future of Socialism*, p. 343.

[93] Interview with R. Plant, House of Lords, 23 February 2015.

[94] R. Plant, 'Democratic Socialism and Equality'.

[95] S. Fielding, *The Labour Governments 1964–70: Labour and Cultural Change*.

[96] A. Crosland, *The Future of Socialism*, p. 214.

[97] S. Meredith, 'Mr Crosland's Nightmare? New Labour and Equality in Historical Perspective', *British Journal of Politics and International Relations*, p. 245, 2006.

[98] Cited in E. Shaw, *Losing Labour's Soul?*, p. 166, London: Routledge, 2008.

[99] Cited in E. Shaw, *Losing Labour's Soul?*, p. 102.

[100] Interview with R. Plant, House of Lords, 23 February 2015.

[101] http://news.bbc.co.uk/1/hi/programmes/world_at_one/our_archive/1153981.stm.

[102] www.theguardian.com/politics/2005/sep/26/schools.labour.

[103] A. Crosland, *Socialism Now*.

[104] R. Hattersley, *Who Goes Home? Scenes from a Political Life*, p. 179, London: Little Brown, 1995.

[105] A. Crosland, 1975, 'Social Democracy in Europe', Tract 438, London: Fabian Society, 1975.

[106] Interview with D. Lipsey, House of Lords, 2 March 2015.

[107] J. Le Grand, *The Strategy of Equality: Redistribution and the Social Services*, London: Allen and Unwin, 1982.

[108] A. Crosland, 'Social Democracy in Europe', p. 9.

[109] E. Luard, *Socialism Without the State*, Basingstoke: Macmillan, 1978. The Callaghan Government recognised this by addressing the decline of school standards as outlined in Callaghan's 1977 speech at Ruskin College, and by considering proposals for council house sales of which Crosland was personally sceptical.

[110] D. Leonard (ed.), *Crosland and New Labour*, Basingstoke: Macmillan, 1999; S. Meredith, 'Mr Crosland's Nightmare? New Labour and Equality in Historical Perspective', *British Journal of Politics and International Relations*.

[111] A. Crosland, *The Future of Socialism*, p. 114.

[112] D. Reisman, *Anthony Crosland and the Mixed Economy*.

[113] D. Reisman, *Anthony Crosland and the Mixed Economy*, p. 116.

[114] D. Marquand, *The Progressive Dilemma: From Lloyd George to Kinnock*, London: Heinemann, 1991.

[115] T. Blair, interview on *The World This Weekend*, BBC Radio 2, 14 December 1995.

[116] G. Stedman-Jones, 'Why is the Labour Party in such a mess?', in G. Stedman-Jones, *Languages of Class: Studies in English Working-Class History 1832–1982*, Cambridge: Cambridge University Press, 1983.

[117] A. B. Atkinson, *Public Economics in an Age of Austerity*, p. 19, London: Routledge, 2014.

[118] A. B. Atkinson, *Public Economics*.

[119] R. Wilkinson and K. Pickett, *The Spirit Level*.

[120] T. Piketty, *Capital in the Twenty-First Century*, p. 116, Cambridge, MA: Harvard University Press, 2014.

[121] A.B. Atkinson, *Inequality: What Can Be Done?*.

[122] This point was brought home to me in discussions with my colleague Thomas Aubrey.

[123] N. Bosanquet, and P. Townsend, *Labour and Inequality: Sixteen Fabian Essays*, London: Fabian Society, 1982.

[124] B. Donoughue, *Prime Minister: The Conduct of Policy under Harold Wilson and James Callaghan*, p. 75, London: Jonathan Cape, 1987.

[125] S. Meredith, 'Mr Crosland's Nightmare? New Labour and Equality in Historical Perspective', *British Journal of Politics and International Relations*.

[126] A. Crosland, 'Equality in Hard Times', *Socialist Commentary*, October 1976; B. Donoughue, *Prime Minister: The Conduct of Policy under Harold Wilson and James Callaghan*, p. 75, London: Jonathan Cape, 1987; S. Meredith, 'Mr Crosland's Nightmare? New Labour and Equality in Historical Perspective', *British Journal of Politics and International Relations*.

[127] R. Plant, 'Democratic Socialism and Equality'.

[128] A. Crosland, *The Future of Socialism*, p. 140.

[129] R. Plant, 'Democratic Socialism and Equality', p. 154.

[130] Interview with D. Marquand, 24 July 2015.

[131] E. Shaw, *Losing Labour's Soul?*, p. 167.

[132] P. Clarke, *Liberals and Social Democrats*, Cambridge: Cambridge University Press, 1978.

[133] T. Hunt, 'Reviving our Sense of Mission: Designing a New Political Economy', in R. Philpot (ed.), *The Purple Book: A Progressive Future for Labour*, p. 65, London: Biteback Books, 2011.

[134] *British Social Attitudes 31*, London: National Centre for Social Research, 2014.

[135] B. Jackson, 'Revisionism Reconsidered: "Property-Owning Democracy" and Egalitarian Strategy in Post-War Britain', *Twentieth Century British History*, Volume 16 (4), 2005.

[136] B. Jackson, *Equality and the British Left*, p. 222.

[137] Interview with R. Plant, House of Lords, 23 February 2015.

[138] Interview with R. Plant, House of Lords, 23 February 2015.

[139] S. Griffiths, 'New Labour, New Liberalism and Revisionism's Second Wave', in S. Griffiths and K. Hickson, *British Party Politics and Ideology After New Labour*, p. 72, Basingstoke: Palgrave Macmillan, 2014.

[140] Interview with R. Plant, House of Lords, 23 February 2015.

[141] S. Soroka and C. Wlezien, 'On the Limits to Inequality in Representation', pp. 319–27, *Political Science and Politics* 41 (2), 2008.

[142] www.bsa.natcen.ac.uk/media/38972/bsa32_fullreport.pdf.

[143] Interview with R. Plant, House of Lords, 23 February 2015.

[144] Interview with R. Plant, House of Lords, 23 February 2015.

[145] Cited in A. Arblaster, 'Anthony Crosland: Labour's Last "Revisionist"', p. 419, *Political Quarterly*, Volume 48 (4), October 1977.

[146] R.H. Tawney, *Equality*, p. 22.

[147] E. Durbin, *The Politics of Democratic Socialism*, pp. 269–70, London: Labour Book Service, 1940; quoted in R. Behrens, 'The Centre: Social Democracy and Liberalism', in L. Tivey and A. Wright (eds), *Party Ideology in Britain*, Basingstoke: Macmillan, 1989; L. Hobhouse, *Liberalism*, Oxford: Oxford University Press, 1967.

[148] E. Durbin, *The Politics of Democratic Socialism*, pp. 269–70; quoted in R. Behrens, 'The Centre: Social Democracy and Liberalism'.

[149] A. Crosland, 'Social Democracy in Europe', p. 3.

[150] R.H. Tawney, *Equality*, p. 22.

[151] P. Sloman, 'Rethinking a Progressive Moment: The Liberal and Labour Parties in the 1945 General Election', *Historical Research*, Volume 84, pp. 722–44, 2011. As Sloman notes, historians disagree on this point: Ross McKibbin insists that there was a 'radicalisation of public opinion' at the end of the Second World War; Fielding and Nick Tiratsoo claim that Attlee's victory was spurred by antipathy towards the Conservative party and an appetite for practical social reforms including implementation of the Beveridge report.

[152] B. Magee, 'Tony Crosland As I Knew Him', *Political Quarterly*, Volume 81 (2), April–June 2010.

Chapter Four

[1] A. Crosland, *The Future of Socialism*, p. 354, London: Jonathan Cape, 1956.

[2] A. Crosland, *The Conservative Enemy*, p. 239, London: Jonathan Cape, 1962.

[3] Cited in P. Gay, *The Dilemma of Democratic Socialism*, p. 247, New York: Collier Books, 1970.

[4] A. Crosland, *The Future of Socialism*, p. 156.

[5] R. Hofstadter, *The American Political Tradition and the men who made it*, p. 451, New York: Anchor, 1948.

[6] P. Clarke cited in E. Robinson and J. Twyman, 'Speaking at Cross Purposes? The Rhetorical Problems of Progressive Politics', *Political Studies Review*, Volume 12, p. 53, 2014.

[7] J. Cronin, *New Labour's Pasts: The Labour Party and its Discontents*, p. 34, Harlow: Pearson Education, 2004.

[8] P. Addison, *No Turning Back: The Peacetime Revolutions of Post-War Britain*, Oxford: Oxford University Press, 2010.

[9] Cited in P. Addison, *No Turning Back: The Peacetime Revolutions of Post-War Britain*, pp. 9–10.

[10] P. Addison, *No Turning Back: The Peacetime Revolutions of Post-War Britain*, p. 10.

[11] In this book, the terms 'social democracy' and 'democratic socialism' are used interchangeably as they are in Crosland's writings. There is evidence that in the final stage of his career, Crosland preferred to define himself as a democratic socialist to distinguish his politics from the insular, conservative right-wing of the Labour party in the 1970s.

[12] R. Plant, 'Democratic Socialism and Equality', in D. Lipsey and D. Leonard (eds), *The Socialist Agenda: Crosland's Legacy*, London: Jonathan Cape, 1981.

[13] H.M. Drucker, *Doctrine and Ethos in the Labour Party*, Edinburgh: Mainstream Press, 1978.

[14] D.W. Brogan, 'The Future is Behind Us? On the North Atlantic Left', p. 66, *Encounter*, Issue 1, 1960.

[15] G. Radice, *Labour's Path to Power: The New Revisionism*, London: Macmillan, 1989; A. Crosland, *The Future of Socialism*.

[16] M. Freeden, *The New Liberalism: An Ideology of Social Reform*, pp. 255–6, Oxford: Clarendon Press, 1978.

[17] A. Grimes, 'Introduction', in L.T. Hobhouse, *Liberalism*, pp. 4–5, Oxford/New York: Oxford University Press, 1964.

[18] M. Freeden, *The New Liberalism: An Ideology of Social Reform*, p. 257.

[19] M. Freeden, *The New Liberalism: An Ideology of Social Reform*, p. 257.

[20] R. Wicks, 'Revisionism in the 1950s: The Ideas of Anthony Crosland', in C. Navari (ed.), *British Politics and the Spirit of the Age*, p. 212, Keele: Keele University Press, 1996.

[21] D. Lipsey and D. Leonard, *The Socialist Agenda: Crosland's Legacy*, p. 1, London: Jonathan Cape, 1981.

[22] H. Pelling, *A Short History of the Labour Party*, p. 42, London: Macmillan, 1961.

[23] W.H. Greenleaf, *The British Political Tradition Volume II: The Ideological Heritage*, p. 360, London: Routledge, 1983.

[24] Cited in A. Crosland, *The Future of Socialism*, p. 48.

[25] H.M. Drucker, *Doctrine and Ethos in the Labour Party*, p. 27; J.M. Winter, *Socialism and the Challenge of War: Ideas and Politics in Britain 1912–18*, London: Routledge and Kegan Paul, 1974.

[26] H. Pelling, *A Short History of the Labour Party*, p. 44.

[27] Cited in H.M. Drucker, *Doctrine and Ethos in the Labour Party*, pp. 27–8.

[28] D. Marquand, 'Review of Speak for England! A New History of the Labour Party by Martin Pugh', *New Statesman*, 2 April 2010.

[29] A. Crosland, 'The Future of the Left', *Encounter*, March 1960, p. 4.

[30] H. Pelling, *A Short History of the Labour Party*, p. 44.

[31] H. Pelling, *A Short History of the Labour Party*, p. 45.

[32] H. Kohn, *Political Ideologies of the Twentieth Century*, p. 7, New York: Harper Torchbooks, 1966.

[33] T. Nairn cited in R. Desai, *Intellectuals and Socialism*, p. 6, London: Lawrence and Wishart, 1991.

[34] A. Crosland, *The Future of Socialism*, p. 44.

[35] R.H.S. Crossman, *New Fabian Essays*, London: Fabian Society, 1952.

[36] 'Labour's Clause Four and Britain's Left of Centre', *The Reformer*, Spring 1995.

[37] 'Labour's Clause Four and Britain's Left of Centre', *The Reformer*, Spring 1995.

[38] Cited in B. Pimlott, *Labour and the Left in the 1930s*, p. 198, Cambridge: Cambridge University Press, 1978.

[39] A. Crosland, *The Conservative Enemy*, pp. 44–45.

[40] H. Dalton, *Practical Socialism for Britain*, London: George Routledge and Sons, 1935; G.D.H Cole, *Great Britain in the Post-War World*, London: Gollancz, 1942; H.M. Drucker, *Doctrine and Ethos in the Labour Party*, p. 27.

[41] H.M. Drucker, *Doctrine and Ethos in the Labour Party*, p. 25.

[42] D. Howell, *British Social Democracy: A Study in Development and Decay*, London: Croom Helm, 1976.

[43] H.M. Drucker, *Doctrine and Ethos in the Labour Party*, pp. 72–3; B. Wootton, *Plan or No Plan*, London: Gollancz, 1934.

[44] P. Gordon Walker, *Political Diaries 1932–1971*, London: The Historian's Press, 1991, p. 258.

[45] L. Black, *Redefining British Politics: Culture, Consumerism and Participation 1954–70*, p. 18, Basingstoke: Palgrave Macmillan, 2010.

[46] H.M. Drucker, *Doctrine and Ethos in the Labour Party*, p. 29.

[47] J.P. Mackintosh, 'Socialism or Social Democracy? The Choice for the Labour Party', *Political Quarterly*, Volume 43 (4), pp. 437–8, 1972; H.M. Drucker, *Doctrine and Ethos in the Labour Party*, p. 28.

[48] Cited in R. Toye, 'The Forgotten Revisionist: Douglas Jay and Britain's Transition to Affluence 1951–1964', in L. Black and H. Pemberton (eds) *An Affluent Society? Britain's Post-War 'Golden age' Revisited*, p. 56, London: Ashgate, 2004.

[49] B. Pimlott, *Labour and the Left in the 1930s*, in L. Black and H. Pemberton (eds) *An Affluent Society? Britain's Post-War 'Golden age' Revisited*, p. 39, London: Ashgate, 2004.

[50] H. Gaitskell, 'Socialism and Nationalisation', Tract 300, London: Fabian Society, 1956.

[51] R.H. Tawney, *The Attack and Other Papers*, pp. 92–8, London: Allen and Unwin, 1953.

[52] Cited in A. Crosland, 'The Future of the Left'.

[53] A. Crosland, 'Can Labour Win?', pp. 14–15, London: The Fabian Society, 1960.

[54] A. Crosland, 'Can Labour Win?', p. 15.

[55] L. Black, *The Political Culture of the Left in Affluent Britain 1951–64*, p. 136, Basingstoke: Palgrave Macmillan, 2002.

[56] Cited in P. Addison, *No Turning Back: The Peacetime Revolutions of Post-War Britain*, p. 16.

[57] P. Addison, *No Turning Back: The Peacetime Revolutions of Post-War Britain*, p. 22.

58 B. Magee, *The New Radicalism*, p. 144, London: Secker and Warburg, 1962.

59 A. Crosland, *The Conservative Enemy*, p. 129.

60 R. Barker, *Political Ideas in Modern Britain*, p. 182, London: Routledge, 1978.

61 A. Crosland, *The Future of Socialism*, p. 165.

62 D. Reisman, *Anthony Crosland and the Mixed Economy*, p. 195, Basingstoke: Macmillan, 1997.

63 A. Crosland, diary entry, 22 June 1947, Crosland archive 16/1, LSE.

64 Interview with D. Leonard, 11 February 2015. Crosland and Richard Crossman were the most popular speakers at Fabian summer schools in the 1950s; Roy Jenkins was then thought to be rather boring and pedestrian.

65 A. Crosland, *The Future of Socialism*, p. 439.

66 Cited in S. Lukes, 'The Future of British Socialism', in B. Pimlott (ed.), *Fabian Essays in Socialist Thought*, p. 275, London: Heinemann, 1984.

67 Interview with R. Hattersley, 6 March 2015.

68 M. Francis, 'Mr Gaitskell's Ganymede: Reassessing Crosland's *The Future of Socialism*', *Contemporary British History*, Volume 11 (2), 1997.

69 Cited in R. Toye, 'The Forgotten Revisionist: Douglas Jay and Britain's Transition to Affluence 1951–1964', p. 197.

70 A. Crosland, 'Britain in 1970' speech, undated, Crosland archive 13/21, speeches 1940–67, LSE.

71 P. Jay, 'Booster Shot', *New Statesman*, 22 March 1974.

72 A. Crosland, 'Britain in 1970 speech', undated, Crosland archive 13/21, speeches 1940–67, LSE.

73 A. Crosland, *The Future of Socialism*, pp. 521–2.

74 A. Crosland, Selection Speech to the South Gloucestershire Constituency Labour Party Selection Meeting, Crosland archive 13/21, LSE.

75 Interview between A. Crosland and George Gale, London BBC, 25 April 1974, Crosland archive 13/20 (326), LSE.

76 J. Campbell, *Roy Jenkins: A Well-Rounded Life*, p. 181, London: Jonathan Cape, 2014.

77 J. Campbell, *Roy Jenkins: A Well-Rounded Life*, p.181.

78 D. Reisman, *Anthony Crosland: The Mixed Economy*, p. 54.

79 J. Harris, *William Beveridge: A Biography*, Oxford: Oxford University Press, 1978.

80 A. Crosland, *The Future of Socialism*, p. 54.

81 J. Harris, *William Beveridge: A Biography*; J. Nuttall, 'Tony Crosland and the Many Falls and Rises of British Social Democracy', *Contemporary British History*, Volume 18 (4), pp. 52–79, 2004.

82 B. Harrison, *Seeking a Role: The United Kingdom 1951–70*, p. 176, Oxford: Oxford University Press, 2009.

83 A.J. Ayer, *Language, Truth and Logic*, London: Dover Publications, 1952.

84 P. Marris, 'Just Rewards: Meritocracy Fifty Years Later', in G. Dench (ed.), *The Rise and Rise of Meritocracy*, p. 158, Oxford: Political Quarterly/ Blackwell Publishing, 2006.

[85] P. Marris, 'Just Rewards: Meritocracy Fifty Years Later', p. 160.

[86] A. Crosland, *The Future of Socialism*, p. 355.

[87] A. Crosland, 'Social Democracy in Europe', Tract 438, London: Fabian Society, p. 16, 1975.

[88] D. Reisman, *Anthony Crosland and the Mixed Economy*, p. 85.

[89] A. Crosland, *The Future of Socialism*, p. 339; D. Reisman, *Anthony Crosland and the Mixed Economy*.

[90] S. Beer, *British Politics in the Collectivist Age*, London: Random House, 1969; H. Pelling, *A Short History of the Labour Party*.

[91] M. Kenny, *The First New Left*, London: Lawrence and Wishart, 1995; R. Miliband, *Parliamentary Socialism: A Study in the Politics of Labour*, London: The Merlin Press, 1972.

[92] A. Warde, *Consensus and Beyond: The Development of Labour Party Strategy Since the Second World War*, p. 43, Manchester: Manchester University Press, 1982.

[93] D. Thomson, 'The Idea of Equality', in D. Thomson (ed.), *Political Ideas*, p. 199, London: Penguin Books, 1966.

[94] H.V. Emy, *Radicals, Liberals and Social Politics 1892–1914*, p. 105, Cambridge: Cambridge University Press, 1973.

[95] H.V. Emy, *Radicals, Liberals and Social Politics 1892–1914*, p. 110.

[96] P. Sloman, *The Liberal Party and the Economy 1929–64*, p. 201, Oxford: Oxford University Press; C.A.R. Crosland, *Britain's Economic Problem*, London: Jonathan Cape, 1953.

[97] H. Campbell-Bannerman, *The Manchester Guardian*, 1903 cited in P. Sloman, 'Partners in Progress? British Liberals and the Labour Party Since 1918', *Political Studies Review*, p. 42, Volume 12, 2014.

[98] S. Crosland, *Tony Crosland*, p. 94.

[99] H. Kohn, *Political Ideologies of the Twentieth Century*, pp. 64–65.

[100] A. Warde, *Consensus and Beyond: The Development of Labour party Strategy Since the Second World War*, p. 43.

[101] This section of the chapter is based on the account of revisionism in A. Warde, *Consensus and Beyond: The Development of Labour Party Strategy Since the Second World War*, pp. 44–58.

[102] Cited in N. Thompson, *Political Economy and the Labour Party*, p. 170, London: Routledge, 2006.

[103] A. Crosland, *The Future of Socialism*, p. 461.

[104] This section was based on the account of 'Social Reformism' in A. Warde, *Consensus and Beyond: The Development of Labour Party Strategy Since the Second World War*, pp. 44–58.

[105] A. Warde, *Consensus and Beyond: The Development of Labour Party Strategy Since the Second World War*, p. 66.

[106] A. Warde, *Consensus and Beyond: The Development of Labour Party Strategy Since the Second World War*, p. 66.

[107] R.H. Tawney, 'We Mean Freedom' in *The Attack and Other Papers*, p. 83.

[108] D. Thomson, 'The Idea of Equality', in D. Thomson (ed.), *Political Ideas*, p. 199.

[109] G. de Ruggiero, *The History of European Liberalism*, p. 155, London: Oxford University Press, 1927.

[110] S. Collini, *Liberalism and Sociology: L.T. Hobhouse and Political Argument in England 1880–1914*, pp. 128–9, Cambridge: Cambridge University Press, 1979.

[111] A. Grimes, 'Introduction', in L.T. Hobhouse, *Liberalism*, p. 5, Oxford/New York: Oxford University Press, 1964.

[112] S. Collini, *Liberalism and Sociology: L.T. Hobhouse and Political Argument in England 1880–1914*, p. 121.

[113] P. Sloman, 'Partners in Progress? British Liberals and the Labour Party since 1918'.

[114] A.R. Morton, 'After Socialism? The Future of Radical Christianity', University of Edinburgh Centre for Theology and Public Issues, Occasional Paper 32, Edinburgh: University of Edinburgh, 1994.

[115] J. Harris, 'Social Policy, Saving, and Sound Money', in P. Clarke and C. Trebilcock, *Understanding Decline: Perceptions and Realities of British Economic Performance*, pp. 172–3, Cambridge: Cambridge University Press, 1997.

[116] Cited in R. Desai, *Intellectuals and Socialism*, p. 5.

[117] P. Clarke, *Keynes: The Twentieth Century's Most Influential Economist*, p. 68, London: Bloomsbury, 2009.

[118] H. Pelling, *The History of the Labour Party*, 1965.

[119] M. Freeden, *The New Liberalism: An Ideology of Social Reform*, p. 257.

[120] A. Grimes, 'Introduction', in L.T. Hobhouse, *Liberalism*, p. 7.

[121] Cited in S. Collini, *Liberalism and Sociology: L.T. Hobhouse and Political Argument in England 1880–1914*, p. 128.

[122] L.T. Hobhouse, *Liberalism*.

[123] D. Nicholls, 'Positive Liberty 1880–1914', *The American Political Science Review*, p. 117, Volume 56, (1), March 1962.

[124] A. Grimes, 'Introduction', in L.T. Hobhouse, *Liberalism*, p. 6.

[125] T.H. Green, *Works*, p. 371, London: Longmans and Green, 1885.

[126] D. Nicholls, 'Positive Liberty 1880–1914', *The American Political Science Review*, p. 122.

[127] B. Jackson, 'Socialism and the New Liberalism', in B. Jackson and M. Stears (eds), *Liberalism as Ideology: Essays in Honour of Michael Freeden*, Oxford: Oxford University Press, 2012.

[128] Cited in S. Collini, *Liberalism and Sociology: L.T. Hobhouse and Political Argument in England 1880–1914*, p. 247.

[129] P. Clarke, 'The Progressive Movement in England', *Transactions of the Royal Historical Society*, Volume 24, p. 162, 1974; S. Collini, *Liberalism and Sociology: L.T. Hobhouse and Political Argument in England 1880–1914*, p. 137, Cambridge: Cambridge University Press, 1979.

[130] Cited in P. Clarke, 'The Progressive Movement in England', p. 162.

[131] Cited in P. Clarke, 'The Progressive Movement in England', p. 178.

[132] A. Thorpe cited in P. Sloman, 'Partners in Progress? British Liberals and the Labour Party Since 1918', p. 43.

[133] P. Sloman, 'Partners in Progress? British Liberals and the Labour Party since 1918', p. 43.

[134] D. Nicholls, 'Positive Liberty 1880–1914', *The American Political Science Review*, p. 125.

[135] P. Clarke, 'The Progressive Movement in England', p. 165.

[136] P. Clarke, 'The Progressive Movement in England', p. 167.

[137] Cited in S. Collini, *Liberalism and Sociology: L.T. Hobhouse and Political Argument in England 1880–1914*, p. 72.

[138] P. Clarke, 'The Progressive Movement in England'.

[139] Cited in P. Clarke, 'The Progressive Movement in England', p. 167.

[140] R.H. Tawney, *Equality*; P. Clarke, 'The Progressive Movement in England'.

[141] P. Clarke, 'The Progressive Movement in England', p. 170.

[142] Cited in A. Crosland, *The Future of Socialism*, p. 44.

[143] R.H. Tawney, *Socialist Commentary*, cited in A. Crosland, *The Future of Socialism*, p. 54.

[144] D. Nicholls, 'Positive Liberty 1880–1914'.

[145] Cited in D. Nicholls, 'Positive Liberty 1880–1914', p. 124.

[146] E. Dell, *A Strange Eventful History: Democratic Socialism in Britain*, London, Harper Collins: 2000.

[147] B. Harrison, *Seeking a Role: The United Kingdom 1951–70*, p. 442.

[148] R. Desai, *Intellectuals and Socialism*, p. 3.

[149] D. Lipsey and D. Leonard, *The Socialist Agenda: Crosland's Legacy*.

[150] A. Crosland, Note to Hugh Gaitskell, November 1960, Crosland 6/1 (13), LSE.

[151] A. Crosland, *The Conservative Enemy*, p. 121.

[152] A. Crosland, *The Future of Socialism*, p. 177.

[153] A. Crosland, *The Future of Socialism*, p. 177.

[154] R. Behrens, 'The Centre: Social Democracy and Liberalism', in L. Tivey and A. Wright (eds), *Party Ideology in Britain*, pp. 75–6, Basingstoke: Macmillan, 1989.

[155] A. Crosland, *The Future of Socialism*, p. 177.

[156] A. Crosland, *The Future of Socialism*, p. 247.

[157] A. Crosland, *The Future of Socialism*, p. 248.

[158] R. Behrens, 'The Centre: Social Democracy and Liberalism', p. 80.

[159] R. Behrens, 'The Centre: Social Democracy and Liberalism', p. 89; L. Hobhouse, *Liberalism*.

[160] P. Sloman, 'Partners in Progress? British Liberals and the Labour Party Since 1918', p. 47.

[161] A. Crosland, 'Social Democracy in Europe', p. 6.

[162] Interview with R. Plant, House of Lords, 23 February 2015.

[163] Cited in S. Fielding, *The Labour Governments 1964–70: Labour and Cultural Change*, p. 195, Manchester: Manchester University Press, 2003.

[164] A. Crosland, 'Social Democracy in Europe'.

[165] A. Crosland, *The Future of Socialism*, p. 198.

[166] Interview between A. Crosland and George Gale, London BBC, 25 April 1974, Crosland archive 13/20 (326), LSE.

[167] Interview with B. Donoughue, 26 February 2015; B. Donoughue, *Prime Minister: The Conduct of Policy under Harold Wilson and James Callaghan*, p. 108, London: Jonathan Cape, 1987.

[168] Interview with D. Lipsey, House of Lords, March 2015.

[169] Cited in D. Reisman, *Anthony Crosland and the Mixed Economy*, p. 96.

[170] A. Crosland, *The Conservative Enemy*, p. 39.

[171] P. Sloman, 'Partners in Progress? British Liberals and the Labour Party Since 1918', p. 44.

[172] J. Meade, *Efficiency, Equality, and the Ownership of Property*, London: Routledge, 1964.

[173] R. Barker, 'Political Ideas in Post-War Britain', p. 183.

[174] A. Crosland, *The Future of Socialism*, p. 361.

[175] A. Crosland, 'Policies for the People, by the People', *Socialist Commentary*, p. 5, November 1971.

[176] A. Crosland, 'Policies for the People, by the People', p. 5.

[177] G. Gallop, 'A Lecture on Labour Party Revisionism', Nuffield College, Oxford, Crosland archive 17/3, LSE.

[178] D. Marquand, *The Progressive Dilemma: From Lloyd George to Neil Kinnock*, London: Heinemann, 1991.

[179] R. Behrens, 'The Centre: Social Democracy and Liberalism', p. 82; L. Hobhouse, *Liberalism*.

[180] D. Piachaud, 'Revitalising Social Policy', *Political Quarterly*, Volume 62 (2), p. 224, 1991.

[181] E. Durbin, *The Politics of Democratic Socialism*, London: Labour Book Service, 1940.

[182] Cited in R. Skidelsky, *Britain Since 1900: A Success Story?*, p. 132, London: Vintage Books, 2014.

[183] A. Crosland, *The Future of Socialism*, p. 354.

[184] A. Crosland, *The Future of Socialism*, p. 355.

[185] A. Crosland, *The Future of Socialism*, p. 355.

[186] This argument is subsequently developed by Crosland in *The Conservative Enemy*.

[187] J. Tomlinson, 'The Decline of the Empire and the Economic "Decline" of Britain', *Twentieth Century British History*, Volume 14 (3), pp.202–4, 2003; M. Shanks, *The Stagnant Society*, London: Harmondsworth, 1961; A. Shonfield, *British Economic Policy Since the War*, London: Harmondsworth, 1958.

[188] J. Tomlinson, *The Labour Governments 1964–70: Economic Policy*, Manchester: Manchester University Press, 2004.

[189] J. Vaizey, 'Anthony Crosland: A Profile', *Encounter*, p. 87, August 1977.

[190] S. Crosland, *Tony Crosland*, p. 62.

[191] A. Crosland, *The Future of Socialism*, p. 356.

[192] A. Crosland, *The Future of Socialism*, pp. 356–7.

[193] B. Jackson, 'Socialism and the New Liberalism'.

[194] P. Sloman, 'Partners in Progress? British Liberals and the Labour Party Since 1918', p. 42.

[195] A. Crosland, *The Future of Socialism*, pp. 313–14.

[196] Cited in A. Briggs, 'The Labour Party as Crucible', in G. Dench (ed.), *The Rise and Rise of Meritocracy*, p. 19, Oxford: Political Quarterly/Blackwell Publishing, 2006.

[197] M. Pugh, *Speak for England: A Short History of the Labour Party*, London: Vintage, 2011.

[198] A. Crosland, *The Future of Socialism*, p. 73.

[199] S. Fielding, *The Labour Governments 1964–70: Labour and Cultural Change*.

[200] A. Crosland, *The Future of Socialism*, p. 253.

[201] A. Crosland, *The Future of Socialism*, p. 253.

[202] A. Crosland, *The Future of Socialism*, p. 319.

[203] A. Crosland, *The Future of Socialism*, p. 319.

[204] A. Crosland, *The Future of Socialism*, p. 70.

[205] A. Crosland, *The Future of Socialism*, p. 70.

[206] A. Crosland, *The Future of Socialism*, p. 70.

[207] Cited in E. Shaw, *The Labour Party Since 1979: Crisis and Transformation*, p. 5, London: Routledge, 1996.

[208] D. Marquand, 'How liberalism lost its way', *New Statesman*, 12–18 September 2014.

[209] P. Clarke, *Liberals and Social Democrats*, Cambridge: Cambridge University Press, 1978; S. Beer, *British Politics in the Collectivist Age*, New York: Knopf, 1965.

[210] T.H. Marshall, *Social Citizenship*, Cambridge: Cambridge University Press, 1950; A. Warde, *Consensus and Beyond: The Development of Labour Party Strategy Since the Second World War*, p. 66.

[211] A. Crosland, *The Future of Socialism*, p. 79.

[212] A. Crosland, *The Future of Socialism*, p. 79.

[213] A. Crosland, *The Future of Socialism*, p. 81.

[214] W. Beveridge, Cmd 6404, 'Social Insurance and the Allied Services', London: HMSO, 1942.

[215] A. Crosland, *The Future of Socialism*, pp. 84–5.

[216] J. Nuttall, *Psychological Socialism*.

[217] R. Desai, *Intellectuals and Socialism*, pp. 76–7.

[218] Cited in R. Desai, *Intellectuals and Socialism*, p. 77.

[219] A. Crosland, *The Future of Socialism*, p. 80.

[220] Cited in A. Crosland, *The Future of Socialism*, p. 63.

[221] A. Crosland, *The Future of Socialism*, p. 62.

[222] A. Crosland, *The Future of Socialism*, p. 62.

[223] A. Crosland, *The Future of Socialism*, p. 80.

[224] P. Sloman, 'Partners in Progress? British Liberals and the Labour Party Since 1918', pp. 45–6.

[225] D. Goodhart, *A Post-Liberal Future*, London: Demos, 2012.

[226] H. Kohn, *Political Ideologies of the Twentieth Century*, p. 124.

[227] D. Goodhart, *A Post-Liberal Future*.

228 H. Pemberton, L. Black and P. Thane (eds), *Reassessing 1970s Britain*, Manchester: Manchester University Press, 2013.

229 J. Gray, *Post-Liberalism: Studies in Political Thought*, London: Routledge, 1993; D. Goodhart, *A Post-Liberal Future*; D. Marquand, 'How liberalism lost its way'.

230 D. Runciman, 'Socialism in One Country', *London Review of Books*, Volume 33 (15), 11 July 2011.

231 D. Goodhart, *A Post-Liberal Future*.

232 L.T. Hobhouse, *The Elements of Social Justice*, New York: Holt and Company, 1922.

233 P. Addison, *No Turning Back: The Peacetime Revolutions of Post-War Britain*.

234 Cited in P. Addison, *No Turning Back: The Peacetime Revolutions of Post-War Britain*, p. 196.

235 Cited in P. Addison, *No Turning Back: The Peacetime Revolutions of Post-War Britain*, pp. 196–7.

236 D. Marquand, *The Unprincipled Society*, London: 1988.

237 P. Collins and R. Reeves, *The Liberal Republic*, London, Demos: 2009.

238 P. Collins and R. Reeves, *The Liberal Republic*.

239 A. Sen, *Development as Freedom*, p. 119, Oxford: Oxford University Press, 1999.

240 J. Fishkin, *Bottlenecks: A New Theory of Equal Opportunity*, Oxford: Oxford University Press, 2014.

241 J. Gray, *After Social Democracy*, London: Demos, 1996.

242 D. Marquand, 'Moralists and Hedonists', in A. Seldon and D. Marquand (eds), *The Ideas That Shaped Post-War Britain*, London: Fontana, 1996.

243 J. Hacker, 'What's Predistribution Got To Do With It?: Assessing New New Labour', *New Statesman*, 21 April 2015.

244 M. Mazzucato, *The Entrepreneurial State: Debunking Public Versus Private Sector Myths*, Anthem Press, 2013; J. Hacker, 'What's Predistribution Got To Do With It?: Assessing New New Labour'.

Chapter Five

1 A. Crosland, *The Future of Socialism*, p. 179, London: Jonathan Cape, 1956.

2 A. Crosland, *The Future of Socialism*, pp. 214–15.

3 Cited in G. Williams, 'Anthony Crosland: The Forgotten Man in Labour Politics?', Trinity College Oxford Report 2010–11, www.darkoptimism. org/TrinityReport2010-11.pdf.

4 A. Gamble, *Between Europe and America: The Future of British Politics*, Basingstoke: Palgrave Macmillan, 2003.

5 A. Wright, 'Whither Labour: Seeking reinvention and a realistic radicalism', *Juncture*, p. 5, London: Institute of Public Policy Research, 2015.

6 B. Magee, *The New Radicalism*, London: Secker and Warburg, 1962.

[7] Cited in D. Marquand, *Ramsay MacDonald*, p. 219, London: Jonathan Cape, 1977.

[8] D. Reisman, *Anthony Crosland: The Mixed Economy*, Basingstoke: Macmillan, 1997.

[9] S. Crosland, *Tony Crosland*, p. 60, London: Jonathan Cape, 1982.

[10] A. Crosland, letter to his mother, 22 October 1962, Crosland archive 10/1, LSE.

[11] A. Crosland, letter to his mother, 10 November 1962, Crosland archive 10/1, LSE.

[12] Interview with D. Marquand, 24 July 2015.

[13] H. Pelling, *America and the British Left: From Bright to Bevan*, p. 152, London: Adam and Charles Black, 1956.

[14] H. Pelling, *America and the British Left: From Bright to Bevan*, p. 150.

[15] Cited in P. Jones, *America and the British Labour Party: The Special Relationship at Work*, p. 27, London: IB Tauris, 1997.

[16] Cited in P. Jones, *America and the British Labour Party: The Special Relationship at Work*, p. 27.

[17] H. Pelling, *America and the British Left: From Bright to Bevan*, p. 151.

[18] O. Hatherley, '"Lower than Vermin". Nye: The Political Life of Aneurin Bevan', *London Review of Books*, 7 May 2015.

[19] B. Pimlott, 'Hugh Was That? Review of Hugh Gaitskell by Brian Brivati', *Independent on Sunday*, 29 September 1996.

[20] H. Pelling, *America and the British Left: From Bright to Bevan*, p. 151.

[21] A. Gamble, *Between Europe and America: The Future of British Politics*.

[22] E. Durbin, *The Politics of Democratic Socialism*, p. 77, London: Labour Book Service, 1940.

[23] P. Hennessy, *Having it So Good: Britain in the Fifties*, p. 519, London: Penguin, 2007.

[24] Letter from Daniel Bell to A. Crosland, Crosland archive 10/3, LSE.

[25] A. Crosland, *The Future of Socialism*, p. 215.

[26] A. Crosland, *The Future of Socialism*, p. 145; D. Reisman, *Anthony Crosland: The Mixed Economy*.

[27] A. Crosland, *The Future of Socialism*, pp. 179–80.

[28] Cited in D. Reisman, *Anthony Crosland: The Mixed Economy*, p. 155.

[29] Cited in B. Pimlott, 'Uber-Tony', *London Review of Books*, 3 September 1998.

[30] D. Reisman, *Anthony Crosland: The Mixed Economy*.

[31] Dick Leonard notes that Crosland referred to Sweden or Scandinavia 38 times in *The Future of Socialism* compared to 42 mentions for the United States: D. Leonard, 'Introduction' in D. Leonard (ed.), *Crosland and New Labour*, Basingstoke: Macmillan, 1999; A. Crosland, *The Future of Socialism*, p. 179.

[32] B. Harrison, *Seeking a Role: The United Kingdom 1951–70*, p. 119, Oxford: Oxford University Press, 2009.

[33] Hugh Dalton, an important early influence on Crosland, was said to have displayed violent and extreme anti-German attitudes which may have affected Crosland's view of the SPD in Germany.

[34] D. Sassoon, *One Hundred Years of Socialism*, New York: The New Press, 1996.

[35] Cited in A. Crosland, *The Future of Socialism*, p. 64.

[36] D. Sassoon, *One Hundred Years of Socialism*.

[37] D. Healey, *The Time of My Life*, London: Politicos Publishing, 2006.

[38] G. Esping-Andersen, *Politics Versus Markets*, Cambridge: Polity, 1999; D. Wincott, 'European Social Democracy', in D. Leonard, *Crosland and New Labour*, Basingstoke, Macmillan, 1999.

[39] D. Sassoon, *One Hundred Years of Socialism*; for an incisive discussion of the post-war social democratic dilemma, see P. Jenkins, 'The Social Democratic Dilemma', *New Statesman*, 20 September 1974, Crosland archive 13/20 (349), LSE.

[40] P. Anderson, 'Sweden: Study in Social Democracy', *New Left Review*, p. 34, Volume I/9, May–June 1961.

[41] S. Steinmo, 'The Political Economy of Swedish Success', in W. Schafer and W. Streek (eds), *Politics in the Age of Austerity*, p. 84, Cambridge: Polity Press, 2014.

[42] S. Steinmo, 'The Political Economy of Swedish Success'.

[43] Cited in G. Foote, *The Labour Party's Political Thought*, p. 194, Basingstoke: Macmillan, 1985.

[44] J. Tomlinson, *The Labour Governments 1964–70: Economic Policy*, p. 68, Manchester: Manchester University Press, 2004.

[45] A. Crosland, *The Future of Socialism*, p. 343.

[46] Cited in M. Kogan, 'Anthony Crosland: Intellectual and Politician', *Oxford Review of Education*, p. 75, Volume 32 (1), 2006.

[47] J. Tomlinson, *The Labour Governments 1964–70: Economic Policy*.

[48] S. Steinmo, 'The Political Economy of Swedish Success', pp. 92–3.

[49] Cited in T. Jones, *Remaking the Labour Party: From Gaitskell to Blair*, p. 49, 1996; A. Crosland, 'The Future of the Left', *Encounter*, 1960.

[50] A. Crosland, 'Social Democracy in Europe', Tract 438, London: Fabian Society, p. 11, 1975.

[51] A. Crosland, 'The Future of the Left', p. 9.

[52] A. Crosland, 'The Future of the Left', p. 9.

[53] A. Crosland, 'The Future of the Left', p. 9.

[54] A. Crosland, 'The Future of the Left', p. 9.

[55] D. Sassoon, *One Hundred Years of Socialism*.

[56] Letter from Tore Browaldh to Crosland, 14 October 1952, Crosland archive 10/1, LSE.

[57] H.M. Drucker, 'All the King's Horses', p. 109, in W. Patterson and A. Thomas (eds), *The Future of Social Democracy*, Oxford: Clarendon Press, 1988.

[58] The most notable exception was Douglas Jay who retained an abiding suspicion of Europe symbolised by his habit of taking breakfast cereals

with him on visits to the European continent: H. Parr, *Britain's Policy Towards the European Community: Harold Wilson and Britain's World Role 1964–67*, p. 5, London: Routledge, 2006.

59 H. Morrison, debate on 'Britain and the Common Market', Hansard *Volume 234, pp. 111–207, 2 August 1961.*

60 J. Callaghan, 'Mr Anthony Crosland Tributes', *Hansard*, Volume 926, pp. 1034–41, 21 February 1977.

61 Letter from A. Crosland to Hugh Gaitskell, Crosland archive 6/1 (2), LSE.

62 B. Harrison, *Seeking a Role: The United Kingdom 1951–70*, p. 119.

63 Interview with G. Radice, 3 February 2015.

64 R. Liddle, 'Can the Idea of a United Europe be Revived as a Progressive Left Project? The British Labour Perspective', London: Policy Network, February 2014.

65 P. Jones, *America and the British Labour Party: The Special Relationship at Work*, p. 67.

66 M. Pugh, *Speak for England: A New History of the Labour Party*, London: Vintage, 2011; R. Liddle, 'Can the Idea of a United Europe be Revived as a Progressive Left Project? The British Labour Perspective'.

67 R. Liddle, 'Can the Idea of a United Europe be Revived as a Progressive Left Project? The British Labour Perspective'.

68 V. Bogdanor, 'Entry into the European Community 1971–73', Gresham College Lecture, 11 March 2014.

69 Cited in V. Bogdanor, Entry into the European Community 1971–73'.

70 S. Wall, *The Official History of Britain and the European Community Volume II: From Rejection to Referendum 1963–75*, London: Routledge, 2013. Crosland had also given a speech to the Grimsby Labour Party in which he gave the distinct impression he was becoming 'lukewarm' on Europe.

71 S. Crosland, *Tony Crosland*, p. 220.

72 S. Crosland, *Tony Crosland*, p. 218.

73 Interview with D. Leonard, 11 February 2015; J. Campbell, *Roy Jenkins: A Well-Rounded Life*, London: Jonathan Cape, 2014; K. Jeffreys, *Tony Crosland: A New Biography*, London: John Blake, 1999.

74 D. Reisman, *Anthony Crosland: The Mixed Economy*.

75 Cited in V. Bogdanor, Entry into the European Community 1971–73', Gresham College Lecture, 11 March 2014.

76 Interview with D. Leonard, 11 February 2015.

77 Interview with R. Plant, 23 February 2015.

78 Interview with G. Radice, 3 February 2015.

79 R. Crossman, *The Diaries of a Cabinet Minister Volume III*, p. 535, London: Mandarin, 1991.

80 Interview with D. Leonard, 11 February 2015.

81 Interview with D. Leonard, 11 February 2015.

82 S. Crosland, *Tony Crosland*, p. 170.

83 Interview with D. Leonard, 11 February 2015.

[84] G. Radice, *Friends and Rivals: Crosland, Jenkins and Healey*, London: Abacus, 2003.

[85] Cited in S. Crosland, *Tony Crosland*, pp. 227–9.

[86] V. Bogdanor, Entry into the European Community 1971–73', Gresham College Lecture, 11 March 2014.

[87] Interview with D. Leonard, 11 February 2015.

[88] Cited in G. Radice, *Friends and Rivals: Crosland, Jenkins and Healey*, p. 193.

[89] S. Crosland, *Tony Crosland*; Interview with D. Leonard, 11 February 2015.

[90] S. Crosland, *Tony Crosland*, p. 224.

[91] S. Crosland, *Tony Crosland*, p. 227.

[92] Interview with D. Leonard, 11 February 2015.

[93] Cited in V. Bogdanor, Entry into the European Community 1971–73', Gresham College Lecture, 11 March 2014.

[94] D. Sassoon, 'Reflections on the Labour Party's Programme for the 1990s', *The Political Quarterly*, Volume 62 (2), p. 372, 1991; A. Warde, *Consensus and Beyond: The Development of Labour Party Strategy Since the Second World War*, pp. 87–9, Manchester: Manchester University Press, 1982.

[95] D. Sassoon, 'Reflections on the Labour Party's Programme for the 1990s', p. 372.

[96] A. Gamble, *Between Europe and America: The Future of British Politics*.

Chapter Six

[1] A. Crosland, *The Conservative Enemy*, p. 21, London: Jonathan Cape, 1962.

[2] I. Zweiniger-Barcielowska, 'Rationing, Austerity and the Conservative Party Recovery after 1945', *The Historical Journal*, Volume 37 (1), p. 193, 1994.

[3] A. Crosland, *The Future of Socialism*, p. 61, London: Jonathan Cape.

[4] A. Schlesinger, Jr., 'Crosland's Socialism: A Review of *The Conservative Enemy*', *The New York Review of Books*, 1 June 1963.

[5] H.M. Drucker, *Doctrine and Ethos in the Labour Party*, p. 87, Edinburgh: Mainstream Press, 1978.

[6] A. Crosland, *The Conservative Enemy*, pp. 143–4.

[7] V. Bogdanor, 'Labour in Opposition 1951–64', in V. Bogdanor and R. Skidelsky (eds), *The Age of Affluence*, London: Penguin, 1970.

[8] V. Bogdanor, 'Labour in Opposition 1951–64'.

[9] R. Skidelsky, *Britain Since 1900: A Success Story?*, London: Vintage Books, 2014; F. Williams, *Fifty Years' March: The Rise of the Labour Party*, London: Odhams Press, 1949.

[10] M. Pugh, *Speak for Britain: A New History of the Labour Party*, London: Vintage, 2011.

[11] I. Zweiniger-Barcielowska, 'Rationing, Austerity and the Conservative Party Recovery after 1945', *The Historical Journal*, p. 174.

[12] I. Zweiniger-Barcielowska, 'Rationing, Austerity and the Conservative Party Recovery after 1945', pp. 173–97.

[13] I. Zweiniger-Barcielowska, 'Rationing, Austerity and the Conservative Party Recovery after 1945', p. 186.

[14] M. Pugh, *Speak for Britain: A New History of the Labour Party*, p. 297.

[15] I. Zweiniger-Barcielowska, 'Rationing, Austerity and the Conservative Party Recovery after 1945', p. 181.

[16] M. Pugh, *Speak for Britain: A New History of the Labour Party*.

[17] V. Bogdanor, 'Labour in Opposition 1951–64', p. 81.

[18] T. Bale, *Sacred Cows and Common Sense: The Symbolic Statecraft and Political Culture of the British Labour Party*, London: Ashgate, 1999.

[19] L. Black, *The Political Culture of the Left in Affluent Britain 1951–64*, p. 106, Basingstoke: Palgrave Macmillan, 2002.

[20] Interview with W.T. Rodgers, 2 March 2015.

[21] V. Bogdanor, 'Labour in Opposition 1951–64'.

[22] R.A. Thorpe, *Super-Mac: The Life of Harold Macmillan*, London: Pimlico Press, 2011.

[23] A. Crosland, *The Future of Socialism*, p. 293.

[24] I. Zweiniger-Barcielowska, 'Rationing, Austerity and the Conservative Party Recovery after 1945'.

[25] V. Bogdanor, 'The General Election 1959', Lecture at Gresham College, 11 November 2014.

[26] *Daily Mail* cited in V. Bogdanor, 'The General Election 1959', Lecture at Gresham College, 11 November 2014.

[27] Interview with G. Radice, House of Lords, 16 December 2014.

[28] S. Crosland, *Tony Crosland*, London: Jonathan Cape, 1982; K. Jeffreys, *Anthony Crosland: A New Biography*, London: John Blake, 1999.

[29] A. Shonfield, 'A Deadlock on the Left', pp. 12–13, *Encounter*, Issue 5, 1960.

[30] P. Williams, *Hugh Gaitskell: A Political Biography*, London: Jonathan Cape, 1979.

[31] H.M. Drucker, *Doctrine and Ethos in the Labour Party*, p. 21.

[32] H.M. Drucker, *Doctrine and Ethos in the Labour Party*, pp. 35–7.

[33] A. Shonfield, 'A Deadlock on the Left', p. 13.

[34] S. Crosland, *Tony Crosland*, p. 93.

[35] B. Pimlott, 'Uber-Tony', *London Review of Books*, 3 September 1998.

[36] Quoted in *Life Magazine*, 'British Begin Election Battle', Volume 18 (26), 1945.

[37] Cited in B. Harrison, *Seeking a Role: The United Kingdom 1951–70*, p. 444, Oxford: Oxford University Press, 2009.

[38] Cited in G. Foote, *The Labour Party's Political Thought*, p. 192, Basingstoke: Macmillan, 1985.

[39] A. Crosland, *The Conservative Enemy*, pp. 118–22.

[40] The founding members of the Campaign for Democratic Socialism (CDS) in 1960 were Bill Rodgers, Tony Crosland, Roy Jenkins, Douglas Jay, Patrick Gordon Walker, Dick Taverne, Michael Shanks, Ivan Yates,

Frank Pickstock, Philip Williams, Ron Owen, Brian Walden and Denis Howell. Interview with Lord Bill Rodgers February 2015.

[41] Note from W.T. Rodgers' private papers dated 7 June 1964.

[42] B. Brivati, 'Crosland as Apparatchik', in D. Leonard (ed.), *Crosland and New Labour*, Basingstoke: Macmillan, p. 107, 1999.

[43] Note from W.T. Rodgers' private papers dated 7 June 1964.

[44] Interview with W.T. Rodgers, February 2015. Rodgers recounted that Crosland brought seriousness of purpose to CDS discussions, preventing other members of the Steering Committee from drinking alcohol at their meetings until the important work was done.

[45] Interview with B. Donoughue, 26 February 2015.

[46] A. Crosland, Letter to Hugh Gaitskell, 4 May 1960, Crosland archive 6/1 (2), LSE.

[47] A. Crosland, Letter to Hugh Gaitskell, 4 May 1960, Crosland archive 6/1 (2), LSE.

[48] A. Crosland, Note to Hugh Gaitskell, November 1960, Crosland archive 6/1 (13), LSE.

[49] A. Crosland, Note to Hugh Gaitskell, November 1960, Crosland 6/1 (13), LSE.

[50] P. Gordon Walker, *Political Diaries 1932–1971*, p. 259, London: The Historian's Press, 1991.

[51] A. Crosland, Note to Hugh Gaitskell, November 1960, Crosland 6/1 (13), LSE.

[52] S. Crosland, *Tony Crosland*, p. 88.

[53] Letter from H. Gaitskell to A. Crosland, 4 September 1960, Crosland archive 6/1 (67), LSE.

[54] Letter from H. Gaitskell to A. Crosland, 4 September 1960, Crosland archive 6/1 (67), LSE.

[55] B. Brivati, 'Crosland as Apparatchik', in D. Leonard (ed.), *Crosland and New Labour*, pp.p. 122.

[56] B. Harrison, *Seeking a Role: The United Kingdom 1951–70*, p. 442.

[57] D.W. Brogan, 'The Future is Behind Us? On the North Atlantic Left', *Encounter*, Issue 1, 1960.

[58] Cited in S. Fielding, *The Labour Governments 1964–70: Labour and Cultural Change*, p. 69, Manchester: Manchester University Press, 2003.

[59] D. Potter, *The Times*, 27 April, 1959.

[60] A. Crosland, *The Conservative Enemy*, p. 120.

[61] S. Padgett and W. Patterson, *A History of Social Democracy in Post-War Europe*, p. 4, London: Longman, 1991.

[62] Sheri Berman, *The Primacy of Politics: Social Democracy and the Making of Europe's Twentieth Century*, Cambridge: Cambridge University Press, 2006.

[63] Cited in G. Foote, *The Labour Party's Political Thought*, p. 191.

[64] Cited in D. Marquand, *The Progressive Dilemma: From Lloyd George to Kinnock*, London: Heinemann, 1991.

[65] P. Gay, *The Dilemma of Democratic Socialism*, p. 245, New York: Collier Books, 1970.

[66] S. Berman, *The Primacy of Politics*.

[67] Cited in P. Gay, *The Dilemma of Democratic Socialism*, p. 247.

[68] L. Kolakowski cited in D. Healey, *The Time of My Life*, London: Politicos Publishing, 2006.

[69] W. Beveridge, Cmd 6404, 'Social Insurance and the Allied Services', London: HMSO, 1942.

[70] A. Warde, *Consensus and Beyond: The Development of Labour Party Strategy Since the Second World War*, Manchester: Manchester University Press, 1982.

[71] M. Kenny, *The First New Left*, p. 56, London: Lawrence and Wishart, 1995.

[72] M. Kenny, *The First New Left*; M. Davis, 'Arguing Affluence: New Left Contributions to the Socialist Debate 1957–63', *Twentieth Century British History*, Volume 23 (4), 2012.

[73] M. Kenny, *The First New Left*, p. 56.

[74] M. Kenny, *The First New Left*.

[75] M. Newman, *Ralph Miliband and the Politics of the New Left*, pp. 84–5, London: The Merlin Press, 2002.

[76] Cited in R. Hattersley, *Choose Freedom*, p. 16, London: Michael Joseph, 1987.

[77] A. Crosland, 'The Future of the Left', *Encounter*, pp. 3–13, March 1960.

[78] Interview with D. Marquand, 24 July 2015.

[79] Cited in P. Hennessy, *Having it So Good: Britain in the Fifties*, p. 519, London: Penguin, 2007.

[80] L. Black, *The Political Culture of the Left in Affluent Britain 1951–64*, p. 140.

[81] L. Black, *The Political Culture of the Left in Affluent Britain 1951–64*, p. 124.

[82] L. Black, *The Political Culture of the Left in Affluent Britain 1951–64*, p. 135.

[83] L. Black, *Redefining British Politics: Culture, Consumerism and Participation 1954–70*, p. 67, Basingstoke: Palgrave Macmillan, 2010.

[84] M. Kenny, *The First New Left*.

[85] R. Desai, *Intellectuals and Socialism*, p. 72, London: Lawrence and Wishart, 1991.

[86] P. Anderson, *The Left in the Fifties*, p. 18, *New Left Review*, Volume I (29), January–February 1965.

[87] Cited in Cited in R. Toye, 'The Forgotten Revisionist: Douglas Jay and Britain's Transition to Affluence 1951–1964', p. 54, in L. Black and H. Pemberton (eds), *An Affluent Society? Britain's Post-War 'Golden age' Revisited*, London: Ashgate, 2004.

[88] A. Warde, *Consensus and Beyond: The Development of Labour Party Strategy Since the Second World War*, p. 18; R.H. Tawney, *Equality*, *New Left Review*, Volume I (29), January–February 1965.

89 R.H.S Crossman, *The Diaries of a Cabinet Minister*, London: Jonathan Cape, 1976.

90 K. Marx and F. Engels, *Collected Works Volume 6 1845–48*, London: Harmondsworth, 1970.

91 R.H.S Crossman, *The Diaries of a Cabinet Minister*, p. 264, London: Jonathan Cape, 1976.

92 B. Harrison, *Seeking a Role: The United Kingdom 1951–70*, p. 447.

93 Cited in P. Clarke, *A Question of Leadership: From Gladstone to Thatcher*, London: Penguin, 1991.

94 Cited in N. Tiratsoo, 'Reconstruction, Affluence and Labour Politics', in N. Tiratsoo (ed.), *The Attlee Years*, p. 44, London: Continuum, 1991.

95 D. Leonard, 'Labour and electoral change', p. 44, in D. Lipsey and D. Leonard (eds), *Socialism Now: Crosland's Legacy*, Basingstoke: Macmillan, 1981.

96 A. Crosland, *The Conservative Enemy*, p. 149.

97 A. Crosland, *The Conservative Enemy*, p. 128.

98 A. Crosland, *The Conservative Enemy*, p. 150.

99 A. Crosland, 'Why Labour Lost the Vote: A Review of The British General Election of 1959 by D.E. Butler and Richard Rose', *Observer*, 12 June 1960, Crosland archive 13/20 (150), LSE.

100 A. Crosland, 'Why Labour Lost the Vote: A Review of The British General Election of 1959 by D.E. Butler and Richard Rose'.

101 M. Savage, *Social Class in the 21st Century*, pp. 3–4, London: Penguin, 2015.

102 Cited in S. Fielding, *The Labour Governments 1964–70: Labour and Cultural Change*, p. 66.

103 S. Fielding, *The Labour Governments 1964–70: Labour and Cultural Change*.

104 V. Bogdanor, 'The General Election 1959', Lecture at Gresham College, 11 November 2014.

105 V. Bogdanor, 'The General Election 1959'.

106 Anthony Crosland, 'Socialism In a Prosperous World', *The New Leader*, undated, Crosland archive 3/20 (142), LSE.

107 L. Black, *The Political Culture of the Left in Affluent Britain 1951–64*, p. 125.

108 V. Bogdanor, 'The General Election 1959'.

109 V. Bogdanor, 'The General Election 1959'.

110 V. Bogdanor, 'The General Election 1959'.

111 A. Crosland, 'Can Labour Win?', p. 11, London: The Fabian Society, 1960.

112 A. Crosland, 'Can Labour Win?', p. 11.

113 A. Crosland, *The Conservative Enemy*.

114 Cited in S. Fielding, *The Labour Governments 1964–70: Labour and Cultural Change*, p. 67.

115 *Daily Mail* cited in V. Bogdanor, 'The General Election 1959', Lecture at Gresham College.

[116] *Evening Standard* cited in V. Bogdanor, 'The General Election 1959', Lecture at Gresham College.

[117] A. Crosland, *The Conservative Enemy*, pp. 118–19.

[118] E. Roberts cited in S. Ramsden, 'Remaking Working-Class Community: Sociability, Belonging and "Affluence" in a Small Town, 1930–80', p. 2, *Contemporary British History*, Volume 29 (1), 2014.

[119] A. Crosland, 'Can Labour Win?', p. 10.

[120] N. Tiratsoo, 'Reconstruction, Affluence and Labour Politics', p. 55; P. Willmott, *The Evolution of a Community*, p. 109, London: Routledge & Kegan Paul, 1963.

[121] Cited in S. Lukes, 'The Future of British Socialism', in B. Pimlott (ed.), *Fabian Essays in Socialist Thought*, p. 273, London: Heinemann, 1984.

[122] N. Tiratsoo, 'Reconstruction, Affluence and Labour Politics'.

[123] A. Crosland, *The Conservative Enemy*, p. 159.

[124] A. Crosland, 'How Labour Can Kill the Image that Haunts its Future', *Daily Herald*, 1959.

[125] B. Brivati, *Hugh Gaitskell*, London: Politico's Publishing, 2006; K. Jeffreys, *Anthony Crosland: A New Biography*.

[126] A. Crosland, 'How Labour Can Kill the Image that Haunts its Future'.

[127] V. Bogdanor, 'The General Election 1959', Lecture at Gresham College.

[128] Letter to A. Crosland from Bruce Douglas-Mann MP, undated, Crosland archive 12/2, correspondence 1971–77, LSE

[129] Letter to A. Crosland from Bernard Donaghue, 22 August 1973, Crosland archive 12/2, correspondence 1971–77, LSE.

[130] Letter to A. Crosland from Daniel Bell, undated, Crosland archive 10/1 (18), LSE.

[131] N. Beloff, 'Labour's Nationalisation Proposals', *Observer*, 14 June 1973.

[132] A. Warde, *Consensus and Beyond: The Development of Labour Party Strategy Since the Second World War*, p. 10.

[133] A. Warde, *Consensus and Beyond: The Development of Labour Party Strategy Since the Second World War*.

[134] N. Davenport, *Memoirs of a City Radical*, p. 182, London: Weidenfeld and Nicolson, 1974.

[135] J. Curtice, 'A Defeat to Reckon With: On Scotland, Economic Competence, and the Complexity of Labour's Losses, *Juncture*, 17 June 2015.

[136] P. Addison, *No Turning Back: The Peacetime Revolutions of Post-War Britain*, Oxford: Oxford University Press, 2010.

[137] Savage, M. and Devine, E. 'A New Model of Social Class? Findings from the BBC's Great British Class Survey Experiment', *Sociology*, doi: 10.1177/0038038513481128, 2013.

[138] R. Ford and M. Goodwin, 'Understanding UKIP: Identity, Social Change and the Left Behind', *Political Quarterly*, Volume 85 (3), p. 278, 2014.

[139] R. Ford and M. Goodwin, *Revolt on the Right: Explaining Support for the Radical Right in Britain*, p. 270, London: Routledge, 2014.

[140] R. Ford and M. Goodwin, 'Understanding UKIP: Identity, Social Change and the Left Behind', p. 278.

[141] British Social Attitudes Survey 30, 2013.

[142] G. Evans and J. Mellon, 'Working Class Votes and Conservative Losses: Solving the UKIP Puzzle', *Parliamentary Affairs*, pp. 1–16, Advanced Access, April 2015, doi: 10.1093/pa/gsv005.

[143] A. Lowes and A. Painter, 'Identity Politics', London: Searchlight, 2011.

[144] D. Miller, *Citizenship and National Identity*, Cambridge: Polity Press, 2000.

[145] J. Curtice, 'A Defeat to Reckon With: On Scotland, Economic Competence, and the Complexity of Labour's Losses'.

[146] P. Addison, *No Turning Back: The Peacetime Revolutions of Post-War Britain.*

[147] A. Crosland, *Socialism Now*, p. 100.

[148] A. Crosland, 'Where We Go Wrong', *The Sunday Times*, March 1973.

[149] A. Crosland, Speech to the London Labour Mayors' Association, 9 September 1972, Crosland archive 13/24 (4), LSE.

[150] A. Crosland, Speech to the Young Fabians, 11 November 1972, Crosland archive 13/24 (16), LSE. It is notable that Crosland appears dismissive of the debate about gender equality given that Labour's electoral prospects were harmed by the increasing propensity of women to vote Conservative after 1979.

[151] A. Warde, *Consensus and Beyond: The Development of Labour Party Strategy Since the Second World War*, p. 64.

[152] A. Crosland, Speech to the London Labour Mayors' Association, 9 September 1972, Crosland archive 13/24 (4), LSE.

[153] D. Marquand, *The Progressive Dilemma: From Lloyd George to Kinnock*, p. 86.

[154] J. Cronin, *New Labour's Pasts: The Labour Party and its Discontents*, p. 35, Harlow: Pearson Education, 2004.

[155] J. Cronin, *New Labour's Pasts: The Labour Party and its Discontents*, p. 37.

[156] Cited in P. Clarke, *A Question of Leadership: From Gladstone to Thatcher*, p. 153.

[157] Interview with D. Lipsey, House of Lords, 2 March 2015.

[158] Interview with D. Lipsey, House of Lords, 2 March 2015.

[159] Marxism Today, 'Special Issue: Wrong', November/December 1998; E. Shaw, *Losing Labour's Soul?*, London: Routledge, 2008.

[160] H.M. Drucker, *Doctrine and Ethos in the Labour Party*, pp. 90–1.

[161] B. Brivati, *Hugh Gaitskell.*

[162] The concept of the 'progressive dilemma' was first expounded in David Marquand's book of that title (1991).

[163] H.M. Drucker, *Doctrine and Ethos in the Labour Party.*

Chapter Seven

[1] J.N. Figgis, *Studies of Political Thought from Gerson to Grotius*, p. 1, Cambridge: Cambridge University Press, 1916.

[2] J. Rutherford, 'The First New Left, Blue Labour, and English Modernity', p. 7, *Renewal*, Volume 21 (1), 2013.

[3] R.H. Tawney, 'Equality', London: Harper Collins, 1965.

[4] J. Harris, 'Social Policy, Saving, and Sound Money', p. 182, in P. Clarke and C. Trebilcock (eds), *Understanding Decline: Perceptions and Realities of British Economic Performance*, Cambridge: Cambridge University Press, 1997.

[5] D. Leonard, 'What would Tony Crosland Make of New Labour?', *Guardian*, 17 February 2002.

[6] R. Hattersley, *Who Goes Home? Scenes from a Political Life*, p. 18, London: Abacus, 1995.

[7] This section draws on P. Diamond and R. Liddle, *Beyond New Labour: The Future of Social Democracy*, London: Methuen Politicos, 2008.

[8] See for example S. Holland, *The Socialist Challenge*, London: Quartet Books, 1978.

[9] Cited in S. Fielding, *The Labour Party: Socialism and Society Since 1951*, p. 111, Manchester: Manchester University Press, 1997.

[10] 'Let us work together – Labour's way out of the crisis', *The Labour Party Manifesto*, London: The Labour Party, 1974.

[11] P. Tatchell, *The Battle for Bermondsey*, p. 16, London: Gay Men's Press, 1994.

[12] S. Holland, *The Socialist Challenge*, London: Quartet Books, 1978; A. Crosland, *The Future of Socialism*, London: Jonathan Cape, 1956.

[13] S. Holland, *The Socialist Challenge*, p. 70.

[14] D. Healey, *The Time of My Life*, pp. 467–8, London: Politicos Publishing, 2006.

[15] R. Wicks, 'Revisionism in the 1950s: The Ideas of Anthony Crosland', in C. Navari (ed.), *British Politics and the Spirit of the Age*, Keele: Keele University Press, 1996.

[16] R. Wicks, 'Revisionism in the 1950s: The Ideas of Anthony Crosland'.

[17] R. Wicks, 'Revisionism in the 1950s: The Ideas of Anthony Crosland'.

[18] R. Hattersley, *Choose Freedom*, p. 6, London: Michael Joseph, 1987.

[19] Labour Party, *Meet the Challenge, Make the Change: A New Agenda for Britain*, p. 8, London: The Labour Party, 1989.

[20] S. Griffiths, 'New Labour, New Liberalism, and Revisionism's Second Wave', in S. Griffiths and K. Hickson (eds), *British Party Politics and Ideology After New Labour*, Basingstoke: Palgrave Macmillan, 2009.

[21] B. Gould, *Goodbye to All That*, p. 248, London: Macmillan, 1995.

[22] Cited in C. Haddon, 'The Commission on Social Justice 1992–92', p. 7, London: Institute of Government, July 2014.

[23] C. Hay, 'Labour's Thatcherite Revisionism: Playing the "Politics of Catch-up"', *Political Studies*, pp. 700–7, XLII, 1994; E. Shaw, *The Labour Party since 1979: Crisis and Transformation*, London: Routledge, 1996.

[24] Cited in R. Heffernan, *New Labour and Thatcherism: Political Change in Britain*, p. 129, Basingstoke: Palgrave Macmillan, 1999.

[25] R. Heffernan, *New Labour and Thatcherism: Political Change in Britain*, p. 129.

[26] Cited in R. Heffernan, *New Labour and Thatcherism: Political Change in Britain*, p. 131.

[27] M. Smith, 'Understanding the "Politics of Catch Up": The Modernisation of the Labour Party', *Political Studies*, pp. 708–15, XLII, 1994; S. Fielding, *New Labour: Continuity and Change in the Making of 'New' Labour*, Basingstoke: Palgrave Macmillan, 2003.

[28] Cited in M. Smith, 'Understanding the "Politics of Catch Up": The Modernisation of the Labour Party, p. 709.

[29] T. Homer-Dixon et al., 'A Complex Systems Approach to the Study of Ideology: Cognitive-Affective Structures and the Dynamics of Belief Systems', *Journal of Social and Political Psychology*, Volume 1, 2013.

[30] S. Driver and L. Martell, *New Labour*, Cambridge: Polity Press, 2006.

[31] V. Bogdanor, 'Social Democracy', in A. Seldon (ed.), *Blair's Britain*, Cambridge: Cambridge University Press, 2007.

[32] M. Mullard and R. Swaray, 'New Labour Legacy: Comparing the Labour Governments of Blair and Brown to Labour Governments Since 1945', *Political Quarterly*, Volume 81 (4), 2010.

[33] Gordon Brown's Crosland Memorial Lecture in 1997 was a rare but successful attempt to situate the New Labour approach to economic management and equality of opportunity within a Croslandite framework, although it was not developed subsequently.

[34] J. Cronin, 'The Ironies of New Labour', Paper presented to 'What's Left of the Left Conference', Center for European Studies, Harvard University, 9–10 May 2010.

[35] E. Hobsbawm, 'The Forward March of Labour Halted?', *Marxism Today*, September 1978.

[36] S. Meredith, 'Mr Crosland's Nightmare? New Labour and Equality in Historical Perspective', *British Journal of Politics and International Relations*, Volume 8(2), pp. 238–255, 2006.

[37] P. Addison, *The Road to 1945: British Politics and the Second World War*, London: Jonathan Cape, 1977.

[38] B. Brivati, *The End of Decline: Blair and Brown in Power*, London: Politicos, 2007.

[39] www.theguardian.com/business/economics-blog/2014/apr/24/uk-economy-seven-things-need-to-know-ons-g7; Office for National Statistics, 'Economic Bulletin', 2014.

[40] M. Francis, 'Mr Gaitskell's Ganymede: Reassessing Crosland's *The Future of Socialism*', *Contemporary British History*, Volume 11 (2), 1997.

[41] J. Cronin, 'The Ironies of New Labour'.

[42] H. Pemberton, 'Strange Days Indeed: British Politics in the 1970s', *Contemporary British History*, p. 594, 23 (4), 2009.

[43] B. Brivati and T. Bale (eds), *New Labour in Power*, London: Routledge, 1997.

[44] B. Donoughue, *Downing Street Diary*, London: Politicos, 2006; J. Callaghan, Speech to the Labour Party Conference, 1976.

[45] R. Skidelsky, *Britain Since 1900: A Success Story?*, p. 311, London: Vintage Books, 2014.

[46] J. Cronin, 'The Ironies of New Labour'.

[47] K. Hickson, *The IMF Crisis of 1976 and British Politics*, London: IB Tauris, 2005.

[48] A. Cairncross, *The British Economy Since 1945*, Oxford: Blackwells, 1992.

[49] M. Mullard and R. Swaray, 'New Labour Legacy: Comparing the Labour Governments of Blair and Brown to Labour Governments Since 1945'.

[50] S. Fielding, *The Labour Party: Continuity and Change*.

[51] E.P. Thompson, *The Making of the English Working-Class*, London: Penguin Classics, 2013.

[52] Cited in S. Fielding, *The Labour Governments 1964–70: Labour and Cultural Change*, p. 69, Manchester: Manchester University Press, 2003.

[53] Interview with D. Lipsey, House of Lords, 2 March 2015.

[54] Darendorf's remark was in fact directed towards leading members of the breakaway Social Democratic Party (SDP), whom Darendorf felt were too conservative in their reappraisal of the post-war welfare state and social settlement.

[55] D. Leonard (ed.), *Crosland and New Labour*, Basingstoke: Macmillan, 1999.

[56] D. Leonard, 'What would Tony Crosland Make of New Labour?'.

[57] D. Leonard, 'What would Tony Crosland Make of New Labour?'.

[58] P. Hain, *Back to the Future of Socialism*, p. 37, Bristol: Policy Press, 2015.

[59] J. Gray, 'Ralph Miliband and Sons', *Guardian*, 4 September 2010.

[60] The term 'Blue Labour' was coined by its leading intellectual, the academic Maurice Glasman. The reference to 'Blue' Labour is an allusion to blues music.

[61] M. Pugh, *Speak for Britain! A New History of the Labour Party*, London: Vintage, 2011.

[62] M. Pugh, *Speak for Britain! A New History of the Labour Party*, pp. 71–7.

[63] Interview with D. Lipsey, House of Lords, 2 March 2015.

[64] A. Harrop, 'Crosland and One Nation Labour', *Fabian Review*, London: Fabian Society, October 2013.

[65] P. Collins, 'Labour Needs Something Blue and Something New', *Prospect*, 26 March 2015.

[66] M. Glasman, 'Politics, Employment Policies and the Younger Generation', www.lse.ac.uk/economics/newsEventsSeminars/files/MauriceGlasmanPaper.pdf.

[67] G. Dench, 'Reviewing Meritocracy', in G. Dench (ed.), *The Rise and Rise of Meritocracy*, Oxford: Political Quarterly/Blackwell Publishing, 2006.

[68] A. Finlayson, 'Should the Left go Blue? Making sense of Maurice Glasman', *Open Democracy*, 27 May 2011.

[69] A. Finlayson, 'Should the Left go Blue? Making sense of Maurice Glasman'. Other figures within the Blue Labour camp take a different position: for example, Stuart White, one of the contributors to the Oxford

volume argues that the Left should not abandon universal values and that support for the welfare state must be upheld (M. Beech and K. Hickson, 'Blue or Purple? Reflections on the Future of the Labour Party', pp. 75–87, *Political Studies Review*, Volume 12, 2014).

[70] R. Plant, 'Democratic Socialism and Equality', in D. Lipsey and D. Leonard (eds), *Crosland's Legacy*, Basingstoke: Macmillan, 1981.

[71] D. Goodhart, *A Post-Liberal Future*, p. 32, London: Demos, 2012.

[72] M. Glasman, 'The Good Society, Catholic Social Thought, and the Politics of the Common Good', in I. Geary and A. Pabst (eds), *Blue Labour: Forging a New Politics*, p. 16, London: IB Tauris, 2014.

[73] D. Runciman, 'Socialism in One Country', *London Review of Books*, Volume 33 (15), 11 July 2011.

[74] A. Pabst, 'Introduction', in I. Geary and A. Pabst (eds), *Blue Labour: Forging a New Politics*, p. 1.

[75] J. Rutherford, 'The First New Left, Blue Labour, and English Modernity'.

[76] J. Rutherford, 'The First New Left, Blue Labour, and English Modernity'.

[77] A. Finlayson, 'Should the Left go Blue? Making Sense of Maurice Glasman'.

[78] A. Pabst, 'Introduction', in I. Geary and A. Pabst (eds), *Blue Labour: Forging a New Politics*.

[79] D. Runciman, 'Socialism in One Country'.

[80] D. Runciman, 'Socialism in One Country'.

[81] J. Milbank, 'The Blue Labour Dream', in I. Geary and A. Pabst (eds), *Blue Labour: Forging a New Politics*, p. 29.

[82] A. Pabst, 'Introduction', in I. Geary and A. Pabst (eds), *Blue Labour: Forging a New Politics*, p. 1.

[83] E. West, 'Civil Economy: Blue Labour's Alternative to Capitalism', in I. Geary and A. Pabst (eds), *Blue Labour: Forging a New Politics*. Intriguingly, there are parallels with the critique of untrammelled market liberalism and speeches made by Tony Blair as Shadow Home Secretary in the early 1990s. In a lecture following the murder of the Liverpool toddler, James Bulger, Blair proclaimed: 'We cannot exist in a moral vacuum. If we do not learn and then teach the value of what is right and what is wrong the result is simply moral chaos which engulfs us all.'

[84] J. Milbank, 'The Blue Labour Dream', in I. Geary and A. Pabst (eds), *Blue Labour: Forging a New Politics*, p. 29.

[85] A. Pabst, 'Introduction', in I. Geary and A. Pabst (eds), *Blue Labour: Forging a New Politics*, p. 4.

[86] D. Marquand, 'Review of Speak for England! A New History of the Labour Party by Martin Pugh', *New Statesman*, 2 April 2010.

[87] A. Pabst, 'Introduction', in I. Geary and A. Pabst (eds), *Blue Labour: Forging a New Politics*, p. 7.

[88] M. Kenny, 'Ideological Politics', in *Developments in British Politics* 10, Basingstoke: Palgrave Macmillan, 2016.

[89] H. Kohn, *Political Ideologies of the Twentieth Century*, p. 159, New York: Harper Torchbooks, 1966.

[90] F. Field, 'A Blue Labour Vision of the Common Good', in I. Geary and A. Pabst (eds), *Blue Labour: Forging a New Politics*, pp. 56–7.

[91] M. Kenny and N. Pearce, 'What National Story Does the Left Need to Tell?', *Juncture*, London: Institute for Public Policy Research, 21 May 2015.

[92] R. Ford and M. Goodwin, *Revolt on the Right: Explaining Support for the Radical Right in Britain*, London: Routledge, 2014.

[93] P. Mair, *Ruling the Void*, p. 1, London: Verso Books, 2013.

[94] M. Kenny, 'Ideological Politics'.

[95] D. Miller, *Citizenship and National Identity*, Cambridge: Polity Press, 2000.

[96] M. Beech and K. Hickson, 'Blue or Purple? Reflections on the Future of the Labour Party', p. 78.

[97] R. Philpot (ed.), *The Purple Book: A Progressive Future for Labour*, London: Biteback, 2011.

[98] D. Runciman, 'Socialism in One Country'.

[99] D. Runciman, 'Socialism in One Country'.

[100] D. Runciman, 'Socialism in One Country'.

[101] A. Crosland, *The Future of Socialism*, p. 54.

[102] Cited in M. Beech, *The Political Philosophy of New Labour*, pp. 186–7, London: IB Tauris, 2006.

[103] T. Jones, *Remaking the Labour Party: From Gaitskell to Blair*, London: Routledge, 1996.

[104] A. Power, *Estates on the Edge*, Basingstoke: Palgrave Macmillan, 1999.

[105] D. Lammy, 'A Politics Centred on Relationships', in I. Geary and A. Pabst (eds), *Blue Labour: Forging a New Politics*, p. 65.

[106] R. Reeves, 'Flee your Tents, Oh Israel', in G. Cooke and J. Purnell (eds), *We Mean Freedom*, London: Demos, 2009.

[107] D. Marquand, 'Towards a Realignment of the Mind', London Commonwealth Club, Compass Lecture, 10 February 2011.

[108] B. Jackson, 'We Are All Social Democrats Now', in G. Cooke and J. Purnell (eds), *We Mean Power*, London: Demos, 2009.

[109] B. Jackson, 'We Are All Social Democrats Now'.

[110] D. Marquand, 'Towards a Realignment of the Mind', London Commonwealth Club, 10 February 2011.

[111] J. Cronin, 'The Ironies of New Labour'.

[112] M. Beech and K. Hickson, 'Blue or Purple? Reflections on the Future of the Labour Party', p. 84.

[113] Interview with D. Leonard, 11 February 2015.

[114] G. Eaton, 'We Will Ever See a Thatcher of the Left?', *New Statesman*, 26 February 2015.

[115] Interview with R. Hattersley, 6 March 2015.

[116] A. Harrop, 'Crosland and One Nation Labour'.

[117] E. Miliband, 'Speech to the Labour Party Conference', September 2012.

[118] J. Gaffney and A. Lahel, 'The Morphology of the Labour Party's One Nation Narrative: Story, Plot and Authorship', *Political Quarterly*, Volume 84 (3), November–December 2013; H. Thompson, 'Post-Crisis, Post-

Devolution Politics and the Mansion Tax', *Political Quarterly*, Volume 86 (1), January–March 2015.

[119] J. Cruddas and J. Rutherford, *One Nation: Labour's Political Renewal*, p. 33, London: The Labour Party, 2014.

[120] P. Hain, *Back to the Future of Socialism*.

[121] P. Hain, *Back to the Future of Socialism*, p. 14.

[122] B. Donoughue, *Prime Minister: The Conduct of Policy under Harold Wilson and James Callaghan*, pp. 84–5, London: Jonathan Cape, 1987.

[123] A. Gamble, *Britain in Decline*, Basingstoke: Macmillan, 1983.

[124] Memorandum by the Secretary of State for Foreign and Commonwealth Affairs, 'Economic Strategy – The IMF', Cabinet CP (76) 118, 29 November 1976.

[125] www.nationalarchives.gov.uk/cabinetpapers/themes/sterling-devalued-imf-loan.htm.

[126] Memorandum by the Secretary of State for Energy, 'The Real Choices Facing the Cabinet', CAB/129/193/7, 29 November 1976.

[127] www.nationalarchives.gov.uk/cabinetpapers/themes/sterling-devalued-imf-loan.htm.

[128] See for example: W. Hutton, *The State We're In*, London: Vintage, 1996; D. Marquand, *The Unprincipled Society*, London: Fontana, 1988.

[129] A. Crosland, 'The Transition from Capitalism', in R.H.S. Crossman (ed.), *New Fabian Essays*, London: Turnstile Press, 1952.

[130] S. Fielding, 'Hell, No! Labour's Campaign: The Correct Diagnosis but the Wrong Doctor', in A. Geddes and J. Tonge, *Britain Votes 2015*, Oxford: Oxford University Press/Hansard Society, 2015.

[131] J. Cruddas and J. Rutherford, *One Nation: Labour's Political Renewal*.

[132] S. Wood, 'One Nation Labour: Remarks to One Nation Labour Conference', Queen Mary University of London, April 2013.

[133] E. Miliband, 'Political interview', *Observer*, 11 November, 2011.

[134] J. Cruddas and J. Rutherford, *One Nation: Labour's Political Renewal*.

[135] G. Cooke et al., 'The Condition of Britain: Strategies for Social Renewal', London: Institute for Public Policy Research, 2014.

[136] D. Lipsey, 'The Meritocracy Myth – What Ever Happened to the Old Dream of a Classless Society?', *New Statesman*, 26 February 2015.

[137] H. Thompson, 'Post-Crisis, Post-Devolution Politics and the Mansion Tax'.

[138] D. O'Leary, 'Something New and Something Blue: The Key to Labour's Future', *New Statesman*, 21 May 2015.

[139] A. Gamble, 'The Economy', in A. Geddes and J. Tonge, *Britain Votes 2015*.

[140] G. Radice, 'In Praise of Revisionism: The Social Democratic Challenge Today', Lecture at Policy Network, 14 May 2007.

[141] D. Miliband, 'Political Quarterly Annual Lecture', London School of Economics, 2012.

[142] A. Gamble, *Crisis Without End? The Unravelling of Western Prosperity*, Basingstoke: Palgrave Macmillan, 2014.

[143] D. Miliband, 'Political Quarterly Annual Lecture'.

[144] B. Gould, *A Future for Socialism*, London: Jonathan Cape, 1989; R. Hattersley, *Choose Freedom*.

[145] S. Griffiths, 'New Labour, New Liberalism and Revisionism's Second Wave'.

[146] See for example G. Radice, *Labour's Path to Power: The New Revisionism*, London: Macmillan, 1989.

[147] R. Philpot, 'Introduction', in R. Philpot, *The Purple Book: A Progressive Future for Labour*, p. 12.

[148] A. Crosland, 'Can Labour Win?', p. 19, London: The Fabian Society, 1960.

Chapter Eight

[1] L.T. Hobhouse cited in S. Collini, *Liberalism and Sociology: L.T. Hobhouse and Political Argument in England 1880–1914*, p. 269, Cambridge: Cambridge University Press, 1979.

[2] R.H. Tawney, 'The Choice Before the Labour Party', *Political Quarterly*, Volume 3, 1932.

[3] A. Hindmoor, *Constructing Political Space: New Labour at the Centre*, Oxford: Oxford University Press, 2005.

[4] J. Cronin, 'The Ironies of New Labour', p. 18, , Paper presented to 'What's Left of the Left Conference', Center for European Studies, Harvard University, 9–10 May 2010.

[5] A. Crosland, 'Can Labour Win?', p. 1, London: The Fabian Society, 1960.

[6] G. Esping-Andersen, *The Three Worlds of Welfare Capitalism*, New York: Princeton, NJ: Princeton University Press, 1990.

[7] J. Hills, *Good Times, Bad Times: The Welfare Myth of Them and Us*, Bristol: Policy Press, 2014.

[8] Cited in K. Jeffreys, 'Anthony Crosland: A New Biography', p. 228.

[9] R. McKibbin, *The Ideologies of Class*, Oxford: Clarendon Press, 1990.

[10] K. Jeffreys, *Anthony Crosland: A New Biography*, p. 229, London: John Blake, 1999.

[11] P. Gregg, 'Pre-distribution as a new set of policy tools', Discussion Paper, London: Policy Network, 2012.

[12] P. Gregg, 'Pre-distribution as a new set of policy tools'.

[13] Table 8.1 is taken from R. Lupton, J. Hills, K. Stewart and P. Vizard, 'Labour's Social Policy Record: Policy, Spending and Outcomes 1997–2010', Research Report 1, Centre for the Analysis of Social Exclusion/LSE, June 2013.

[14] J. Hills, *Towards a More Equal Society*, p. 134, Bristol: Policy Press, 2005.

[15] R. Joyce and L. Sibieta, 'An Assessment of Labour's Record on Income Inequality and Poverty', *Oxford Review of Economic Policy*, pp. 178–202, Volume 29 (1), 2013.

[16] J. Lindley and S. Machin, 'Wage inequality in the Labour years', *Oxford Review of Economic Policy*, pp. 165–77, Volume 29 (1), 2013.

[17] R. Joyce and L. Sibieta, 'An Assessment of Labour's Record on Income Inequality and Poverty', pp. 178–202.

[18] R. Joyce and L. Sibieta, 'An Assessment of Labour's Record on Income Inequality and Poverty', p. 183.

[19] K. Jeffreys, *Anthony Crosland: A New Biography*, p. 229.

[20] Organisation for Economic Co-operation and Development (OECD), 'Divided We Stand: Why Inequality Keeps Rising, Country Note – United Kingdom', 5 December 2011, Paris: OECD.

[21] Office for National Statistics, 'The Effects of Taxes and Benefits on Household Income 2012–13', Statistical Bulletin, 26 June 2014, London: ONS.

[22] Office for National Statistics, 'The Effects of Taxes and Benefits on Household Income 2012–13'.

[23] Office for National Statistics, 'The Effects of Taxes and Benefits on Household Income 2012–13'.

[24] G. Esping-Andersen, *The Three Worlds of Welfare Capitalism*.

[25] Office for National Statistics, 'UK Earnings Mobility', 23 September 2014, London: ONS.

[26] Office for National Statistics, 'UK Earnings Mobility'.

[27] OECD, 'Divided We Stand: Why Inequality Keeps Rising, Country Note – United Kingdom'.

[28] OECD, 'Divided We Stand: Why Inequality Keeps Rising, Country Note – United Kingdom'.

[29] OECD, 'Divided We Stand: Why Inequality Keeps Rising, Country Note – United Kingdom'.

[30] H. Thompson, 'Post-Crisis, Post-Devolution Politics and the Mansion Tax', *Political Quarterly*, Volume 86 (1), January–March 2015.

[31] J. Hills et al., *Wealth in the United Kingdom*, Oxford: Oxford University Press, 2014.

[32] J. Hills et al., *Wealth in the United Kingdom*.

[33] J. Hills and H. Glennerster, 'Why the Left Need to Take Wealth Seriously Again', *Juncture*, Volume 20 (1), Summer 2013.

[34] J. Hills et al., *Wealth in the United Kingdom*.

[35] J. Hills et al., *Wealth in the United Kingdom*.

[36] J. Hills and H. Glennerster, 'Why the Left Need to Take Wealth Seriously Again', p. 74.

[37] J. Hills and H. Glennerster, 'Why the Left Need to Take Wealth Seriously Again', p. 74, *Juncture*.

[38] www.whitehouse.gov/the-press-office/2013/12/04/remarks-president-economic-mobility.

[39] J. Hills, *Towards a More Equal Society*.

[40] J. Ostry, A. Berg and C. Tsangarides, 'Redistribution, Inequality and Growth', p. 4, Washington: International Monetary Fund, April 2014.

[41] J. Ostry, A. Berg and C. Tsangarides, 'Redistribution, Inequality and Growth', p. 25.

[42] K. Coutts and G. Gufdgin, 'The Macroeconomic Impact of Liberal Economic Policies in the UK', p. 5, Centre for Business Research, Judge Business School: University of Cambridge, April 2015.

[43] P. Addison, *No Turning Back: The Peacetime Revolutions of Post-War Britain*, Oxford: Oxford University Press, 2010; R. Plant, 'Democratic Socialism and Equality', in D. Lipsey and D. Leonard (eds), *Socialism Now: Crosland's Legacy*, Basingstoke: Macmillan, 1981.

[44] A. Gamble, *Between Europe and America: The Future of British Politics*, Basingstoke: Palgrave Macmillan, 2003.

[45] G. Brown, 'A Modern Agenda for Prosperity and Social Reform', London: Social Market Foundation, 3 February 2003.

[46] D. Marquand, *Decline of the Public: The Hollowing-Out of Citizenship*, pp. 2–3, Cambridge: Polity Press, 2004.

[47] P. Gay, *The Dilemma of Democratic Socialism*, New York: Collier Books, 1970.

[48] G.A. Cohen, *If You're an Egalitarian, How Come You're So Rich*, Cambridge: Harvard University Press, 2000, p. 34.

[49] J. Curtice, 'The Uphill Battle for "Responsible Capitalism"', *Public Policy Research*, Volume 19 (2), pp. 129–30, 2012.

[50] S. Soroka and C. Wlezien, 'Political Institutions and the Opinion–Policy Link', paper presented at the European Consortium for Political Research Joint Sessions of Workshops, St Gallen, Switzerland, 12–17 April 2011.

[51] J. Tomlinson, *The Labour Governments 1964–70: Economic Policy*, Manchester: Manchester University Press, 2004.

[52] G. O'Hara, *Governing Post-War Britain: The Paradoxes of Progress 1951–73*, Basingstoke: Palgrave Macmillan, 2012.

[53] J. Tomlinson, *The Labour Governments 1964–70: Economic Policy*.

[54] See M. Wiener, *English Culture and the Decline of the Industrial Spirit 1850–1980*, Cambridge: Cambridge University Press, 1985; A. Gamble, *Britain in Decline*, Basingstoke: Macmillan, 1983.

[55] R. Heffernan, *New Labour and Thatcherism: Political Change in Britain*, p. 22, Basingstoke: Palgrave Macmillan, 1999.

[56] R. Heffernan, *New Labour and Thatcherism: Political Change in Britain*, p. 22.

[57] J. Cronin, 'The Ironies of New Labour'.

[58] D. Corry, 'Labour and the Economy 1997–2010: More than a Faustian Pact', in P. Diamond and M. Kenny, *Reassessing New Labour: State, Society and Economy Under Blair and Brown*, London: The Political Quarterly, 2011.

[59] D. Corry, A. Valero and J. Van Reenan, 'UK Economic Performance', p. 3, LSE Discussion Paper, March 2011.

[60] D. Corry, A. Valero and J. Van Reenan, 'UK Economic Performance'.

[61] D. Corry, A. Valero and J. Van Reenan, 'UK Economic Performance'.

[62] D. Cobham, C. Adam and K. Mayhew, 'The Economic Record of the 1997–2010 Labour Government: An Assessment', *Oxford Review of Economic Policy*, p. 2, Volume 29 (1), 2013.

[63] A. From, *The New Democrats and the Return to Power*, New York: St Martin's Press, 2013.

[64] D. Sainsbury, *Progressive Capitalism*, p. 85, London: Biteback Books, 2013.

[65] K. Coutts and G. Gudgin, 'The Macroeconomic Impact of Liberal Economic Policies in the UK', p. 5, Centre for Business Research, Judge Business School: University of Cambridge, April 2015.

[66] www.bankofengland.co.uk/publications/Documents/quarterlybulletin/2014/qb14q304.pdf.

[67] For these points and the data I am grateful to my colleague Thomas Aubrey.

[68] C. Crouch, *The Strange Non-Death of Neo-Liberalism*, Cambridge: Polity Press, 2011; A. Gamble, *Crisis Without End? The Unravelling of Western Prosperity*, Basingstoke: Palgrave Macmillan, 2014.

[69] F. Faucher-King and P. Le Gales, *The New Labour Experiment*, Stanford, CA: Stanford University Press, 2010.

[70] A. Gamble, *The Free Economy and the Strong State*, Basingstoke: Palgrave Macmillan, 1994.

[71] A. Gamble, *The Free Economy and the Strong State*.

[72] U. Beck, *Risk Society: Towards a New Modernity*, London: Sage, 1992; A. Giddens, *The Consequences of Modernity*, Cambridge: Polity Press, 1991.

[73] A. Harrop and H. Reed, 'Inequality 2030', Fabian Policy Report, London: Fabian Society, 2015.

[74] B. Ansell and J. Gingrich, 'A Tale of Two Trilemmas', in A. Wren *The Service Economy in Transition*, Oxford: Oxford University Press, 2014.

[75] www.ons.gov.uk/ons/rel/lmac/self-employed-workers-in-the-uk/2014/rep-self-employed-workers-in-the-uk-2014.html.

[76] www.gov.uk/government/uploads/system/uploads/attachment_data/file/377934/bpe_2014_statistical_release.pdf.

[77] www.gov.uk/government/uploads/system/uploads/attachment_data/file/431564/Trade_Union_Membership_Statistics_2014.pdf.

[78] G. Cooke et al., *The Condition of Britain: Strategies for Social Renewal*, London: Institute for Public Policy Research, 2014.

[79] The following section of the chapter on challenges for the next decade draws on data and commentary from: www.fao.org/docrep/meeting/025/md883E.pdf; https://globaltrends2030.files.wordpress.com/2012/11/global-trends-2030-november2012.pdf; L. Byrne, '2020 Vision', *Progress*, September 2006.

[80] P. Mason, *Post-Capitalism: A Guide to Our Future*, London: Allen Lane, 2015.

[81] G. Mulgan, 'Labour Britain', *Fabian Review*, London: The Fabian Society, Summer 2005.

[82] E. Brynjolfsson and A. McFee, *The Second Machine Age: Work, Progress and Prosperity in a Time of Brilliant Technologies*, New York: W.W. Norton, 2014.

[83] https://globaltrends2030.files.wordpress.com/2012/11/global-trends-2030-november2012.pdf.

[84] P. Mason, *Post-Capitalism: A Guide to Our Future*, London: Allen Lane, 2015.

[85] E. Brynjolfsson and A. McFee, *The Second Machine Age: Work, Progress and Prosperity in a Time of Brilliant Technologies.*

[86] www.oxfordmartin.ox.ac.uk/downloads/academic/The_Future_of_Employment.pdf.

[87] L. Abramovsky, R. Griffith and M. Sako, *Off-shoring of Business Services and its Impact on the UK Economy*, London: Advanced Institute of Management Research, November 2004.

[88] L. Abramovsky, R. Griffith and M. Sako, *Off-shoring of Business Services and its Impact on the UK Economy* .

[89] www.demos.co.uk/files/Reinventing_the_firm.pdf?1252652788.

[90] E. Brynjolfsson and A. McFee, *The Second Machine Age: Work, Progress and Prosperity in a Time of Brilliant Technologies.*

[91] D. Rodrik, 'From Welfare State to Innovation State', www.project-syndicate.org/commentary/labor-saving-technology-by-dani-rodrik-2015-01.

[92] https://globaltrends2030.files.wordpress.com/2012/11/global-trends-2030-november2012.pdf.

[93] D. Rodrik, 'From Welfare State to Innovation State', www.project-syndicate.org/commentary/labor-saving-technology-by-dani-rodrik-2015-01.

[94] https://globaltrends2030.files.wordpress.com/2012/11/global-trends-2030-november2012.pdf.

[95] www.fao.org/docrep/meeting/025/md883E.pdf.

[96] W. Carlin and D. Soskice, *Macroeconomics: Institutions, Instability and the Financial System*, Oxford: Oxford University Press, 2013.

[97] J. Hills, *Towards a More Equal Society.*

[98] https://globaltrends2030.files.wordpress.com/2012/11/global-trends-2030-november2012.pdf.

[99] www.fao.org/docrep/meeting/025/md883E.pdf.

[100] https://globaltrends2030.files.wordpress.com/2012/11/global-trends-2030-november2012.pdf.

[101] www.fao.org/docrep/meeting/025/md883E.pdf.

[102] www.fao.org/docrep/meeting/025/md883E.pdf.

[103] https://globaltrends2030.files.wordpress.com/2012/11/global-trends-2030-november2012.pdf.

[104] Z. Darvas and O. Tschekassin, 'Poor and Under Pressure: The Social Impact of Europe's Fiscal Consolidation', Bruegal, March 2015 http://bruegel.org/2015/03/poor-and-under-pressure-the-social-impact-of-europes-fiscal-consolidation/.

[105] https://globaltrends2030.files.wordpress.com/2012/11/global-trends-2030-november2012.pdf.

[106] www.fao.org/docrep/meeting/025/md883E.pdf.

[107] www.fao.org/docrep/meeting/025/md883E.pdf.

[108] Z. Darvas and O. Tschekassin, 'Poor and Under Pressure: The Social Impact of Europe's Fiscal Consolidation'.

[109] https://globaltrends2030.files.wordpress.com/2012/11/global-trends-2030-november2012.pdf.

[110] S. Saggar, *Pariah Politics: Understanding Western Radical Islam and What Should be Done*, Oxford: Oxford University Press, 2008.

[111] www.fao.org/docrep/meeting/025/md883E.pdf.

[112] https://globaltrends2030.files.wordpress.com/2012/11/global-trends-2030-november2012.pdf.

[113] www.fao.org/docrep/meeting/025/md883E.pdf.

[114] A. Gamble, *Between Europe and America: The Future of British Politics*.

[115] https://globaltrends2030.files.wordpress.com/2012/11/global-trends-2030-november2012.pdf.

[116] www.fao.org/docrep/meeting/025/md883E.pdf.

[117] https://globaltrends2030.files.wordpress.com/2012/11/global-trends-2030-november2012.pdf.

[118] *British Social Attitudes 31*, London: National Centre for Social Research, 2014.

[119] M. Naim, *End of Power: From Boardrooms to Battlefields, and Churches to States, Why Being in Charge isn't What it Used to Be*, New York: Basic Books, 2013.

[120] R. E. Lane, *The Loss of Happiness in Market Democracies*, pp. 3–4, Yale: Yale University Press, 2000.

[121] https://globaltrends2030.files.wordpress.com/2012/11/global-trends-2030-november2012.pdf.

[122] G. Mulgan, 'Labour Britain'.

[123] R.E. Lane, *The Loss of Happiness in Market Democracies*, pp. 3–4.

[124] A. Offer, *The Challenge of Affluence: Self-Control and Well-Being in the United States and Britain Since 1950*, Oxford: Oxford University Press, 2006.

[125] R.E. Lane, *The Loss of Happiness in Market Democracies*.

[126] J.M. Keynes, 'The Economic Possibilities for our Grandchildren', in L. Pecchi and G. Piga, *Revisiting Keynes*, Cambridge: MIT Press, 2010.

[127] M. Kaus, *The End of Equality*, New York: Basic Books, 1992.

[128] D. Lipsey, 'Revisionists revise', in D. Leonard (ed.), *Crosland and New Labour*, Basingstoke: Macmillan, 1999.

[129] A. Wright, 'Wither Labour: Seeking Reinvention and a Realistic Radicalism', *Juncture*, London: Institute of Public Policy Research, 2015; A. Gamble, 'On the Future of Social Democracy', *Policy Network Seminar*, London, 2008.

[130] R. Musgrave, 'The Voluntary Exchange Theory of Public Economy', *Quarterly Journal of Economics*, Volume 53, pp. 213–38, 1939.

[131] R.H. Tawney, 'The Choice Before the Labour Party', p. 324.

[132] P. Clarke, *A Question of Leadership: From Gladstone to Thatcher*, London: Penguin, 1991.

[133] Cited in E. Shaw, *The Labour Party Since 1979: Crisis and Transformation*, p. 5, London: Routledge, 1996.

[134] K. Hickson, 'Social Democracy and Happiness'.

[135] J.C.R. Dow and I.D. Saville, *A Critique of Monetary Policy: Theory and British Experience*, Oxford: Oxford University Press, 1990.

[136] J.M. Keynes, *The End of Laissez-Faire: The Economic Consequences of the Peace*, p. 26, London: BN Publishing, 2009.

[137] J.B. Davis (ed.), *The State of Interpretation of Keynes*, p. 209, New York: Springer Science, 1994.

[138] A. Wright, 'Wither Labour: Seeking Reinvention and a Realistic Radicalism'.

[139] J. Kay, *The Truth About Markets*, London: Penguin, 2003; J. Plender, *Capitalism: Money, Morals and Markets*, London: Biteback, 2015; M. Mazzucato, *The Entrepreneurial State: Debunking Public Versus Private Sector Myths*, London: Anthem Press, 2013.

[140] C. Mayer, *A Firm Commitment: Why the Corporation is Failing and How to Restore Trust In It*, Oxford: Oxford University Press, 2014.

[141] M. Porter and M.E. Kramer, 'Creating Shared Value', *Harvard Business Review*, January–February 2010.

[142] I am grateful to Thomas Aubrey for these points.

[143] http://economics.mit.edu/files/1785; J. Schumpeter, 1942.

[144] S. Berman, *The Primacy of Politics: Social Democracy and the Making of Europe's Twentieth Century*, p. 207, Cambridge: Cambridge University Press, 2006.

[145] H. Thompson, 'Post-Crisis, Post-Devolution Politics and the Mansion Tax', p. 14.

[146] H. Thompson, 'Post-Crisis, Post-Devolution Politics and the Mansion Tax'.

[147] M. Keating, *Rescaling the State: The Making of Territory and the Rise of the Meso*, Oxford: Oxford University Press, 2014.

[148] S. Berman, *The Primacy of Politics*.

[149] S. Saggar, *Pariah Politics: Understanding Western Radical Islam and What Should be Done*.

[150] www.newstatesman.com/uk-politics/2012/03/new-times-new-thinking.

[151] J.M. Keynes, 'Economic Possibilities for our Grandchildren'.

[152] www.newstatesman.com/uk-politics/2012/03/new-times-new-thinking.

[153] A.B. Atkinson, *Lectures in Public Economics*, London: Routledge, 2014.

[154] H. Kippin and B. Lucas, 'From Big Society to Social Productivity', London: Royal Society of the Arts, 2011.

[155] A. Crosland, *Socialism Now and Other Essays*, London: Jonathan Cape, 1974.

[156] J. Hills, *Towards a More Equal Society*.

[157] G. Esping-Andersen, *The New Worlds of Welfare Capitalism*.

[158] A. Sen, *The Idea of Justice*, London: Allen Lane, 2009.

[159] B. Jackson, 'Revisionism Reconsidered: "Property-Owning Democracy" and Egalitarian Strategy in Post-War Britain', *Twentieth Century British History*, Volume 16 (4), 2005.

[160] L. T. Hobhouse, *The Crisis of Liberalism: New Issues of Democracy*, London: Williams & Norgate, 1909.

[161] B. Ackerman and A. Alsott, *The Stakeholder Society*, New Haven, CT: Yale University Press, 2001; this liberal egalitarian tradition draws on a multiplicity of writers, notably Rawls and Meade, who directly influenced Crosland.

[162] P. Van Parijs, *Red Freedom for All: What (if Anything) Can Justify Capitalism*, Oxford: Clarendon Press, 1995.

[163] J. Fishkin, *Bottlenecks: A New Theory of Equal Opportunity*, Oxford: Oxford University Press, 2014; B. Ackerman and A. Alsott, *The Stakeholder Society*.

[164] A. Wright, 'Wither Labour: Seeking Reinvention and a Realistic Radicalism'.

[165] J. Hills et al., *Wealth in the United Kingdom*.

[166] T. Atkinson, *Inequality: What Can be Done?*, Princeton, NJ: Princeton University Press, 2015.

[167] B. Ackerman and A. Alsott, *The Stakeholder Society*.

[168] Of course, a universal stakeholder grant would still be dependent on the individual fulfilling certain conditions and obligations, for example refraining from criminal and 'anti-social' activity.

[169] B. Ackerman and A. Alsott, *The Stakeholder Society*.

[170] Cited in A.B. Atkinson, *Inequality: What Can Be Done?*, p. 169.

[171] A. Gamble and R. Prabhakar, 'The New Assets Agenda', p. 200, in G. Dench (ed.), *The Rise and Rise of Meritocracy*, Oxford: Political Quarterly/Blackwell Publishing, 2006.

[172] B. Ackerman and A. Alsott, *The Stakeholder Society*.

[173] Ackerman and Alsott point out that those who have done well out of the capital endowment could effectively pay back the grant through a wealth tax levied at the point of death.

[174] For these points I am grateful to my colleague Thomas Aubrey.

[175] R. Reeves, 'Flee Your Tents, Oh Israel', in G. Cooke and J. Purnell, *We Mean Freedom*, London: Demos, 2009.

[176] J. Hills et al., *Wealth in the United Kingdom*.

[177] J. Hills and H. Glennerster, 'Why the Left Need to Take Wealth Seriously Again'.

[178] J. Hills and H. Glennerster, 'Why the Left Need to Take Wealth Seriously Again'.

[179] J. Hills and H. Glennerster, 'Why the Left Need to Take Wealth Seriously Again'.

[180] J. Hills et al., *Wealth in the United Kingdom*.

[181] B. Ackerman and A. Alsott, *The Stakeholder Society*.

[182] T. Paine, *The Rights of Man*, London: Wordsworth Publishing, 1996.

[183] J. Hills et al., *Wealth in the United Kingdom*, p. 197.

[184] 'An hereditary meritocracy', *The Economist*, 24 January 2015.

185 B. Ackerman and A. Alsott, *The Stakeholder Society*.

186 M. Naim, *The End of Power: From Boardrooms to Battlefields and Churches to States, Why Being in Charge isn't What it Used to Be.*

187 B. Ackerman and A. Alsott, *The Stakeholder Society*.

188 T. Aubrey, 'Britain's Dysfunctional Housing Market: A European Comparison', London: Policy Network, 20 October 2015.

189 T. Aubrey, 'Britain's Dysfunctional Housing Market: A European Comparison', p. 3.

190 P. Brione and C. Nicholson, 'Employee Ownership: Unlocking Growth in the UK Economy', London: Centre Forum, 2012.

191 D. Rodrik, 'From Welfare State to Innovation State', www.project-syndicate.org/commentary/labor-saving-technology-by-dani-rodrik-2015-01.

192 N. Goodway, 'Here's a Radical Sell-off Scheme that Could Speed RBS Back to Popularity', *Evening Standard*, 16 June 2015, www.standard.co.uk/business/markets/nick-goodway-a-radical-selloff-scheme-that-could-speed-rbs-back-to-popularity-10323690.html.

193 P. Gregg, 'Pre-distribution as a new set of policy tools', http://blogs.lse.ac.uk/politicsandpolicy/predistribution.

194 E. Lonergan and M. Blyth, 'Radical but Credible Policies are Available to the Labour Party', *The Financial Times*, 10 September 2015.

195 T. Clark. and A. Dilnot, *Long-Term Trends in British Taxation and Spending*, London: Institute for Fiscal Studies, 2002, www.ifs.org.uk/bns/bn25.pdf.

196 S. Griffiths, 'New Labour, New Liberalism and Revisionism's Second Wave', in S. Griffiths and K. Hickson (eds), *British Party Politics and Ideology After New Labour*, Basingstoke: Palgrave Macmillan, 2009.

197 A. Briggs, 'The Labour Party as Crucible', in G. Dench (ed.), *The Rise and Rise of Meritocracy*, Oxford: Political Quarterly/Blackwell Publishing, 2006.

198 R. Wicks, 'Revisionism in the 1950s: The Ideas of Anthony Crosland', in C. Navari (ed.), *British Politics and the Spirit of the Age*, Keele: Keele University Press, 1996.

199 E. Shaw, *Losing Labour's Soul? New Labour and the Blair Government 1997–2007*, London: Routledge, 2008.

Chapter Nine

1 A. Crosland, *Socialism Now and Other Essays*, p. 168, London: Jonathan Cape, 1974.

2 Letter from Mr Kevin Kavanagh, Crosland archive 6/4 (63), LSE.

3 J.K. Galbraith, www.procon.org/view.resource.php?resourceID=005358.

4 L.T. Hobhouse, *Liberalism*, p. 40, Oxford/New York: Oxford University Press, 1964.

5 Interview with T. Wright, 3 March 2015.

[6] Cited in J. Nuttall, *Psychological Socialism: The Labour Party and Qualities of Mind and Character, 1931 to the Present*, Manchester: Manchester University Press, 2006, p. 12.

[7] Cited in B. Harrison, *Seeking a Role: The United Kingdom 1951–70*, p. 523, Oxford: Oxford University Press, 2009.

[8] S. Crosland, *Tony Crosland*, p. 357, London: Jonathan Cape, 1982.

[9] M. Francis, 'Mr Gaitskell's Ganymede: Reassessing Crosland's *The Future of Socialism*', *Contemporary British History*, Volume 11 (2), 1997.

[10] Interview with D. Marquand, 24 July 2015.

[11] Cited in P. Addison, *No Turning Back: The Peacetime Revolutions of Post-War Britain*, pp. 404–5, Oxford: Oxford University Press, 2010.

[12] H. Pemberton, 'Relative Decline and British Economic Policy in the 1960s', *The Historical Journal*, Volume 47 (4), 2004.

[13] G. Kaufman, 'Power Failure: A Review of *Friends and Rivals* by Giles Radice', *Guardian*, 14 September 2002.

[14] R. Skidelsky, *Britain Since 1900: A Success Story?*, London: Vintage Books, 2014.

[15] Interview with B. Donoughue, 26 February 2015.

[16] V. Boliver and A. Swift, 'Do Comprehensive Schools Reduce Social Mobility?', *British Journal of Sociology*, Volume 62 (1), 2011.

[17] K.O. Morgan, *Ages of Reform: Dawns and Downfalls of the British Left*, p. 136, London: IB Tauris, 2008.

[18] R. Desai, *Intellectuals and Socialism*, pp. 81–2, London: Lawrence and Wishart, 1991.

[19] A. Crosland, 'The Future of the Left', p. 122, *Encounter*, March 1960.

[20] G. Radice, *Labour's Path to Power: The New Revisionism*, London: Macmillan, 1989.

[21] D. Marquand, *The Progressive Dilemma: From Lloyd George to Kinnock*, London: Heinemann, 1991.

[22] Cited in D. Marquand, *The Progressive Dilemma: From Lloyd George to Kinnock*, pp. 22–3.

[23] R. McKibbin, 'With or Without the Workers', *London Review of Books*, 25 April 1991.

[24] B. Magee, 'Tony Crosland As I Knew Him', p. 185, *Political Quarterly*, Volume 81 (2), April–June 2010.

[25] J. Cronin, *New Labour's Pasts: The Labour Party and its Discontents*, p. 48, Harlow: Pearson Education, 2004.

[26] S. Fielding, *The Labour Governments 1964–70: Labour and Cultural Change*, Manchester: Manchester University Press, 2003.

[27] R. Plant, 'Democratic Socialism and Equality', in D. Lipsey and D. Leonard (eds), *Crosland's Legacy*, Basingstoke: Macmillan, 1981.

[28] D. Marquand, 'Moralists and Hedonists', in A. Seldon and D. Marquand (eds), *The Ideas That Shaped Post-War Britain*, London: Fontana, 1996; J. Nuttall, *Psychological Socialism: The Labour Party and Qualities of Mind and Character, 1931 to the present*, p. 10.

[29] D. Marquand, *The Unprincipled Society: New Demands and Old Politics*, London: Jonathan Cape, 1988; J.P. Mackintosh, 'Has Social Democracy Failed in Britain?', *Political Quarterly*, Volume 49 (3), August–October, 1978; B. Walden, 'A Critique of Revisionism', *New Statesman*, 25 June 1971.

[30] A. Crosland, *The Future of Socialism*, p. 515, London: Jonathan Cape, 1956.

[31] A. Crosland, *The Future of Socialism*.

[32] G. Gallop, 'A Lecture on Labour Party Revisionism', Nuffield College, Oxford, Crosland archive 17/3, LSE.

[33] V. Bogdanor, 'Labour in Opposition 1951–64', in V. Bogdanor and R. Skidelsky (eds), *The Age of Affluence*, London: Penguin, 1970.

[34] Letter from Flaubert Henderson to A. Crosland, 7 June 1950, Crosland archive 10/3, LSE

[35] Interview with G. Radice, 10 October 2014.

[36] J. Tomlinson, *The Politics of Decline*, London: Routledge, 2000.

[37] S. Crosland, *Tony Crosland*, p. 128; T. Bale, 'Dynamics of a Non-Decision: The "Failure" to Devalue the Pound, 1964–67', *Contemporary British History*, Volume 10 (2), 1999.

[38] D. MacDougall, *Don and Mandarin: Memoirs of an Economist*, p. 153, London: John Murray, 1987.

[39] R. Crossman, *The Diaries of a Cabinet Minister Volume I*, p. 305, London: Mandarin, 1991.

[40] S. Crosland, *Tony Crosland*, p. 128.

[41] R. Crossman, *The Diaries of a Cabinet Minister Volume II*, p. 576, London: Mandarin, 1991; P. Clarke, *A Question of Leadership: From Gladstone to Thatcher*, pp. 260–1, London: Penguin, 1991.

[42] Cited in P. Clarke, *A Question of Leadership: From Gladstone to Thatcher*, p. 261.

[43] J. Tomlinson, *The Labour Governments 1964–70: Economic Policy*, Manchester: Manchester University Press, 2004.

[44] A. Gamble, *Britain in Decline*, Basingstoke: Macmillan, 1983.

[45] J. Campbell, *Roy Jenkins: A Well-Rounded Life*, London: Jonathan Cape, 2014.

[46] J. Tomlinson, *The Labour Governments 1964–70: Economic Policy*.

[47] J. Tomlinson, *The Labour Governments 1964–70: Economic Policy*.

[48] S. Newton, 'The Sterling Devaluation of 1967, the International Economy and Post-War Social Democracy', p. 944–5, *English Historical Review*, CXXV, 2010.

[49] S. Newton, 'The Sterling Devaluation of 1967, the International Economy and Post-War Social Democracy', p. 944–5.

[50] A. Gamble, *The Free Economy and the Strong State*, Basingstoke: Palgrave Macmillan, 1994.

[51] B. Pimlott, *Labour and the Left in the 1930s*, Cambridge: Cambridge University Press, 1978.

[52] Brian Walden, 'A Critique of Revisionism', *New Statesman*, 25 June 1971, Crosland archive 13/20 (202), LSE.

[53] S. Pollard, *Britain's Pride and Britain's Decline: The British Economy 1870–1914*, London: Edward Arnold, 1989; A. Gamble, *Britain in Decline*; A. Milward, *The United Kingdom and the European Community, Volume I: The Rise and Fall of a National Strategy, 1945–1963*, London: Frank Cass, 2003.

[54] In *Socialism Now* (1974), Crosland explicitly attacks one of the major proponents of the Alternative Economic Strategy, the economist Stuart Holland.

[55] S. Crosland, *Tony Crosland*, p. 356.

[56] T. Benn, *Against the Tide: Diaries, 1973–77*, p. 674, London: Hutchinson, 1989.

[57] Interview with G. Radice, House of Lords, 16 December 2014.

[58] R. Hattersley, *Who Goes Home? Scenes from a Political Life*, p. 175, London: Little Brown, 1995.

[59] Interview with D. Lipsey, House of Lords, 2 March 2015.

[60] Cited in G. Hodgson, *Labour at the Crossroads*, p. 126, Oxford: Martin Robertson, 1981.

[61] P. Jenkins, 'The Social Democratic Dilemma', *New Statesman*, 20 September 1974, Crosland archive 13/20 (349), LSE.

[62] R. Skidelsky, *Britain since 1900: A Success Story?*

[63] A. Warde, *Consensus and Beyond: The Development of Labour Party Strategy Since the Second World War*, Manchester: Manchester University Press, 1982.

[64] P. Jenkins, 'The Social Democratic Dilemma', *New Statesman*, 20 September 1974, Crosland archive 13/20 (349), LSE.

[65] P. Jenkins, 'The Social Democratic Dilemma', *New Statesman*, 20 September 1974, Crosland archive 13/20 (349), LSE.

[66] B. Walden, 'A Critique of Revisionism', *New Statesman*, 25 June 1971, Crosland archive 13/20 (202), LSE.

[67] R.H. Tawney, 'The Choice Before the Labour Party', p. 338, *Political Quarterly*, Volume 3, 1932.

[68] S. Beer, *British Politics in a Collectivist Age*, p. 239, New York: Knopf, 1965.

[69] V. Bogdanor, 'Labour in Opposition 1951–64'.

[70] V. Bogdanor, 'Labour in Opposition 1951–64', p. 113.

[71] B. Pimlott, 'Hugh Was That? Review of Hugh Gaitskell by Brian Brivati', *Independent on Sunday*, 29 September 1996.

[72] E. Shaw, *The Labour Party Since 1979: Crisis and Transformation*, p. 3, London: Routledge, 1996.

[73] J.M. Keynes, 'Liberalism and Labour', *The New Republic*, 3 March 1926.

[74] J.M. Keynes, 'The Dilemma of Modern Socialism', *Political Quarterly*, Volume 3 (3), July–September 1932.

[75] J.M. Keynes, 'Am I a Liberal?', London: Royal Economic Society, 1925.

[76] A. Crosland, 'The Greatness of Keynes: A Review of John Maynard Keynes by R.F. Harrod', *Tribune*, 23 February 1950, Crosland archive 13/20 (60), LSE.

[77] B. Pimlott, *Labour and the Left in the 1930s*, p. 39, Cambridge: Cambridge University Press, 1978.

[78] B. Pimlott, *Labour and the Left in the 1930s*, p. 39.

[79] P. Addison, *No Turning Back: The Peacetime Revolutions of Post-War Britain*.

[80] V. Bogdanor and R. Skidelsky, *The Age of Affluence*, p. 15, London: Penguin, 1970.

[81] Interview with D. Marquand, 24 July 2015.

[82] J. Cronin, *New Labour's Pasts: The Labour Party and its Discontents*, p. 187–8.

[83] P. Mason, 'Keynes and Our Grandchildren: Recapturing an Alternative Vision of Economic Progress', *Juncture/IPPR*, 21 July 2015.

[84] M. Carney, 'Mansion House Speech', the Lord Mayor's Banquet for Bankers and Merchants of the City of London at the Mansion House, 12 June 2014.

[85] G. Mulgan, 'Lessons of Power', *Prospect*, August 2005.

[86] J. Nuttall, 'Tony Crosland and the Many Falls and Rises of British Social Democracy', *Contemporary British History*, Volume 18 (4), pp. 52–79.

[87] J. Nuttall, 'Tony Crosland and the Many Falls and Rises of British Social Democracy', p. 60.

[88] J. Campbell, *Roy Jenkins: A Well-Rounded Life*, p. 180.

[89] K. Jeffreys, 'The Old Right', in R. Plant, M. Beech and K. Hickson (eds.), *The Struggle for Labour's Soul: Understanding Labour's Political Thought Since 1945*, p. 78, London: Routledge, 2004; Interview with G. Radice, House of Lords, 16 December 2014.

[90] Interview with W.T. Rodgers, 2 March 2015.

[91] P. Clarke, *A Question of Leadership: From Gladstone to Thatcher*.

[92] Cited in N. Thomas-Symonds, *Nye: The Political Life of Aneurin Bevan*, p. 187, London: IB Tauris, 2014.

[93] B. Harrison, *Seeking a Role: The United Kingdom 1951–70*, p. 446.

[94] R.H.S. Crossman, 'The Spectre of Revisionism: a reply to Crosland', p. 26, *Encounter*, Issue 4, 1960.

[95] G. Hodgson, *Labour at the Crossroads*, p. 71, Oxford: Martin Robertson, 1981.

[96] A. Crosland, 'On the Left Again: Some Last Words on the Labour Controversy', p. 12, *Encounter*, Issue 8, 1960.

[97] Cited in Susan Crosland, *Tony Crosland*, p. 390.

[98] S. Griffiths, 'New Labour, New Liberalism, and Revisionism's Second Wave', in S. Griffiths and K. Hickson (eds), *British Party Politics and Ideology After New Labour*, Basingstoke: Palgrave Macmillan, 2009.

[99] W.H. Greenleaf, *The British Political Tradition Volume I: The Rise of Collectivism* London: Routledge, 1983.

[100] A. Crosland, *The Future of Socialism*, p. 169.

[101] Cited in G. Radice, *Friends and Rivals: Crosland, Jenkins and Healey*, p. 231, London: Abacus, 2003.

[102] A. Crosland, *The Conservative Enemy*, p. 8, London: Jonathan Cape, 1962.

[103] P. Jenkins, 'The Social Democratic Dilemma', *New Statesman*, 20 September 1974, Crosland archive 13/20 (349), LSE.

[104] See D. Howell, *British Social Democracy: A Study in Development and Decay*, London: Croom Helm, 1976.

[105] J. Nuttall, 'Tony Crosland and the Many Falls and Rises of British Social Democracy', p. 52–79; L. Black, 'Coming to Terms with Affluence: Socialism and Social Change in 1950s Britain', Conference on 'Consensus or Coercion? The State, the People and Social Cohesion in Post-war Britain', London: University College London, 13 March 1999; P. Hennessy, *Having it So Good: Britain in the Fifties*, London: Penguin, 2007.

[106] L. Black, H. Pemberton and P. Thane, *Britain in the 1970s*, Manchester: Manchester University Press.

[107] H. Pemberton, 'Strange Days Indeed: British Politics in the 1970s', *Contemporary British History*, p. 583.

[108] L. Black, H. Pemberton and P. Thane, *Britain in the 1970s*.

[109] Cited in P. Addison, *No Turning Back: The Peacetime Revolutions of Post-War Britain*, pp. 404–5.

[110] B. Brivati, *Hugh Gaitskell*, London: Politicos Publishing, 2006.

[111] R. Plant, 'Democratic Socialism and Equality'.

[112] K. Jeffreys, *Anthony Crosland: A New Biography*, pp. 225–32, London: John Blake, 1999.

[113] D. Lipsey and D. Leonard (eds), *Crosland's Legacy*, Basingstoke: Macmillan, 1981.]]

[114] Interview with D. Lipsey, House of Lords, 2 March 2015.

[115] Interview with W.T. Rodgers, 2 March 2015; Interview with R. Hattersley, 6 March 2015.

[116] Interview with B. Donoughue, 26 February 2015.

[117] B. Donoughue, *Downing Street Diary*, p. 385, London: Politicos, 2006.

[118] Interview with D. Leonard, 11 February 2015.

[119] Cited in A. Briggs, 'The Labour Party as Crucible', p. 25, in G. Dench (ed.), *The Rise and Rise of Meritocracy*, Oxford: Political Quarterly/Blackwell Publishing, 2006.

[120] 'Anthony Crosland: The Man Who Never Was', Profile, *New Statesman*, 28 September 1973.

[121] K. Jeffreys, *Anthony Crosland: A New Biography*, pp. 225–32.

[122] R.H. Tawney, 'Lecture: Poverty as an Industrial Problem', London: London School of Economics, 1913.

[123] J. Fishkin, *Bottlenecks: A New Theory of Equal Opportunity*, Oxford: Oxford University Press, 2014.

[124] A. Sen, *The Idea of Justice*, p. 112, London: Allen Lane, 2009.

[125] J. Fishkin, *Bottlenecks: A New Theory of Equal Opportunity*.

[126] A. Gamble and R. Prabhakar, 'The New Assets Agenda', in G. Dench (ed.), *The Rise and Rise of Meritocracy*, Oxford: Political Quarterly/ Blackwell Publishing, 2006.

[127] B. Barber, *Strong Democracy: Participatory Politics for a New Age*, pp xiii, Berkeley: University of California Press.

[128] M. Kenny and N. Pearce, 'What National Story Does the Left Need to Tell', *Juncture*, London: Institute for Public Policy Research, 21 May 2015.

[129] M. Kenny, *The Politics of English Nationhood*, Oxford: Oxford University Press, 2014.

[130] B. Pimlott, 'Uber-Tony', *London Review of Books*, 3 September 1998; Cited in P. Hain, *Back To The Future Of Socialism*, p. 9, Bristol: Policy Press, 2015.

[131] A. Gamble, 'Progressive Politics: A New Beginning', *Policy Network*, 23 September 2015.

[132] K. Morgan, *Ages of Reform*, p. 145.

[133] R.H. Tawney, 'The Choice Before the Labour Party', p. 332.

[134] T. Wright, 'Wither Labour: Seeking Reinvention and a Realistic Radicalism', *Juncture*, London: Institute of Public Policy Research, 2015.

[135] K. Morgan, *Ages of Reform*, p. 145.

Index